Fodor's 94
Chicago

D1036520

Fodor's Travel Publications, Inc.
New York • Toronto • London • Sydney • Auckland

Copyright © 1994
by Fodor's Travel Publications, Inc.

Fodor's Chicago

Editor: Andrew Collins
Area Editor: Elizabeth Gardner
Editorial Contributors: Paul A. Camp, Don Davenport, Mark Kollar, Caroline Liou, Dominic A. Pacyga, Marcy Pritchard, Anne Schamburg, Barbara Shortt, Doris L. Taub, Phil Vettel, Mary Wagner
Creative Director: Fabrizio La Rocca
Cartographer: David Lindroth
Illustrators: Joseph Sipri, Karl Tanner
Cover Photograph: Brooks/Masterfile
Design: Vignelli Associates

Special Sales

Contents

3 Exploring Chicago 52

Sightseeing Checklists 113

4 Shopping 121

5 Sports, Fitness, Beaches 132

6 Dining 137

7 Lodging 174

8 The Arts and Nightlife 195

9 Excursions from Chicago 209

Index 232

Maps

Foreword

The Chicago most visitors see first is the commercial and cultural heart of the city, the Downtown and Near North areas that contain the world-famous architecture, the impressive skyline, the department stores, major hotels, and fine restaurants that together define a great American city. This Chicago is the primary focus of the present guide, which takes a close look at the town, gives extensive information on places to stay, and provides reviews of more than 130 recommended places to eat throughout the city.

Yet there is another, equally interesting Chicago, a vibrant Chicago of the neighborhoods and their distinctive populations, and this guide takes the reader into some of those neighborhoods and shows how the tides of immigration have led to change, development, and curious ethnic juxtapositions. Quite a few of the restaurants recommended here are located in those neighborhoods, too.

Fodor's Chicago '94, through its walking tours and essays, examines the two Chicagos—the downtown and the neighborhoods—and tries to suggest the greater political and human entity that is the foremost city of the American Middle West.

While every care has been taken to assure the accuracy of the information in this guide, the passage of time will always bring change, and consequently the publisher cannot accept responsibility for errors that may occur.

All prices and opening times quoted here are based on information supplied to us at press time. Hours and admission fees may change, however, and the prudent traveler will avoid inconvenience by calling ahead.

Fodor's wants to hear about your travel experiences, both pleasant and unpleasant. When a hotel or restaurant fails to live up to its billing, let us know and we will investigate the complaint and revise our entries where the facts warrant it.

Send your letters to the editors of Fodor's Travel Publications, 201 East 50th Street, New York, NY 10022.

Highlights '94 and Fodor's Choice

Highlights '94

The **Chicago Bulls** snared their third consecutive National Basketball Association championship in 1993, a feat unequaled since the 1960s. The entire city united to watch the team knock off the New York Knicks in the division playoffs and the Phoenix Suns in the finals. The final victory celebration was a bit more sedate than 1992's fiasco, when more than a thousand people were arrested for looting and vandalism; thousands of police officers in riot gear, at a cost of $1 million a day, saw to restoring order. Nonetheless, in the wake of this year's victory, three people were killed by random gunfire on the city's South and West sides and more than 600 were arrested in rioting and looting.

Another major sports triumph has been snagging the opening ceremonies and the first five games of 1994's **World Cup soccer match.** Soldier Field is the setting, June 17–July 2 is the time. Soccer fans should reserve early; nonfans might plan on visiting at a later date.

Mayor Richard M. Daley is still hot on two "megaprojects": opening a **third airport** within Chicago's city limits and legalizing **casino gambling.** The state legislature nixed his proposal to build an airport on the city's southeast side, and the new facility, if ever built, now seems likely to land on a "green grass" location far south of the city proper.

Daley's still fond of the Lake Calumet site, though; he proposed it as one possible location for a riverboat casino and theme park—now that Governor James Edgar has turned him down on a land-based casino. Illinois politicos seem to feel there's something intrinsically less sinful about gambling on the water, though the distinction is obscure to those who believe any kind of casino will result in increased crime and that gambling addiction will suck tourism dollars away from existing attractions. When some legislators balked at the notion of gambling on either Lake Michigan or the Chicago River, Daley and developers proposed the ultimate absurdity: building a man-made lake near downtown to facilitate casino boats. At press time, the whole question had been put on indefinite hold as legislators grapple with the deeper problem of balancing the state budget.

The **Chicago Transit Authority** (CTA) has enacted major changes in the routes of its elevated trains. This should ease life for visitors in 1994. Biggest news: There's finally rapid-transit service: the Orange Line, between Midway-Airport and the Loop. Brand-new, it's fully wheelchair accessible except where it follows the older Loop tracks. At this writing, we can't yet compare its travel time with a taxi or shuttle van, but at under $2, the price is right.

Another alteration of interest is the creation of the Howard–Dan Ryan line from the halves of two existing lines. Baseball fans can use it to go between Wrigley Field and Comiskey Park without changing trains, and it stops in Chinatown along the way. The other two halves—high in crime and not recommended to out-of-towners—were combined into the Lake Englewood–Jackson Park route. In addition to the rerouting, the CTA is attempting to install new signage, which, unfortunately, may cause more confusion rather than foster clarity. Taking a leaf out of Boston's book, it's attempting to reidentify the various El routes by color. For example, the Howard–Dan Ryan is now called the Red Line and the Congress–Douglas–O'Hare is the Blue Line. Two caveats, though: The CTA is strapped for cash, so much of the Red Line signage is blue, some of the Purple Line signage is red, and the Brown Line might be labeled with blue or yellow occasionally. Furthermore, it will take years for residents to adapt to the new nomenclature, so when requesting directions to the Red Line, call it the "Howard line" or the "State Street subway." Good luck!

Travelers through **O'Hare** will notice two big changes: The International Terminal, four years and $620 million in the making, finally opened for incoming flights in May 1993 and for departures in October 1993. The new terminal, with glass walls and exposed structural beams, is designed by Chicago-based architects Perkins and Will. International travelers will find it a delightful contrast to the dingy, dark cinderblock structure that preceded it. A brand-new, $127-million "people-mover" train has replaced the interterminal shuttle buses. The run between Terminal 1 and remote parking takes less than 8 minutes. A big drawback for tourists, though: The train whizzes right past car rental parking, because no station was built there. Officials say one may be built eventually; meantime, the usual company shuttle vans will whisk you to your rental car.

Visitors to the **River North gallery district** have several new choices this year. A branch of the restaurant **Planet Hollywood,** bankrolled by a number of movie stars, is scheduled to open on Wells Street near Ed Debevic's. Bulls superstar **Michael Jordan** opened his warehouse-size restaurant at LaSalle and Illinois during the 1993 playoff season (*see* Dining). And around the corner at Clark and Ohio streets is **Capone's Chicago,** which opened in June 1993 to the Office of Tourism's chagrin. It's one of the city's few genuine "tourist attractions," built almost solely for out-of-towners. For $4.75, you get a 45-minute show about the history of Chicago's gangster past, with slides, film clips, music, and rather unrealistic Disney World–style animated mannequins. Some find it fascinating, others silly.

Fodor's Choice

No two people will agree on what makes a perfect vacation, but it's fun and helpful to know what others think. We hope you'll have a chance to experience some of Fodor's Choices yourself while visiting Chicago. For detailed information about each entry, refer to the appropriate chapters in this guidebook.

Activities

Exploring the tomb of Unis-ankh in "Inside Ancient Egypt" at the Field Museum of Natural History

Singing "Take Me out to the Ballgame" during the seventh-inning stretch at Wrigley Field

Watching the animals in a "thunderstorm" in the rain forest at the Brookfield Zoo

Turn-of-the-Century Architecture

Fisher Building

Monadnock Building

Robie House

The Rookery

Modern Architecture

Northwestern Atrium Center

State of Illinois Center

333 West Wacker Drive

Moments

Feeding time at the coral reef of the John G. Shedd Aquarium

The skylit sculpture court at the Art Institute

The winter orchid show at the Chicago Botanic Garden

Sights

Chicago River from the Michigan Avenue Bridge

Chicago skyline from Olive Park

Chicago skyline from South Lake Shore Drive

The panoramic view of the city from the top of the John Hancock Building

Hotels

The Drake (*Very Expensive*)

The Four Seasons (*Very Expensive*)

Chicago Hilton and Towers (*Expensive*)

The Claridge (*Moderate*)

The Raphael (*Moderate*)

Restaurants

Everest (French, *Very Expensive*)

Spiaggia (Italian, *Very Expensive*)

Charlie Trotter's (American, *Expensive–Very Expensive*)

Yoshi's Cafe (French, *Expensive–Very Expensive*)

Arun's (Thai, *Expensive*)

Morton's of Chicago (Steak House, *Expensive*)

Vivere (Italian, *Expensive*)

Frontera Grill (Mexican, *Moderate*)

Taylor Street Bistro (French, *Moderate*)

Ed Debevic's (American 1950s, *Inexpensive*)

Lou Mitchell's (American, *Inexpensive*)

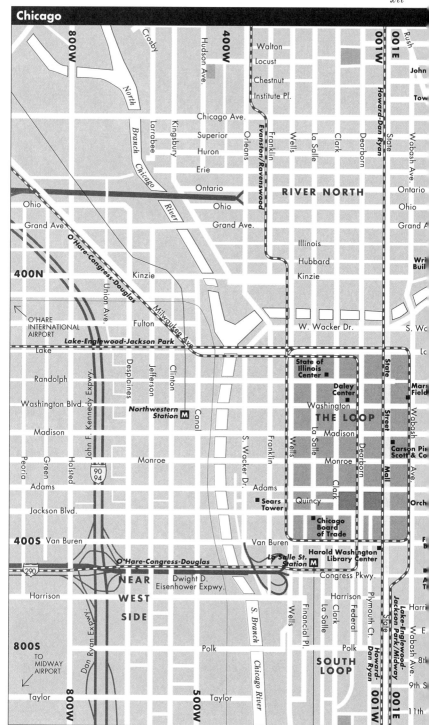

Chicago

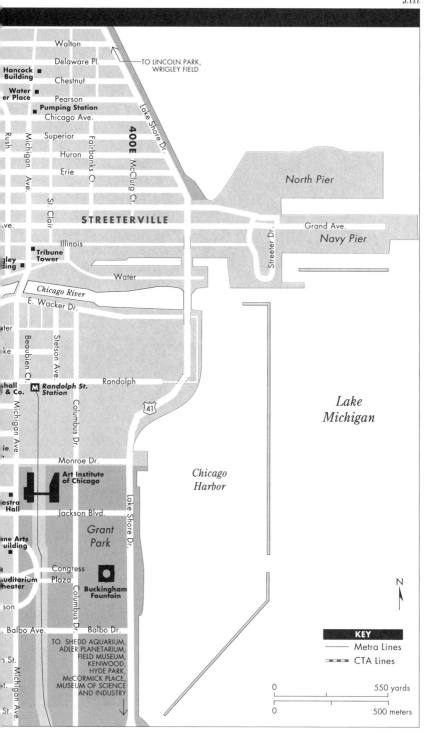

Walton

Delaware Pl.

TO LINCOLN PARK,
WRIGLEY FIELD

Hancock Building

Chestnut

Water er Place

Pearson

Pumping Station

Chicago Ave.

Superior

Huron

Erie

400E

Rush

Michigan Ave.

Fairbanks Ct.

McClurg Ct.

St. Clair

STREETERVILLE

ve.

North Pier

Grand Ave.

Navy Pier

Streeter Dr.

Illinois

gley ding

Tribune Tower

Water

Chicago River

E. Wacker Dr.

ater

ke

Beaubien Ct.

Stetson Ave.

Randolph

M Randolph St. Station

Columbus Dr.

41

Lake Michigan

Michigan Ave.

ie

Monroe Dr.

Art Institute of Chicago

Lake Shore Dr.

Chicago Harbor

estra Hall

Jackson Blvd.

Grant Park

ne Arts uilding

Congress Plaza

Columbus Dr.

N

uditorium heater

Buckingham Fountain

son

Balbo Ave.

Balbo Dr.

TO SHEDD AQUARIUM,
ADLER PLANETARIUM,
FIELD MUSEUM,
KENWOOD,
HYDE PARK,
McCORMICK PLACE,
MUSEUM OF SCIENCE
AND INDUSTRY

n St.

Michigan Ave.

t.

St.

KEY
— Metra Lines
▬▬▬ CTA Lines

0   550 yards

0   500 meters

World Time Zones

International Date Line

MONDAY
SUNDAY

+12 +13 -9 -7 -5 -4 -3

+11 +12 -11 -10 -8 -6 -4 -3:30

+11 +12

-10

-5 -4 -3

-5 -4 -3

-3

1 Auckland
2 Honolulu
3 Anchorage
4 Edmonton
5 Los Angeles
6 Los Angeles
7 Denver
8 Denver
9 Chicago
10 Dallas
11
12
13
14
15
16
17
18
19 Bogotá
20 Lima
21
22 Caracas
23
24 Buenos Aires

Numbers below vertical bands relate each zone to Greenwich Mean Time (0 hrs.).
Local times frequently differ from these general indications,
as indicated by light-face numbers on map.

Algiers, **29**	Berlin, **34**	Delhi, **48**	Istanbul, **40**
Anchorage, **3**	Bogotá, **19**	Denver, **8**	Jerusalem, **42**
Athens, **41**	Budapest, **37**	Djakarta, **53**	Johannesburg, **44**
Auckland, **1**	Buenos Aires, **24**	Dublin, **26**	Lima, **20**
Baghdad, **46**	Caracas, **22**	Edmonton, **7**	Lisbon, **28**
Bangkok, **50**	Chicago, **9**	Hong Kong, **56**	London (Greenwich), **27**
Beijing, **54**	Copenhagen, **33**	Honolulu, **2**	Los Angeles, **6**
	Dallas, **10**		Madrid, **38**
			Manila, **57**

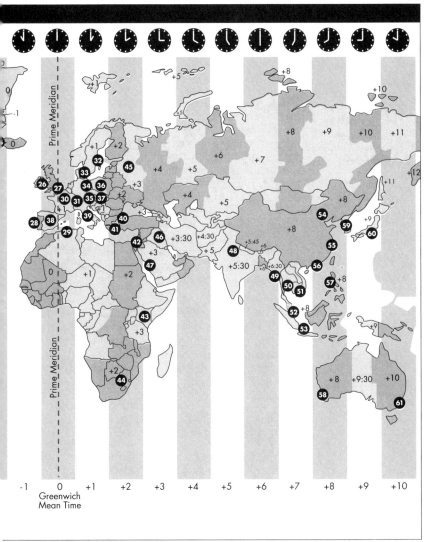

Mecca, **47**	Ottawa, **14**	San Francisco, **5**	Toronto, **13**
Mexico City, **12**	Paris, **30**	Santiago, **21**	Vancouver, **4**
Miami, **18**	Perth, **58**	Seoul, **59**	Vienna, **35**
Montréal, **15**	Reykjavík, **25**	Shanghai, **55**	Warsaw, **36**
Moscow, **45**	Rio de Janeiro, **23**	Singapore, **52**	Washington, D.C., **17**
Nairobi, **43**	Rome, **39**	Stockholm, **32**	Yangon, **49**
New Orleans, **11**	Saigon (Ho Chi Minh	Sydney, **61**	Zürich, **31**
New York City, **16**	City), **51**	Tokyo, **60**	

Introduction

*By Elizabeth
Gardner*

*Elizabeth Gardner
grew up just outside
Chicago in what is
now the Oak Park
Historic District.*

few years ago, the *Chicago Tribune* ran a piece in its Sunday magazine about what Chicago would be like without Lake Michigan. The artist's rendering showed a one-street town with a tumbleweed in the foreground. In many ways, Chicago *is* Lake Michigan. Whereas some cities radiate from a central hub, Chicago flattens out along the lakeshore like a string bean. On sunny summer weekends the whole city heads to the lakefront parks to swim (yes, you can swim in the lake, although the water could be cleaner), to sunbathe, to bicycle, to roller-skate, to stroll, to jog, and just to soak up the atmosphere. Whatever the summer weather, it's always "cooler near the lake." In winter, many fleeting snowfalls come from the "lake effect," when cold clouds hit the warmer air above the water. The lake's moods range from glassy calm to roiling tempest, and the population reacts accordingly.

The city owes its origins to Lake Michigan. Chicago was born as a shipping center when it was discovered that a series of rivers and one portage could connect the lake with the Mississippi River. Any water traffic between the east coast and the country's heartland had to pass through this damp, marshy land, christened Checagou or "place of the wild onion" by local Indians. In 1833 Chicago officially became a city. In 1836 ground was broken to turn the portage into a canal that was finally finished in 1848. The Illinois and Michigan Canal still links the Des Plaines and Illinois rivers.

People who like cities generally love Chicago. To urbanites, it's got everything: architectural wonders old and new, gracious parks, cultural institutions that rival the world's finest, outstanding restaurants, classic and avant-garde theater, music from heavy metal to weary blues, nightlife, streetlife, urban grit, and urban sophistication. Because the city is not as large or famous as New York, many Chicagoans suffer from "Second City" complex, a fear that out-of-towners won't appreciate their city's charms. But they're worrying needlessly, for the charms—from the stunning sweep of the skyline to the elegance of Michigan Avenue's shops to the tree-lined streets of the outlying neighborhoods—are hard to miss.

A number of events have left their mark on the city's history. The Great Fire of 1871 razed nearly every building between Roosevelt Road and Fullerton Avenue—a sizable chunk of the city, leaving behind a virtual blank canvas on which architects could design (*see* "The Builders of Chicago" in Chapter 2). Such giants as Louis Sullivan and Daniel H. Burnham began experimenting with the steel frames that even today define the term "skyscraper." In these architects' wake came droves of carpenters, masons, and other laborers, who flocked here to build the new Chicago. Their arrival was nothing new to Chicago, which welcomed successive waves of Germans, Swedes, Poles, Irish, Jews, and Italians throughout the 19th and early 20th centuries.

Many of these immigrants came to work in the burgeoning industries here, and their eventual uprising against wretched labor conditions had a profound impact upon the city—and the country. When Upton Sinclair published his landmark novel *The Jungle*, describing the lives of Chicago's stockyard and meatpacking workers, the public outcry was so great that it led to the 1906 passage of the federal Pure Food and Drug Act. The Haymarket Riot of May 4, 1886, began as a demonstration by workers in sympathy with strikers at the McCormick Reaper plant and ended with a bomb explosion and a melee that killed four workers and seven policemen. The Haymarket became a rallying point for the world labor movement when eight "anarchists" were convicted of the bombing in a blatantly unjust trial, and four were executed. (Governer John P. Altgeld pardoned the others in 1893, committing political suicide in the process.)

The lawless era of Prohibition will forever be linked with Chicago in people's minds. Today's city hall would like people to forget the notorious criminals who subverted the police and courts and terrorized ordinary citizens here. The tourism council's "brief history" of the city breathes not a word about gangsters. But Al Capone and John Dillinger are more famous than Chicago luminaries Frank Lloyd Wright and Ludwig Mies van der Rohe (at least, they've had more movies made about them). According to a history of the city published in 1929, murders in Cook County rose from 190 in 1920 to 399 in 1928, and felony convictions fell almost 50%. And almost 24,000 felony charges were dropped or modified in 1923 alone, due primarily to "friendly" judges. If it didn't actually create the term "racketeer," Chicago played a key role in defining it.

Like so many American cities, Chicago saw its middle class flee to the suburbs during the postwar prosperity of the 1950s and the turbulence of the 1960s. Some neighborhoods turned from rich to poor, although many ethnic enclaves on the northwest and southwest sides remained relatively stable. But in the 1970s, young "urban pioneers" began to creep back to the city, picking up run-down properties for a song and renovating them into showplaces. Meanwhile, new groups of immigrants—Vietnamese, Thai, Cambodian, Hmong, Russian Jews—were finding their niches in the city. Today each of Chicago's dozens of neighborhoods has a distinct character: the wealthy socialite Gold Coast; "lakefront liberal" Lincoln Park and Lakeview; white-ethnic

Bridgeport, Ukrainian Village and Blue Island; black middle-class South Shore; integrated Hyde Park and Beverly; and battle-scarred ghettos such as North Lawndale and Austin. Black people and white people, divided as often by an economic abyss as by skin color, coexist with caution, although overt hatred has in many cases been replaced by the pragmatic need to get along in a city where neither group predominates. (Black and white each account for about 40% of Chicago's 2.6 million people.)

Nonetheless, factions abound. The North Side and the South Side are two different worlds. You're a White Sox fan or a Cubs fan, not both (unless one of the teams is down to the wire in a serious pennant race—a once-in-a-blue-moon event that sucks in even the nonfan). The conflicts on the city council, although currently muted, are legendary. Even in a city chronically strapped for cash, don't try to suggest closing an under-used public school or cutting service to a redundant El stop, except over the ward alderman's dead body.

It's true that Chicagoans can be contentious, territorial, and possessive. Although the city's official motto is "Urbs in Horto" (City in a Garden), its unofficial one is "Ubi est Meus?" (Where's Mine?). But to visitors, Chicagoans are as friendly and open as big-city dwellers can be. Perhaps the one thing that unites many of them is unparalleled civic chauvinism. Don't be shy about asking directions or questions; people will probably tell you more than you really want to know. You'll find the city straightforward and unpretentious: For every club imported from the coast where your outfit has to pass muster with the doorman, there are a hundred corner bars where you'll be welcome in anything from a tux to a T-shirt. To meet the real Chicago, try to get away from downtown a little and venture into the 'hoods, preferably with a local guide. (*See* Chapter 3 for some of our favorites.) And if you get lost, just remember the one Chicago rule: The lake is east.

1 Essential Information

Before You Go

Visitor Information

For information on the city, contact the **Chicago Office of Tourism** (806 N. Michigan Ave., Water Tower in the Park, Chicago, IL 60611, tel. 312/280–5740 or 800/487–2446).

If you plan on traveling outside Chicago, contact the **Illinois Bureau of Tourism** (310 S. Michigan Ave., Chicago, IL 60601, tel. 800/233–0121) for a free packet on travel in Illinois.

Tours and Packages

Should you buy your travel arrangements packaged or do it yourself? There are advantages either way. Buying packaged arrangements saves you money, particularly if you can find a program that includes exactly the features you want. You also get a pretty good idea of what your trip will cost from the outset. Generally, you have two options: fully escorted tours and independent packages. Escorted tours are most often via motorcoach, with a tour director in charge. They're ideal if you don't mind having limited free time and traveling with strangers. Your baggage is handled, your time rigorously scheduled, and most meals planned. Such tours are therefore the most hassle-free way to see a destination, as well as generally the least expensive. Independent packages allow plenty of flexibility. They generally include airline travel and hotels, with certain options available, such as sightseeing, car rental, and excursions. Such packages are usually more expensive than escorted tours, but your time is your own.

While you can book directly through tour operators, you will pay no more to go through a travel agent, who will be able to tell you about tours and packages from a number of operators. Whatever program you ultimately choose, be sure to find out exactly what is included: taxes, tips, transfers, meals, baggage handling, ground transportation, entertainment, excursions, sports or recreation (and rental equipment if necessary). Ask about the level of hotel used, its location, the size of its rooms, the kind of beds, and its amenities, such as pool, room service, or programs for children, if they're important to you. Find out the operator's cancellation penalties. Nearly everyone charges them, and the only way to avoid them is to buy trip-cancellation insurance. Also ask about the single supplement, a surcharge assessed to solo travelers. Some operators do not make you pay it if you agree to be matched up with a roommate of the same sex, even if one is not found by departure time. Remember that a program that has features you won't use may not be the most cost-wise choice for you.

Fully Escorted Tours Escorted tours are usually sold in three categories: deluxe, first-class, and tourist or budget class. The most important differences are the price, of course, and the level of accommodations. Some operators specialize in one category, while others offer a range.

Contact **Maupintour** (Box 807, Lawrence, KS 66044, tel. 913/843–1211 or 800/255–4266) in the deluxe category; **Globus-Gateway** (95-25 Queens Blvd, Rego Park, NY 11374, tel.

718/268–7000 or 800/221–0900); **Brendan Tours** (15137 Califa St., Van Nuys, CA 91411, tel. 818/785–9696 or 800/421–8446); **Mayflower Tours** (1255 Warren Ave., Downers Grove, IL 60515, tel. 708/960–3430 or 800/323–7604) in the first-class category; and **Cosmos,** a sister company of Globus (*see above*), in the budget category.

Most itineraries are jam-packed with sightseeing, so you see a lot in a short amount of time (usually one place per day). To judge just how fast-paced the tour is, review the itinerary carefully. If you are in a different hotel each night, you will be getting up early each day to head out, travel to your next destination, do some sightseeing, have dinner, and go to bed; then you'll start all over again. If you want some free time, make sure it's mentioned in the tour brochure; if you want to be escorted to every meal, confirm that any tour you consider does that. Also, when comparing programs, be sure to find out if the motorcoach is air-conditioned and has a restroom on board. Make your selection based on price and stops on the itinerary.

Independent Packages   Independent packages are offered by airlines, tour operators who may also do escorted programs, and any number of other companies from large, established firms to small, new entrepreneurs.

Airlines offering packages to the city include **America West** (tel. 800/356–6611), **American Airlines Fly AAway Vacations** (tel. 800/321–2121), **Continental's Grand Destinations** (tel. 800/634–5555), **Delta Dream Vacations** (tel. 800/872–7786), and **United** (tel. 800/328–6877). **Supercities** (7855 Haskell Ave., Van Nuys, CA 91406, tel. 818/988–7844 or 800/333–1234) offers packages with a choice of hotels. **Amtrak** (tel. 800/872–7245) also offers hotel and sightseeing packages.

Their programs come in a wide range of prices based on levels of luxury and options—in addition to hotel and airfare, sightseeing, car rental, transfers, admission to local attractions, and other extras. Note that when pricing different packages, it sometimes pays to purchase the same arrangements separately, as when a rock-bottom promotional airfare is being offered, for example. Again, base your choice on what's available at your budget for the destinations you want to visit.

Special-Interest Travel   Special-interest programs may be fully escorted or independent. Some require a certain amount of expertise, but most are for the average traveler with an interest and are usually hosted by experts in the subject matter. When the program is escorted, it enjoys the advantages and disadvantages of all escorted programs; because your fellow travelers are apt to be passionate or knowledgeable about the subject, they can prove as enjoyable a part of your travel experience as the destination itself. The price range is wide, but the cost is usually higher—sometimes a lot higher—than for ordinary escorted tours and packages, because of the expert guiding and special activities.

Music   **Dailey-Thorp** (315 West 57th St., New York, NY 10019, tel. 212/307–1555) offers opera and other performing arts tours to Chicago periodically. Call for details on this year's itineraries.

Historic Homes   **Adventures in Elegance** (1187 Wilmette Ave., Wilmette, IL 60091, tel. 708/615–2251 or 800/666–2251) offers tours of private historic homes and mansions along Chicago's elegant

North Shore. Tours are led by an historian who discusses the architectural and historic significance of homes and other points of interest along the shore, within the city limits and into the suburbs.

Art The **Art Institute of Chicago** (Michigan Ave. at Adams St., Chicago, IL 60603, tel. 312/443–3944 or 800/676–6101) offers weekend packages to Chicago that include hotel accommodations and free admission to the Institute's superb museum (*see* Chapter 3, Exploring Chicago).

Tips for British Travelers

Government Tourist Office Contact the **United States Travel and Tourism Administration** (Box 1EN, London WIA 1EN, tel. 071/495–4466).

Passports and Visas British subjects need a valid 10-year passport. A visa is not necessary unless (1) you are planning to stay more than 90 days, (2) your trip is for purposes other than vacation, (3) you have at some time been refused a visa, or refused admission, to the United States or have been required to leave by the U.S. Immigration and Naturalization Service, or (4) you do not have a return or onward ticket. You will need to fill out the Visa Waiver Form 1–94W, supplied by the airline.

To apply for a visa or for more information, call the **U.S. Embassy's Visa Information Line** (tel. 0891/200–290; calls cost 48p per minute or 36p per minute cheap rate). If you qualify for visa-free travel but want a visa anyway, you must apply in writing, enclosing an SAE, to the U.S. Embassy's Visa Branch (5 Upper Grosvenor St., London W1A 2JB), or, for residents of Northern Ireland, to the U.S. Consulate General (Queen's House, Queen St., Belfast BT1 6EO). Submit a completed Nonimmigrant Visa Application (Form 156), a valid passport, a photograph, and evidence of your intended departure from the United States after a temporary visit. If you require a visa, call 0891/234–224 to schedule an interview.

Customs British visitors aged 21 or over may import the following into the United States: 200 cigarettes or 50 cigars or 2 kilograms of tobacco; one U.S. liter of alcohol; gifts to the value of $100. Restricted items include meat products, seeds, plants, and fruits. Never carry illegal drugs.

Insurance Most tour operators, travel agents, and insurance agents sell specialized policies covering accident, medical expenses, personal liability, trip cancellation, and loss or theft of personal property. Some policies include coverage for delayed departure and legal expenses, winter-sports, accidents, or motoring abroad. You can also purchase an annual travel-insurance policy valid for every trip you make during the year in which it's purchased (usually only trips of less than 90 days). Before you leave, make sure you will be covered if you have a preexisting medical condition or are pregnant; your insurers may not pay for routine or continuing treatment, or may require a note from your doctor certifying your fitness to travel.

The **Association of British Insurers,** a trade association representing 450 insurance companies, advises extra medical coverage for visitors to the United States.

For advice by phone or a free booklet, "Holiday Insurance," that sets out what to expect from a holiday-insurance policy and gives price guidelines, contact the Association of British Insurers (51 Gresham St., London EC2V 7HQ, tel. 071/600–3333; 30 Gordon St., Glasgow G1 3PU, tel. 041/226–3905; Scottish Provincial Bldg., Donegall Sq. W, Belfast BT1 6JE, tel. 0232/249176; call for other locations).

Tour Operators Tour operators offering packages to Chicago include **British Airways Holidays** (Atlantic House, Hazelwick Ave., Crawley, West Sussex RH10 1NP, tel. 0293/611611), **Kuoni Travel** (Kuoni House, Dorking, Surrey RH5 4AZ, tel. 0306/742222), and **North American Vacations** (Acorn House, 172/174 Albert Rd., Jarrow, Tyne & Wear NE32 5JA, tel. 091/483–6226).

Car Rentals Major firms include **Alamo** (tel. 0800/272–200), **Budget** (tel. 0800/181–181), **EuroDollar** (tel. 0895/233–300), **Europcar** (tel. 081/950–5050), and **Hertz** (tel. 081/679–1799). In the United States you must be 21 to rent a car; some companies rent only to those over 25, or charge extra for those under 25. Extra costs cover child seats, compulsory for under 5s (about $3 per day), and additional drivers (around $8 per day). For more details, *see* Car Rentals, *below.* To pick up your reserved car, you will need the reservation voucher, a passport, a United Kingdom driver's license, and a travel insurance policy covering each driver.

Hints for Travelers with Disabilities Main information sources include the **Royal Association for Disability and Rehabilitation** (RADAR, 25 Mortimer St., London W1N 8AB, tel. 071/637–5400), which publishes travel information for the disabled in Britain, and **Mobility International** (228 Borough High St., London SE1 1JX, tel. 071/403–5688), the headquarters of an international membership organization that serves as a clearinghouse of travel information for people with disabilities.

When to Go

Chicago has activities and attractions to keep visitors busy at any time of year. Travelers whose principal concern is comfortable weather for touring the city may prefer spring or fall, when moderate temperatures make it a pleasure to be out and about. Late fall in Chicago sees lavish Christmas decorations in the stores of the Magnificent Mile and the State Street Mall.

Summertime brings many opportunities for outdoor recreation, although temperatures will climb into the 90s in hot spells, and the humidity can be uncomfortably high. Lake Michigan has a moderating effect on the city's weather, keeping it several degrees cooler in summer, a bit warmer in winter.

Winters can see very raw weather and the occasional newsmaking blizzard, and temperatures in the teens are to be expected; wintertime visitors should come prepared for the cold. Yet mild winters, with temperatures in the 30s, are common, too. There are January sales to reward those who venture out, and many indoor venues let one look out on the cold in warm comfort.

Climate What follows are the average daily maximum and minimum temperatures for Chicago.

Jan.	32F	0C	May	65F	18C	Sept.	73F	23C
	18	− 8		50	10		58	14
Feb.	34F	1C	June	75F	24C	Oct.	61F	16C
	20	− 7		60	16		47	8
Mar.	43F	6C	July	81F	27C	Nov.	47F	8C
	29	− 2		66	19		34	1
Apr.	55F	13C	Aug.	79F	26C	Dec.	36F	2C
	40	4		65	18		23	− 5

Information Sources For current weather conditions for cities in the United States and abroad, plus the local time and helpful travel tips, call the **Weather Channel Connection** (tel. 900/932–8437; 95¢ per minute) from a touch-tone phone.

Festivals and Seasonal Events

Chicagoans love celebrations. Spring and summer are the festival seasons, while celebrations move indoors for the winter. The following is a sampling of the many events in Chicago. For precise dates and details, contact the Chicago Office of Tourism (*see* Government Tourist Offices, *above*) or consult one of Chicago's local events calenders: The Reader, and *New City,* two free weekly newspapers distributed on Thursday in many stores in Hyde Park, the Loop, and the North Side; the "Friday" section of the Friday *Chicago Tribune;* and the "Weekender" section of the Friday *Chicago Sun-Times.*

Month of Feb.: Black History Month celebrations at the Museum of Science and Industry (57th St. and Lake Shore Dr., tel. 312/684–1414), the DuSable Museum (740 E. 56th Pl., tel. 312/947–0600), the Chicago Cultural Center (78 E. Washington St., tel. 312/269–2900), the Field Museum (Roosevelt Rd. at Lake Shore Dr., tel. 312/922–9410), the Art Institute of Chicago (Michigan Ave. at Adams St., tel. 312/443–3600) and other Chicago cultural institutions include arts and crafts exhibitions and theater, music, and dance performances.

Mid-Feb.–Early Mar.: Azalea and Camellia Show at Lincoln Park Conservatory (2400 N. Stockton Dr., tel. 312/294–4770).

Early Feb.: Chicago International Auto Show previews next year's domestic and imported models (McCormick Pl., 2300 S. Lake Shore Dr., tel. 312/698–6630).

Late Feb.–mid-Mar.: Medinah Shrine Circus at Medinah Temple (600 N. Wabash Ave., tel. 312/266–5000).**Mar. 17:** The Chicago River is dyed green and the center stripe of Dearborn Street is painted the color of the Irish for a **St. Patrick's Day parade** from Wacker Drive to Van Buren Street.

Late Mar.–early Apr.: Spring and Easter Flower Show blooms at the Lincoln Park Conservatory.

Mid-May: International Art Exposition in Donnelley International Hall at McCormick Place (2300 S. Lake Shore Dr., tel. 312/787–6858).

Mid-May: See masterpieces by Frank Lloyd Wright and other Prairie School architects on the **Wright Plus House Walk,** Oak Park (tel. 708/848–1978).

Late May: Festival of Illinois Film and Video Artists, a two-day visual arts display, has events at various theaters (tel. 312/663–1600).

Late May: Chicago Blues Festival in Grant Park, a three-day, three-stage event featuring blues greats from Chicago and around the country (tel. 312/744–0571).

Memorial Day: Buckingham Fountain, in Grant Park, is turned on. Colored lights nightly, 9–10, through Labor Day.

Early June: Body Politic Street Festival takes over the 2200 North block of Lincoln Avenue with food and theatrics (tel. 312/348–7901).

Early June: 57th Street Art Fair (Ray School yard, 57th St., and Kimbark Ave.), one of the major juried art fairs in the Midwest, selects exhibitors from applicants from all over the country. Offerings include paintings, sculpture, jewelry, ceramics, and clothing and textiles (tel. 312/744–3315).

Mid-June: Printer's Row Book Fair, a two-day event in the historic Printer's Row District, is built around books and the printer's and binder's arts. Clowns, jugglers, and food vendors weave their way through displays from major and specialty booksellers and craftspeople demonstrating book-related arts (Dearborn St. between Harrison St. and Polk St., tel. 312/663–1595).

Mid-June: The Boulevard–Lakefront Bicycle Tour brings 5,000 cyclists to the city's network of boulevards and parks for a 35-mile ride (tel. 312/427–3325).

Mid-June: Chicago Gospel Fest brings its joyful sounds to Grant Park (tel. 312/744–5368).

June 17–July 5: Opening ceremonies and five games of **World Cup Soccer** come to Soldier Field (tel. 312/923–1994).

Late June: Grant Park Symphony Orchestra and Chorus give four concerts weekly through mid-August (tel. 312/294–2420).

Late June–early Sept: Ravinia Festival, Highland Park, hosts a variety of classical and popular musical artists in a pastoral setting north of the city (tel. 312/728–4642).

All summer: Noontime music and dance performances are held outdoors weekdays at the Daley Plaza Civic Center (Washington St. between Dearborn and Clark Sts.) and at the First National Bank of Chicago Plaza (Dearborn St. at Madison St.).

July 3: Evening fireworks along the lakefront; bring a blanket and a portable radio to listen to the *1812 Overture* from Grant Park (tel. 312/744–3315).

Early July: Taste of Chicago (Columbus Dr. between Jackson and Randolph) feeds 4 million curious visitors with specialties from scores of Chicago restaurants.

Late July: Air and water show along the Near North lakefront at North Avenue features precision flying teams and antique and high-tech aircraft going through their paces.

Late July: Chicago to Mackinac Island Boat Race originates at Belmont Harbor (Monroe St. Harbor, tel. 312/861–7777).

Mid-Aug.: Venetian Night features fireworks and boats festooned with lights (Monroe St. Harbor, Grant Park, tel. 312/744–3315).

Late Aug.: Chicago Triathlon participants plunge in at Oak Street Beach for a one-mile swim, followed by a 10-kilometer run and a 25-mile bike race on Lake Shore Drive.

Labor Day: *Chicago Tribune* **Ribfest** in Grant Park (tel. 312/222–3232) sees some 500 avid barbecuers and their friends generate a dense, aromatic cloud of hickory smoke seasoned with beer that hovers over the central city.

Labor Day weekend: Chicago Jazz Festival, Grant Park.

Mid-Sept.: International New Art Forms Exposition comes to Navy Pier (tel. 312/787–6858).

Mid-Sept.: Viva Chicago, a festival of Latin music, comes to Grant Park (tel. 312/744–8520).

Late Sept.–early Oct.: Oktoberfest brings out the best in beer and German specialties at the Berghoff Restaurant (17 W. Adams St., tel. 312/427–3170) and Chicago area pubs.

Columbus Day: Columbus Day Parade on Dearborn Street from Wacker Drive to Congress Street.

Mid-Oct.: International Antiques Show, Navy Pier (tel. 312/787–6858).

Late Oct.: Chicago Marathon starts at Daley Bicentennial Plaza and follows a course through the city (tel. 312/951–0660).

Late Oct.–early Nov.: Chicago International Film Festival brings new American and foreign films to the Music Box and Biograph theaters (tel. 312/644–3400).

Thanksgiving Weekend: Friday marks the illumination of **Chicago's Christmas tree** in the Daley Center Plaza (Washington St. between Dearborn and Clark Sts.). The **Christmas parade,** with balloons, floats, and Santa travels down Michigan Avenue on Saturday.

Late Nov.–Dec.: Christmas Around the World display at the Museum of Science and Industry features trees decorated in the traditional styles of more than 40 countries.

Late Nov.–early Dec.: The Goodman Theatre (200 S. Columbus Dr., tel. 1312/443–3800) presents *A Christmas Carol,* and *The Nutcracker* is performed at the Arie Crown Theatre at McCormick Place (2300 S. Lake Shore Dr., tel. 312/791–6000).

Late Dec.–early Jan.: Christmas Flower Show at Lincoln Park Conservatory.

What to Pack

Clothing Pack light, because porters and luggage carts are hard to find. Be prepared for cold, snowy weather in the winter and hot, sticky weather in the summer. Jeans (shorts in summer) and T-shirts or sweaters and slacks are fine for sightseeing and informal dining. Men will need jackets and ties, women dresses, for many expensive restaurants. In winter take boots or a sturdy pair of shoes with nonslip soles for icy sidewalks, and a hat to protect your ears from the numbing winds that buffet Michigan Avenue. In summer, bring a swimsuit for Lake Michigan swimming or sunning.

Miscellaneous Bring an extra pair of eyeglasses or contact lenses. If you have a health problem that may require you to purchase a prescription drug, pack enough to last the duration of the trip. And don't forget to pack a list of the addresses of offices that supply refunds for lost or stolen traveler's checks.

Luggage Free baggage allowances on an airline depend on the airline, *Regulations* the route, and the class of your ticket. In general, on domestic flights you are entitled to check two bags—neither exceeding 62 inches, or 158 centimeters (length + width + height), or weighing more than 70 pounds (32 kilograms). A third piece may be brought aboard as a carryon; its total dimensions are generally limited to less than 45 inches (114 centimeters), so it will fit easily under the seat in front of you or in the overhead compartment. There are variations, so ask in advance. The single rule, a Federal Aviation Administration safety regulation that pertains to carry-on baggage on U.S. airlines, requires that carryons be properly stowed and allows the airline to limit allowances and tailor them to different aircraft and operational conditions. Charges for excess, oversize, or overweight pieces vary, so inquire before you pack.

Safeguarding Your Luggage Before leaving home, itemize your bags' contents and their worth; this list will help you estimate the extent of your loss if your bags go astray. To minimize that risk, tag them inside and out with your name, address, and phone number. (If you use your home address, cover it so that potential thieves can't see it.) At check-in, make sure that the tag attached by baggage handlers bears the correct three-letter code for your destination. If your bags do not arrive with you, or if you detect damage, do not leave the airport until you've filed a written report with the airline.

Insurance In the event of loss, damage, or theft on domestic flights, airlines limit their liability to $1,250 per passenger. Excess-valuation insurance can be bought directly from the airline at check-in but leaves your bags vulnerable on the ground. Your own homeowner's policy may fill the gap; or you may want special luggage insurance. Sources include **The Travelers Companies** (1 Tower Sq., Hartford, CT 06183, tel. 203/277–0111 or 800/243–3174) and **Wallach and Company, Inc.** (107 W. Federal St., Box 480, Middleburg, VA 22117, tel. 703/687–3166 or 800/237–6615), underwritten by Lloyds, London.

Traveler's Checks

The most widely recognized are **American Express, Thomas Cook, Visa,** and those issued by major commercial banks such as **Citibank** and **Bank of America.** American Express also issues *Traveler's Cheques for Two,* which can be counter-signed and used by you or your traveling companion. Some checks are free; usually the issuing company or the bank at which you make your purchase charges 1%–1¹/₂% of the checks' face value as a fee. Be sure to buy a few checks in small denominations to cash toward the end of your trip, when you don't want to be left with more foreign currency than you can spend. Always record the numbers of checks as you spend them, and keep this list separate from the checks.

Getting Money from Home

Cash Machines Automated-teller machines (ATMs) are proliferating; many are tied to international networks such as **Cirrus** and **Plus.** You can use your bank card at ATMs away from home to withdraw money from an account and get cash advances on a credit-card account (providing your card has been programmed with a personal identification number, or PIN). Check in advance on limits on withdrawals and cash advances within specified periods. Remember that on cash advances you are charged interest from the day you get the money from ATMs as well as from tellers. And note that transaction fees for ATM withdrawals outside your home turf will probably be higher than for withdrawals at home.

For specific Cirrus locations in the United States and Canada, call 800/424–7787 (for U.S. Plus locations, 800/843–7587), and press the area code and first three digits of the number you're calling from (or the calling area where you want an ATM).

American Express Cardholder Services The company's **Express Cash** system lets you withdraw cash and/or traveler's checks from a worldwide network of 57,000 American Express dispensers and participating bank ATMs. You must *enroll first* (call 800/227–4669 for a form and allow two weeks for processing). Withdrawals are charged not to your card but to a designated bank account. You can withdraw up to $1,000 per seven-day period on the basic card, more if your card is gold or platinum. There is a 2% fee (minimum $2.50, maximum $10) for each cash transaction, and a 1% fee for traveler's checks (except for the platinum card), which are available only from American Express dispensers.

At AmEx offices, cardholders can also cash personal checks for up to $1,000 in any seven-day period; of this $200 can be in cash, more if available, with the balance paid in traveler's checks, for which all but platinum cardholders pay a 1% fee. Higher limits apply to the gold and platinum cards.

Wiring Money You don't have to be a cardholder to send or receive an **American Express MoneyGram** for up to $10,000. To send one, go to an American Express MoneyGram agent, pay up to $1,000 with a credit card and anything over that in cash, and phone a transaction reference number to your intended recipient, who needs only present identification and the reference number to the nearest MoneyGram agent to pick up the cash. There are MoneyGram agents in more than 60 countries (call 800/543–4080 for locations). Fees range from 5% to 10%, depending on the amount and how you pay. You can't use American Express, which is really a convenience card—only Discover, Master-Card, and Visa credit cards.

You can also use **Western Union.** To wire money, take either cash or a check to the nearest office. (Or you can call and use a credit card.) Fees are roughly 5%–10%. Money sent from the United States or Canada will be available for pickup at agent locations in Chicago within minutes. There are approximately 20,000 agents worldwide (call 800/325–6000 for locations).

Traveling with Cameras, Camcorders, and Laptops

Film and Cameras If your camera is new or if you haven't used it for a while, shoot and develop a few rolls of film before leaving home. Pack some lens tissue and an extra battery for your built-in light meter, and invest in an inexpensive skylight filter, to both protect your lens and provide some definition in hazy shots. Store film in a cool, dry place—never in the car's glove compartment or on the shelf under the rear window.

Films above ISO 400 are more sensitive to damage from airport security X-rays than others; very high speed films, ISO 1,000 and above, are exceedingly vulnerable. To protect your film, don't put it in checked luggage; carry it with you in a plastic bag and ask for a hand inspection. Such requests are honored at American airports. Don't depend on a lead-lined bag to protect film in checked luggage—the airline may very well turn up the dosage of radiation to see what you've got in there. Airport metal detectors do not harm film, although you'll set off the alarm if you walk through one with a roll in your pocket. Call the Kodak Information Center (tel. 800/242–2424) for details.

Camcorders Before your trip, put new or long-unused camcorders through their paces, and practice panning and zooming. Invest in a sky-light filter to protect the lens, and check the lithium battery that lights up the LCD (liquid crystal display) modes. As for the rechargeable nickel-cadmium batteries that are the camera's power source, take along an extra pair, so while you're using your camcorder you'll have one battery ready and another recharging.

Videotape Unlike still-camera film, videotape is not damaged by X-rays. However, it may well be harmed by the magnetic field of a walk-through metal detector. Airport security personnel may want you to turn the camcorder on to prove that that's what it is, so make sure the battery is charged when you get to the airport.

Laptops Security X-rays do not harm hard-disk or floppy-disk storage. Most airlines allow you to use your laptop aloft but request that you turn it off during takeoff and landing so as not to interfere with navigation equipment. Make sure the battery is charged when you arrive at the airport, because you may be asked to turn on the computer at security checkpoints to prove that it is what it appears to be. If you're a heavy computer user, consider traveling with a backup battery.

Car Rentals

All major car-rental companies are represented in Chicago, including **Avis** (tel. 800/331–1212, 800/879–2847 in Canada); **Budget** (tel. 800/527–0700); **Dollar** (tel. 800/800–4000); **Hertz** (tel. 800/654–3131, 800/263-0600 in Canada); and **National** (tel. 800/227–7368). Local and lower-cost companies include **Airways** (tel. 312/332–3434), **Fender Benders** (tel. 312/569–2678), and **Rent-a-Wreck** (tel. 800/535–1391). Unlimited-mileage rates range from about $35 per day for an economy car to $45 for a large car; weekly unlimited-mileage rates range from about $125 to $250. This does not include taxes, which in Chicago total 18% on car rentals.

Extra Charges Picking up the car in one city and leaving it in another may entail drop-off charges or one-way service fees, which can be substantial.

Cutting Costs If you know you will want a car for more than a day or two, you can save by planning ahead. Major international companies have programs that discount their standard rates by 15%–30% if you make the reservation before departure (anywhere from two to 14 days), rent for a minimum number of days (typically three or four), and prepay the rental. Ask about these advance-purchase schemes when you call for information. More economical rentals are those that come as part of fly/drive or other packages, even those as bare-bones as the rental plus an airline ticket (*see* Tours and Packages, *above*).

Other sources of savings are the companies that operate as wholesalers—companies that do not own their own fleets but rent in bulk from those that do and offer advantageous rates to their customers. Rentals through such companies must be arranged and paid for in advance. Among them is **Auto Europe** (Box 1097, Camden, ME 04843, tel. 207/236–8235 or 800/223–5555, 800/458–9503 in Canada). Ask if unlimited mileage is available, and find out about any required deposits, cancellation penalties, and drop-off charges.

One last tip: Remember to fill the tank when you turn in the vehicle, to avoid being charged for refueling at what you'll swear is the most expensive pump in town.

Insurance and Collision Damage Waiver The standard rental contract includes liability coverage (for damage to public property, injury to pedestrians, etc.) and coverage for the car against fire, theft (not included in certain countries), and collision damage with a deductible—most commonly $2,000–$3,000, occasionally more. In the case of an accident, you are responsible for the deductible amount unless you've purchased the collision damage waiver (CDW). However, Illinois has outlawed the sale of CDW altogether; coverage is included in the price of the rental.

Traveling with Children

Publications *Local Guides* *Chicago Parent* (141 S. Oak Park Ave., Oak Park, IL 60302, tel. 708/386–5555) is a monthly publication with events and resource listings that is available free at locations throughout the city.

Newsletter *Family Travel Times*, published 10 times a year by Travel With Your Children (TWYCH, 45 W. 18th St., 7th Floor Tower, New York, NY 10011, tel. 212/206–0688; annual subscription $55), covers destinations, types of vacations, and modes of travel.

Books *Great Vacations with Your Kids*, by Dorothy Jordon and Marjorie Cohen ($13; Penguin USA, 120 Woodbine St., Bergenfield, NJ 07621, tel. 800/253–6476) and *Traveling with Children— And Enjoying It*, by Arlene K. Butler ($11.95 plus $3 shipping per book; Globe Pequot Press, Box 833, Old Saybrook, CT 06475, tel. 800/243–0495, or 800/962–0973 in CT) help plan your trip with children, from toddlers to teens.

Tour Operators **GrandTravel** (6900 Wisconsin Ave., Suite 706, Chevy Chase, MD 20815, tel. 301/986–0790 or 800/247–7651) offers international and domestic tours for grandparents traveling with their grandchildren. The catalogue, as charmingly written and illustrated as a children's book, positively invites armchair traveling with lap-sitters aboard. **Rascals in Paradise** (650 5th St., Suite 505, San Francisco, CA 94107, tel. 415/978–9800, or 800/872–7225) specializes in programs for families.

Getting There *Air Fares* On domestic flights, children under 2 not occupying a seat travel free, and older children currently travel on the "lowest applicable" adult fare.

Baggage The adult baggage allowance applies for children paying half or more of the adult fare. Check with the airline for particulars.

Safety Seats The FAA recommends the use of safety seats aloft and details approved models in the free leaflet "Child/Infant Safety Seats Recommended for Use in Aircraft" (available from the Federal Aviation Administration, APA–200, 800 Independence Ave. SW, Washington, DC 20591, tel. 202/267–3479). Airline policy varies. U.S. carriers must allow FAA-approved models, but because these seats are strapped into a regular passenger seat, they may require that parents buy a ticket even for an infant under 2 who would otherwise ride free.

Facilities Aloft Airlines do provide other facilities and services for children, such as children's meals and freestanding bassinets (to those sitting in seats on the bulkhead, where there's enough legroom to accommodate them). Make your request when reserving.

The annual February/March issue of *Family Travel Times* gives details of the children's services of dozens of airlines ($10; *see above*). "Kids and Teens in Flight" (free from the U.S. Department of Transportation, tel. 202/366–2220) offers tips for children flying alone.

Lodging **The Ritz-Carlton** (160 E. Pearson St., Chicago, IL 60611, tel. 312/266–1000 or 800/621–6906) provides many children's services, from complimentary strollers to a children's menu, and kids stay free in their parents' room. At the **Drake** (140 E. Walton Place, Chicago, IL 60611, tel. 312/787–2200), children under 18 stay free, and there is a children's menu in the restaurant. Most **Days Inn** hotels (tel. 800/325–2525) charge only a nominal fee for children under 18 and allow kids 12 and under to eat free; many offer efficiency-type apartments, too. Many other Chicago hotels offer family plans in which kids stay free or at nominal cost in their parents' room (*see* Chapter 7); inquire when making reservations.

Baby-Sitting Services Make child-care arrangements with your hotel or through **American Registry for Nurses and Sitters** (3921 N. Lincoln Ave., Chicago, IL 60613, tel. 312/248–8100) and **Art Resource Studio** (537 W. Diversey Pkwy., Chicago, IL 60614, tel. 312/975–1671), with weekday craft workshops and drop-off care on weekends. Call ahead, as hours vary.

Hints for Travelers with Disabilities

Access Living (310 S. Peoria, Suite 201, Chicago, IL 60607) offers personal-attendant referrals for disabled travelers.

Organizations Several organizations provide travel information for people with disabilities, usually for a membership fee, and some publish newsletters and bulletins. Among them are the **Information Center for Individuals with Disabilities** (Fort Point Pl., 27–43 Wormwood St., Boston, MA 02210, tel. 617/727–5540 or 800/462–5015 in MA between 11 and 4, or leave message; TDD/TTY tel. 617/345–9743); **Mobility International USA** (Box 3551, Eugene, OR 97403, voice and TDD tel. 503/343–1284), the U.S. branch of an international organization based in Britain (*see below*) and present in 30 countries; **MossRehab Hospital Travel Information Service** (1200 W. Tabor Rd., Philadelphia, PA 19141, tel. 215/456–9603, TDD tel. 215/456–9602); the **Society for the Advancement of Travel for the Handicapped** (SATH, 347 5th Ave., Suite 610, New York, NY 10016, tel. 212/447–7284, fax 212/725–8253); the **Travel Industry and Disabled Exchange** (TIDE, 5435 Donna Ave., Tarzana, CA 91356, tel. 818/368–5648); and **Travelin' Talk** (Box 3534, Clarksville, TN 37043, tel. 615/552–6670).

Travel Agencies and Tour Operators **Directions Unlimited** (720 N. Bedford Rd., Bedford Hills, NY 10507, tel. 914/241–1700), a travel agency, has expertise in tours and cruises for the disabled. **Evergreen Travel Service** (4114 198th St. SW, Suite 13, Lynnwood, WA 98036, tel. 206/776–1184 or 800/435–2288) operates Wings on Wheels Tours for those in wheelchairs, White Cane Tours for the blind, and tours for the deaf and makes group and independent arrangements for travelers with any disability. **Flying Wheels Travel** (143 W. Bridge St., Box 382, Owatonna, MN 55060, tel. 800/535–6790 or 800/722–9351 in MN), a tour operator and travel agency, arranges international tours, cruises, and independent travel itineraries for people with mobility disabilities. **Nautilus,** at the same address as TIDE (*see above*), packages tours for the disabled internationally.

Publications In addition to the fact sheets, newsletters, and books mentioned above are several free publications available from the Consumer Information Center (Pueblo, CO 81009): "New Horizons for the Air Traveler with a Disability," a U.S. Department of Transportation booklet describing changes resulting from the 1986 Air Carrier Access Act and those still to come from the 1990 Americans with Disabilities Act (include Department 608Y in the address), and the Airport Operators Council's *Access Travel: Airports* (Dept. 5804), which describes facilities and services for the disabled at more than 500 airports worldwide.

Twin Peaks Press (Box 129, Vancouver, WA 98666, tel. 206/694–2462 or 800/637–2256) publishes the *Directory of Travel Agencies for the Disabled* ($19.95), listing more than 370 agencies worldwide; *Travel for the Disabled* ($19.95), listing some 500 access guides and accessible places worldwide; the *Directory of Accessible Van Rentals* ($9.95) for campers and RV travelers worldwide; and *Wheelchair Vagabond* ($14.95), a collection of personal travel tips. Add $2 per book for shipping.

Hints for Older Travelers

Organizations The **American Association of Retired Persons** (AARP, 601 E St. NW, Washington, DC 20049, tel. 202/434–2277) provides independent travelers the Purchase Privilege Program, which offers discounts on hotels, car rentals, and sightseeing, and the AARP Motoring Plan, provided by Amoco, which furnishes domestic trip-routing information and emergency road-service aid for an annual fee of $39.95 per person or couple ($59.95 for a premium version). AARP also arranges group tours, cruises, and apartment living through AARP Travel Experience from American Express (400 Pinnacle Way, Suite 450, Norcross, GA 30071, tel. 800/927–0111); these can be booked through travel agents, except for the cruises, which must be booked directly (tel. 800/745–4567). AARP membership is open to those 50 and over; annual dues are $8 per person or couple.

Two other membership organizations offer discounts on lodgings, car rentals, and other travel products, along with such nontravel perks as magazines and newsletters. The **National Council of Senior Citizens** (1331 F St. NW, Washington, DC 20004, tel. 202/347–8800) is a nonprofit advocacy group with some 5,000 local clubs across the United States; membership costs $12 per person or couple annually. **Mature Outlook** (6001 N. Clark St., Chicago, IL 60660, tel. 800/336–6330), a Sears Roebuck & Co. subsidiary with 800,000 members, charges $9.95 for an annual membership.

Note: When using any senior-citizen identification card for reduced hotel rates, mention it when booking, not when checking out. At restaurants, show your card before you're seated; discounts may be limited to certain menus, days, or hours. If you are renting a car, ask about promotional rates that might improve on your senior-citizen discount.

Educational Travel **Elderhostel** (75 Federal St., 3rd floor, Boston, MA 02110, tel. 617/426–7788) is a nonprofit organization that has offered inexpensive study programs for people 60 and older since 1975.

Programs are held at more than 1,800 educational institutions in the United States, Canada, and 45 other countries; courses cover everything from marine science to Greek myths and cowboy poetry. Participants generally attend lectures in the morning and spend the afternoon sightseeing or on field trips; they live in dorms on the host campuses. Fees for programs in the United States and Canada, which usually last one week, run about $300, not including transportation.

Tour Operators **Saga International Holidays** (222 Berkeley St., Boston, MA 02116, tel. 800/343–0273), which specializes in group travel for people over 60, offers a selection of variously priced tours and cruises covering five continents. If you want to take your grandchildren, look into **GrandTravel** (*see* Traveling with Children, *above*).

Further Reading

Chicago has been celebrated and vilified in fiction and nonfiction. For the flavor of the city a century ago, pick up Theodore Dreiser's *Sister Carrie,* the story of a country innocent who falls from grace in Chicago. Upton Sinclair's portrayal of the meatpacking industry's squalor and employee exploitation raised a public outcry in his novel *The Jungle.*

More recently, native Chicagoan Saul Bellow has set many novels in the city, most notably in *The Adventures of Augie March.* Richard Wright's explosive *Native Son* and James T. Farrell's *Studs Lonigan* depict racial clashes in Chicago from both the black and white sides, respectively. The works of long-time resident Nelson Algren show the city at its grittiest: *The Man with the Golden Arm, A Walk on the Wild Side,* and *Chicago: City on the Make.* On a lighter note, two series of detective novels use a Chicago backdrop: Sara Paretsky's "V.I. Warshawski" novels and the "Monsignor Ryan" mysteries of Andrew Greeley. Greeley has set other novels in Chicago as well, including *Lord of the Dance.*

Chicago was once the quintessential newspaper town; the play *The Front Page,* by Ben Hecht and Charles MacArthur, is set here. Local reporters have penned some excellent chronicles, including *Fabulous Chicago,* by Emmett Dedmon, *Division Street,* by Studs Terkel, and *Boss,* a portrait of the late Mayor Richard J. Daley, by Mike Royko. Lois Willie's *Forever Open, Clear and Free* is a superb history of the fight to save Chicago's lakefront parks.

If you're an architecture buff, you can choose from among three excellent guidebooks by Ira J. Bach, former director of city development: *Chicago's Famous Buildings, Chicago on Foot,* and *Chicago's Public Sculpture.* David Lowe's *Lost Chicago* is a fascinating and heartbreaking history of vanished buildings.

Arriving and Departing

By Plane

Flights are either nonstop, direct, or connecting. A **nonstop** flight requires no change of plane and makes no stops. A **direct** flight stops at least once and can involve a change of plane, although the flight number remains the same; if the first leg is late, the second waits. This is not the case with a **connecting** flight, which involves a different plane and a different flight number.

Airports and Airlines Chicago has two national airports and one regional airport. **O'Hare International Airport,** one of the world's busiest, is 20 miles from downtown in the far northwestern corner of the city. **Midway Airport,** on Chicago's Southwest Side, about 7 miles from downtown, is smaller, relatively uncrowded and lacks O'Hare's confusion. **Meigs Field,** just south of Downtown, serves commuter airlines with flights to downstate Illinois and Wisconsin. Every national airline, most international airlines, and a number of regional carriers fly into Chicago.

Cutting Flight Costs The Sunday travel section of most newspapers is a good source of deals. When booking, particularly through an unfamiliar company, call the Better Business Bureau to find out whether any complaints have been registered against the company, pay with a credit card if you can, and consider trip-cancellation and default insurance.

Promotional Airfares All the less expensive fares, called promotional or discount fares, are round-trip and involve restrictions. The exact nature of the restrictions depends on the airline, the route, and the season and on whether travel is domestic or international, but you must usually buy the ticket—commonly called an APEX (advance purchase excursion) when it's for international travel—in advance (seven, 14, or 21 days are usual). You must also respect certain minimum- and maximum-stay requirements (for instance, over a Saturday night or at least seven and no more than 30, 45, or 90 days), and you must be willing to pay penalties for changes. Airlines generally allow some changes for a fee. But the cheaper the fare, the more likely the ticket is to be nonrefundable; it would take a death in the family for the airline to give you any of your money back if you had to cancel. The lowest fares are also subject to availability; because only a certain percentage of the plane's total seats will be sold at that price, they may go quickly.

Consolidators Consolidators or bulk-fare operators—also known as bucket shops—buy blocks of seats on scheduled flights that airlines anticipate they won't be able to sell. They pay wholesale prices, add a markup, and resell the seats to travel agents or directly to the public at prices that still undercut the airline's promotional or discount fares. You pay more than on a charter but ordinarily less than for an APEX ticket, and, even when there is not much of a price difference, the ticket usually comes without the advance-purchase restriction. Moreover, although tickets are marked nonrefundable so you can't turn them in to the airline for a full-fare refund, some consolidators sometimes give you your money back. Carefully read the fine print detailing penalties for changes and cancellations. If you doubt the reliability of a company, call the airline once you've made your booking and confirm that you do, indeed, have a reservation on the flight.

The biggest U.S. consolidator, C.L. Thomson Express, sells only to travel agents. Well-established consolidators selling to the public include **UniTravel** (Box 12485, St. Louis, MO 63132, tel. 314/569–0900 or 800/325–2222); **Council Charter** (205 E. 42nd St., New York, NY 10017, tel. 212/661–0311 or 800/800–8222), a division of the Council on International Educational

Exchange and a longtime charter operator now functioning more as a consolidator; and **Travac** (989 6th Ave., New York, NY 10018, tel. 212/563–3303 or 800/872–8800), also a former charterer.

Charter Flights Charters usually have the lowest fares and the most restrictions. Departures are limited and seldom on time, and you can lose all or most of your money if you cancel. (Generally, the closer to departure you cancel, the more you lose, although sometimes you will be charged only a small fee if you supply a substitute passenger.) The charterer, on the other hand, may legally cancel the flight for any reason up to 10 days before departure; within 10 days of departure, the flight may be canceled only if it becomes physically impossible to operate it. The charterer may also revise the itinerary or increase the price after you have bought the ticket, but if the new arrangement constitutes a "major change," you have the right to a refund. Before buying a charter ticket, read the fine print for the company's refund policy and details on major changes. Money for charter flights is usually paid into a bank escrow account, the name of which should be on the contract. If you don't pay by credit card, make your check payable to the escrow account (unless you're dealing with a travel agent, in which case, his or her check should be payable to the escrow account). The Department of Transportation's Consumer Affairs Office (I–25, Washington, DC 20590, tel. 202/366–2220) can answer questions on charters and send you its "Plane Talk: Public Charter Flights" information sheet.

Charter operators may offer flights alone or with ground arrangements that constitute a charter package. Well-established charter operators include **Council Charter** (205 E. 42nd St., New York, NY 10017, tel. 212/661–0311 or 800/800–8222), now largely a consolidator, despite its name, and **Travel Charter** (1120 E. Long Lake Rd., Troy, MI 48098, tel. 313/528–3500 or 800/521–5267), with Midwestern departures. **DER Tours** (Box 1606, Des Plains, IL 60017, tel. 800/782–2424), a charterer and consolidator, sells through travel agents.

Discount Travel Travel clubs offer their members unsold space on airplanes,
Clubs cruise ships, and package tours at nearly the last minute and at well below the original cost. Suppliers thus receive some revenue for their "leftovers," and members get a bargain. Membership generally includes a regular bulletin or access to a toll-free telephone hot line giving details of available trips departing anywhere from three or four days to several months in the future. Packages tend to be more common than flights alone, so if airfares are your only interest, read the literature before joining. Reductions on hotels are also available. Clubs include **Discount Travel International** (114 Forrest Ave., Suite 203, Narberth, PA 19072, tel. 215/668–7184; $45 annually, single or family), **Moment's Notice** (425 Madison Ave., New York, NY 10017, tel. 212/486–0503; $45 annually, single or family), **Travelers Advantage** (CUC Travel Service, 49 Music Sq. W, Nashville, TN 37203, tel. 800/548–1116; $49 annually, single or family), and **Worldwide Discount Travel Club** (1674 Meridian Ave., Miami Beach, FL 33139, tel. 305/534–2082; $50 annually for family, $40 single).

Smoking Since February 1990, smoking has been banned on all domestic flights of less than six hours duration; the ban also applies to domestic segments of international flights aboard U.S. and foreign carriers. On a flight on which smoking is permitted, a seat in a no-smoking section must be provided for every passenger who requests one, and the section must be enlarged to accommodate such passengers if necessary as long as they have complied with the airline's deadline for check-in and seat assignment. If smoking bothers you, request a seat far from the smoking section.

From the Airport to Downtown Chicago
By Public Transit Chicago Transit Authority's (CTA) rapid transit station is located on O'Hare Airport's baggage claim level. This is the cheapest ($1.50) way to get from the airport to the city, and convenient if you're heading to the North Side or Downtown and you don't have much luggage. Travel time is 40–60 minutes. From the first stop in the Loop (Washington and Dearborn Streets) you can take a taxi to your hotel or change to other transit lines.

In mid-1993, a new CTA transit line opened between Midway Airport and the Loop. The stop at Adams Street and Wabash Avenue is the closest to the hotels on south Michigan Avenue; for others, the simplest strategy is to alight anywhere in the Loop and hail a cab.

By Bus **Continental Airport Express** (tel. 312/454–7799) coaches provide service from both airports to major downtown and Near North hotels; call for reservations. The trip downtown from O'Hare takes an hour or longer, depending on traffic conditions and your destination; the fare is $13.00. When taking the coach to O'Hare to catch a departing flight, be sure to allow at least 1½ hours. The trip downtown from Midway takes about half an hour; the fare is $9.50.

CW Limo (tel. 312/493–2700) offers moderately priced express van service from both airports to locations in Hyde Park and the South Side. Vans leave O'Hare about every 45 minutes, and the travel time to Hyde Park is about an hour; the fare is $12.50. CW serves Midway with five vans daily, at Midway's traffic peaks; the fare is $9. If you're going from the South Side to Midway, call 24 hours in advance.

By Taxi Metered taxicab service is available at both O'Hare and Midway airports. Trips to and from O'Hare incur a $1 surcharge. Expect to pay about $28–$32 plus tip from O'Hare to Near North and Downtown locations, about $14 plus tip from Midway. Some cabs participate in a share-a-ride program that combines two or three individuals going from the airport to Downtown; the cost per person is substantially lower than the full rate.

By Rental Car Leaving the airport, follow the signs to I–90 east, the Kennedy Expressway, which merges with I–94, the Edens Expressway. Take the eastbound exit at Ohio Street for Near North locations, the Washington or Madison Street exits for Downtown. After you exit, continue east about a mile to get to Michigan Avenue.

By Car

Travelers coming from the east can take the Indiana Toll Road (I–80/90) westbound for about 30 miles to the Chicago Skyway (also a toll road), which runs into the Dan Ryan Expressway (I–90/94). Take the Dan Ryan north (westbound) just past the turnoff for I–290 to any of the Downtown eastbound exits

(Monroe, Madison, Washington, Randolph, Lake) and drive east about a mile to reach Michigan Avenue. If you are heading to the Near North, take the Ohio Street exit eastbound and continue straight through local streets for about a mile to reach Michigan Avenue. Travelers coming from the south should take I–57 northbound to the Dan Ryan Expressway.

From the west, follow I–80 eastbound across Illinois to I–55, the major artery from the southwest. Continue east on I–55 to Lake Shore Drive. Those coming from areas due west of Chicago may prefer to pick up I–290 eastbound, which forks as it nears the city, heading to O'Hare in one direction (where it meets I–90) and to downtown Chicago in the other (where it ends).

From the north, take I–90 eastbound, which merges with I–94 south (eastbound) to form the Kennedy Expressway (I–90/94) about 10 miles north of Downtown. (I–90/94 is called the Kennedy Expressway north of I–290 and the Dan Ryan Expressway south of I–290).

By Train

Amtrak (800/872–7245) offers nationwide service to Chicago's Union Station (Jackson and Canal Sts., tel. 312/558–1075). Some trains travel overnight, and you can sleep in your seat or book a roomette at additional cost. Most trains have attractive diner cars with acceptable food, but you may prefer to bring your own.

By Bus

Greyhound (630 W. Harrison St., tel. 800/231–2222) has nationwide service to its main terminal in the Loop and to neighborhood stations at the 95th Street and Dan Ryan Expressway CTA station, and at the Cumberland CTA station near O'Hare Airport. The Harrison Street terminal is far from most hotels, so plan on another bus or a cab to your hotel.

Indian Trails, Inc. (tel. 312/928–8606 for 95th St. terminal or 312/408–5971 for Harrison St. terminal) serves Chicago from Indiana and Michigan, sharing Greyhound's terminal facilities at 630 West Harrison Street and at 95th Street and the Dan Ryan Expressway.

Staying in Chicago

Important Addresses and Numbers

Tourist Information The **Chicago Office of Tourism** is housed in the Historic Water Tower, in the middle of the Magnificent Mile (806 N. Michigan Ave., tel. 312/280–5740). There are two walk-in centers: the **Chicago Cultural Center** (78 E. Washington St.); and the **Pumping Station** (163 E. Pearson St.).

The **Mayor's Office of Special Events General Information and Activities** (121 N. La Salle St., tel. 312/744–3315) will tell you about city-sponsored events of interest.

The **State of Illinois Office of Tourism** (310 S. Michigan Ave.) maintains a **Tourism Hotline** (tel. 800/223–0121).

Emergencies **Police, fire, ambulance** (tel. 911).

Hospitals In the Near North or north, **Northwestern Memorial Hospital** (Superior St. at Fairbanks Ct., tel. 312/908–2000). In the Loop, **Rush Presbyterian St. Luke's** (1753 W. Congress Pkwy., tel. 312/942–5000). In Hyde Park and the South Side, **Michael Reese Hospital** (Lake Shore Dr. at 31st St., tel. 312/791–2000), or the **Bernard Mitchell Hospital at the University of Chicago** (5841 S. Maryland Ave., tel. 312/702–1000). Michael Reese and other hospitals sponsor storefront clinics for fast treatment of minor emergencies. Call the hospitals for information, or check the Chicago Consumer Yellow Pages under "Clinics."

Dentists The **Chicago Dental Society Emergency Service** (tel. 312/726–4321 or 312/836–7300) makes referrals at all hours.

24-Hour **Osco** (call 800/654–6726 for nearest location). **Walgreen's** (757 *Pharmacies* N. Michigan Ave., at Chicago Ave., tel. 312/664–8686).

Opening and Closing Times

Banks are generally open 8:30–3; a few open for a half day on Saturday and close on Wednesday. Many banks in the Loop and Near North stay open until 5 PM.

The main **U.S. Post Office** (433 W. Van Buren St., tel. 312/765–3210) is open weekdays until 9, Saturday until 5, closed Sunday. The post office at O'Hare International Airport is open daily 24 hours.

Chicago City Hall (121 N. La Salle St., tel. 312/744–5000) is open weekdays, closed on city holidays.

Stores Most department stores, except those in Water Tower Place, are open Monday–Saturday from 9:45 to 5:30 or 6, Thursday until 7. Sunday hours at Magnificent Mile department stores are usually noon–5. Loop department stores are closed Sunday except once a month (designated Super Sunday); the newspapers announce the specific day. Lord & Taylor and Marshall Field at the Water Tower are open Monday–Saturday 10–8 and Sunday noon–6.

Getting Around

Chicago's streets follow a grid pattern. Madison Street is the baseline for streets and avenues that run north/south; Michigan Avenue, for example, is North Michigan Avenue above Madison Street, South Michigan Avenue below it. House numbers start at the baseline and climb in each direction, generally by 100 a block; thus the Fine Arts Building at 410 South Michigan Avenue is four blocks south of Madison Street.

For streets that run east–west, State Street is the baseline; 18th Street, for example, is East 18th Street east of State Street and West 18th Street west of State Street. House numbers start at the baseline and rise in each direction, east and west.

"The Loop" denotes the section of downtown that is roughly encircled by the elevated tracks, although the Loop boundaries actually exceed the tracks. They are Michigan Avenue on the east, Wacker Drive on the north and west, and Congress on the south.

By Train and Bus Chicago's extensive public transportation network includes buses and rapid transit trains, both subway and elevated. The **Chicago Transit Authority (CTA)** publishes an excellent map of the transit system, available on request from the CTA (Merchandise Mart, Chicago, IL 60654). The **RTA Travel Information Center** (tel. 312/836–7000) provides information on how to get around on city, suburban, and commuter transit and bus lines.

In 1990 the CTA restructured its fares, and the result is likely to confuse the uninitiated. The basic fare is $1.50 for rapid transit trains and buses during morning and afternoon rush hours; at other times, the bus fare is $1.25. Tokens, which can be used on either buses or trains, offer a substantial discount: a roll of 10 tokens costs $12.50. Tokens can be bought at currency exchanges and Jewel and Dominick's supermarkets. Transfers, which must be bought when you board the bus or train, cost an extra 30¢; they can be used twice within a two-hour time period but not twice on the same route. Children ages 7–11 travel for less than half fare (65¢ at press time). Children under 7 travel free. Several different weekly and monthly passes are available, but tokens are the most economical option for those staying in the city for only a short time.

Most, but not all, rapid transit lines operate 24 hours; some stations are closed at night. (In general, late-night CTA travel is not recommended.) To transfer between the Loop's elevated ("El") lines and subway lines, or between rapid transit and bus service, you must use a transfer; be sure to *buy the transfer when you board the first conveyance.* Buses generally stop on every other corner northbound and southbound (on State Street they stop at every corner). Eastbound and westbound buses generally stop on every corner. Buses generally run either north or south from the Loop. Principal transfer points are on Michigan Avenue at the north side of Randolph Street for northbound buses, Adams and Wabash for westbound buses and the El, and State and Lake streets for southbound buses.

By Car Chicago's extensive network of buses and rapid transit rail, as well as the availability of taxis and limousine services (often priced competitively with metered cabs) make having a car in Chicago unnecessary, particularly for those whose visit is confined to the Loop, Near North, and Lakefront neighborhoods. If your business or interests take you to the suburbs, you may want to rent a car for that part of your trip. Chicago traffic is often heavy, on-street parking is nearly impossible to find, parking lots are expensive, congestion creates frustrating delays, and other drivers may be impatient with those who are unfamiliar with the city and its roads. During the 1990s, extensive repair work is planned for several of the city's major arteries, including Lake Shore Drive and the Kennedy Expressway (I–90/94). Similar work on the Dan Ryan Expressway in 1988–1989 caused a nightmare of snarled traffic during rush hours. In these circumstances, the visitor to Chicago may find a car to be a liability rather than an asset.

By Taxi Chicago taxis are metered, with fares beginning at $1.20 for the first $1/5$ mile and 20¢ for each additional $1/6$ mile or minute of waiting time. A charge of 50¢ is made for each additional passenger between the ages of 12 and 65, and a charge of 25¢ per bag may be levied when luggage is bulky. Taxi drivers expect a 15% tip. The principal taxi companies are **American United Cab Co.** (tel. 312/248–7600), **Flash Cab** (tel. 312/561–1444), **Yellow Cab Co.** (tel. 312/829–4222), and **Checker Cab Co.** (tel. 312/829–4222).

Guided Tours

Orientation Tours **Chicago Motor Coach Co.** Double-decker buses take visitors on
By Land one-hour narrated tours of Chicago landmarks. Climb on at the Sears Tower (Jackson Blvd. and Wacker Dr.), the Field Museum (Lake Shore Dr. at E. Roosevelt Rd.), Orchestra Hall (220 S. Michigan Ave.), or the Water Tower (Michigan Ave. at Pearson St.). *Tel. 312/922–8919. Daily 10–4. Cost: $7 adults, $5 senior citizens.*

American Sightseeing. The North tour along State Street and North Michigan Avenue includes the John Hancock Center, Water Tower Place, and the Lincoln Park Conservatory. The South tour covers the financial district, Grant Park, the University of Chicago, the Museum of Science and Industry, and Jackson Park. Tours leave from the Congress Hotel (530 S. Michigan Ave.), or you can arrange to be picked up at your hotel (downtown or Near North only). *Tel. 312/427–3100. Cost: $15 adults, $7.50 children 5–14. For a combined 4-hour tour of north and south: $25 adults, $12.50 children 5–14. Two-hour tours leave daily 9:30, 11:30, 1:30, and 3:30 during the summer, 10 and noon in winter.*

By Boat Boat tour schedules vary by season; be sure to call for exact times and fares.

Wendella Sightseeing Boats (400 N. Michigan Ave., tel. 312/337–1446). Guided tours traverse the Chicago River to south of the Sears Tower and through the locks; on Lake Michigan, they travel between the Adler Planetarium on the south and Oak Street Beach on the north. Available April–October. Ninety-minute tours at 10, 11:30, 1:15, 3 and 7:30; cost: $9 adults, $8 senior citizens, $4.50 children 11 and under. Two-hour evening tours at 7:30; cost: $11 adults, $5.50 children 11 and under. Wendella also offers an unscheduled, but fairly frequent, one-hour tour on Lake Michigan only; cost: $7 adults, $3.50 children. All tours leave from lower Michigan Avenue at the foot of the Wrigley Building on the north side of the river.

Mercury Skyline Cruises (tel. 312/332–1353 for recorded information or 312/332–1368). A 90-minute river and lake cruise departs at 10, 11:30, 1:15, 3:15, and 7:30; cost: $9 adults, $4.50 children under 12. Tickets can be obtained one hour before departure time. One-hour lakefront cruises are available evenings: daily 5–9 PM and weekends 9:30, 10, and 11 PM. A one-hour Chicago River cruise begins at noon, weekends only, June–August; cost: $6 adults, $3 children under 12. Cruises leave from Wacker Drive at Michigan Avenue (the south side of the Michigan Avenue bridge).

Shoreline Marine (tel. 312/222–9328). Half-hour boat trips on Lake Michigan are offered daily between Memorial Day and Labor Day. Tours leave from the Adler Planetarium (1800 S. Lake Shore Dr.) at quarter past the hour daily, 12:15–9:15; from the Shedd Aquarium 11:15–5:15; and in the evening from Buckingham Fountain, 6:15–11:15. Cost: $6 adults, $3 children.

Interlude Enterprises (tel. 312/641–7245). Tours focusing on Chicago architecture leave from the southeast corner of Wabash Avenue and Wacker Drive by the Wabash Avenue bridge, Monday–Saturday, every two hours from 9:30 AM to 7:30 PM. Tours run from mid-April to early November, depending on the weather. Reservations can be made from one week in advance to 10 AM the day of the tour. Cost: $6 for the tour plus $5.50 for lunch, or you can bring your own.

Special-Interest Tours **Pumping Station** (806 N. Michigan Ave., tel. 312/467–7114). Tour the facility at the historic Water Tower and see *Here's Chicago!*, a multimedia show about the city. Shows begin every half hour Monday–Thursday 10–5:30, Friday and Saturday 10–6:30. Cost: $5.75 adults, $4.50 children.

Newspaper Tours. The *Chicago Tribune* offers free weekday tours of its Freedom Center production facility (777 W. Chicago Ave., tel. 312/222–2116). Reservations must be made in advance of your visit.

Chicago Mercantile Exchange (30 S. Wacker Dr., tel. 312/930–8249). The visitors' gallery, which offers a view of the often frenetic trading floor, is open 7:30–3:15; a presentation explains the activity on the floor below.

Walking Tours The **Chicago Architecture Foundation** gives several tours, such as walking tours of Loop architecture and tours of historic houses, on a daily or weekly schedule, depending on the season. Other tours are offered on an occasional, seasonal, or prescheduled basis, including Graceland Cemetery, Frank Lloyd Wright's Oak Park buildings, and bicycle tours of Lincoln Park and Oak Park. Tour departure times vary; prices run about $5–$10 per person. For information, write or call the foundation at the Tour Center (224 S. Michigan Ave., tel. 312/922–8687), where most tours originate.

Friends of the Chicago River (407 S. Dearborn St., Chicago 60605, tel. 312/939–0490) offers walking tours along the river April–July, September, and October, Saturday at 10 AM. The tours last two hours and cost $5. There are seven different tours; call in advance to find out which tour is being offered and where it starts. The organization also has maps of the routes available for a small donation.

Credit Cards

The following credit-card abbreviations are used in this book: AE, American Express; D, Discover; DC, Diners Club; MC, MasterCard; V, Visa.

2 Portraits of Chicago

Chicago

By Studs Terkel

A writer, a broadcaster, and of late a film actor, Studs Terkel has come to be a virtual symbol of Chicago. His newest collection of oral histories is The Great Divide: Second Thoughts on the American Dream.

Janus, the two-faced god, has both blessed and cursed the city-state Chicago. Though his graven image is not visible to the naked eye, his ambiguous spirit soars atop Sears, Big Stan, and Big John. (Our city is street-wise and alley-hip of the casually familiar. Thus the Standard Oil Building and the John Hancock are, with tavern gaminess, referred to as Big Stan and Big John. Sears is simply that; never mind Roebuck. Ours is a one-syllable town. Its character has been molded by the muscle rather than the word.)

Our double-vision, double-standard, double-value, and double-cross have been patent ever since—at least, ever since the earliest of our city fathers took the Pottawattomies for all they had. Poetically, these dispossessed natives dubbed this piece of turf *Chikagou.* Some say it is Indian lingo for "City of the Wild Onion"; some say it really means "City of the Big Smell." "Big" is certainly the operative word around these parts.

Nelson Algren's classic *Chicago: City on the Make* is the late poet's single-hearted vision of his town's doubleness. "Chicago . . . forever keeps two faces, one for winners and one for losers; one for hustlers and one for squares . . . One face for Go-Getters and one for Go-Get-It-Yourselfers. One for poets and one for promoters. . . . One for early risers, one for evening hiders."

It is the city of Jane Addams, settlement worker, and Al Capone, entrepreneur; of Clarence Darrow, lawyer, and Julius Hoffman, judge; of Louis Sullivan, architect, and Sam Insull, magnate; of John Altgeld, governor, and Paddy Bauler, alderman. (Paddy's the one who some years ago observed, "Chicago ain't ready for reform." It is echoed in our day by another, less paunchy alderman, Fast Eddie.)

Now, with a new kind of mayor, whose blackness is but one variant of the Chicago norm, and a machine—which like the old gray mare ain't what it used to be—creaking its expected way, all bets are off. Race, though the dominant theme, is but one factor.

It is still the arena of those who dream of the City of Man and those who envision a City of Things. The battle appears to be forever joined. The armies, ignorant and enlightened,

This essay is drawn from Studs Terkel's Chicago, *which was originally published in 1986, when the late Harold Washington was mayor of Chicago.*

clash by day as well as night. Chicago is America's dream, writ large. And flamboyantly.

It has—as they used to whisper of the town's fast women—a reputation.

Elsewhere in the world, anywhere, name the city, name the country, Chicago evokes one image above all others. Sure, architects and those interested in such matters mention Louis Sullivan, Frank Lloyd Wright, and Mies van der Rohe. Hardly anyone in his right mind questions this city as the architectural Athens. Others, literary critics among them, mention Dreiser, Norris, Lardner, Algren, Farrell, Bellow, and the other Wright, Richard. Sure, Mencken did say something to the effect that there is no American literature worth mentioning that didn't come out of the palatinate that is Chicago. Of course, a special kind of jazz and a blues, acoustic rural and electrified urban, have been called Chicago style. All this is indubitably true.

Still others, for whom history has stood still since the Democratic convention of 1968, murmur: Mayor Daley. (As our most perceptive chronicler, Mike Royko, has pointed out, the name has become the eponym for city chieftain; thus, it is often one word, "Maredaley.") The tone, in distant quarters as well as here, is usually one of awe; you may interpret it any way you please.

An English Midlander, bearing a remarkable resemblance to Nigel Bruce, encounters me under London's Marble Arch: "Your mayor is my kind of chap. He should have bashed the heads of those young ruffians, though he did rather well, I thought." I tell him that Richard J. Daley died several years ago and that our incumbent mayor is black. He finds this news somewhat startling.

"Really?" He recovers quickly: "Nonetheless, I do like your city. I was there some thirty-odd years ago. Black, is he?"

Yeah, I tell him, much of the city is.

He is somewhat Spenglerian as he reflects on the decline of Western values. "Thank heavens, I'll not be around when they take over, eh?"

I nod. I'm easy to get along with. "You sound like Saul Bellow," I say.

"Who?"

"Our Nobel laureate. Do you realize that our University of Chicago has produced more Nobel Prize winners than any other in the world?"

"Really?"

"Yeah."

He returns to what appears to be his favorite subject: gumption. "Your mayor had it. I'm delighted to say that our lady prime minister has it, too."

I am suddenly weary. Too much Bells Reserve, I'm afraid. "So long, sir. I'll see you in Chicago."

"Not likely; not bloody likely."

In Munich, a student of the sixties, now somewhat portly and balding, ventures an opinion. Not that I asked him. Chicago does that to strangers as well as natives.

"Your Mayor Daley vas bwutal to those young pwotesters, vasn't he?"

Again I nod. Vat could I say?

But it isn't Daley whose name is the Chicago hallmark. Nor Darrow. Nor Wright. Nor is it either of the Janes, Addams or Byrne. It's Al Capone, of course.

I n a Brescian trattoria, to Italy's north, a wisp of an old woman, black shawl and all, hears where I'm from. Though she has some difficulty with English (far less than I have with Italian), she thrusts both hands forward, index fingers pointed at me: *Boom, boom,* she goes. I hold up my hands. We both laugh. It appears that Jimmy Cagney, Edward G. Robinson, and Warner Brothers have done a real job in image making.

Not that Al and his colleagues didn't have palmy days during what, to others, were parlous times. Roaring Twenties or Terrible Thirties, the goose always hung high for the Boys. I once asked a casual acquaintance, the late Doc Graham, for a résumé. Doc was, as he modestly put it, a dedicated heist man. His speech was a composite of Micawber and Runyon:

"The unsophisticated either belonged to the Bugs Moran mob or the Capone mob. The fellas with talent didn't belong to either one. We robbed both."

Wasn't that a bit on the risky side?

"Indeed. There ain't hardly a one of us survived the Biblical threescore and ten. You see this fellow liquidated, that fellow—shall we say, disposed of? Red McLaughlin was the toughest guy in Chicago. But when you seen Red run out of the drainage canal, you realized Red's *modus operandi* was unavailing. His associates was Clifford and Adams. They were set in Al's doorway in his hotel in Cicero. That was unavailing."

Was it a baseball bat Al used?

"You are doubtless referring to Anselmi and Scalisi. They offended Al. This was rare. Al Capone usually sublet the matter. Since I'm Irish, I had a working affiliate with Bugs Moran. Did you know that Red and his partners once stole the Checker Cab Company? They took machine guns, went up, and had an election. I assisted in that operation."

What role did the forces of law and order play?

"With a bill, you wasn't bothered. If you had a speaking acquaintance with Mayor Thompson, you could do no wrong. Al spoke loud to him." . . .

Chicago is not the most corrupt of cities. The state of New Jersey has a couple. Need we mention Nevada? Chicago, though, is the Big Daddy. Not more corrupt, just more theatrical, more colorful in its shadiness.

It's an attribute of which many of our Respectables are, I suspect, secretly proud. Something to chat about in languorous moments. Perhaps something to distract from whatever tangential business might have engaged them.

Consider Marshall Field the First. The merchant prince. In 1886, the fight for the eight-hour day had begun, here in Chicago. Anarchists, largely German immigrants, were in the middle of it for one reason or another.

There was a mass meeting; a bomb was thrown; to this day, nobody knows who did it. There was a trial. The Haymarket Eight were in the dock. With hysteria pervasive—newspaper headlines wild enough to make Rupert Murdoch blush—the verdict was in. Guilty.

Before four of them were executed, there was a campaign, worldwide, for a touch of mercy. Even the judge, passionate though he was in his loathing of the defendants, was amenable. A number of Chicago's most respected industrialists felt the same way. Hold off the hooded hangman. Give 'em life, what the hell. It was Marshall Field I who saw to it that they swung. Hang the bastards. Johnny Da Pow had nothing on him when it came to power.

Lucy Parsons, the youngest widow of the most celebrated of the hangees, Albert—an ex-soldier of the Confederacy—lived to be an old, old woman. When she died in the forties and was buried at Waldheim Cemetery, my old colleague Win Stracke sang at the services. Though Parsons sang "Annie Laurie" on his way to the gallows, Win sounded off with "Joe Hill." It was a song, he said, that Lucy liked. When I shake hands with Win, I shake hands with history. That's what I call continuity.

The Janus-like aspect of Chicago appeared in the being of John Peter Altgeld. One of his first acts as governor of Illinois in 1893 was an 18,000-word message, citing chapter and verse, declaring the trial a frame-up. He pardoned the three survivors. The fourth had swallowed a dynamite cap while in the pokey.

Though it ended his political life, Altgeld did add a touch of class to our city's history. He was remembered by Vachel

Lindsay as Eagle Forgotten. Some kid, majoring in something other than business administration or computer programming, might come across this poem in some anthology. Who knows? He might learn something about eagles.

Eagles are a diminished species today, here as well as elsewhere. On occasion, they are spotted in unexpected air pockets. Hawks, of course, abound, here as well as elsewhere. Some say this is their glory time. So Dow-Jones tells us. Observe the boys and girls in commodities. Ever ride the La Salle Street bus? Bright and morning faces; *Wall Street Journals* neatly folded. The New Gatsbys, Bob Tamarkin calls them. Gracelessness under pressure.

Sparrows, as always, are the most abundant of our city birds. It is never glory time for them. As always, they do the best they can. Which isn't very much. They forever peck away and, in some cock-eyed fashion, survive the day. Others—well, who said life was fair? They hope, as the old spiritual goes, that His eye is on all the sparrows and that He watches over them. And you. And me . . .

On a hot summer day, the lake behaves, the beach is busy, and thousands find cool delight. All within sight of places where ads are created telling you Wendy's is better than Burger King, where computers compute like crazy, and where billions of pages are Xeroxed for one purpose or another, or for no purpose at all. All within one neighborhood. It's crazy and phenomenal. No other city in the world has a neighborhood like this. Visitors, no matter how weary-of-it-all and jaded, are always overawed. You feel pretty good; and, like a spoiled débutante, you wave a limp hand and murmur: It *is* rather impressive, isn't it? . . .

But those damn bridges. Though I haven't searched out any statistics, I'll bet Chicago has more bridges than Paris. When up they go and all traffic stops, you lean against the railing and watch the boats: pulp paper from Canada for the *Trib* and *Sun-Times*, and ore from where?—the Mesabi iron range?—and all sorts of tugs easing all sorts of lake vessels, bearing all sorts of heavy stuff, big-shouldered stuff. You may not feel particularly chesty, yet there's a slight stirring, a feeling of Chicago's connection with elsewhere.

However—and what an infuriating however—when a lone sailboat comes through with two beautiful people sporting Acapulco or Palm Beach tan, she in a bikini and he in Calvin Klein shorts, and the two, with the casualness and vast carelessness of a Tom and Daisy Buchanan, wave at the held-up secretaries, file clerks, and me, I look around for a rock to throw, only to realize I'm not Walter Johnson, and I settle for a mumbled *sonofabitch* and I'm late for lunch. *Sonofabitch.*

There's no other city like this, I tell you.

And taxi drivers.

When, in eighth-grade geography, Miss O'Brien, her wig slightly askew, quizzed you ferociously on populations of the world's great cities, you had to, with equal ferocity, look them up in the atlas. Thanks to Third World hackies, you can save an enormous amount of time and energy.

You peek up front toward the driver and you see the name Ahmed Eqbal. Naturally, you ask him what's the population of Karachi and he tells you. With great enthusiasm. If his surname is Kim, you'll find out that Seoul is close to seven million. If the man driving at an interesting speed is Marcus Olatunji, you might casually offer that Ibadan is bigger than Lagos, isn't it? If his name has as many syllables as a Welsh town's, you simply ask if Bangkok has changed much; has its population really experienced an exponential growth?

Of course, all shortcuts to knowledge have their shortcomings. Sometimes he'll whirl around, astonished, and in very, very precise British English ask, "How do you *know* that?" A brief cultural exchange ensues as suddenly you cry out, Watch out! We missed an articulated bus with a good one-tenth of an inch to spare. If it's a newspaper circulation truck, God help the two of us.

Chicago's traffic problem is hardly any problem at all—if you forget about storms, light rains, accidents, and road construction—when compared with other great cities. In contrast to New York's cacophony of honks and curses, ours is the song of the open road. Mexico City is not to be believed. Ever been to Paris where the driver snaps his fingers, frustrated, as you successfully hop back onto the curb? Need we mention the Angeleno freeway? . . .

So we're reminiscing about one thing or another, Verne and I. Vernon Jarrett knocks out a *Sun-Times* column: reflections of black life in Chicago and elsewhere. I can't get that Jubilee Night, '38, out of my mind. He tells me of that same celebratory moment in Paris, Tennessee, along the IC tracks. Hallelujah and hope. We see our reflections in the mirror behind the bar and neither of us looks too hopeful. Hallelujah for what?

"The ghetto used to have something going for it," he says. "It had a beat, it had a certain rhythm and it was all hope. I don't care how rough things were. They used to say, If you can't make it in Chicago, you can't make it anywhere. You may be down today; you're gonna be back up tomorrow."

The lyric of an old blues song is rolling around in my head like a loose cannonball:

I'm troubled in mind, baby, I'm so blue,
But I won't be blue always
You know the sun, the sun gonna shine
In my back door someday.

"You had the packinghouses going, you had the steel mills going, you had secondary employment to help you 'get over.' "

Oh, there's still a Back of the Yards, all right, but where are the yards? And Steeltown. Ever visit South Chicago these days? Smokestacks with hardly an intimation of smoke. A town as silent, as dead as the Legionnaires' fortress in *Beau Geste.* Where the executioner's ax fell upon Jefferson and Johnson as upon Stasiak, Romano, and Polowski.

"Now it's a drag," says Verne. "There are thousands of people who have written off their lives. They're serving out their sentences as though there were some supreme judge who said, 'You're sentenced to life imprisonment on earth and this is your cell here.' What do you do if you've got a life sentence? You play jailhouse politics. You hustle, you sell dope, you browbeat other people, you abuse other cellmates, you turn men into weaklings, and girls you overcome.

"If I'm feeling good and want to have my morale lowered, all I have to do is drive out Madison Street on a bright, beautiful day and look at the throng of unemployed young guys in the weird dress, trying to hang on to some individuality. Can't read or write; look mean at each other. You see kids hating themselves as much as they hate others. This is one thing that's contributed to the ease with which gangs kill each other. Another nigger ain't nothin'."

Is it possible that ol' Hightower, the pub-crawling buddy of Dude and me during those Jubilee hours on a June night so long ago, has a signifying grandson among the wretched and lost on some nonsignified corner somewhere on the West Side?

From the year one we've heard Lord Acton cited: Power corrupts and absolute power corrupts absolutely. You're only half right, Your Lordship, if that. In a town like Chicago, Johnny Da Pow and a merchant prince and, in our day, a Croation Sammy Glick run much of the turf because of another kind of corruption: the one Verne Jarrett observed. Powerlessness corrupts and absolute powerlessness corrupts absolutely. You see, Lord A knew nothing of Cabrini-Green. Or—*memento mori*—47th and South Parkway, with exquisite irony renamed Martin Luther King, Jr., Drive. Mine eyes haven't seen much glory lately.

However—there's always a however in the city Janus watches over . . .

Somethin's happenin' out there not covered by the six-o'clock news or a Murdoch headline. There is a percolating and bubbling in certain neighborhoods that may presage unexpected somethings for the up-againsters. A strange something called self-esteem, springing from an even stranger something called sense of community.

Ask Nancy Jefferson. It happened at the Midwest Community Council on the West Side. She's director of this grassroots organization. "This morning I had a young man. He had taken some money from us. I didn't think I'd see him again. I spread the warning: 'Watch out; he's a bad egg.' Today, out of the clear blue sky, he walked into my office. He says, 'I want to pay back my debt at fifty dollars a month. I've gotten a job. I didn't want to see you until I got a job.' I didn't know what made him come back. Was it the spirit of the community?"

In South Chicago, a bit to the southeast, Fast Eddie is finding out about UNO. That's the United Neighborhood Organization. While the alderman was busy giving Harold a hard time, his Hispanic constituents in the Tenth Ward were busy giving Waste Management, Inc., a hard time. The multinational toxic dumper was about to dump some of the vile stuff in the neighborhood. Hold off, big boy, said Mary Ellen Montez, a twenty-six-year-old housewife. So far, she and her neighbors are doing a far better job than Horatio ever did at the bridge.

UNO's grassroots power is being felt in Pilsen, too, where rehabs are springing up without the dubious touch of gentrification. The community folk are there because they're there and that's where they intend to stay. No shoving out in these parts. And no yuppies need apply.

Farther west, the South Austin Community Council, when not challenging joblessness and street crime, has sent housewives and suddenly redundant steelworkers to Springfield as well as to City Hall to lobby for the Affordable Budget, so that gas and electric bills don't destroy those whom God has only slightly blessed with means. They're not waiting for the hacks to fight for it; they're do-it-yourselfers.

Talk about fighting redundancy, the Metro Seniors are among the most militant. Never mind the wheelchairs, crutches, tea, and sympathy. They bang away everywhere, with or without canes and walkers: Keep your grubby hands off Medicare and Social Security. Ever hear of the time they marched into official sanctums with a cake: Cut the cake but not the COLA (cost-of-living adjustment)? The hacks ate that cake more slowly and thoughtfully than ever. There are 7,500 such scrappers in town, the youngest sixty-five. They may not have heard "Me and Bobby McGee," but they sure know the lyric: "Freedom's just another word for nothin' left to lose."

All sorts of new people from Central America and Southeast Asia, together with the more settled have-nots, are at it in Uptown with ONE (Organization of the North East). Tenants' rights, lousy housing, ethnic identity—name it; if it's an elementary right, they're battling for it.

And let's not forget all those nimble neighborhood organizers coming out of Heather Booth's Midwest Academy. Their style is sixties hipness, Saul Alinsky's Actions (political jujitsu, he called it), and eighties hard-earned awareness. They're all over town, astirring.

This is house-to-house, block-by-block, pavement-pounding, church-meeting, all-kinds-of-discussion stuff that may, as we wake up some great gettin'-up morning, reveal a new kind of Chicago. Nick Von Hoffman, who for a time was Alinsky's right arm, said it: "You who thought of yourself, up to that moment, as simply being a number, suddenly spring to life. You have that intoxicating feeling that you can make your own history, that you really count."

Call it a backyard revolution if you want to. It will sure as hell confute the Johnny Da Pows of our day, the merchant princes and the Fast Eddies. And, incidentally, lay the ghost of Lord Acton: less powerlessness that corrupts and more power than may ennoble.

Perhaps mine eyes may yet see the glory.

Neighborhoods of the Southwest Side

By Dominic A. Pacyga

An urban historian who teaches at Columbia College in Chicago, Dominic A. Pacyga is the coauthor of Chicago: City of Neighborhoods.

Chicago is proud of its ethnic neighborhoods. The "City of the Big Shoulders" is also the city of the blues and the polka, the jig and the tarantella. Tacos, kielbasa, Irish meat pies, and soul food are the sustenance of Chicago beyond the Loop and the high-rise towers of the lakefront. On Chicago streets newspapers in Polish, Lithuanian, Arabic, Spanish, German, and Greek are sold alongside the better-known English-language dailies, and a black newspaper, the *Chicago Defender*, makes its voice heard throughout the city. Many of the churches whose spires dot the cityscape can trace their origins to the arrival in Chicago of a particular national group. Schools, hospitals, museums, monuments, even street names (Emerald Avenue, King Drive, Lituanica Street, Pulaski Road) speak to the influence of ethnic groups on the city's history and political life.

As the city grew along with the Industrial Revolution of the 19th century, its neighborhoods became mazes of railroads, mills, factories, and packinghouses that reached across the Illinois prairie. The huge industrial complexes attracted workers from all over the United States, Europe, and Asia. Every major wave of migration that affected the United States after 1825 had a part in transforming Chicago. In recent years Arab, Vietnamese, Mexican, and Chinese immigrants have joined the descendants of the Germans, Irish, Swedes, Poles, Jews, Italians, and black Americans who made earlier journeys in search of peace and prosperity. And each group has left its mark on the city: Hispanic and Vietnamese cultural centers and museums have now joined the long-established Polish Museum on the Northwest Side, the Balzekas Museum of Lithuanian Culture on the Southwest Side, and the DuSable Museum of African American Culture on the South Side.

Chicago's communities have not always lived in harmony. Clashes between white ethnic groups have marked the history of the city, and relationships between whites and blacks exploded in a calamitous race riot in 1919. Although much has changed over the last 30 years, Chicago is still known as the nation's most segregated city. Yet its pluralism re-

---

The communities described in this essay are shown in the Chicago Neighborhoods map. A note following the essay gives directions and suggestions for visiting these neighborhoods, which are not covered in the tours of Chapter 3.

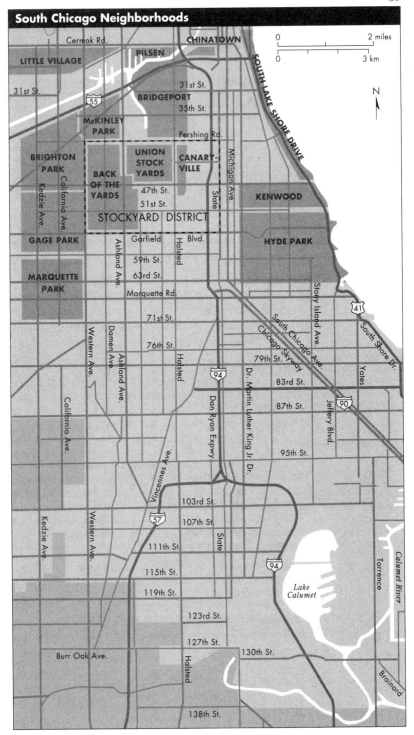

South Chicago Neighborhoods

0 ____ 2 miles
0 ____ 3 km

N

Cermak Rd.
CHINATOWN
PILSEN
LITTLE VILLAGE
31st St.
BRIDGEPORT
31st St.
35th St.
McKINLEY PARK
Pershing Rd.
BRIGHTON PARK
UNION STOCK YARDS
CANARY-VILLE
BACK OF THE YARDS
KENWOOD
47th St.
51st St.
STOCKYARD DISTRICT
GAGE PARK
Garfield Blvd.
HYDE PARK
59th St.
63rd St.
MARQUETTE PARK
Marquette Rd.
71st St.
76th St.
79th St.
83rd St.
87th St.
95th St.
103rd St.
107th St.
111th St.
115th St.
119th St.
123rd St.
127th St.
130th St.
138th St.
Burr Oak Ave.

SOUTH LAKE SHORE DRIVE
Michigan Ave.
State
Ashland Ave.
Halsted
Kedzie Ave.
California Ave.
Western Ave.
Damen Ave.
Ashland Ave.
California Ave.
Kedzie Ave.
Western Ave.
Vincennes Ave.
Halsted
Dan Ryan Expwy.
Dr. Martin Luther King Jr. Dr.
State
Chicago Skyway
South Chicago Ave.
Stony Island Ave.
South Shore Dr.
Jeffery Blvd.
Yates
Torrence
Calumet River
Brainard
Lake Calumet

55
41
94
57
90

mains intact and healthy. Polish, Hmong, Greek, Arabic, and other languages mix freely with English, and summer in Chicago is a time when ethnic and community street fairs attract crowds.

The neighborhoods that lie like a fan to the southwest of the meeting of State Street and Archer Avenue have seen a succession of working-class ethnic populations. Archer Avenue, which runs roughly parallel to the South Branch of the Chicago River and the Chicago Sanitary and Ship Canal, is part of a huge transportation corridor that includes rail lines and the Stevenson Expressway (I–55). On this corridor much of the industrial history of the city took place.

Father Jacques Marquette and the explorer Louis Jolliet, who first arrived in the area in 1673, suggested the construction of a canal to connect Lake Michigan with the Illinois River. Begun in 1836, the monumental task took 12 years to complete. The Illinois–Michigan Canal gave Chicago commercial transportation to the hinterlands, and the canal and the river soon teemed with barges, docks, and factories. The activity quickly brought the railroads as well to the Archer Avenue corridor. By the turn of the century, the larger Chicago Sanitary and Ship Canal had also been constructed.

Irish workers made up a large portion of those who came to dig the Illinois–Michigan Canal, many of them having worked on the Erie Canal. The "canal" Irish tended to settle along the river in the area known originally as Hardscrabble or Lee's Farm; the building of the canal brought a change in name to Bridgeport. This workingclass community anchored the northern end of Archer Avenue. St. Bridget's Church at Archer Avenue and Arch Street stands as a reminder of the canal workers who flocked to Chicago before the Civil War. The present structure of 1906 resembles a cathedral built by Irish monks in Novara, Italy, in 1170; its survival in the face of the construction of the Stevenson Expressway in 1964 is a tribute to the efforts of its pastor and to Bridgeport's political clout. (Planners swung the expressway directly behind St. Bridget's and its Shrine of Our Lady of the Highway.)

The river and the canal soon attracted Chicago's most famous industry: Meat packing plants opened along the South Branch and fouled the river with pollution. The packinghouses in turn attracted skilled German and Bohemian butchers and brought more Irish to Bridgeport. On Christmas Day, 1865, the Union Stock Yard opened west of Halsted Street, between Pershing Road (39th Street) and 47th Street, just to the south of Bridgeport. The huge livestock market became the center of the nation's meat packing industry. In time, an immigrant city grew up around the more than 400 acres of livestock pens, chutes, and railroad yards. Bridgeport's Irish, Germans, and Bohemians found themselves surrounded by Poles, Lithuanians, Slovaks, Italians, French Canadians, black Americans, and others; this was the beginning of the ethnic mélange of the South Side.

In 1905 the Chicago stockyards were rocked by the publication of Upton Sinclair's muckraking novel *The Jungle*. Sinclair portrayed the life of a Lithuanian immigrant family that lived in Back of the Yards, just to the southwest of the stockyards and Bridgeport. The Chicago stockyards soon had an international reputation for unwholesome practices, and it was not the last time the area was looked upon unfavorably in literature or in the press.

In fact the area contains four of the most written about, most famous neighborhoods in the history of urban America. Bridgeport, McKinley Park, Back of the Yards, and Canaryville surround the old Union Stock Yard. Bridgeport, the oldest settlement, predates the founding of the stockyards; much of its fame rests on its workingclass ethnicity and its peculiar brand of politics. Richard J. Daley, its best-known political son, was only one of four Chicago mayors born and raised in Bridgeport, who together ran the city from the death of Anton Cermak in 1933 until the election of Jane Byrne in 1979. For many people, the name Bridgeport still means politics, especially Irish machine politics.

Bridgeport today has more than a dozen resident ethnic groups, some of them the overflow from neighboring communities. Pilsen, to the north, across the Chicago River, was once the center of Chicago's lumber industry; by 1900 it had become the largest Bohemian community outside Chicago; today it is the home of the city's principal concentration of Mexicans. Chinatown, to the northeast, its heart at the intersection of Cermak Road and Wentworth Avenue, was once occupied by Germans and Irish; Italians followed them before the Chinese arrived after 1900. The Chinatown community today is a growing and prosperous one, with a good deal of cohesion, and new immigrants have helped to solidify the Asian presence in the inner city.

Canaryville, to the south of Bridgeport, between Pershing Road and 49th Street, Halsted and the old New York Central Railroad yards, is a largely Irish-American neighborhood with many Mexicans and Appalachian whites. Here, at the corner of 45th Street and Lowe Avenue, is St. Gabriel's, perhaps the most famous church in the Stock Yard District. One of John Root's finest designs, the Romanesque structure was built in 1887–1888 with financial help from the packinghouse owners who were close friends of Fr. Maurice Dorney, the founder of the parish in 1880.

The neighborhoods that once surrounded the stockyards have more than 30 Roman Catholic churches and many Protestant houses of worship. Each is a monument to the faith and community-building spirit of an ethnic group that settled in the area. Polish packinghouse workers, who came to the area in large numbers between 1880 and 1920, alone built six of the structures. Today many of the old national parishes are of mixed ethnicity; many have services in the language of their founders, as well as in English and Spanish. Worshipers entering the magnificent church of St. John of God at 52nd Street and Throop, across the street from Sherman Park, are greeted by the flags of Poland, Mexico, the United States, and the Vatican.

The Stock Yard District, once known as Town of Lake, a suburb of Chicago until it was annexed in 1889, behaved in some ways like a city in itself. As its residents moved to the south and west after World War I, out of the core neighborhoods of wooden two-flats and cottages in close proximity to the stockyards and the packinghouses, they created suburbs in the new neighborhoods of the Southwest Side, principally along Archer Avenue. These areas are part of Chicago's "bungalow belt."

During the 1920s bungalows appeared throughout the Southwest, Northwest, and Southeast sides. The single-family dwellings, with their small front- and backyards, were the pre-Depression equivalent of suburban sprawl. Today they comprise much of Chicago's second tier of ethnic neighborhoods: Brighton Park, Gage Park, and Marquette Park all owe their existence to the movement away from the stockyard communities of Bridgeport, McKinley Park, Back of the Yards, and Canaryville. And the movements of ethnic groups can be traced across the Southwest Side in the churches and other institutions they left behind.

The Lithuanian community, for example, organized its first church, St. George's, in 1892 in Bridgeport. (The present structure was dedicated in 1902.) A second Lithuanian parish, Providence of God, was founded in 1900, north of St. George's in the Pilsen community. Three more Lithuanian parishes opened in 1904, including Holy Cross in Back of the Yards. Ten years later the Lithuanian community was supporting 10 Roman Catholic parishes, a consequence of the large East European emigration to America that took place before 1914. These arrivals became part of Chicago's first tier of ethnic neighborhoods.

As Lithuanians settled into better jobs following World War I, many of them decided to move away from the old industrial districts, and they looked to the bungalow belt for newer, more spacious housing. In the 1920s the Marquette Park area near the intersection of Marquette Road and California Avenue attracted Lithuanian Americans. A Lithuanian order of religious sisters had laid the foundation for the community in 1911 by opening the Academy of St. Casimir (later Maria High School). In 1928 ground was broken for a Lithuanian parish, Nativity B.V.M., at 68th Street and Washtenaw, and the parish quickly became a central institution in the Lithuanian community. In the same year the Sisters of St. Casimir opened Holy Cross Hospital near the church and the high school.

The large institutional base drew more Lithuanians to the neighborhood throughout the interwar period. After World War II, another major emigration from Eastern Europe rejuvenated the Lithuanian community, and Marquette Park became its new center. The present Nativity Church, designed by John Mulokas and dedicated on May 12, 1957, is a striking example of Lithuanian architecture. Its dedication to Our Lady of Siluva celebrates the site of a famous Shrine to the Blessed Virgin in Lithuania.

The movement of Lithuanians away from the inner city has been typical of that of ethnic groups that originally settled in the area. By 1988 many of the Marquette Park Lithuanians were relocating in the southwest suburbs near Lemont. Yet the neighborhood they left behind continues to nourish the community; many people and cultural institutions choose to stay in Chicago, and Marquette Park remains the Lithuanian "gold coast."

The Union Stock Yard closed its gates on August 1, 1971, after 105 years of active livestock trading. In reality the meat packing business had begun to leave the city nearly 20 years earlier, when Wilson and Company announced the closing of its huge Chicago plant. By the early 1960s the big packers had left the city, and Chicago was facing its first post-industrial crisis. The area west of the Union Stock Yard, formerly the center of one of the nation's great industries, now resembled a ghost town.

Recent years have seen a partially successful attempt to redevelop some of the land the stockyards and packing-houses had occupied. A visit to the Old Stone Gate at Exchange and Peoria, which marks the entrance to the area, will show you industrial buildings mixed with open prairie and abandoned packinghouse buildings. Yet the new industries, important as they are to the city's economic base, employ only a fraction of the number of workers formerly employed by Chicago's most infamous industry. Meanwhile, new immigrants from Poland, Mexico, and elsewhere continue to come to the district in search of employment.

The economic future of Chicago's Southwest Side looked bleak just a few years ago. Now a resurgent Midway Airport at 55th Street and Cicero and a new rapid transit line that is scheduled to open by 1993 have infused the local economy with optimism. Bridgeport, in part because of its proximity to downtown and an excellent public transportation system that will improve when the Southwest Rapid Transit opens, is already witnessing economic rebirth. Areas a little farther down Archer Avenue should see new development as Midway Airport increases its capacity and the rapid transit line reaches them. The entire area along the canal and the river is now part of the Illinois–Michigan Canal National Heritage Corridor, and there are plans for riverfront parks and other amenities. In the shadow of great economic, cultural, and social change, Chicago's ethnic communities continue to maintain their heritage in the old and the new neighborhoods.

The Southwest Side is easily accessible by public or private transportation. The Archer Avenue (No. 62) bus, which can be boarded on State Street, makes its way southwest through the corridor. The Dan Ryan Rapid Transit Line will take you to Chinatown (Cermak Avenue) or to Comiskey Park (35th Street), the home of the Chicago White Sox. By automobile, you can take Archer and turn down Halsted Street (800 W), Ashland Avenue (1600 W), Western Avenue (2400 W), or another major street and follow it until you find an interesting side street or attraction to explore. If you continue west on Archer past Kedzie Avenue, stop at the Dom Podhalan or Polish Highlanders Hall at 4808 South Archer Avenue; it is as authentic a Polish mountain chalet as you are likely to see this side of the Odra River. A visit to the Balzekas Museum of Lithuanian Culture at 6500 South Pulaski Road would be worthwhile (*see* Sightseeing Checklists in Chapter 3). Wonderful and inexpensive Lithuanian restaurants line 71st Street from Western to California avenues (2600 W). Some of the best Middle Eastern restaurants in Chicago are located along 63rd Street between Western and Central Park avenues (3600 W). While the Northwest Side, along Milwaukee Avenue, is famous for Polish cuisine, the South Side holds its own: Tatra Inn serves a satisfying smorgasboard at 6038 South Pulaski. Mexican restaurants abound in Back of the Yards near the intersection of Ashland Avenue and 47th Street and in Pilsen along 18th Street and on Blue Island Avenue. Mi Pueblo, at 2908 West 59th Street, resembles a Mexican hacienda. The Southwest Side Italian community is well represented with restaurants along Oakley Avenue (2300 W), Western just north of 26th Street, and on 63rd Street, where Palermo's at 3715 West 63rd Street and Little Joe's at 63rd Street and Richmond are noteworthy. Many of the churches hereabouts have beautiful interiors, and Sunday is the best time to visit them, when services are scheduled. At other times of the week, you may find the church you want to see closed unless you call in advance of your visit.

The Builders of Chicago

By Barbara Shortt

A practicing architect and an architectural historian, Barbara Shortt writes frequently on architecture and travel.

When Mrs. O'Leary's cow kicked over the lantern and started the Great Chicago Fire of 1871, she set the scene for the birth of a Modern Architecture that would influence the entire globe. If Chicago today is a world capital of modern architecture landmarks—a city whose buildings embody contemporary architectural history from its beginnings in the 1880s—it is thanks to this cataclysmic fire and a unique set of cultural circumstances that were fueled by the new wealth of the thriving port city. In 1871 Chicago was isolated from European and East Coast opinion. At the same time, it was not uncivilized frontier, nor had it been traumatized by the Civil War. And it was strongly conscious of being the metropolis of the American heartland. Yet it had absolutely no existing architectural tradition; physically and aesthetically, it was wide open.

Because Chicago had been built mainly of wood, it was wiped out by the fire. Virtually the only building left standing downtown, where it still dominates the intersection of North Michigan and Chicago avenues, was the bizarre yellow stone Water Tower of 1869. Oscar Wilde, that infamous aesthete, called it a "monstrosity" when he visited Chicago in 1882. Today, with its fake battlements, crenellations, and turrets, it looks like a transplant from Disneyland rather than a real part of a vibrant and serious city. It serves now as a tourist information center, and even amid the amazingly varied architecture of central Chicago it appears to be an anachronism.

In the years following the fire, many remarkable people flocked to the building opportunity in the city that sprawled for miles along the western shore of Lake Michigan and inland along the branches of the Chicago River. A brilliant engineer named William LeBaron Jenney and a young Bostonian trained at MIT and Paris named Louis Sullivan, who would become a great architect, philosopher, writer, and teacher, were joined by a group of ingenious architects and engineers from diverse parts of America and Europe: Dankmar Adler (from Denmark), William Holabird (from New York), John Wellborn Root, Frank Lloyd Wright (from Wisconsin), Henry Hobson Richardson (from Louisiana via Boston and Paris), Daniel H. Burnham, and Martin Roche, among others. During the 1880s and 1890s in Chicago, these men did nothing less than create the foundations of modern architecture and construction.

The skyscraper was born here. The "curtain-wall," a largely glass exterior surface that does not act as a "wall" supporting the building but is supported on the floors from within, originated here. Modern metal-frame, multistory construction was created here. The Chicago Window—a popular window design used in buildings all over America (until air-conditioning made it obsolete), consisting of a large fixed glass panel in the center, with a narrow operable sash on each side—was developed here. Chicago builders also discovered how to fireproof the metal structures that supported their buildings, which would otherwise melt in fires and bring total collapse: They covered the iron columns and beams with terra-cotta tiles that insulated the structural metal from heat.

Philosophically, the Chicago architects believed they were creating a democratic architecture to express the soul of American civilization, an architecture pragmatic, honest, healthy, and unashamed of wealth and commerce. Louis Sullivan, a philosopher, a romantic, and a prolific writer (his most famous book on architecture, *Kindergarten Chats*, is a Socratic dialogue), originated and propagated the ideas that "form follows function" and "a building is an act." For Sullivan, social purpose and structure had to be integrated to create an architecture of human satisfaction.

Technologically, the Chicago School, as they became known, were aware of the latest developments in European iron structures, such as the great railroad stations. Jenney had his engineering degree from Paris in 1856—he was older than the others, many of whom worked for him—yet he, Richardson, and John Root were the only conventionally well educated men of the group. At the same time, they had in Chicago a daring and innovative local engineering tradition. Jenney, a strict rationalist, incarnated this no-nonsense tradition and gave romantics like Sullivan and, later on, Sullivan's disciple Wright the tools with which to express their architectural philosophy.

The term *Chicago School of Architecture* refers to the work of these men, whose offices served as their true school: Jenney and Mundie, Root and Burgee, Adler and Sullivan, Holabird and Roche, Burnham and Root, H. H. Richardson, and Frank Lloyd Wright. In many instances it requires a scholarly effort to figure out precisely who did what, as they worked for and with one another, living in each other's pockets, shifting partnerships, arguing the meaning of what they did as well as how best to do it. Jenney and Adler were essentially engineers uninterested in decoration; with the exception of Richardson's Romanesque motifs, Sullivan's amazing ornament, and Wright's spatial and ornamental forms, these builders did not have distinct, easily discernible "styles." It becomes an academic exercise to try to identify their individual efforts.

The Chicago School's greatest clients were wealthy businessmen and their wives. The same lack of inhibition that led Mrs. Potter Palmer and Mrs. Havemeyer to snap up Impressionist paintings that had been rejected by French academic opinion (and today are the core of the Art Institute collection) led sausage magnates to hire young, inventive, local talent to build their mansions and countinghouses. Chicagoans may have been naive, but history has vindicated their taste.

Although they started building in the 1870s, nothing of note remains from before 1885. The oldest important structure is H. H. Richardson's massive granite Italian Romanesque-inspired Glessner House, with its decorative interiors derived from the innovative English Arts and Crafts movement. The only Richardson building left in Chicago, the Glessner House is considered by some his highest creation; Wright was influenced by its flowing interior space. At the corner of 18th Street and the Prairie Avenue Historic District, it now houses the offices of the Chicago Architecture Foundation.

Downtown, Richardson designed a Wholesale Building for Marshall Field that was later demolished. An addition to the Field store in the same architectural vocabulary, done by Burnham in 1893 and now part of the Marshall Field block, stands at the corner of Wabash and Washington streets. Burnham completed the block in 1902–1907, but in the airy, open, metal-frame, Chicago Window style.

In 1883 William LeBaron Jenney invented the first "skyscraper construction" building, in which a metal structural skeleton supports an exterior wall on metal shelves. (The metal frame or skeleton, a sort of three-dimensional boxlike grid, is still used today.) His earliest surviving metal-skeleton structure, the Second Leiter Building of 1891, is now Sears, Roebuck and Company, at the southeast corner of State and Van Buren streets in the Loop. The granite-face facade is extremely light and open, suggesting the metal frame behind. The building looks so modern that it comes as a shock to realize it is nearly a century old.

At 209 South La Salle Street, the Rookery Building of 1886, a highly decorated, structurally transitional building by Burnham and Root, employs masonry bearing walls (brick, terra-cotta, and stone) on the two major street facades and lots of iron structure (both cast-iron columns and wrought-iron beams) elsewhere. Here the decoration emphasizes the structural elements—pointing out, for example, the floor lines. Note also how specially shaped bricks are used at the edges of the window openings and to make pilasters. The plan, a freestanding square "donut," was unusual at the time. A magnificent iron and glass skylight covers the lower two stories of the interior courtyard, which was renovated in 1905 by Frank Lloyd Wright, who designed light fixtures and other decorative additions.

The nearby Marquette Building of 1894 at 140 South Dearborn Street, by Holabird and Roche, is almost a prototype for the modern office building, with its skeleton metal frame covered by decorative terra-cotta and its open, cellular facade with Chicago Windows. The marble lobby rotunda has Tiffany mosaic portraits of Indian chieftains and Père Marquette, a hymn to local history.

The most advanced structure from this period, one in which the exterior wall surface is freed of all performance of support, is Burnham's Reliance Building of 1895 at 36 North State Street. Here the proportion of glass to solid is very high, and the solid members are immensely slender for the era. Today the white terra-cotta cladding needs cleaning, and the building's seedy condition mars its beauty; the casual observer would be surprised to learn that most critics consider it the masterpiece of the Chicago School's office buildings.

To appreciate fully the giant leap taken by the architects of the Reliance, look at Burnham and Root's Monadnock Building of 1889–1892, at 53 West Jackson Boulevard. Its 16 stories are supported by conventional load-bearing walls, which grow to six feet thick at the base! While elegant in its stark simplicity (the result of a cheap-minded entrepreneur who had all the decoration removed from the plans while Root was traveling), its ponderousness contrasts sharply with the delicate structure and appearance of the Reliance Building. The Monadnock Building may have been the swan song of conventional building structure in Chicago, yet its verticality expressed the aspirations of the city.

Jenney's Manhattan Building of 1890, at 431 South Dearborn Street, with its variously shaped bay windows, was the first tall building (16 stories) to use metal-skeleton structure throughout; it is admired more for its structure than for its appearance. Both it and the equally tall Monadnock would never have come into being without Elisha Otis's elevator invention, which was already in use in New York City in buildings of 9 or 10 stories at most.

The impetus toward verticality was an essential feature of Chicago commercial architecture. Verticality seemed to embody commercial possibility, as in "the sky's the limit!" Even the essential horizontality of the 12-story, block-long Carson Pirie Scott store is offset by the rounded corner tower at the main entrance.

The Chicago School created new decorative forms to apply to their powerful structures, and they derived them largely from American vegetation rather than from classical motifs. The apogee of this lush ornament was probably reached by Sullivan in his Carson Pirie Scott and Company store of 1899–1904 at State and Madison streets. The cast-iron swirls of rich vegetation and geometry surround the ground-floor show windows and the entrance, and they grow to the second story as well, with the architect's initials,

LHS, worked into the design. (A decorative cornice that was originally at the top was removed.) The facade of the intermediate floors is extremely simple, with wide Chicago Windows surrounded by a thin line of delicate ornament; narrow vertical and horizontal bands, all of white terra-cotta, cover the iron structure behind.

Terra-cotta plaques of complex and original decoration cover the horizontal spandrel beams (the beams that cover the outer edges of the floors, between the vertical columns of the facades) of many buildings of this era, including the Reliance and the Marquette. Even modest residential and commercial structures in Chicago began to use decorative terra-cotta, which became a typical local construction motif through the 1930s.

Adler and Sullivan's Auditorium Building of 1887–1889 was a daring megastructure sheathed in massive granite, the same material Richardson used, and its style derives from his Romanesque forms. Here the shades of stone color and the rough and polished finishes provide contrasts. Built for profit as a civic center at South Michigan Avenue and Congress Street, facing Lake Michigan, the Auditorium Building incorporated a theater, a hotel, and an office building; complex engineering solutions allowed it to carry heavy and widely varying loads. Adler, the engineer, devised a hydraulic stage lift and an early air-conditioning system for the magnificent theater. Sullivan freely decorated the interiors with his distinctive flowing ornamental shapes.

In the spirit of democracy and populism, Adler wanted the Auditorium to be a "people's theater," one with lots of cheap seats and few boxes. It is still in use today as the Auditorium Theater, Adler's belief in the common man having been upheld when thousands of ordinary Chicagoans subscribed to the restoration fund in 1968. The rest of the building is now Roosevelt University.

Frank Lloyd Wright, who had worked for a year on the Auditorium Building in Adler and Sullivan's office, remained in their employ and in 1892 designed a house for them in a wealthy area of the Near North Side of town. The Charnley House, 1365 North Astor Street, built of long, thin, yellowish Roman brick and stone, has a projecting central balcony and shows a glimmer of Wright's extraordinary later freedom with volumes and spaces. The Charnley House, with its exquisite interior woodwork and the exterior frieze under the roof, has now been completely restored. Soon after the Charnley House project, Wright left Adler and Sullivan to work on his own.

Wright's ability to break apart and recompose space and volume, even asymmetrically, was given full range in the many houses he built in and around Chicago. What became typical of American domestic "open plan" interiors (as opposed to an arrangement of closed, boxlike rooms) derived from Wright's creation, but they could never have been practical without the American development of central heating, which eliminated the need for a fire in each room.

Wright was the founder of what became known as the Prairie School, whose work consisted largely of residences rather than buildings intended for commerce. Its principal characteristic was a horizontality evocative of the breadth of the prairies that contrasted with the lofty vertical shafts of the business towers. Like his teacher Sullivan, Wright also delighted in original decorative motifs of geometric and vegetable design.

The opening of the Lake Street el railway west to the new suburb of Oak Park gave Wright an enormous opportunity to build. In 1889 he went to live there at 951 Chicago Avenue, where he created a studio and a home over the next 22 years. Dozens of houses in Oak Park, of wood, stucco, brick, and stone, with beautiful leaded- and stained-glass windows and carved woodwork, were designed or renovated by him. He was almost obsessional in his involvement with his houses, wanting to design and control the placement of furniture and returning even after his clients had moved in. For Wright a house was a living thing, both in its relationship to the land and in its evolution through use.

Yet Wright's masterpiece in Oak Park is not a house but the Unitarian Unity Temple of 1906, at Kenilworth Avenue and Lake Street, a short walk from the Oak Park Avenue el stop. Because of intense budget limitations, he built it of the daring and generally abhorred material, poured concrete, and with only the simplest details of applied wood stripping. Nevertheless, Wright's serene creation of volume and light endures to this day. It is lit by high windows from above and has operable colored-glass skylights inserted into the "coffers" of the Roman-style "egg-crate" ceiling, intended for ventilation as well as light. The design of the windows and skylights echoes the designs applied to the walls, the door grilles, the hinges, the light fixtures; everything is integrated visually, no detail having been too small to consider.

Unity Temple was built on what became known as an H plan, which consisted of two functionally separate blocks connected by an entry hall. The Unity Temple plan has influenced the planning of public buildings to the present day. Recently restored to its original interior greens and ochers, Unity Temple is definitely worth a pilgrimage.

On the South Side of Chicago is the most famous of all Wright's houses, the Robie House of 1909, now on the University of Chicago campus, at 5757 South Woodlawn Avenue. Its great horizontal overhanging roof lines are echoed by the long limestone sills that cap its low brick walls. Wright designed everything for the house, including the furniture. Wright's stock has soared of late: A single lamp from the Robie House sold at auction recently for three-quarters of a million dollars!

The World's Columbian Exposition of 1893 was held at Midway Park in South Chicago. For complex political reasons, the planning was turned over mainly to eastern architects, who brought the influence of the international Beaux-Arts style to Chicago. A furious Louis Sullivan prophesied that "the damage wrought to this country by the Chicago World's Fair will last half a century." He wasn't entirely wrong in his prediction; the classicist style vied sharply over the next decades with the native creations of the Chicago and Prairie schools, all the while incorporating their technical advances. But the city fathers succumbed to the "culture versus commerce" point of view; thus most of the museums and public buildings constructed before World War II in Chicago were built in classical Greek or Renaissance styles.

Many of these public buildings are fine works in their own right, but they do not contribute to the development of 20th-century architecture. The most notable of them, the Public Library of 1897, at 78 East Washington Street, by Shepley, Rutan and Coolidge, has gorgeous interiors of white and green marble and glass.

Many of Chicago's museums are situated in Grant Park and along Lake Shore Drive, magnificent points from which to view the city skyline. The park and the drive were built on landfill in the 1910s and 1920s after the tracks of the Illinois Central Railroad along the old lakefront had been bridged over. Lake Shore Drive, with its parks and beaches, seems such an integral part of today's city that it is hard to imagine a Chicago without it. Daniel Burnham called for this development in his "Chicago Plan" of 1909.

In 1922 an important international competition offered a prize of $100,000 for the design of a Tribune Building that would dominate the Chicago River just north of the Loop. Numerous modernist plans were submitted, including one by Walter Gropius, of the Bauhaus. Raymond Hood's Gothic design—some called it Woolworth Gothic—was chosen. The graceful and picturesque silhouette of the Tribune Tower was for many years the symbol of Chicago, not to be overshadowed until general construction resumed, following World War II. More important, the Tribune Building moved the center of gravity of downtown Chicago north and east, causing the Michigan Avenue bridge to be built and opening the Near North Side to commercial development along Michigan Avenue.

The postwar Chicago School was dominated by a single personality who influenced modern architecture around the world: Ludwig Mies van der Rohe. The son of a stonemason, Mies was director of the Bauhaus in Dessau, Germany, the world's leading modern design center, from 1930 until Nazi pressure made him leave in 1937. On a trip to the United States he met John Holabird, son of William, who invited him to head the School of Architecture at the Armour Institute, later the Illinois Institute of Technology. Mies accepted—and redesigned the entire campus as part of the deal. Over the next 20 years he created a School of Architecture that disseminated his thinking into architecture offices everywhere.

Whatever Mies owed to Frank Lloyd Wright, such as Mies's own open-plan houses, his philosophy was very much in the tradition of Chicago, and the roots of Bauhaus architecture can be traced to the Chicago School. Mies's attitudes were profoundly pragmatic, based on solid building techniques, technology, and an appreciation of the nature of the materials used. He created a philosophy, a set of ethical values based on a purist approach; his great aphorisms were "Less is more" and "God is in the details." He eschewed applied ornament, however, and in that sense he was nothing like Wright. All Mies's "decoration" is generated by fine-tuned structural detail. His buildings are sober, sometimes somber, highly orderly, and serene; their aesthetic is based on the almost religious expression of structure.

The campus of IIT was built in 1942–1958 along South State Street, between 31st and 35th streets. Mies used few materials in the two dozen buildings he planned here: light cream colored brick, black steel, and glass. Quadrangles are only suggested, space is never rigidly defined. There is a direct line of descent from Crown Hall (1956), made of black steel and clear glass, with its longspan roof trusses exposed above the level of the roof, to the great convention center of 1970 on South Lake Shore Drive at 23rd Street, McCormick Center by C. F. Murphy, with its great exposed black steel space-frame roof and its glass walls.

Age requirements forced Mies to retire from IIT in 1958, but his office went on to do major projects in downtown Chicago, along Lake Shore Drive, and elsewhere. He had impressed the world in 1952 with his black steel and clear glass twin apartment towers, set at right angles to one another, almost kissing at the corner, at 860–880 North Lake Shore Drive. Later he added another, darker pair just to the north, 900–910.

In 1968 Heinrich and Schipporeit, inspired by "860" and by Mies's Berlin drawings of 1921 for a free-form glass skyscraper, built Lake Point Tower. This dark bronze metal and glass trefoil shaft, near the Navy Pier at East Grand Avenue, is a graceful and dramatic joy of the Chicago skyline. It is one of the few Chicago buildings, along with Bertram Goldberg's Marina City of 1964—twin round concrete towers on the river between State and Dearborn streets—to break with strict rectilinear geometry.

Downtown, Mies's Federal Center is a group of black buildings around a plaza, set off by a bright red steel Alexander Calder stabile sculpture, on Dearborn Street between Jackson Boulevard and Adams Street. The Dirksen Building, with its courthouse, on the east side of Dearborn, was built in 1964; the Kluczynski office building at the south side of the plaza and the single-story Post Office to the west were added through 1975. The north side of the large Federal Plaza is enclosed by the Marquette Building of 1894, thereby integrating the past with the present.

The IBM Building of 1971, the last office building designed by Mies, is a dark presence north of the river, between Wabash and State streets.

Perhaps the most important spinoff of Miesian thinking was the young firm of Skidmore, Owings & Merrill, which bloomed after the war. Their gem of the postwar period was the Inland Steel Building of 1957, at 30 West Monroe Street, in the Loop. The bright stainless-steel and pale green glass structure, only 18 stories high, with exposed columns on the long facade and a clear span in the short dimension, has uninterrupted interior floor space. It is considered a classic.

SOM became the largest architecture firm in America, with offices in all major cities. In Chicago the firm built, among other works, the immensely tall, tapering brown Hancock Tower of 1965–1970, with its innovative exterior criss-cross wind-bracing, and the even taller Sears Tower (1970–1975), with two of its nine shafts reaching to 1,450 feet, now the tallest structure in the world. SOM may have achieved the epitome of the vertical commercial thrust of the Chicago School.

Meanwhile, Mies's Federal Plaza started a Chicago tradition, that of the outdoor plaza with a focus of monumental art. These plazas are real, usable, and used; they are large-scale city gathering places, not the mingy setbacks of New York office megaliths, and they shape the architectural and spatial character of downtown Chicago.

A string of plazas, featuring sculptures by Picasso and Dubuffet and mosaic murals by Chagall, leads one up Dearborn and Clark streets, to the Chicago River. At the river one finds more outdoor space. The south bank quays, one level down from the street, are a series of imaginatively landscaped gardens. Here one can contemplate the ever-changing light on the river and the 19th-century riveted-iron drawbridges, which prefigure Calder's work. Other monumental outdoor sculpture downtown includes Joan Miró's *Chicago* and Claes Oldenburg's *Batcolumn.*

The Jean Dubuffet sculpture stands before the State of Illinois Building of 1985 at the corner of Randolph and Clark streets. Here there are really two plazas: one outdoors, the other inside the stepped-back, mirrored-glass and pink-paneled irregular donut of a building. This wild fantasy is the work of Helmut Jahn, a German who came to Chicago in the 1960s to study at IIT. His colorful, lighthearted, mirrored Chicago buildings provide a definite counterpoint to the somber Mies buildings of the 1950s and 1960s, and they appear everywhere, influencing the design and choice of materials of the architecture of the 1980s.

Jahn's first important contribution to the Chicago scene was a sensitive addition to the Board of Trade in 1980. The Board of Trade was housed in an architectural landmark at 141 West Jackson Boulevard, at the foot of La Salle Street, a jewel of Art Deco design by the old Chicago firm of Holabird and Root in 1930. Murphy/Jahn's glittering addition echoed numerous features of the original structure. Both parts of the building have sumptuous interior atrium spaces. Marble, nickel, and glass motifs from the earlier edifice are evoked and reinterpreted—but not copied—in the high-tech addition. Within the new atrium, framed by highly polished chromium-plated trusses and turquoise panels, hangs a large Art Deco painting that was found in the older building during renovation. This complex captures the spirit of Chicago architecture: Devoted to commerce, it embraces the present without denying the past.

Next came Jahn's sleek, curving Xerox Center of white metal and reflective glass, at Monroe and Dearborn streets (1980). Mirrored glass, introduced by Jahn, has become one of the favorite materials in new Chicago commercial buildings. It is successful as a foil to the dark Miesian buildings, especially along the river, where it seems to take on a watery quality on an overcast day. His latest accomplishment is the elegant but playful high-tech United Airlines Terminal 1 at O'Hare (1987). The terminal has been praised as a soaring technological celebration of travel, in the same splendid tradition as the 19th-century European iron and glass railroad stations that Jenney had studied.

Two disparate threads of architectural creation are weaving the modern tissue of Chicago, providing aesthetic tension and dynamism, much as in the period following the World's Columbian Exposition of 1893. The solid, muscular past provides an armature that can support diversity and even fantasy without cracking apart. Yet Chicago is a down-to-earth place whose greatest creations have been products of a no-nonsense approach. "The business of Chicago is business"; when Chicago becomes selfconsciously "cultural," it fares less well.

Chicago is a city with a sense of continuity, where the traditions of design are strong. Money and technology have long provided a firm support for free and original intellectual thought, with a strong populist local bias. Chicagoans talk of having a "second city" mentality, yet at the same time they have a strong sense of self; perhaps being "second" has indeed freed them to be themselves.

3 Exploring Chicago

O BOARD O

Chicago's variety is dazzling. The canyons of the Loop bustle with bankers, lawyers, traders, brokers, politicians, and wheeler-dealers of all kinds, transacting their business in buildings that make architecture buffs swoon. Equally busy but sunnier is the Near North (near the Loop, that is), where the smart shops of Michigan Avenue give way on either side to the headquarters of myriad trade associations, advertising agencies, one of the nation's leading teaching hospitals, and cathedrals of the Roman Catholic and Episcopal churches.

Cultural life flourishes. The Shubert, Auditorium, and Goodman theaters, the Chicago bases for Broadway-scale shows, have been joined by more than 40 little theaters based in the neighborhoods, where young actors polish their skills. The art galleries of Ontario and Superior streets are alive and well, augmented by a large new neighborhood of galleries in resurgent River North. The Lyric Opera has extended its season into January, offering nine productions annually that play to houses averaging 95% full; Chicago Opera Theatre augments the Lyric's offerings with a spring season of smaller works. Chicago Symphony subscriptions are a sellout; the Ravinia Festival and the Grant Park Concerts pack people in. Music lovers hungry for more turn to smaller performing groups: the Orpheus Band, Music of the Baroque, the Chicago Brass Ensemble, Concertante di Chicago, and dozens more.

The city's skyline is one of the most exciting in the world. In the last two decades the Sears Tower, the Amoco Building, the John Hancock Building, The Associates Center, the NBC Building, Illinois Center, 333 West Wacker, the CNA Building, Lake Point Towers, and others have joined such legendary structures as the Chicago Board of Trade, Railway Exchange Building, and the Wrigley Building.

Leave downtown and the lakefront, however, and you soon encounter a city of neighborhoods: bungalows, two-flats, three-flats, and six-flats, churches and shopping strips with signs in Polish, Spanish, Chinese, Arabic, Hebrew, or Korean, and an ethnic community life that remains vibrant.

The neighborhoods are the part of Chicago that a visitor rarely sees. Yet it is in the neighborhoods that one can encounter the life of ordinary people, enjoy a great ethnic feast for a pittance, and visit the museums and churches that house cultural artifacts reflecting the soul and spirit of the community. The Chicago of the neighborhoods is the underpinning of the world-class city, and both must be experienced to understand the real Chicago.

In the tours that follow, we explore in depth the many faces of Chicago. We'll begin **Downtown,** in the heart of the world-class city, visiting handsome old landmark buildings and shimmering new ones, the centers of business and trade and the mainstays of culture, new residential areas and renewed older districts. Our visit to **Downtown South** shows how old forms take on new functions that merge with the life of the central city.

Then we'll head south to **Hyde Park,** home of the University of Chicago, and **Kenwood.** We'll see turn-of-the-century mansions and workingmen's cottages, we'll look at the process of urban renewal and the changes it has wrought in the neighborhood, and we'll ramble through museums, churches, and bookstores.

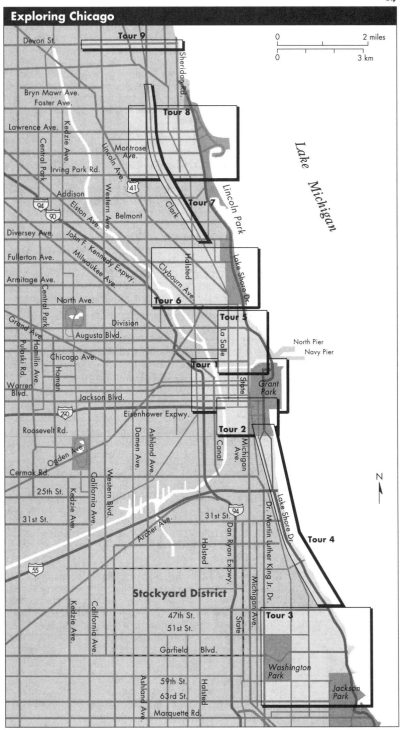

Exploring Chicago

Tour 9

Devon St.

Tour 8

Bryn Mawr Ave.
Foster Ave.

Lawrence Ave.

Kedzie Ave.

Central Park

Lincoln Ave.

Montrose Ave.

Tour 7

Irving Park Rd.

Addison

41

Western Ave.

Belmont

Clark

Lincoln Park

Lake Michigan

0   2 miles

0   3 km

Sheridan Rd.

Elston Ave.

94

90

Diversey Ave.

John F. Kennedy Expwy.

Milwaukee Ave.

Fullerton Ave.

Armitage Ave.

Central Park

North Ave.

Tour 6

Halsted

Clybourn Ave.

Lake Shore Dr.

Grand Ave.

Hamlin Ave.

Pulaski Rd.

Division

Augusta Blvd.

Tour 5

La Salle

North Pier
Navy Pier

Chicago Ave.

Homan

Tour 1

State

Grant Park

Warren
Blvd.

Jackson Blvd.

290

Eisenhower Expwy.

Tour 2

Roosevelt Rd.

Michigan Ave.

Ogden Ave.

Canal

Cermak Rd.

Damen Ave.

Ashland Ave.

Western Blvd.

25th St.

Kedzie Ave.

California Ave.

31st St.

Archer Ave.

31st St.

94

Dan Ryan Expwy.

Halsted

Michigan Ave.

Dr. Martin Luther King Jr. Dr.

Lake Shore Dr.

Tour 4

N

55

Stockyard District

47th St.

51st St.

State

Tour 3

Kedzie Ave.

California Ave.

Garfield   Blvd.

Washington Park

Ashland Ave.

59th St.

63rd St.

Halsted

Marquette Rd.

Jackson Park

We'll head north again via **South Lake Shore Drive,** viewing Chicago's splendid skyline along the way.

In the **Near North,** we'll explore the riches of **Michigan Avenue** and the side streets of **Streeterville,** then proceed to **River North,** to see how the rehabilitation process has transformed an area of factories and warehouses into a neighborhood of up-scale shopping strips and more than 50 art galleries.

In **Lincoln Park,** we'll visit the campuses of the old McCormick Seminary and De Paul University. Then we'll head up North Lincoln Avenue for a stop at the historic Biograph Theatre and a look at the shops. We'll explore the Old Town Triangle, visiting one of the oldest and most expensive streets in Chicago and contrasting the religious expressions found in St. Michael's Church with those at the Midwest Buddhist Temple. Finally, we'll look at the oldest park in Chicago's "emerald necklace."

We'll take a bus or a car the length of **North Clark Street** to see how the continuing waves of immigration leave their mark on the face of the city.

Further north, we'll visit **Argyle Street** and **Uptown** for a brief look at how the immigrant Vietnamese have created an economic miracle in one of Chicago's most depressed neighborhoods.

Finally, we'll visit **Devon Avenue,** on the city's far north side, to see how immigrants from the Indian subcontinent live virtually side by side with Orthodox Jews newly arrived from Russia. Here we'll find different customs and cultures in juxtaposition, and we'll sample their ethnic cuisines.

Highlights for First-Time Visitors

Art Institute of Chicago (Tour 1: Downtown)

Chicago Historical Society (Tour 6: Lincoln Park)

Door of Carson Pirie Scott building (Tour 1: Downtown)

Field Museum of Natural History
(Tour 4: South Lake Shore Drive)

Grant Park (Tour 2: Downtown South)

Lobbies of The Rookery and the Chicago Board of Trade
(Tour 1: Downtown)

Museum of Science and Industry
(Tour 3: Hyde Park and Kenwood)

Picasso sculpture in Daley Center (Tour 1: Downtown)

The Robie House (Tour 3: Hyde Park and Kenwood)

Shedd Aquarium (Tour 4: South Lake Shore Drive)

Tour 1: Downtown

Numbers in the margin correspond to points of interest on the Tour 1: Downtown map.

Downtown Chicago, aka the Loop, is a city lover's delight. It comprises the area south of the Chicago River, west of Lake Michigan, and north of the Congress Parkway/Eisenhower Expressway. Downtown Chicago's western boundary used to be the Chicago River, but the boundary continues to push westward even as this book is written. Handsome new skyscrapers line every foot of South Wacker Drive east and west of the river, and investors have sent construction crews across the bridges in search of more land to fuel the expansion.

We begin our tour on North Michigan Avenue at South Water Street. You can reach it from the north via the No. 2, 3, 11, 145, 146, 147, 151, or 157 bus; get off before the bridge, cross it, and walk the short block to South Water Street. Coming from the south, you can take the No. 3, 6, 56, 141, 145, 146, 147, 151, or 157 bus; get off at Lake Street and walk one block north to South Water Street. If you arrive by car, you'll want to park it, for this tour is best done on foot. If possible, take this tour on a weekday; the lobbies of many of the office buildings discussed here are closed on weekends, and these interiors are some of the most interesting sights in the Loop.

On the southwest corner of the intersection stands the elegant Art Deco **Carbide and Carbon Building** (233 N. Michigan Ave.). Designed by the Burnham Brothers in 1929, its sleek gold and black exterior is accented by curving, almost lacy brasswork at the entrance. Inside, the lobby is splendid, with more burnished brass, glass ornamentation, and marble.

Walk south on Michigan Avenue, turn right on Lake Street, and continue to State Street and the north end of the **State Street Mall.** Built a decade ago with federal funds, the mall was intended to revive the faltering State Street shopping strip by providing trees, sculptures, and outdoor cafés to encourage shoppers to visit the area and patronize the stores. Because of restrictions on the federal grant, however, the street could not be made a true pedestrian mall; closed to private vehicles, it remained open to police cars, emergency vehicles, and buses. The mall has been a spectacular failure. The improvements and amenities were minimal: The new hexagonal gray concrete bricks are no more appealing than the original sidewalk, the few pieces of sculpture are undistinguished, and the outdoor cafés fail to thrive amid the exhaust fumes of the buses. The exodus of better stores to North Michigan Avenue and elsewhere has continued.

Turn left onto this urban paradise and walk half a block to the **Chicago Theatre** (175 N. State St.). Threatened with demolition a few years ago, the 70-year-old theater was saved through the efforts of a civic-minded consortium that bought the building and oversaw a multimillion-dollar restoration. It has had several different managers who have been unable to make the theater a financial success. National tours of singers, musicals, and variety acts are booked sporadically. Next door, the **Page Brothers Building** is one of only two buildings in Chicago known to have a cast-iron front wall. Notice the delicate detail work on the horizontal and vertical bands between the windows. The building behind the facade, now being renovated, will become part of a new Chicago Theatre complex. Notice also the very handsome building, directly across State Street, that houses WLS-TV.

Continue south, turn left on Randolph Street, and walk to Michigan Avenue. On the northwest corner, the **Associates Center** (150 N. Michigan Ave.), the office building with the distinctive diamond-shape, angled face visible for miles, is the first building in Chicago to be wired for computer use (outlets in every office eliminate the need for costly cabling). An amusing sculpture sits in its small plaza.

❺ Two blocks east, the **Amoco Building** (200 E. Randolph St.), formerly the Standard Oil Building, was for a short time the largest marble-clad building in the world. Unfortunately, the thin slabs of marble, unable to withstand Chicago's harsh climate, began to warp and fall off soon after the building was completed. A two-year, $60-million project to replace the marble with light-colored granite was completed in 1992. The building looks as striking as it did before, but its massive presence is best viewed from a distance. The building sits on a handsome but rather sterile plaza, and Harry Bertoia's wind chime sculpture in the reflecting pool makes interesting sounds when the wind blows. Next door is the **Prudential Building,** replaced as Chicago's tallest building in the late '60s by the John Hancock. Behind it rises a postmodern spire added in 1990.

Return west on Randolph Street to Michigan Avenue, walk south a block, and turn right onto East Washington Street, to **❻** the **Chicago Cultural Center** (78 E. Washington St., tel. 312/269–2900 or 312/346–3278). When you've stepped inside the Romanesque-style entrance, notice the marble and the mosaic work before you climb the curving stairway to the third floor. There you will see a splendid back-lit Tiffany dome, restored during the 1977 renovation of the building. This is Preston Bradley Hall, used for public events. Other parts of the building were modeled on Venetian and ancient Greek elements. If you love Tiffany domes, you will find another one on the second floor. More than an architectural marvel, the Cultural Center offers concerts and changing exhibitions. Civil War buffs will enjoy the artifacts on display in the Grand Army of the Republic room. Here also is the new home of the **Museum of Broadcast Communications,** where you can see artifacts, audiotapes, and videotapes from the history of television and radio. There's a miniature TV studio where you can make a tape of yourself as a news anchor. *Tel. 312/629–6000. Admission free. Open Mon.–Sat. 10–4:30, Sun. noon–5.*

Turn right on leaving the Cultural Center from the Washington **❼** Street side, walk to Wabash Avenue, and enter **Marshall Field's & Co.** (111 N. State St.). This mammoth store, now undergoing a massive renovation, boasts some 500 departments, and it's a great place for a snack (the Crystal Palace ice cream parlor) or a meal (the grand Walnut Room or Hinky Dink Kenna's in the basement). Another spectacular Tiffany dome can be found on Field's southwest corner, near State and Washington streets. A recent multimillion-dollar renovation spruced up the entire store, though the synthetic look of the new atrium clashes drastically with the rest of the building's turn-of-the-century charm.

Across State Street is a vacant lot known as "Block 37," cleared a few years ago by developers and then abandoned when their deal fell through. Conscious that the space could become an eyesore, the city and several corporate sponsors have taken steps to use it for the civic good. During summer, it's an outdoor art gallery for the works of high school students, and in winter it's converted to "Skate on State," a small rink with free admission and skates available at a nominal charge. At this writing, the fate of the lot is undetermined.

Amoco Building, **5**
Art Institute of Chicago, **23**
Associates Center, **4**
AT&T Building, **17**
Auditorium Theatre, **41**
Berghoff Restaurant, **28**

Buckingham Fountain, **42**
Carbide and Carbon Building, **1**
Carson Pirie Scott, **22**
Chicago Board of Trade, **34**
Chicago City Hall-Cook County Building, **10**
Chicago Cultural Center, **6**

Chicago Mercantile Exchange, **18**
Chicago Temple, **8**
Civic Opera House, **13**
CNA Building, **38**
Daley Center, **9**
Dawn Shadows, **19**
Federal Center and Plaza, **29**

Fine Arts Building, **40**
First National Bank Plaza, **20**
Fisher Building, **36**
Harold Washington Library Center, **37**
Main Post Office, **45**
Marquette Building, **27**
Marshall Field's, **7**

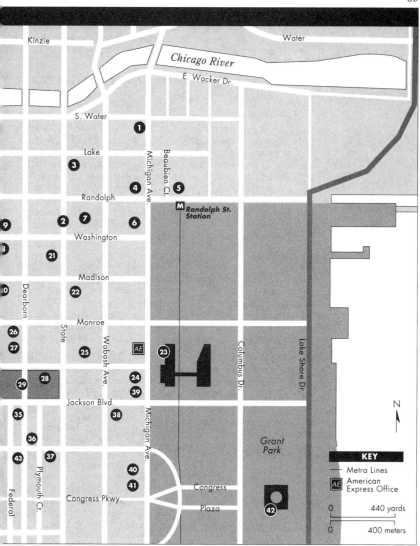

Kinzie

Water

Chicago River

E. Wacker Dr.

S. Water

1

Lake

3

4

Beaubien Ct.

5

Michigan Ave.

Randolph

M *Randolph St. Station*

9

2

7

6

Washington

3

21

Madison

0

Dearborn

22

Monroe

26

State

25

Wabash Ave.

AE

23

Columbus Dr.

Lake Shore Dr.

27

29

28

Jackson Blvd.

35

38

24

39

36

43

37

Plymouth Ct.

Grant Park

40

41

Congress

Federal

Congress Pkwy.

Plaza

42

N

KEY

— Metra Lines

AE American
Express Office

0   440 yards

0   400 meters

Metropolitan
Detention Center, **43**

Monadnock
Building, **35**

Northwestern Atrium
Center, **14**

One Financial
Place, **44**

Orchestra Hall, **24**

Page Brothers
Building, **3**

Palmer House, **25**

Presidential
Towers, **16**

Railway Exchange
Building, **39**

Reliance Building, **21**

The Rookery, **30**

Sears Tower, **31**

Social Security
Building, **15**

State of Illinois
Center, **11**

State Street Mall, **2**

311 South Wacker
Drive, **32**

333 West Wacker
Drive, **12**

Union Station, **33**

Xerox Building, **26**

⑧ Further west on Washington Street, we come to the **Chicago Temple** (77 W. Washington St.), whose beautiful spire can be seen only at some distance (the bridge across the river at Dearborn Street is a good spot for viewing it). In the plaza is Joan Miró's sculpture *Chicago* (1982).

⑨ Directly opposite is the **Daley Center,** named for the late Mayor Richard J. Daley, where the Cook County court system is headquartered. The building is constructed of a steel known as Corten, which was developed as a medium that would weather naturally and attractively (and weathering has certainly improved its appearance). In the plaza is a sculpture by Picasso that is made of the same material. Known simply as "the Picasso," it provoked an outcry when it was installed in 1967. Speculation about what it is meant to represent (knowledgeable observers say it is the head of a woman; others have suggested it is a pregnant cow) has diminished but not ended. In the plaza, as well, is an eternal flame dedicated to the memory of American soldiers who died in Korea and Vietnam. In summertime the plaza hosts concerts, dance presentations, and a weekly farmer's market.

⑩ Directly across Clark Street from the Daley Center is the **Chicago City Hall–Cook County Building,** a handsome neo-classical structure, designed by Holabird and Roche in 1911, whose appearance is generally ignored by the citizens who rush in and out to do business with the City. Inside are spacious halls, high ceilings, plenty of marble, and lots of hot air, for this is where the Chicago City Council holds its infamous meetings.

Head north on Clark for a block and you'll reach the much-dis-
⑪ cussed **State of Illinois Center** (100 W. Randolph St.). Governor James Thompson, who personally selected the Helmut Jahn design for the building, hailed it in his dedication speech in 1985 as "the first building of the twenty-first century." Those who work there, and many ordinary Chicagoans as well, have groaned in response, "I hope not." It is difficult to say more about the design of the building than to point out that it presents multiple shapes and faces. Narrow alternating vertical strips of mirrored and plain glass give the impression of taffeta streamers flying from a giant maypole. Some people love it and some do not; the structure's sky blue, white, and red exterior colors have elicited such adjectives as "garish" and "tacky." Its enormous interior atrium embraces a volume of 8 million cubic feet. The dramatically patterned circular floor at its base and the soaring vistas, with handsome exposed elevators and a skylighted glass dome, are impressive.

On the northwest corner of Randolph and Clark streets stands *Monument to a Standing Beast,* a sculpture by Jean Dubuffet. Its curved shapes, in white with black traceries, set against the curving red, white, and blue of the center, merely add to the visual cacophony. In another setting it might be a pleasing and enjoyable work.

Now let's look at a building roughly contemporary to the State of Illinois Center that has had a very different public reception. Head west on Randolph Street, turn right on La Salle Street, left on Lake Street, and walk two blocks to Franklin Street.
⑫ The building at **333 West Wacker Drive,** designed by Kohn, Pedersen, Fox in 1983 and constructed on a triangular plot, is a softly curving building with forest green marble columns, a

spacious plaza, and a shimmering green glass skin. Its unpromisingly irregular shape, dictated by the parcel on which it sits, is particularly lovely seen at sunset from the bridge over the Chicago River at Orleans Street, when the river and surrounding buildings are mirrored in the glass.

A two-block walk south on Wacker Drive will take you to the ⑬ **Civic Theatre** and, a bit farther on, the **Civic Opera House** (20 N. Wacker Dr., tel. 312/332–2244), where Chicago's Lyric Opera gives its performances. Built by the utilities magnate and manipulator Samuel Insull, the handsome Art Deco building is also an elegant older office building. The Civic Opera House is very grand indeed, with marble floors and pillars in the main hall, crystal chandeliers, and a marvelous sweeping staircase to the second floor. Lyric Opera performances are oversubscribed (subscriptions are willed to succeeding generations), so you can't expect simply to drop in on one of the productions during the season that runs from late September through January. Nevertheless, if you stop by the corner of Madison Street and Wacker Drive early on the evening of a performance, you may find ticket holders with the extra ticket to sell.

At press time (spring 1993), the Lyric had bought the building that houses its auditorium and the neighboring theater and was planning to demolish the latter starting in March 1994 to create more backstage space for its increasingly grand productions. The change was expected to leave Chicago without a major dance space, and organizations such as the Hubbard Street Dance Company and Ballet Chicago were searching for a home for their 1994 season.

We'll turn right onto Madison Street and continue west to Clinton Street and the eastern end of the smashing **Northwestern Atrium Center** (500 W. Madison St.), which replaced the old Northwestern Station and serves as one of several stations throughout the city for commuter trains to outlying suburban areas. The building combines a boxlike office tower with glass half-cylinders piled one atop the other at the lower levels. Broad contrasting horizontal bands of mirrored and smoked glass alternate up the building for a ribbon effect that is reminiscent of a similar theme—by the same architects—at the State of Illinois Center. Inside, the marble floors and exposed girders, painted a soft grayish blue, remind you of the appearance of the grand old railroad stations in this country and in Europe. The girders seen against the rippling exterior glass make beautiful geometric patterns. The area over the entrance simulates a rose window in steel and clear glass. The gates to the tracks, elevated above street level to allow street traffic to proceed east and west via underpasses, are reached by going up one level and heading to the north end of the building. Go up another flight for a grand view northward looking out over the tracks; this level is the entrance to the office spaces of the building.

⑮ One block west is the **Social Security Building** (600 W. Madison St.), once a distant outpost in a dangerous neighborhood that was selected by the federal government because it was a low-rent district. Today the structure is one of several good-looking contemporary and renovated buildings in the area. Of interest here is the Claes Oldenburg sculpture *Batcolumn*, a gigantic baseball bat that failed to get critical acclaim when it was unveiled in 1977. Yet a 100-foot-high baseball bat is an amusing sight, and the current development west of the river will allow even more people the opportunity for a twice-daily smile at this whimsical construction.

Directly across from the *Batcolumn* are the buildings that make up the **Presidential Towers** residences. The easternmost and main building of the four is at 555 West Madison Street. Best seen from a distance, these attractive, if not architecturally distinguished, structures have lured some suburbanites back to the city and persuaded other young adults not to move away. The amenities are good: an upscale supermarket, several fast food restaurants, a drug store, and other shops catering to the daily needs of the residents. The complex extends west to Desplaines Street and south to Monroe Street, with the buildings aligned on a southwesterly diagonal. The developers were threatened with foreclosure on some government loans because of their failure to provide low-income housing as was stipulated in their loan agreements. At press time (spring 1993), both sides were restructuring the agreement.

To the east of Presidential Towers, just opposite the Northwestern Atrium Center, is the ugly, windowless, poured-concrete **AT&T Building.** All that can be said in its defense is that when it was built, it must have seemed unlikely that visitors would stray so far from the heart of downtown.

As you recross the river on Madison Street, regard the pale grape colored buildings to your right; they are the twin towers of the **Chicago Mercantile Exchange** (10 and 30 S. Wacker Dr.). The visitor's gallery of the Merc, open weekdays from 7:30 AM to 3:15 PM, looks down on the frenetic activity on the trading floor. Here is where hog belly futures (they have to do with the supermarket price of bacon), soybeans, and dollars are traded on national and international markets.

Stop at the northwest corner of Madison and Wells streets for a look at a Louise Nevelson sculpture of 1983—a vigorous, forceful construction of darkened steel incongruously titled *Dawn Shadows.*

Farther along Madison Street, the **First National Bank of Chicago,** designed by Perkins and Will in 1973, was a sensation when it was built because this structure slopes upward from its base in a shape that looks like an ornate letter A. Today it's just another good-looking downtown office building. On your left is the very different recent addition to the First National complex, **3 First National Plaza.**

Now turn right onto Dearborn Street. Halfway down the block is the famous **First National Bank Plaza,** which runs the length of the block from Dearborn to Clark streets. In the summer the plaza is the site of outdoor performances by musicians and dancers and a hangout for picnickers and tanners. In any season you can visit the Chagall mosaic known as *The Four Seasons* (1974) at the northeast end of the plaza, between Madison and Monroe streets on Dearborn Street. It is said that when Chagall arrived in Chicago to install the mosaic, he found it a more vigorous city than he had remembered, and he began immediately to modify the work to reflect the stronger and more vital elements he found around him. Not one of Chagall's greatest works, it is nevertheless a pretty, pleasing, sometimes lyrical piece.

Across Dearborn from the Bank Plaza is the turquoise-tinted **Inland Steel Building,** a 1957 homage to steel and glass by Skidmore, Owings & Merrill. The supporting columns are outside the curtain wall, and there are none in the interior, so office spaces are completely open. All the elevators, stairs, and service areas are in the taller structure behind the building proper.

㉑ If you continue east on Madison Street and turn left on State Street, you'll come to the **Reliance Building** (32 N. State St.). Designed by Daniel Burnham in 1890, it was innovative for its time in its use of glass as well as terra-cotta for its exterior, and once it was quite beautiful. Today, the building is not much to look at; the street level houses the kind of sleazy shop that is typical of State Street, and the whole building needs a good cleaning.

㉒ Return to Madison Street to find **Carson Pirie Scott** (1 S. State St.), known to architecture students as one of Louis Sullivan's outstanding works. The building illustrates the Chicago Window, a large fixed central window with smaller movable windows on each side. Notice also the fine exterior ornamentation at street level, particularly the exquisite work over the entrance on the southeast corner of Madison and State streets. Dedicated shoppers may be less interested in the architecture of the building than in its contents; Chicago's "second" department store (always mentioned after Marshall Field & Co.) would be a standout anywhere else. Its Corporate Level offers tasteful clothing for male and female executives, while its main-floor InPulse store lures the teenage set.

From the south end of Carson's, head east on Monroe Street and south on Michigan Avenue to Adams Street and the impos-
㉓ ing entrance to the marvelous **Art Institute of Chicago.** You'll recognize the Art Institute by its guardian lions on each side of the entrance. (The lions have a special place in the hearts of Chicagoans, who outfitted them with Chicago Bears helmets when the Bears won the Superbowl.) A map of the museum, available at the Information Desk, will help you find your way to the works or periods you want to visit. The Art Institute has outstanding collections of Medieval and Renaissance paintings as well as Impressionist and Postimpressionist works. Less well-known are its fine holdings in Asian art and its photography collection. Be sure to visit the Rubloff paperweight collection; a Chicago real estate magnate donated these shimmering, multicolored functional objects. The Thorne Miniature Rooms show interior decoration in every historical style; they'll entrance anyone who's ever furnished a dollhouse or built a model. And don't miss the Stock Exchange room, a splendid reconstruction of the trading floor of the old Chicago Stock Exchange, which was demolished in 1972. The Daniel F. and Ada L. Rice Building, opened in September 1988, has three floors of exhibition galleries, a large space for temporary exhibitions, and a skylit central court dotted with sculpture and plantings.

If you have a youngster with you, make an early stop at the Children's Museum downstairs. Your child will be given a set of Gallery Games, including "I Spy" (which challenges small folk to locate particular works in the museum's collections),

"Scrutinize" (which includes a set of postcards to be taken home), and "Bits and Pieces." The delightful and informative games will keep kids from becoming hopelessly bored as you tramp through the galleries. The museum store has an outstanding collection of art books, calendars, merchandise related to current exhibits, and an attractive selection of gift items. *S. Michigan Ave. at Adams St., tel. 312/443–3600. Admission: $6 adults, $3 children and senior citizens, free Tues. Open weekdays 10:30–4:30 (Tues. until 8), Sat. 10–5, Sun. noon–5. Closed Dec. 25.*

Time Out   From Memorial Day to mid-September, an outdoor **café** in the **Art Institute's courtyard** is a charming spot for lunch. In more inclement weather, there's the **Court Cafeteria,** offering snacks and family fare; **Restaurant on the Park** offers a more upscale menu.

㉔ **Orchestra Hall** (220 S. Michigan Ave., tel. 312/435–6666), opposite the Art Institute, is the home of the internationally acclaimed Chicago Symphony Orchestra. Don't expect to find symphony tickets at the box office; subscription sales exhaust virtually all the available tickets. (You'll have better luck at hearing the symphony during the summer if you make the trek to Ravinia Park in the suburb of Highland Park. *See* Chapter 9.) Sometimes it pays to stop by Orchestra Hall about an hour before a concert; there may be last-minute ticket returns at the box office, or there may be street-corner vendors. If you'd like to see the inside of Orchestra Hall, regardless of who's performing, buy a ticket to one of the recitals that are scheduled frequently, particularly on Sunday afternoons. For an incredible view, get a balcony ticket. The balconies are layered one atop the other in dramatic fashion, and because the seats are steeply banked, the view is splendid and the acoustics are excellent.

㉕ The **Palmer House** (17 E. Monroe St., tel. 312/726–7500), one of Chicago's grand old hotels, is reached by returning to Adams Street and proceeding west one block. Cross Wabash Avenue, turn right, and enter about halfway down the block. The ground-floor level is an arcade with patterned marble floors and antique lighting fixtures where you'll find upscale shops, restaurants, and service establishments. But it's the lobby—up one flight of stairs—that you must see: Richly carpeted, outfitted with fine furniture, and lavishly decorated (look at the ceiling murals), this room is one of the few remaining examples of the opulent elegance that was once de rigueur in Chicago's fine hotels.

Exit the Palmer House on the State Street side, walk north to **㉖** Monroe Street, and turn left. The **Xerox Building** (55 W. Monroe St.) was designed in 1982 by the same firm (Murphy/Jahn) that would be responsible three years later for the State of Illinois Center. The building's wraparound aluminum and glass wall extends from the Monroe Street entrance around the corner onto Dearborn Street, communicating both vitality and beauty.

㉗ Now head south half a block on Dearborn Street. The **Marquette Building** (140 S. Dearborn St.) of 1894, by Holabird and Roche, features an exterior terra-cotta bas relief and interior reliefs and mosaics depicting scenes from early Chicago history.

Continue south to Adams Street and then jog a bit eastward to ㉘ have a look at the westernmost building of the **Berghoff Restaurant** (17 W. Adams St.). Although at first glance it appears as though the front is masonry, it is in fact ornamental cast iron. The practice of using iron panels cast to imitate stone was common in the latter part of the 19th century (this building was constructed in 1872), but this building and the **Page Brothers Building** on State Street, built in the same year, are the only examples known to have survived. The iron front on the Berghoff building was discovered only a few years ago, and other such buildings may yet be extant, waiting to be found.

㉙ Return now to Dearborn Street and the **Federal Center and Plaza.** The twin Federal Buildings, the Kluczyinski (219 S. Dearborn St.) and the Dirksen (230 S. Dearborn St.), built in 1964, are classic examples of the trademark Mies van der Rohe glass and steel box. In the plaza, on the southwest side of Dearborn and Adams streets, is the wonderful Calder stabile *Flamingo*, dedicated on the same day in 1974 as Calder's *Universe* at the Sears Tower. It is said that Calder had a grand day, riding through Chicago in a brightly colored circus bandwagon accompanied by calliopes, heading from one dedication to the other.

㉚ Continue west on Adams Street. At La Salle Street is **The Rookery** (209 S. La Salle St.), an imposing redstone building designed in 1886 by Burnham and Root. The Rookery was built partly of masonry and partly of the more modern steel frame construction. The magnificent lobby was remodeled in 1905 by Frank Lloyd Wright. The building has recently reopened following a $2.5 million renovation that restored the Rookery's airy marble and gold-leaf lobby to its 1905 appearance. The result is a marvelous and lighthearted space that should not be missed.

Cross La Salle Street and head west on the little two-block lane called Quincy Street. At its terminus on Franklin you will be ㉛ directly opposite the entrance to the **Sears Tower** (233 S. Wacker Dr.). A Skidmore, Owings & Merrill design of 1974, Sears Tower has 110 stories and is almost 1,500 feet tall. Although this is the world's tallest building, it certainly isn't the world's most livable one. Despite costly improvements to the Wacker Drive entrance (most of the street traffic is on the Franklin Street side) and the main floor arcade area, the building doesn't really attract the passerby.

Once inside, you'll probably be baffled by the escalators and elevators that stop on alternate floors (the elevators have double cars, one atop the other, so that when one car has stopped, say, at 22, the other is at 21). If you need to go to the upper reaches of the building (other than to go via direct express elevator to the 103rd-floor Skydeck), you'll find that you have to leave one elevator bank, walk down the hall and around a corner, and find another to complete your trip. Stories have been told about new employees on the upper stories spending their entire lunch hour trying to find a way out. In high winds the building sways noticeably at the upper levels and, most alarming, in 1988 there were two occasions on which windows were blown out. According to the architects and engineers, the odds against this happening even once were astronomical; imagine how red their faces must have been the second time it happened. When it did happen, the streets surrounding the building were littered with shards of glass, and papers were sucked out of offices that had lost their windows. On a clear day, however, the view from the Skydeck is unbeatable. (Check the visibility ratings at the security desk before you decide to ride up and take it in.) And don't miss the Calder mobile sculpture *Universe* in the lobby on the Wacker Drive side. *Skydeck: tel. 312/875–9696. Admission: $6 adults, $3.25 children 5–17, under 5 free. Open daily, Oct.–Apr. 10–10, May–Sept. 9 AM–11 PM.*

32 A block south on Wacker Drive is **311 South Wacker Drive,** designed by Kohn Pedersen Fox and completed in 1990. This tower is the first of three intended for the site; the other two are on hold until the economy picks up. The building's most distinctive feature is the "white castle" crown, which is blindingly lighted at night. (During migration season so many birds killed themselves crashing into the illuminated tower that the building management was forced to tone down the lighting, though it wasn't turned off.) The interior has a spectacular winter garden atrium entry with palm trees: a perfect spot for lunch in the colder months.

From the south end of the Sears Tower we'll head west on Jackson Boulevard and across the river to Canal Street. The won-
33 derful old (1917) **Union Station** (210 S. Canal St.) is everything a train station should be, with a 10-story dome over the main waiting room, a skylight, columns, and gilded statues. Amtrak trains arrive and depart from here.

34 We return east on Jackson to the **Chicago Board of Trade** (141 W. Jackson Blvd., tel. 312/435–3500), one of the few important Art Deco buildings in Chicago (the Civic Opera House and the Carbide and Carbon building are the others). It was designed in 1930 by the firm of Holabird and Root; at the top is a gilded statue of Ceres, the Roman goddess of agriculture, an apt overseer of the frenetic commodities trading that goes on within. The observation deck that overlooks the trading floor is open to the public weekdays, 9 AM–2 PM. The lobby is well worth your attention.

Farther east, taking up a good portion of the block from Jackson Boulevard to Van Buren Street, is the massive, darkly
35 handsome **Monadnock Building** (53 W. Jackson Blvd.). The north half was built by Burnham and Root in 1891, the south half by Holabird and Roche in 1893. This is the tallest building ever constructed entirely of masonry. The problem with all-masonry buildings is that the higher they go, the thicker the walls at the base must be to support the upper stories, and the Monadnock's walls at the base are six feet thick. Thus you can see why the introduction of the steel frame began a new era in construction. The building was recently and tastefully renovated inside (the original wrought-iron banisters, for example, have been retained) and cleaned outside, restoring it to its former magnificence from the rather dilapidated and slightly creepy hulk it had become. This is a popular office building for lawyers because of its proximity to the federal courts in the Kluczynski Building.

36 Across the street is the **Fisher Building** (343 S. Dearborn St.), designed by D. H. Burnham & Co. in 1896. This Gothic-style building, exquisitely ornamented in terra-cotta, is for some reason (perhaps because of favorable rents) the headquarters of dozens of arts and other not-for-profit organizations. Turn left onto Van Buren Street for a view of the beautifully carved cherubs frolicking over what was once a side entrance to the building, now glassed in.

Taking up the entire block between Van Buren and Congress streets, the new **Harold Washington Library Center** is a post-modern homage to classical-style public buildings. Chosen from six proposals submitted to a design competition, the granite and brick structure has some of the most spectacular terra-cotta work seen in Chicago since the 19th century: ears of corn, faces with puffed cheeks (representing the Windy City), and the logo of the Chicago Public Library are a few of the building's embellishments. In its final stages of construction, the building looked so much like the vintage skyscrapers around it that visitors mistook it for a renovation project. The library's interior is for the most part disappointingly cramped, and many Chicago residents point to abbreviated hours, broken equipment, and unshelved books as evidence that the city's investment in the library was more show than substance. But there's hope; at this writing a bill was pending in the state legislature to give the library enough money to extend its hours. The center's holdings include more than 2 million books and special collections on Chicago Theater, Chicago Blues, and the Civil War. For a special treat, check out the children's library on the second floor, an 18,000-square-foot haven for the city's youngsters that includes a charming storytelling alcove. The primary architect was Thomas Beeby, of the Chicago firm Hammond Beeby Babka, who now heads the School of Architecture at Yale University. *400 S. State St., tel. 312/747–4050. Admission free. Open Tues., Thurs. 11–7; Wed., Fri., Sat. 9–5. Tours given daily; call for information.*

Proceed east again on Jackson Boulevard to Wabash Avenue for a look at the rust-color **CNA Building.** On no one's list of landmarks, the structure is interesting principally because it leaves such a noticeable mark on the skyline. Chicagoans who thought the color was an undercoat of rustproofing paint that would be covered over by something more conventional were wrong.

Farther along Jackson Boulevard, at Michigan Avenue, is the **Railway Exchange Building** (80 E. Jackson Blvd.; enter on Michigan Ave.), better known as the Santa Fe building, because of the large "Santa Fe" sign atop it that is part of the nighttime skyline. Designed in 1904 by Daniel Burnham, who later had his office there, it underwent an extensive and very successful renovation a few years ago. The interior atrium is spectacular. The **Chicago Architecture Foundation (CAF) Shop and Tour Center** is located here (tel. 312/922–3432 or 312/922–8687 for recorded information). CAF tours of the Loop originate at the center.

One block south is the **Fine Arts Building** (410 S. Michigan Ave.). Notice first the handsome detailing on the exterior of the building; then step inside to see the marble and the woodwork in the lobby. The motto engraved in the marble as you enter says, "All passes—art alone endures." The building once housed artists and sculptors in its studios; today its principal tenants are professional musicians and those who cater to musicians' needs. A fine little music shop is hidden away on the ninth floor, and violin makers and other instrument repair shops are sprinkled about. The building has an interior courtyard, across which strains of piano music and soprano voices compete with tenors as they run through exercises and arias. The ground floor of the building, originally the Studebaker Theatre (the building was constructed to house the showrooms of the Studebaker Co., then makers of carriages), was converted into four cinemas in 1982, and the individual theaters have preserved much of the beautiful ornamentation of the original. The Fine Arts Theatres are an asset to the city for their exceptional selection of foreign films, art films, and movies by independent directors.

Continue on Michigan Avenue to the Congress Parkway and **Roosevelt University,** a massive building that houses the remarkable **Auditorium Theatre** (430 S. Michigan Ave.). Built in 1889 by Dankmar Adler and Louis Sullivan, the hall seats 4,000 people and has unobstructed sightlines and near-perfect acoustics. The interior ornamentation, including arched rows of lights along the ceiling, is breathtaking. Though it's normally closed to the public unless there's a show or concert, ask for a tour of this elegant hall that was allowed to fall into disrepair and even faced demolition in the 1950s and early 1960s. (Determined supporters raised $3 million to provide for the restoration, which was undertaken by Harry Weese in 1967.) Another beautiful, though less well-known, space is the library on the 10th floor of the building.

Head east on Congress Parkway to Columbus Drive and, set in its own plaza, **Buckingham Fountain.** When dedicated in 1927, it was the world's largest decorative fountain. Given to Chicago by philanthropist Kate Sturges Buckingham in memory of her brother Clarence, it was patterned on one of the fountains at Versailles. The central jet can shoot up to 135 feet. Between Memorial Day and Labor Day you can see it in all its glory, when it's elaborately illuminated at night.

Return west on Congress Parkway to Dearborn Street and look ahead and to your right. The odd, triangular, poured-concrete building looming up on the right-hand side of Clark Street is the **Metropolitan Detention Center** (71 W. Van Buren St.). A jail (rather than a penitentiary, where convicted criminals are sent), it holds people awaiting trial as well as those convicted and awaiting transfer. When erected in 1975, it brought an outcry from citizens who feared large-scale escapes by dangerous criminals. (Their fears have not been realized.) The building was designed by the same Harry Weese who saved the Auditorium Theatre; with its long, slit windows (5 inches wide, so no bars are required), it looks like a modern reconstruction of a medieval fort, where slits in the walls permitted archers to shoot at approaching invaders.

Continue west on Congress to the striking building of 1985 by Skidmore, Owings & Merrill known as **One Financial Place** (440 S. La Salle St.), which has an exterior and interior of Italian red granite and marble. Among its striking features is the arched section that straddles the rushing traffic on the Congress Parkway/Eisenhower Expressway below. The building's tenants include the Midwest Stock Exchange, whose visitor's gallery is open weekdays, 8:30–4, and the La Salle St. Club, which offers limited but elegant hotel accommodations and is the home of the superb Everest restaurant (*see* Chapter 6).

Another walk west across the river will take you to Chicago's **Main Post Office** (433 W. Van Buren St.), the world's largest. Tours of this mammoth, highly automated facility are given weekdays at 10:30 AM or 12:30 PM (*see* Chicago for Free).

Tour 2: Downtown South

Numbers in the margin correspond to points of interest on the Tour 2: Downtown South map.

The Downtown South area, bounded by Congress Parkway/Eisenhower Expressway on the north, Michigan Avenue on the east, Roosevelt Road on the south, and the Chicago River on the west, presents a striking and often fascinating contrast to the downtown area we have just visited. Once a thriving commercial area and the center of the printing trades in Chicago, it fell into disrepair as the printing industry moved south in search of lower costs. Sleazy bars, pawnbrokers, and pornographic shops filled the area behind what was then the Conrad Hilton Hotel, crowding each other on Wabash Avenue and State Street and on the side streets between. Homeless winos found a place to sleep at the Pacific Garden Mission (646 S. State St.). Declining business at the mammoth Hilton meant decreasing revenues; floors were closed off, too expensive to maintain, and the owners considered demolishing the building.

Then, about a decade ago, investors became interested in renovating the run-down yet sturdy loft and office buildings in the old printing district. With the first neighborhood rehab efforts just beginning, Michael Foley, a young Chicago restaurateur from an old Chicago restaurant family, opened a restaurant on the edge of the redevelopment area. The innovative cuisine at Printer's Row (*see* Chapter 6) attracted favorable notice, and the restaurant became a success; soon other restaurants, shops, and businesses moved in, and today the Printer's Row district is a thriving urban neighborhood enclave.

At about the time that the first renovations were being undertaken in Printer's Row, a consortium of investors, aided by preferential interest rates from downtown banks, obtained a large parcel of land in the old railroad yards to the south and put up an expansive new development. This was Dearborn Park, affordable housing targeted at young middle-class families. Although its beginnings were rocky—the housing was attractive but there was no supermarket, no dry cleaner, and no public school nearby—Dearborn Park, too, became successful.

To the west, the architect and developer Bertrand Goldberg (of Marina City fame) acquired a sizable tract of land between Wells Street and the Chicago River. Driven by a vision of an innovative, self-contained city within a city, Goldberg erected the futuristic River City, the massed, almost cloudlike complex that seems to rise from the river at Polk Street. This development has been less commercially successful than Dearborn Park, yet the willingness of a developer to make an investment of this size in the area was an indication that the neighborhood south of downtown was here to stay.

Spurred by signs of revitalization all around, the owners of the Conrad Hilton scrapped their plans to abandon the hotel and instead mounted a renovation of tremendous proportion. Now one of the most beautifully appointed hotels in the city, the Chicago Hilton and Towers once again attracts the business it needs to fill its thousands of rooms.

We'll begin our tour of Downtown South at the corner of Balbo Drive and Michigan Avenue. You can drive here—traffic and parking conditions are far less congested in the Downtown South area than they are in Downtown—or you can take the Jeffery Express (No. 6) bus from the north (catch it at State and Lake streets) or from Hyde Park.

East of the intersection of Balbo Drive and Michigan Avenue ❶ is the heart of beautiful **Grant Park.** On a hot summer night during the last week of August 1968, the park was filled with young people protesting the Vietnam War and events at the Democratic presidential nominating convention that was taking place at the Conrad Hilton Hotel down the street. Rioting broke out; heads were cracked, protesters were dragged away screaming, and Mayor Daley gave police the order to "shoot to kill." Later investigations into the events of that evening determined that a "police riot"—not the misbehavior of the protesters, who had been noisy but not physically abusive—was responsible for the violence that erupted. Those who remember those rage-filled days cannot visit this idyllic spot without recalling that time.

Today Grant Park is a lovely mix of gardens (especially above Monroe Street and around the fountain), tennis courts, softball diamonds, and a field surrounding the Petrillo bandshell, at Columbus Drive and Monroe Street, where outdoor concerts are held. While it's not as heavily used as Lincoln or Jackson parks, Grant Park is home to several blockbuster events: the Grant Park Society Concerts held four times a week in the summer; notable blues, jazz, and gospel festivals; and the annual Taste of Chicago, a vast picnic featuring foods from more than 70 restaurants that precedes a fireworks show on July 3 (*see* Festivals and Seasonal Events in Chapter 1).

❷ The **Blackstone Hotel** (636 S. Michigan Ave.), on the northwest corner of the intersection, is rich with history. Presidential candidates have been selected here, and presidents have stayed here. Note the ornate little roofs that cap the first-floor windows. Inside, the elegant lobby has impressive chandeliers, sculptures, and handsome woodwork. Next door is the **Blackstone Theatre,** another vintage building, where Broadway-bound shows were once booked; the theater was recently acquired by De Paul University for its own use and that of local theater companies.

❸ Head north on Michigan Avenue to the **Spertus Museum of Judaica,** a small museum housed in Spertus College. The permanent collections include Medieval Jewish art, which is surprisingly like the better-known Christian art of the same period, without the central Christian themes and imagery. The museum regularly mounts exhibitions on topics broadly relevant to Judaism; a recent one displayed photographs by late author Jerzy Kosinski. *618 S. Michigan Ave., tel. 312/922–9012. Admission: $3.50 adults, $2 children; Fri. free. Open Sun.–Thurs. 10–5, Fri. 10–3.*

Continue to the corner of Harrison Street, turn left, and walk ❹ three blocks to Dearborn Street. The pioneering **Printer's Row**

Restaurant (550 S. Dearborn St.) is a wonderful place to stop for an elegant (but not inexpensive) lunch during the week.

⑤ Nearby on Dearborn Street is the **Hyatt on Printer's Row** (538 S. Dearborn St.). Beautifully appointed, the hotel is located in a group of renovated old buildings that have been interconnected. On the corner is the **Prairie Restaurant** (500 S. Dearborn St.).

Turn left and walk west to Federal Street and turn left again. On your right as you head south is a massive beige-gray brick renovated apartment complex, **Printer's Square** (640–780 S. Federal St.).

⑥

Continue south, turn west on Polk, and walk to Wells Street. **⑦** Turn left at Wells Street and continue to the entrance to **River City** (800 S. Wells St.). Apartments, all with curving exterior walls (making it a bit difficult to place square or rectangular furniture), ring the circumference of the building. Interior spaces are used for shops, walkways, and tenant storage closets. The building boasts a state-of-the-art health club. The west side of River City fronts on the river, providing a splendid view for apartment dwellers on that side, and 70 spaces for mooring boats are available. If you'd like to take a tour, speak to the guard.

Taylor Street, south of the River City entrance, will take you east to Sherman Street; turn left on Sherman Street, right on Polk Street, and left on Dearborn Street. If you're driving, this is a good place to park. We'll walk up the west side of Dearborn Street to the end of the block and return on the east side.

⑧ The first building on your left is the grand old **Franklin Building** (720 S. Dearborn St.), originally "The Franklin Co.: Designing, Engraving, Electrotyping" and now condominium apartments. The decorative tilework on the facade leads up to the scene over the front door, *The First Impression;* representing a medieval event, it illustrates the first application of the printer's craft. Above the entryway is the motto "The Excellence of Every Art Must Consist in the Complete Accomplishment of Its Purpose."

⑨ Next door, **Sandmeyer's Bookstore** (714 S. Dearborn St.) has an iron stairway set with glass bricks and a fine selection of books about Chicago.

In June this street is the locale of the Printer's Row Book Fair, a weekend event where dealers offer a wide variety of books and prints and where demonstrations of the papermaking and bookbinding crafts are given. Street performers and food vendors add to the festivity.

⑩ Across the street a rehabbed brick building is hung with banners announcing **Grace Place** (637 S. Dearborn St.). This is not the newest condo on the block but a consortium of two churches: Grace Episcopal Church and Christ the King Lutheran Church. Each of the congregations is too small to support its own church building, so the two have joined together to share facilities.

Another renovated building (705 S. Dearborn St.) houses **Paper Row,** a card and gift shop, and **Wine Plus,** a wine merchant. The distinguished **Prairie Ave. Bookshop** (707 S. Dearborn St.) concentrates on new and out-of-print books about

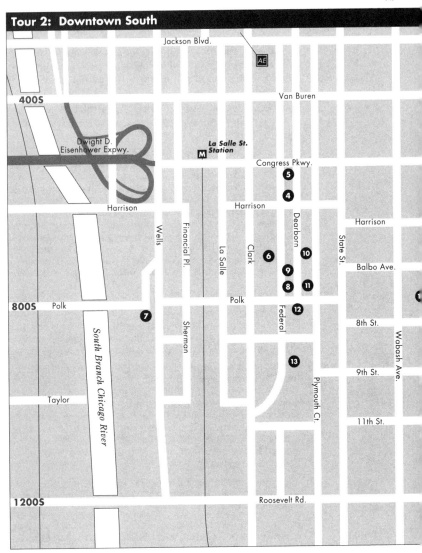

Blackstone Hotel, **2**

Chicago Hilton and
Towers, **14**

Dearborn Park, **13**

Dearborn Station, **12**

Donohue Building, **11**

Franklin Building, **8**

Grace Place, **10**

Grant Park, **1**

Hyatt on
Printer's Row, **5**

Printer's Row
Restaurant, **4**

Printer's Square, **6**

River City, **7**

Sandmeyer's
Bookstore, **9**

Spertus Museum of
Judaica, **3**

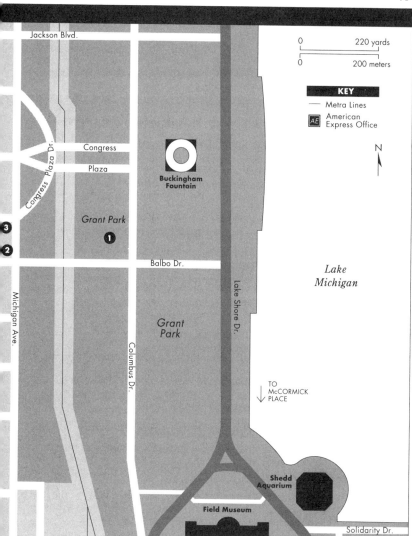

architecture, planning, and design. These shops are part of the

11 grand **Donohue Building,** whose main entrance is at 711 South Dearborn Street. The entrance is flanked by marble columns topped by ornately carved capitals, with tile work over the entrance set into a splendid granite arch. Note also the beautiful ironwork and woodwork in the doors and frames of the shops as you proceed south.

Time Out For a quick pick-me-up, stop at the **Deli on Dearborn** (723 S. Dearborn St.) or at the **Moonraker Restaurant and Tavern** (733 S. Dearborn St.). In summer, you can sit outside at either establishment, although the cool interior of the Moonraker may be more welcome after a tramp through the city streets.

12 The recently restored **Dearborn Station** (47 W. Polk St.) at the foot of Dearborn Street, designed in Romanesque-Revival style in 1885 by the New York architect Cyrus L. W. Eidlitz, has a red sandstone and red brick facade ornamented with terra-cotta. The striking features inside the station are the brass fixtures set against the cream and white walls and woodwork and the white, rust, and jade marble floor. Since its opening in 1985, Dearborn Station has been successful in attracting office tenants, less so in attracting retail tenants. At press time (spring 1993), the space was about 75% rented, and a 10,000-square-foot specialty food store was scheduled to open by summer of 1993. *Open 7:30 AM–9 PM weekdays, 7:30 AM–6 PM weekends.*

Walk east, turn right on Plymouth Court, and look south, where

13 you can see **Dearborn Park.** A planned mix of high-rise, low-rise, and single-family units, some in red brick and some in white, the development has a tidy look. The residents are enthusiastic about Dearborn Park, and they have developed a warm and supportive community life.

Walk down Plymouth Court to 9th Street and turn left. Walk one block to State Street and turn left again. Look at the attractive high rise on the northeast corner. Built recently on a site that would have been unthinkable only a few years earlier, this building has reinforced the resurgent residential community of the area. If you look to the south from here, you can see that redevelopment is under way now in many of the nearby buildings. The Cineplex Odeon (826 S. Wabash Ave.) opened in 1988 and shows first-run movies on five screens.

14 Walk east on 8th Street, across Wabash Avenue, to the **Chicago Hilton and Towers** (720 S. Michigan Ave.). Enter by the revolving doors, head a bit to your right and then straight, and stroll through the opulent lobby, tastefully done in shades of mauve and soft sea green. Notice the gilded horses that flank the main entrance on the inner wall and the sweeping stairway to your right off the main entrance that leads to the Grand Ballroom. Sneak a peek at the Grand Ballroom if possible; there isn't a more spectacular room in the city. On opening night at the Opera, when a midnight supper and dance is held here, a brass quintet stationed at the top of this stairway plays fanfares as the guests arrive. Be sure not to miss the exquisite Thai hanging on the north wall of the lobby (directly behind and above the concierge's desk).

Time Out The **Lobby Cafe** at the Hilton has an attractive light lunch and dinner menu. The food is good, and the setting is wonderful for those who enjoy people-watching. Should you prefer a cocktail in the lobby lounge, choose a table by the windows looking out on Michigan Avenue, sit back, relax, and listen to the music of the string ensemble that plays here afternoons until 5 PM.

When you're ready to leave, the Jeffery Express (No. 6) bus to Hyde Park stops on Balbo Drive, directly across Michigan Avenue from the Hilton. Or you can catch any bus that stops on the northeast corner and then transfer to a Michigan Avenue bus at Randolph Street.

Tour 3: Hyde Park and Kenwood

Numbers in the margin correspond to points of interest on the Tour 3: Hyde Park and Kenwood map.

Site of the World's Columbian Exposition of 1893, residence at the turn of the century of the meat-packing barons Swift and Armour, home of the University of Chicago, locale of five houses designed by Frank Lloyd Wright, and the nation's oldest stable racially integrated neighborhood, Hyde Park and the adjoining Kenwood are important historically, intellectually, and culturally.

Although farmers and other settlers lived in Hyde Park in the early 1800s and Chicago's oldest Jewish congregation was founded here in 1847, the growth and development of the area really got under way as a result of two events: the World's Columbian Exposition of 1893 and the opening of the University of Chicago in 1892. The Columbian Exposition, whose influence on American public architecture was to prove far-reaching, brought about the creation of the Midway Plaisance and the construction of numerous buildings, of which the Museum of Science and Industry is the most famous survivor. The Midway Plaisance, surrounding the heart of the 1893 fair, still runs along the southern edge of the University of Chicago's original campus. Another legacy from the exposition was the civic moniker "The Windy City," used by *New York Sun* editor Charles Dana to ridicule Chicago's bid for hosting the exposition.

The University of Chicago was built through the largesse of John D. Rockefeller. Coeducational from the beginning, it was known for progressive education. The campus covers 184 acres, dominating the life of Hyde Park and South Kenwood. Much of the original campus was designed by Henry Ives Cobb, also responsible for the Newberry Library at the corner of Dearborn and Walton streets on the Near North Side. The university's stately gothic quadrangles recall the residential colleges in Cambridge, England, and the Ivy League schools of the East Coast. But the material is Indiana limestone, and the U. of C. retains a uniquely Midwestern quality.

The university boasts 61 Nobel laureates as graduates, resident researchers, or faculty members. Its schools of economics, law, business, and medicine are world famous. The University of Chicago Hospitals are leading teaching institutions. It was at U. of C. in 1990 that a baby received a successful transplant of a section of her mother's liver—the first operation of its kind. Perhaps the most world-altering event to take place at U. of C. (or anywhere else, for that matter) was the first self-sustaining nuclear chain reaction in 1942, created by Enrico Fermi and his team of physicists under an unused football stadium. Although the stadium is gone, there's a plaque on the spot now, near the Crerar Science Library.

In the 1890s the university embarked on a program to build housing for its faculty members, and the mansions that line Woodlawn Avenue are the result. Then the neighborhood began to attract well-to-do private individuals who commissioned noted architects to construct homes suitable to persons of great wealth. Many of their houses still stand in Kenwood.

With the coming of the Depression, followed by World War II, the neighborhood entered a period of decline. Grand homes fell into disrepair as the numbers of those with the resources to maintain them dwindled. Wartime housing shortages led to the conversion of stately houses into multifamily dwellings.

Alarmed by the decline of the neighborhood, concerned citizens formed the Hyde Park-Kenwood Community Conference. Aided by $29 million from the University of Chicago, which was anxious that it might not be able to retain—never mind recruit—faculty members, this group set about restoring the neighborhood. Prizes were offered to those who would buy and "deconvert" rooming houses, and the city was pressured to enforce the zoning laws.

The effort that was to have the most lasting effect on the neighborhood was urban renewal, one of the first such undertakings in the nation. Again with the backing and support of the University of Chicago, 55th Street from Lake Park Avenue to Cottage Grove Avenue was razed. Most of the buildings on Lake Park Avenue and on many streets abutting 55th Street and Lake Park Avenue were torn down as well. With them went the workshops of painters and artisans, the quarters of "little magazines" (some 20 chapters of James Joyce's *Ulysses* were first published at one of them), the Compass Theatre—where Mike Nichols and Elaine May got their start—and Second City (since relocated to Lincoln Park), and more than 40 bars where jazz and blues could be heard nightly. In their place came town houses designed by I. M. Pei and Harry Weese and a shopping mall designed by Keck and Keck. Cynics have described the process as one of "blacks and whites together, shoulder to shoulder—against the poor."

In the end, these efforts were successful beyond the wildest imaginings of their sponsors, but more than 20 years elapsed before the neighborhood regained its luster. The 18-room houses on Woodlawn Avenue that sell today for $600,000 could still be had for $35,000 in the early 1960s.

To reach the start of our Hyde Park tour if you're arriving by car, take Lake Shore Drive south to the 57th Street exit and turn left into the parking lot of the Museum of Science and Industry. Or you can take the Illinois Central Gulf (ICG) RR train from Randolph Street and Michigan Avenue; get off at the 55th Street stop and walk east through the underpass two blocks, then south two blocks.

❶ Our exploration of Hyde Park and Kenwood begins at the **Museum of Science and Industry,** built for the Columbian Exposition as a Palace of Fine Arts. Plan on at least half a day to explore this hands-on museum, where you can visit a U-505 submarine, descend into a coal mine, experience an auditory miracle in the whispering gallery, learn how telephones work, trace the history of computing and the development of computer hardware, explore spacecraft and the history of space exploration, visit "Main Street of Yesterday," learn how the body works, and much more. The Omnimax Theater shows science and space-related films on a giant screen. *5700 S. Lake Shore Dr., tel. 312/684–1414. Admission: $5 adults, $2 children; Thurs. free. Open Memorial Day–Labor Day, daily 9:30–5:30; Labor Day–Memorial Day, weekdays 9:30–4, weekends and holidays 9:30–5:30.*

Exiting the museum, cross 56th Street, and head west. Turn right under the viaduct and go north on Lake Park Avenue.
② You'll pass the **Hyde Park Historical Society** (5529 S. Lake Park Ave., tel. 312/493–1893), a research library halfway down the block.

③ Just north stands the **Chevrolet building** (5508 S. Lake Park Ave.), named for the car dealership that formerly occupied it. The beautiful terra-cotta border decorates an otherwise functional building, one of only two buildings in the area left standing after urban renewal.

Head west on 55th Street to one of the happy results of urban renewal, **1400–1451 East 55th Street,** an apartment building
④ designed by I. M. Pei. He also designed the town houses that border it on the north, between Blackstone and Dorchester avenues. Turn right and head up Blackstone Avenue, passing a variety of housing between 55th and 51st streets. Although these houses command prices in the hundreds of thousands of dollars today, they were originally cottages for workingmen, conveniently located near the cable-car line that ran west on 55th Street.

Continue north on Blackstone Avenue to 53rd Street, Hyde Park's main shopping strip. Across the street and ½ block east
⑤ is **Harper Court.** Another product of urban renewal, Harper Court was built to house craftspeople who were displaced from their workshops on Lake Park Avenue. Despite subsidized rents, it never caught on with the craftspeople, who moved elsewhere, while Harper Court evolved into a successful shopping center and community gathering place.

Time Out | **Café Coffee** (5211 S. Harper) serves an invigorating selection of coffees, pastries, and snacks. Those who are very hungry might prefer the **Valois Cafeteria** (1518 E. 53rd St.) ½ block away, where inexpensive meals are served all day.

Leaving the north exit of Harper Court, go west to Woodlawn
⑥ Avenue and turn right. The **Heller House** (5132 S. Woodlawn Ave.) was built by Frank Lloyd Wright in 1897; note the plaster naiads cavorting at the top. Now proceed south on Woodlawn
⑦ Avenue to 55th Street. On the east side of the street is **St. Thomas the Apostle Church and School** (5467 S. Woodlawn Ave.), built in 1922 and now a national landmark. Note its terra-cotta ornamentation.

Now we come to the northern edge of the University of Chicago campus. A walking tour of the campus is offered daily (tel. 312/702–8374), but if you'd like to see things on your own, con-

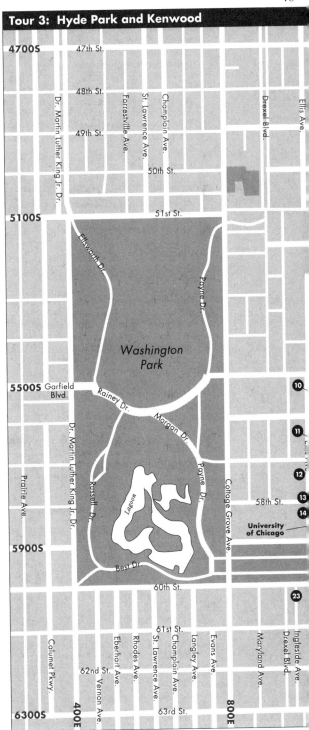

Tour 3: Hyde Park and Kenwood

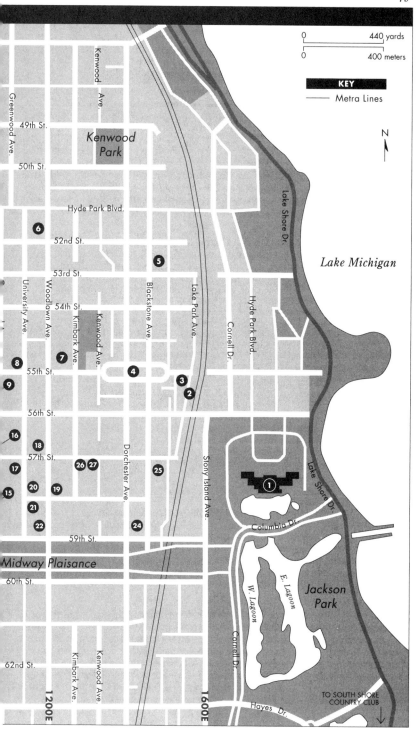

8 tinue west to University Avenue and the **Lutheran School of Theology** (1100 E. 55th St.). Built in 1968 by the firm of Perkins and Will, the massive structure seems almost to float from its foundation, lightened by the transparency of its smoked-glass exteriors. Across the street is **Pierce Hall** (5514 S. University Ave.), a student dormitory designed by Harry Weese.

9 One block west on Greenwood Avenue, between 55th and 56th streets, is the **David and Alfred Smart Museum of Art.** Founded in 1974 with a gift from the Smart Family Foundation, whose members David and Alfred founded *Esquire* magaine, the museum and an adjacent sculpture garden display the fine-arts holdings of the university. The 5,000-piece permanent collection is diverse and includes works by Old Masters; photographs by Walker Evans; furniture by Frank Lloyd Wright; sculptures by Degas, Matisse, Rodin, and Henry Moore; ancient Chinese bronzes; and modern Japanese ceramics. *5550 S. Greenwood Ave., tel. 312/702–0200. Admission free. Open Tues.–Fri. 10–4, weekends noon–6.*

10 Walk west on 55th Street to Ellis Avenue and the **Court Theatre** (5535 S. Ellis Ave., tel. 312/753–4472), a professional repertory company that specializes in revivals of the classics. An intimate theater, the Court offers unobstructed sight from every seat in the house. A flag flies atop the theater when a show is on.

11 Continue south on Ellis Avenue about 1/2 block beyond 56th Street; on your left is the Henry Moore sculpture *Nuclear Energy,* commemorating the first controlled nuclear chain reaction, which took place below ground roughly where the sculpture stands, in the locker room under the bleachers of what was then Stagg Field. Across 57th Street, set into the small quad-
12 rangle on your right, is the **John Crerar Science Library** (5730 S. Ellis Ave., tel. 312/702–7715). Inside the library is John David Mooney's splendid sculpture *Crystara,* composed of enormous Waterford crystal pieces made to order for this work, which was commissioned for the site.

13 Farther down the block is the **University of Chicago Bookstore,** which has, in addition to scholarly books, a large selection of general-interest books, an outstanding collection of cookbooks, and clothing, mugs, and other souvenirs. *970 E. 58th St., tel. 312/702–8729. Open Mon.–Sat. 8:30–5.*

14 On the east side of Ellis Avenue at 58th Street is **Cobb Hall,** home of the Renaissance Society. The society was founded in 1915 to identify living artists whose work would be of lasting significance and influence. It was among the first hosts of works by Matisse, Picasso, Braque, Brancusi, and Miró. Come here to see what the next generation of great art may look like. *Cobb Hall 418, 5811 S. Ellis Ave., tel. 312/702–8670. Admission free. Open Tues.–Fri. 10–4, weekends noon–4.*

North of Cobb Hall is the **University of Chicago Administration Building.** Between the two is a small passageway to the **quadrangle** of the university. Here is a typical college campus, green and grassy, with imposing neo-Gothic buildings all around. Tucked into the southwest corner between two other buildings
15 is **Bond Chapel** (1025 E. 58th St.), a lovely Gothic-style chapel. The fanciful gargoyles outside belie the simple interior of dark wood, stained glass, and delicate ornamentation. The effect is one of intimacy and warmth.

Cross the quadrangle and head east to the circular drive. Bear left, then turn left at the intersecting road. Follow this path north, and you will pass a reflecting pool (Botany Pond) before you exit through the wrought-iron gate. Directly ahead is the ⓰ **Joseph Regenstein Library,** framed in the gate. The "Reg," the main library of the university, was designed by Skidmore, Owings, and Merrill and built in 1970.

Turn right on 57th Street and continue east. The massive building on the corner, **Mandel Hall** (5706 S. University Ave., tel. ⓱ 312/702–8068; enter on 57th St.), is a gem of a concert hall that has been tastefully restored. Peek in, if you can, for a glimpse of gold leaf and soft greens against the dark wood of the theater. Professional musical organizations, including ensembles from the Chicago Symphony and such groups as Les Arts Florissants from France, perform in the 900-seat hall throughout the year. The building also houses the student union.

Continue east on 57th Street one block to Woodlawn Avenue. ⓲ On the northwest corner is the **First Unitarian Church** (5750 S. Woodlawn Ave., tel. 312/324–4100), whose graceful spire is visible throughout the area. Turn right on Woodlawn Avenue and head south, noting the stately brick mansions that line both sides of the street. To the north the building at 5605 is on the National Register of Historic Places. Many of the buildings were built by the University of Chicago in the 1890s to provide housing for professors. Professors continue to live in several of them; others have been repurchased by the university for institutional use.

Continue south on Woodlawn Avenue to Frank Lloyd Wright's ⓳ **Robie House.** Built in 1909, Robie House exemplifies the Prairie style. Its cantilevered roof offers privacy while allowing in light. The house sits on a pedestal; Wright abhorred basements, thinking them unhealthful. You can tour Robie House and examine the interiors, including the built-in cupboards, the leaded-glass windows, and the spacious kitchen. Rescued by the university from the threat of demolition, the building now houses the university alumni office and is used for small official dinners and receptions. *5757 S. Woodlawn Ave., tel. 312/702–8374. Free tours daily at noon.*

Cross Woodlawn Avenue and continue west one block to the ⓴ **Chicago Theological Seminary** (5757 S. University Ave.). Its basement accommodates the **Seminary Cooperative Bookstore** (tel. 312/752–4381), which includes an extensive selection of books in the humanities among its wide offerings. Defying the rules of marketing, this store—which does not advertise, is not visible from the street, and has no parking—has more sales per square foot than any other bookstore in Chicago. Upstairs in the chapel is the Reneker organ, donated by the widow of a university trustee. Free concerts are given Tuesday at noon on this exquisitely handcrafted replica of an 18th-century organ.

㉑ Across 58th Street is the **Oriental Institute,** which focuses on the history, art, and archaeology of the ancient Near East, including Assyria, Mesopotamia, Persia, Egypt, and Syro-Palestine. Permanent displays include statuary, small-scale amulets, mummies, limestone reliefs, gold jewelry, ivories, pottery, and bronzes from the 2nd millennium BC through the 13th century AD. *1155 E. 58th St., tel. 312/702–9520 or 312/702–9521 for re-*

corded information. Admission free. Open Tues. and Thurs.–
Sat. 10–4, Wed. 10–8:30, Sun. noon–4.

Go down University Avenue one block to 59th Street. To your **22** left, set back on a grassy expanse, is the neo-Gothic **Rockefeller Memorial Chapel** (5850 S. Woodlawn Ave., designed by Bertram Goodhue and named in honor of the founder of the university. The interior, which recently underwent extensive structural and cosmetic renovation, has a stunning vaulted ceiling; hand-sewn banners decorate the walls. A university carillonneur gives regular performances on the carillon atop the chapel. Tours of the chapel are given by appointment (tel. 312/702–8374).

Continue south again, crossing 59th Street and entering the **Midway Plaisance.** Created for the World's Columbian Exposition, this green, hollowed-out strip of land was intended to replicate a Venetian canal. When the "canal" was filled with water, houses throughout the area were flooded as well, and the idea had to be abandoned. At the western end of the Plaisance, by Cottage Grove Avenue, you can see Lorado Taft's masterpiece *The Fountain of Time,* completed in 1922. Taft (1830–1926) was one of the most distinguished sculptors and teachers of his time. Like many, he got his start by creating pieces for the Columbian Exposition. One of these, the *Fountain of the Great Lakes*, is now at the Art Institute. Other works adorn Chicago's parks and public places, as well as those of other cities.

Heading west on 60th Street, you'll pass the **School of Social Service Administration** (969 E. 60th St.), an undistinguished example of the work of Mies van der Rohe. One block farther, **23** at 60th Street and Ingleside Avenue, is **Midway Studios,** the home and workplace of Lorado Taft. A National Historic Landmark since 1966, the building now houses the university's studio-art program and serves as an exhibit space for student works. *6016 S. Ingleside Ave., tel. 312/753–4821. Admission free. Open weekdays 9–5.*

On 60th Street between Ellis and University avenues is the **Laird Bell Law Quadrangle** (1111 E. 60th St.). This attractive building, with fountains playing in front, is the work of Finnish architect Eero Saarinen. Two blocks farther east, between Kimbark Street and Kenwood Avenue, is the **New Graduate Residence Hall** (1307 E. 60th St.). This poured-concrete structure, elaborately ornamented, is reminiscent of the American embassy in New Delhi, India—unsurprisingly, architect Edward Durrell Stone designed both.

Cross the Midway again to 59th Street and continue east. The **24** neo-Gothic structure just past Dorchester Avenue is **International House** (1414 E. 59th St., tel. 312/753–2270), where many foreign students live during their tenure at the university. It was designed in 1932 by the firm of Holabird and Roche. Continue east to Blackstone and turn left. **5806 South Blackstone Avenue,** a house designed in 1951 by Bertrand Goldberg of Marina City and River City fame, is an early example of the use of solar heating and natural cooling.

Continue north on Blackstone Avenue to 57th Street and turn **25** right. **Powell's Bookstore** (1501 E. 57th St., tel. 312/955–7780) generally has a box of free books out front, and inside you'll find a tremendous selection of used and remaindered books, especially art books, cookbooks, and mysteries. Walk west on 57th Street to Dorchester Avenue; on your left, at **5704 South Dorchester Avenue,** is an Italian-style villa constructed before the Chicago Fire. The two houses at **5642** and **5607 South Dorchester Avenue** also predate the fire.

On 57th Street, spanning the block between Kenwood Avenue and Kimbark Street, is the **Ray School** complex. One of the best public elementary schools in the city, Ray hosts the annual Hyde Park Art Fair, one of the oldest (1947) annual outdoor art-fairs in the country.

㉖ Farther west is **O'Gara & Wilson Book Shop Ltd.** (1311 E. 57th St., tel. 312/363–0993), which has another outstanding selection
㉗ of used books. Nearby is **57th Street Books** (1301 E. 57th St., tel. 312/684–1300), a cooperatively owned bookstore that is sister to the Seminary Cooperative Bookstore on University Avenue and that specializes in current books of general interest. Copies of the *New York Times Book Review* and the *New York Review of Books* are always on a table toward the rear, next to the coffeepot. An extensive children's section has its own room, where reading aloud to youngsters is encouraged.

Time Out This street has several spots where you can get a quick bite and rest your feet. **Medici Pan Pizza** (1327 E. 57th St.) has sandwiches and snacks as well as pizza, as does **Edwardo's** (1321 E. 57th St.). For a caffeine jolt, try **Caffe Florian** (1450 E. 57th St.). Breakfast fare is your best bet at **Ann Sather** (1329 E. 57th St.).

To get back to the museum and our starting point, backtrack east on 57th Street, go under the viaduct, and cross Stony Island Avenue. The museum will be in front of you, and to the right are the lagoons of Jackson Park.

Tour 4: South Lake Shore Drive

The South Lake Shore Drive tour offers spectacular views of the downtown skyline; it serves as a bonus for those who have visited Hyde Park and Kenwood and are returning north via car or the Jeffery Express (No. 6) bus or (during the afternoon rush hour) the Hyde Park Express (No. 2). If you followed Tour 1 (*see above*) or Tour 5 (*see below*), you will have visited some of the skyscrapers described here. This driving tour allows you to see these buildings from a distance, and in relation to the surrounding skyline.

Enter Lake Shore Drive at 57th Street northbound, with the lake to your right. At 35th Street you will pass, on your left, the **Stephen Douglas Memorial.** Douglas was the U.S. Senator who debated the merits of slavery with Abraham Lincoln; you can see the monument, Douglas at the top, from the drive, but you'd have to go inland to Lake Park Avenue to visit the lovely park and gardens there.

Directly ahead, the **Sears Tower** (233 S. Wacker Dr.) is the world's tallest building. In case the perspective makes it appear unfamiliar, you can recognize it by the angular setbacks that narrow the building as it rises higher. To its left is the "white castle" top of **311 S. Wacker,** which is blindingly lighted at night (*see* Tour 1). Ahead and to your right is the low-rise, dark **McCormick Place Convention Hall** (2300 S. Lake Shore Dr.); to the left, the low-rise **McCormick Place North** is the latest addition to the complex, its completion having been delayed by almost a year because of political machinations and scandals, in true Chicago style.

The rust-color building to the east is the **CNA Building** (55 E. Jackson Blvd.). When it was newly constructed, Chicagoans believed that the color was that of a first coat of rustproofing paint. They were wrong. The **Associates Center** (150 N. Michigan Ave.), is the building with the more or less diamond-shape, angled face at the top (*see* Tour 1).

The tall white building to the right of the Associates Center is the **Amoco Building** (200 E. Randolph St.), with its new granite exterior (*see* Tour 1). Next to the Amoco Building is the severe gray **Prudential Building,** with its postmodern annex rising behind it.

The building with the twin antennae, to the right of the Amoco Building, is the **John Hancock Center** (875 N. Michigan Ave.), the world's third-tallest building, at 98 stories (*see* Tour 5). Off to the right, seemingly out in the lake, are the sinuous curves of **Lake Point Towers** condominium apartments (505 N. Lake Shore Dr.).

Coming up on the left, the building with the massive columns on an ancient Grecian model is **Soldier Field** (425 E. McFetridge Dr.), the home of the Chicago Bears. A new stadium on the near west side is in the planning stages, and many Chicagoans look forward to having Lake Shore Drive to themselves again on fall and winter Sunday afternoons. To visit the three museums on Chicago's museum campus, turn right into the drive that's just past Meigs Field, drive to the end, and park. Or follow the signs to the left that lead to the Field Museum parking lot.

On your left as you turn onto the peninsula is the **John G. Shedd Aquarium.** The dazzling new **Oceanarium,** with two beluga whales and several Pacific dolphins, is the big draw here. But don't miss the sharks, tarpon, turtles, and myriad smaller fish and other aquatic forms in the coral-reef exhibit. Hundreds of other watery "cages" display fish from around the world, some bizarre and many fantastically beautiful. *1200 S. Lake Shore Dr., tel. 312/939–2426. Admission: $3 adults, $2 children and senior citizens. Separate admission for Oceanarium, $4. Open daily 9–5.*

At the far end of the peninsula is the **Adler Planetarium,** featuring exhibits about the stars and planets and a popular program of Sky Shows. Past shows have included "The Space Telescope Story" and "Planetary Puzzles." *1300 S. Lake Shore Dr., tel. 312/322–0304 (general information), 312/322–0300 (Sky Show information), or 312/322–0334 (information on current month's skies). Admission to planetarium free. Sky Show admission: $4 adults, $2 children 6–17. Open Mon.–Thurs. and weekends 9–5, Fri. 9–9.*

The **Field Museum of Natural History,** located across Lake Shore Drive from the aquarium and accessible through a pedestrian underpass, is one of the country's great natural-history museums. From the reconstructed Pawnee earth-lodge (completed with the assistance of the Pawnee tribe of Oklahoma) to the Mastaba tomb-complex from ancient Egypt, the size and breadth of the museum's collections are staggering. The Mastaba complex alone includes a working canal, a living marsh where papyrus is grown, a shrine to the cat goddess Bastet, burial-ceremony artifacts, and 23 mummies. The museum's gem room contains more than 500 gemstones and jewels. Place for Wonder, a three-room exhibit for children, lets youngsters handle everything on display, including a 1/2-ton stuffed polar bear, shells, animal skins, clothing and toys from China, aromatic scent jars, and gourds. Music, dance, theater, and film performances are also scheduled. *Lake Shore Dr. at E. Roosevelt Rd., tel. 312/922–9410. Admission: $10 families, $4 adults, $3 students and senior citizens; free Thurs. Open daily 9–5.*

After you've had your fill of museums, retrieve your car and continue north. As you round the curve past the Shedd Aquarium, look to your right for a view of the harbor. Off to the left looms the handsome, massive complex of the **Chicago Hilton and Towers** (720 S. Michigan Ave.), and soon thereafter the **Buckingham Fountain** will appear immediately to your left. To the far right, at the north and east, you can just see the ornate towers of **Navy Pier** (*see* Tour 5).

Having reached the Loop, we've come to the end of the South Lake Shore Drive tour.

Tour 5: Near North

Numbers in the margin correspond to points of interest on the Tour 5: Near North map.

Some of the most beautiful and interesting sights in Chicago are within a short walk of the multitude of hotels on the Near North Side. If business has brought you here, and you have a few hours to kill between meetings, you can wander over to the lakefront and Navy and North piers, browse the shops and museums of Michigan Avenue, or take a turn around the galleries of River North. If you have a whole day to spend, you can do all three comfortably. For more information on shopping Michigan Avenue, *see* Chapter 4.

Magnificent Mile/Streeterville The **Magnificent Mile,** a stretch of Michigan Avenue between the Chicago River and Oak Street, got its name from the swanky shops that line both sides of the street (*see* Chapter 4) and from its once-elegant low-rise profile, which used to contrast sharply with the canyons of the Loop. Unfortunately, a parade of new high rises is making the Mag Mile more canyon-like each year, but you can still see patches of what the entire street used to look like.

To the east of the Magnificent Mile is swanky **Streeterville,** which began as a disreputable landfill presided over by notorious lowlife "Cap" Streeter and his wife Maria. The couple set out from Milwaukee in the 1880s on a small steamboat bound for Honduras. When their boat was stranded on a sandbar between Chicago Avenue and Oak Street, Streeter claimed the "land" as his own, seceding from both the city of Chicago and the state of Illinois. After building contractors were invited to dump their debris on his "property," the landfill soon mushroomed into 186 acres of saloons and shanties. Today this once-infamous area is filled with high-rise apartment buildings and a smattering of older structures, and has attracted young professionals who work nearby. Where Cap Streeter's own shanty once sat is the John Hancock Center.

West of Streeterville, from Michigan Avenue to Dearborn Street, is a peculiar stretch that mixes a few skyscrapers, lots of parking lots and garages, a sprinkling of shops and restaurants, and some isolated examples of the stone town houses that once filled the neighborhood. Despite its lack of cohesion the area is the seat of various types of power, containing as it does two cathedrals and the headquarters of the American Medical Association, housed in a sterile new high rise at Wabash and Grand avenues.

❶ Our tour starts at the north side of the **Michigan Avenue Bridge,** which spans the Chicago River. The sculptures on the four pylons of the bridge represent major Chicago events: its discovery by Marquette and Jolliet, its settlement by du Sable, the Fort Dearborn Massacre of 1812, and the rebuilding of the city after the fire. The site of the fort is just across the river, where 360 North Michigan Avenue now stands.

Around the bridge are several notable skyscrapers, old and
❷ new. On the west side of Michigan Avenue is the **Wrigley Building** (400 N. Michigan Ave., tel. 312/923–8080), corporate home of the Wrigley chewing-gum empire. It was built in the early 1920s by the architectural firm of Graham Anderson Probst and White, the same firm that designed the Merchandise Mart (*see below*) and Union Station. The building is sheathed in terra cotta that's remained remarkably white, considering the pollution around it. Its wedding-cake embellishments and clock tower make it an impossible structure to overlook. The building is brightly illuminated at night.

Looking west you'll see the twin "corncobs" of Bertrand Gold-
❸ berg's **Marina City,** built in the early 1960s. Many architects love the complex, but engineers aren't so sure. If you get up close you can see patches in the concrete of the balconies. When it was first built Marina City was popular with young professionals who worked in the area; today it's less soughtafter, although it does have the dubious distinction of housing the only bowling alley in downtown Chicago. Just east of it is Mies van der Rohe's boxlike **IBM Building.** Next to that is the headquarters of the *Chicago Sun-Times*.

❹ Across Michigan Avenue is the crenellated **Tribune Tower** (435 N. Michigan Ave., tel. 312/222–3232). In 1922 *Tribune* publisher Colonel Robert McCormick chose this Gothic design for the building that would house his paper, after rejecting a slew of functional modern designs. Look for chunks of material taken from other famous buildings, such as Westminster Abbey and St. Peter's Basilica, embedded in the exterior wall of the tower. On the ground floor, behind plate-glass windows, are the studios of WGN radio, part of the *Tribune* empire that also includes WGN-TV, cable-television stations, and the Chicago Cubs. (Modesty was not one of Colonel McCormick's prime traits: WGN stands for the *Trib*'s self-bestowed nickname, World's Greatest Newspaper.)

❺ Behind the Tribune Tower is the new **NBC Tower** (200 E. Illinois St.). This 1989 limestone-and-granite edifice by Skidmore Owings and Merrill looks suspiciously like the 1930s-vintage Rockefeller Center complex in New York, another of NBC's

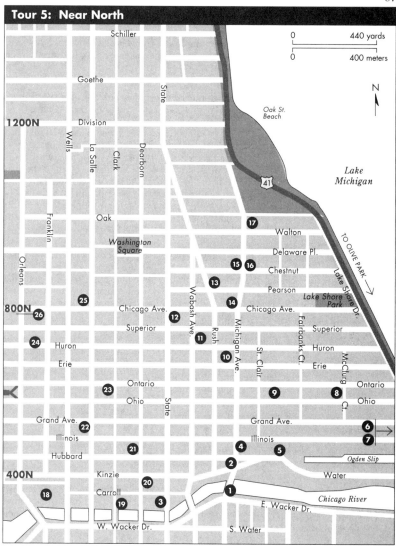

Tour 5: Near North

Schiller

Goethe

State

1200N

Division

Wells

La Salle

Clark

Dearborn

Franklin

Oak

Orleans

Washington Square

Chicago Ave.

Superior

Huron

Erie

Ontario

Ohio

Grand Ave.

Illinois

Hubbard

400N

Kinzie

Carroll

W. Wacker Dr.

Oak St. Beach

Lake Michigan

Walton

Delaware Pl.

Chestnut

Pearson

Chicago Ave.

Superior

Huron

Erie

Ontario

Ohio

Grand Ave.

Illinois

Ogden Slip

Water

Chicago River

E. Wacker Dr.

S. Water

Wabash Ave.

Rush

Michigan Ave.

St. Clair

Fairbanks Ct.

McClung Ct.

State

Lake Shore Dr.

TO OLIVE PARK

Lake Shore Park

0   440 yards
0   400 meters

N

17   15 16   13 14   12 11 10   25 26 24   23   22 21   20 19 3   18   2 4 5   9 8   6 7   1

Anti-Cruelty Society Building, **22**

Courthouse Place, **21**

Drake Hotel, **17**

Fourth Presbyterian Church, **15**

Holy Name Cathedral, **12**

John Hancock Center, **16**

Marina City, **3**

May Weber Museum of Cultural Arts, **8**

Merchandise Mart, **18**

Michigan Avenue Bridge, **1**

Moody Bible Institute, **25**

Museum of Contemporary Art, **9**

Navy Pier, **6**

NBC Tower, **5**

North Pier, **7**

Quaker Oats Building, **19**

Quigley Seminary, **13**

River North Concourse, **26**

Rock and Roll McDonald's, **23**

St. James Cathedral, **11**

SuHu, **24**

Terra Museum of American Art, **10**

33 West Kinzie Street, **20**

Tribune Tower, **4**

Water Tower, **14**

Wrigley Building, **2**

homes. The gift shop on the ground floor stocks NBC memorabilia.

As you look east you'll see that the riverbanks have been turned into a landscaped promenade. The arc of water that occasionally shoots across the river from the south side is Centennial Fountain.

For a lakefront detour, go down the steps beside the Tribune Tower at Grand Avenue and walk east, under Lake Shore Drive ❻ and across a large parking lot, to **Navy Pier.** Constructed in 1916 as a commercial-shipping pier, it was renamed in honor of the Navy in 1927 (the Army got Soldier Field). Currently under construction to become a European-style garden, with plantings and fountains, it's a wonderful place to enjoy the lake breezes and take in the skyline. The boats that dock there offer brunch, lunch, and dinner cruises at premium prices. The food's better on land, but the voyage can be pleasant on a hot summer night. Operators include *Spirit of Chicago* (tel. 312/836–7899) and *Odyssey* (tel. 708/990–0800).

Time Out   Just south of Navy Pier is **Rocky and Sons Fish House,** which offers various forms of fried fish in a ramshackle building that looks like something from Maine or Cape Cod. Eat your fish on the waterfront and watch the ducks converge for a handout. Sodas (Rocky's sells only coffee) and nonfish items can be had at the adjacent snack wagon.

For more conventional fare, head west on Illinois Street to ❼ **North Pier.** This fairly recent shopping complex in an old building offers interesting stores, a food court, waterside dining in several restaurants, a miniature golf course, and the **Chicago Children's Museum.** The museum contains exhibits on African art, architecture, and a recycling center, but the big draws are the three hands-on exhibits for children 2–12 and a "touch and feel" exhibit for preschoolers. *435 E. Illinois St. (N. Pier building), tel. 312/527–1000. Admission: $3.50 adults, $2.50 children. Thurs.* PM *free. Open Tues.–Fri. 12:30–4:30 and Thurs. 5* PM*–8* PM*, weekends 10–4:30.*

As you leave North Pier, walk north on McClurg Court to Ontario Street. Turn left and you'll find the tiny **May Weber Mu-** ❽ **seum of Cultural Arts,** which changes exhibits every three months; recent shows have explored the textiles and household arts of Japan and the crafts of the Yoruba tribe. *299 E. Ontario St., tel. 312/787–4477. Admission: $1. Open Wed.–Sun. noon–5.*

❾   Farther west on Ontario is the **Museum of Contemporary Art.** Started by a group of art patrons who found the great Art Institute unresponsive to modern work, this museum concentrates on 20th-century art, principally works created after 1940. Limited display space means that the collection of more than 4,000 works can be shown only in rotation; about six major exhibitions and 12 smaller ones are mounted each year. Because the museum closes in preparation for major exhibitions, be sure to call before planning a visit. The museum may move in 1996 to larger quarters on the site of the old armory on Chicago Avenue. *237 E. Ontario St., tel. 312/280–5161. Admission: $6 adults; $3 students, senior citizens, and children under 16; free Tues. Open Tues.–Sat. 10–5, Sun. noon–5.*

If you see lots of people in white coats in the neighborhood, don't be surprised. Stretching east of Michigan Avenue from Ontario to Chicago avenues are the buildings of one of the city's most prominent medical centers, **Northwestern Memorial Hospital.** The complex includes a veteran's hospital, a rehabilitation hospital, and a women's hospital, plus outpatient buildings. The downtown campus of Evanston's **Northwestern University,** including the law school and business school, is also here.

Continue west to Michigan Avenue, cross it and turn right for
⑩ the third museum in the Near North, the **Terra Museum of American Art.** Daniel Terra, Ambassador-at-Large for Cultural Affairs under Ronald Reagan, made his collection of American art available to Chicago in 1980; in 1987, the collection was moved here from Evanston. Subsequent acquisitions by the museum have added to the superb collection here, which includes works by Whistler, Winslow Homer, three generations of Wyeths, Sargent, and Mary Cassatt. *664 N. Michigan Ave., tel. 312/664–3939. Admission: $4 adults, $2.50 senior citizens, $1 children 12–18. Open Wed.–Sun. 10–5, Tues. 10–8.*

⑪ Two blocks west of Michigan Avenue at Huron Street is the **St. James Cathedral** (65 E. Huron St., tel. 312/787–7360). First built in 1856, the original St. James was largely destroyed by the Chicago Fire in 1871. The second structure from 1875 is Chicago's oldest Episcopal church.

Time Out	In sunny weather the plaza just east of St. James is a great place to eat a sandwich while you people-watch. For great fixings, try **L'Appetito** (Wabash Ave. and Huron St.), a take-out deli that has some of the best Italian subs in Chicago.

Another block west and one block north is the Catholic strong-
⑫ hold, **Holy Name Cathedral** (735 N. State St., tel. 312/787–8040). This yellow-stone Victorian cathedral built between 1874 and 1875 is the principal church of the archdiocese of Chicago. Although the church is grand inside, the exterior is somewhat disappointing.

Go east on Chicago Avenue to Rush Street and turn left (north).
⑬ At Pearson and Rush streets is **Quigley Seminary,** a 1918 Gothic-style structure. Its chapel is a little jewel, with perfect acoustics and a splendid rose window.

Continue east on Pearson Street to **Water Tower Park,** one of Chicago's icons. One of the few buildings to survive the fire of
⑭ 1871, the **Water Tower** houses a 37-foot pipe once used to equalize water pressure for the matching **pumping station** across the street. Today the water tower and pumping station house the **Chicago Office of Tourism** and the **visitors center,** respectively.

A block north on the west side of Michigan Avenue is the
⑮ **Fourth Presbyterian Church** (126 E. Chestnut Street). The courtyard of the church, a grassy spot adorned with simple statuary and bounded by a covered walkway, is an oasis amid Michigan Avenue's commercial bustle; many a weary shopper has found respite here. The courtyard is situated between the church and the rectory. The granite church itself is a prime example of the Gothic Revival style popular at the turn of the century. Noontime organ concerts are given occasionally in the sanctuary.

⓰ Across Michigan Avenue towers the 98-story **John Hancock Center,** which briefly held the title of world's tallest building when it was completed in 1969. The crisscross braces help keep the building from swaying in the high winds that come off the lake, although people who live in the apartments on the upper floors have learned not to keep anything fragile on a high shelf. There's an observation deck on the 96th floor that charges admission, although you can see the same view in a more festive setting by having an exorbitantly priced drink in the bar that adjoins **The 95th** restaurant (*see* Chapter 6). *Tel. 312/751–3681. Observation deck admission: $3.65 adults, $2.35 students 5–17 and senior citizens. Open daily 10–midnight.*

⓱ At the head of the Magnificent Mile is the **Drake Hotel** (140 E. Walton Pl.), one of the city's oldest and grandest; take a look in the marble-and-oak lobby, complete with cherub-laden fountain, even if you're not staying here. The lobby is one of the city's most popular spots for afternoon tea. In nice weather you can cross Oak Street in front of the Drake's main entrance and take the underground passage that leads to Oak Street Beach and the lakefront promenade. (Watch out for speeding bicyclists, skateboarders, and Rollerbladers.)

River North Bounded on the south and west by branches of the Chicago River, River North has eastern and northern boundaries that are harder to define than those of Streeterville and the Magnificent Mile. As in many neighborhoods, the limits have expanded as the area has grown more attractive; today they extend roughly to Oak Street on the north and Clark Street on the east. Richly served by waterways and by railroad tracks that run along its western edge, the neighborhood was settled by Irish immigrants in the mid-19th century. As the 20th century approached and streetcar lines came to Clark, La Salle, and Wells streets, the area developed into a vigorous commercial, industrial, and warehouse district.

But as economic conditions changed and factories moved away, the neighborhood fell into disuse and disrepair. Despite its location less than a mile from Michigan Avenue and the bustling downtown, River North became just another deteriorated urban area, the deterioration underscored by the depressed quality of life in the massive Cabrini-Green public-housing project at the neighborhood's northern and western fringe.

As commerce moved away, artists and craftspeople moved into River North, attracted by the spacious abandoned storage areas and shop floors and the low rents. Developers began buying up properties with an eye toward renovation. Today, although some buildings remain unrestored, and patches of the neighborhood retain their earlier character, the area has gone through a renaissance. Scores of art galleries, dozens of restaurants, and numerous trendy shops have opened here, bringing life and excitement to a newly beautiful neighborhood. Walking through River North, one is aware of the almost complete absence of contemporary construction; the handsome buildings are virtually all renovations of properties nearly a century old. However, rising rents have combined with the recession to drive out some small retailers, and at press time many renovated spaces stood empty.

The typical River North building, made of the famed Chicago red brick, is a large, rectangular, solidly built structure with high ceilings and hardwood floors. Even those buildings of the period that were intended to be strictly functional were planned with an often loving attention to detail in the fine woodwork in doors and door frames, in the decorative patterns set in the brickwork, in the stone carvings and bas reliefs, and in the wrought-iron and handsome brass ornamentation.

⑱ Our tour begins on the plaza of the massive **Merchandise Mart,** on the river between Orleans and Wells streets. The mart contains more square feet than any other building in the country except the Pentagon. Built by the architectural firm of Graham Anderson Probst and White in 1930, it's now owned by the Kennedys, of political fame. Inside are wholesale showrooms for all sorts of merchandise, much of it related to interior decoration. You can view the showrooms either accompanied by an interior designer or on one of the Mart's tours. The first two floors of the mart were converted into a retail shopping mall in late 1991. Most of the shops here are representatives of national chains. The anchor is a branch of the downtown department store Carson Pirie Scott. The somewhat macabre row of heads on the plaza is the Merchandise Mart Hall of Fame, installed at Joseph P. Kennedy's behest in 1953. The titans of retail portrayed here include Marshall Field, F. W. Woolworth, and Edward A. Filene. *13-156 The Merchandise Mart, tel. 312/644–4664. Showrooms open for tours only. Admission to tours: $7 adults, $5.50 seniors and students. Children under 16 not admitted on tours. Tours given Mon., Wed., Fri. 10 and 1:30; closed major holidays.*

The nondescript building to the west is the **Apparel Center,** the Mart's equivalent for clothing.

From the plaza, walk north on Wells Street to Kinzie Street. Turn east on Kinzie Street, cross Clark Street, and look to your right to see two recent additions to Chicago's architectural **⑲** scene. At the river's edge is the **Quaker Oats building,** a massive, glass-skin box designed by Skidmore, Owings & Merrill that was built to house the company's world headquarters after decades in the nearby Merchandise Mart. In the lobby there's an immense replica of the famous Quaker Oats box. This handsome office building dwarfs the Japanese **Hotel Nikko** (320 N. Dearborn St.) to the east. The hotel was built by a consortium headed by Japan Air Lines to provide both top-quality Japanese-style accommodations to Japanese businessmen and luxury Western-style facilities to traveling Americans (*see* Chapter 7).

Before you turn left on Dearborn Street, notice the splendid **⑳** ornamental brickwork of **33 West Kinzie Street,** a Dutch Renaissance–style building. Once a commercial building, it was twice renovated and is now the home of Harry Caray's restaurant, owned by the famed sportscaster (*see* Chapter 6).

Proceed north to Hubbard Street, turn left, and pause at **㉑** **Courthouse Place** (54 W. Hubbard St.), a splendid granite building that has been beautifully renovated; notice the bas reliefs over the arched, pillared doorway. Inside, the restored lobby has black-and-white pictures of the original site. Continuing west you come to Clark Street, where you can see a remnant of the neighborhood's former condition, a sleazy porno peep-show shop, two doors down from **Quadrant** (406 N.

Clark Ave.), a trendy snack shop featuring a large selection of homemade muffins.

Go north on Clark Street to Grand Avenue. Turn left and continue one block west to La Salle Street. The funny, charming ㉒ edifice on the southwest corner is the **Anti-Cruelty Society building** (153 W. Grand Ave., tel. 312/644–8338), designed by whimsical Chicago architect Stanley Tigerman.

Walk north on La Salle to Ontario Street and turn right. The ㉓ **Rock and Roll McDonald's** at Clark Avenue and Ontario Street has a standard McD's menu (with slightly higher prices), 24-hour service, and a profusion of rock-and-roll artifacts, '50s and '60s kitsch, and just plain bizarre items to entertain you while you eat. Jukeboxes blast at all hours, and vintage '50s cars often crowd the parking lot on Saturday night. It's one of the highest-grossing McDonald's franchises in the world, so the company lets the operator decorate as he pleases. Even if you don't like the food, it's worth sticking your head in the door just to admire the Howdy Doody puppets, the '59 Corvette, and the rest of the collection.

One more block east, at Ontario and Dearborn streets, is the Romanesque pile that used to house the Chicago Historical Society before it moved to its Lincoln Park location. After several incarnations, it has become **Excalibur,** a dance club popular with young professionals and visiting suburbanites.

Now double back and head west on Ontario Street. At Wells Street, turn right, and walk to Huron Street. Huron, Superior (one block north), and Hudson (a north–south street west of ㉔ Orleans) streets form an area known as **SuHu**—a word play on New York's SoHo, for this, too, is an arts district, home of more than 50 art galleries, showing every kind of work imaginable. Don't be shy about walking in and browsing; a gallery's business is to sell the works it displays, so most galleries welcome interested visitors and, time permitting, the staff will discuss the art they are showing. On Friday evening many galleries schedule openings of new shows and serve refreshments; you can sip jug wine as you stroll through the newly hung exhibit. Consider a gallery tour an informal, admission free alternative to a museum visit. Although each gallery sets its own hours, most are open weekdays and Saturday 10–5 or 11–5 and are closed Sunday. For announcements of openings and other news of the art scene, write for the *Chicago Gallery News,* 107 West Delaware Place, Chicago, IL 60610, or stop by and pick up a copy at the Pumping Station (*see above*).

Virtually every building on Superior Street between Orleans and Franklin streets houses at least one gallery. At 301 West Superior is **Eva Cohon** (tel. 312/664–3669), with contemporary American and Canadian painting, sculpture, and works on paper. At 311 West Superior Street is **East West Contemporary Art** (tel. 312/664–8003) with works by Chinese artists.

Nestled under the El tracks at Superior and Franklin streets is **Brett's Kitchen,** an excellent spot for a sandwich or an omelet during the week.

Go north on Franklin Street to Chicago Avenue. Two blocks ㉕ east on Chicago Avenue is the **Moody Bible Institute** (820 N. La Salle St., tel. 312/329–4000), a massive contemporary brick structure. Other campus buildings spread out behind it to the north. Here students of various conservative Christian denominations study and prepare for religious careers.

Backtrack to Orleans Street. The bleak high rises you see to the northwest are the southeastern edge of the infamous **Cabrini Green** public-housing project—so close to the affluence of River North but a world away. Cabrini Green is one of many war zones created in Chicago by public housing. Although some believe it's only a matter of time before the project is razed to accommodate developers of luxury properties who are eyeing the land, relocating the hundreds of people who live there is a political hot potato few want to face. Meanwhile the residents struggle to raise families amid squalor and disrepair, and gang violence claims several lives every year.

26 The **River North Concourse** (750 N. Orleans St. at Chicago Ave.) houses many galleries along with a collection of stores and businesses. The striking lobby is done in exposed brick and glass block, and a bank of television monitors decorates the Orleans Street entrance.

To return by public transportation to Michigan Avenue in the Near North, take the eastbound Lincoln (No. 11) bus at the intersection of Chicago Avenue and La Salle Street. The bus travels Chicago Avenue to Michigan Avenue and turns south on Michigan Avenue. Or you can take the Chicago (No. 66) bus from the same stop, eastbound to Michigan Avenue and transfer to the Water Tower Express (No. 125) for points north between Chicago Avenue and Walton Street.

Tour 6: Lincoln Park

Numbers in the margin correspond to points of interest on the Tour 6: Lincoln Park map.

In the early years of the 19th century the area bounded by North Avenue (1600 N.) on the south, Diversey Parkway (2800 N.) on the north, the lake on the east, and the Chicago River on the west was a sparsely settled community of truck farms and orchards that grew produce for the city of Chicago, 3 miles to the south. The original city burial ground was located on the lakefront at North Avenue. The park that today extends from North Avenue to Hollywood Avenue (5700 N.) was established in 1864, after the city transferred about 20,000 bodies to Graceland and Rosehill cemeteries, then far north of the city limits (*see* Tour 7). Many of the dead were Confederate soldiers who perished at Camp Douglas, the Union's infamous prison camp on the lakefront several miles south. Called Lincoln Park after the then recently assassinated president, this swath of green became the city's first public playground. The neighborhood adjacent to the original park also became known as Lincoln Park (to the confusion of some visitors).

By the mid-1860s the area had become more populated. Germans predominated, and there were Irish and Scottish immigrants. The construction in 1860 of the Presbyterian Theological Seminary (later the McCormick Seminary, which moved to Hyde Park in 1977) brought modest residential construction. By the end of the century, immigrants from Eastern Europe—Poles, Slovaks, Serbs, Hungarians, Romanians, and some Italians as well—had swelled the population, and much of the housing stock in the western part of the neighborhood dates from this period.

Between the world wars, expensive new construction, particularly along the lakefront and the park, was undertaken in Lincoln Park. At the same time, the once elegant houses to the west that had begun to deteriorate were being subdivided into rooming houses—a process that was occurring at roughly the same period in Hyde Park, 10 miles to the south. By 1930 a group of blacks had moved to the southwestern corner of Lincoln Park. Italians were feared because the "black hand" was active here. The St. Valentine's Day Massacre and the FBI shooting of John Dillinger at the Biograph Theatre took place on North Lincoln Avenue.

Following World War II, the ethnic groups that had been first to arrive in Lincoln Park, having achieved some affluence, began to leave for the suburbs and the northern parts of the city. Poor Appalachians, Hispanics, and blacks, who did not have the resources to maintain their homes, moved in. By 1960 nearly a quarter of the housing stock in Lincoln Park had been classified as substandard.

As housing prices fell, artists and others who appreciated the aesthetic value of the decaying buildings and were willing to work to restore them moved to the southeastern part of the area. The newcomers joined established residents in forming the Old Town Triangle Association; residents to the north, who had successfully resisted subdivision, formed the Mid-North Association. Neighborhood institutions, including De Paul University, the McCormick Seminary, four hospitals, a bank, and others dismayed by the decline of the area, formed the Lincoln Park Conservation Association in 1954. As the University of Chicago had done in Hyde Park, this association began exploring the possibilities of urban renewal as a means of rejuvenating the area.

As renewal plans progressed, blacks and Hispanics became incensed by what appeared to be minority removal, but the sit-ins and demonstrations that followed were ultimately unsuccessful. The original buildings along North Avenue were bulldozed and replaced with anonymous modern town-house developments, and many north–south streets were blocked off at North Avenue to create an enclosed community to the north.

Since the 1960s the gentrification of Lincoln Park has moved steadily westward, spreading as far as Clybourn Avenue, formerly a light industrial strip.

Our tour is divided into three parts. First we'll explore North Lincoln Avenue, the "main drag" of Lincoln Park, which is full of shops, restaurants, and theaters. The Biograph Theatre, where John Dillinger met his end, still stands here. DePaul University rules the center of the neighborhood. Then we'll see the Old Town Triangle, which has some of the oldest streets in Chicago and some of the most expensive, and accommodates a diverse population. Here you'll see some prime examples of gentrification. Finally we'll visit the lakefront and see several attractions in the city's oldest and most popular park.

DePaul and North Lincoln Avenue Our tour starts at the DePaul University campus. The CTA is the best way to get here from the Loop and the Near North Side. Take the Howard A or B train or the Ravenswood A or B train to Fullerton Avenue. Sheffield Avenue will be the nearest north–south street. If you're driving, take Lake Shore Drive to Fullerton Avenue and drive west on Fullerton Avenue to Sheffield Avenue. Parking is scarce, especially evenings and weekends, so public transit or a cab is recommended.

The massive brick complex extending halfway down the block on the southwest corner of Fullerton and Sheffield avenues, now known as the **Sanctuary** (2358 N. Sheffield Ave.), was built in 1895 as the St. Augustine Home for the Aged.

Walk south on Sheffield Avenue and turn left onto Belden Avenue. Continue east to the entrance to the **DePaul University** campus. Begun in 1898, the university today enrolls about 12,000 students, many of whom commute from neighboring suburbs. DePaul has a large continuing-education program, and thousands of Chicago adults attend the many evening and weekend classes. This portion of the campus is the former **McCormick Seminary** grounds, where antislavery groups met during the Civil War and Chicagoans sought refuge from the Great Fire in 1871. Note the elegant New England–style church on your right as you enter. The small street inside the U on your left is Chalmers Place. The massive Queen Anne building on the north side has decorative shingles aligned in rows of different shapes; at the west end of the building is a great turret. Now enter the cul-de-sac, whose brick houses, more than 100 years old and once faculty residences at McCormick Seminary, are now privately owned. Note the semicircular brickwork around the windows. At the west end of the street is the Gothic seminary building. Continue south past the seminary, east on Chalmers Place, and south again to exit the university grounds where you entered on Belden Avenue.

Continue east on Belden Avenue and turn left onto Halsted Street. Walk north to the intersection of Fullerton Avenue, Halsted Street, and Lincoln Avenue.

Lincoln Avenue is a diagonal that creates a three-way intersection with Fullerton Avenue and Halsted Street. To the southeast, where Halsted Street and Lincoln Avenue come together at a point is the huge **White Elephant Children's Memorial Resale Shop** (2380 N. Lincoln Ave., tel. 312/281–3747), which carries every kind of used merchandise imaginable: furniture, clothing, kitchenware, china, books, and more.

We'll head up the east side of Lincoln Avenue and return on the west side. This shopping strip tells a good deal about the neighborhood. Upscale and trendy without being avant-garde, the strip caters to well-educated young and middle-age professionals, emphasizing recreation and leisure-time needs over more mundane requirements. You'll be hard pressed to find a drugstore or a shoemaker's shop on this strip: those conveniences have moved to Clark Street, several blocks east, or to Sheffield Avenue.

The **Biograph Theater** (2433 N. Lincoln Ave., tel. 312/348–1350), where gangster John Dillinger met his end at the hands of the FBI, is now on the National Register of Historic Places. The Biograph shows first-run movies with an emphasis, as you might expect from the neighborhood, on foreign and art films.

Tour 6: Lincoln Park

Apollo Theatre
Center, **7**

Biograph Theater, **5**

Bookseller's Row, **6**

Chess Pavilion, **28**

Chicago Academy of
Sciences, **12**

Chicago Historical
Society, **23**

Crilly Court, **20**

DePaul University, **2**

1800 North Hudson
Avenue, **18**

1800 North
Sedgwick, **15**

1838 and 1836 North
Lincoln Park West, **13**

Green, Inc., **21**

Lincoln Park
Conservatory, **26**

Lincoln Park Zoo, **24**

Marge's Pub, **14**

McCormick
Seminary, **3**

Midwest Buddhist
Temple, **17**

Moody Memorial
Church, **22**

North Avenue
Beach, **27**

Omiyage, **8**

Potbelly Sandwich
Works, **11**

St. Michael's
Church, **19**

Sanctuary, **1**

Shakespeare
Garden, **25**

Threepenny Theatre, **9**

2312-2310 North
Lincoln Avenue, **10**

White Elephant
Children's Memorial
Resale Shop, **4**

Wisconsin Street, **16**

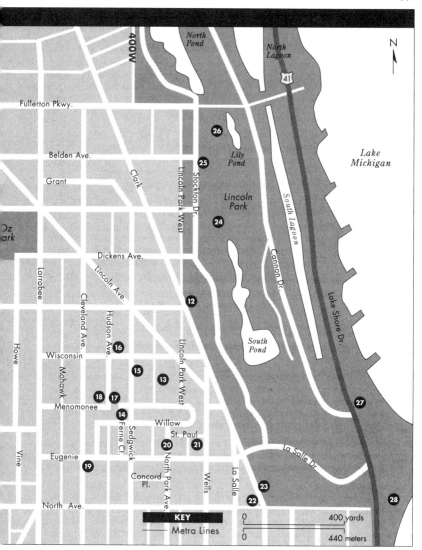

Fullerton Pkwy.

Belden Ave.

Grant

Clark

400W

North Pond

North Lagoon

41

Lake Michigan

26

Lily Pond

25

Stockton Dr.

Lincoln Park West

Lincoln Park

24

N

South Lagoon

Oz ark

Dickens Ave.

Lincoln Ave.

Larrabee

Cleveland Ave.

Hudson Ave.

12

Lincoln Park West

Cannon Dr.

Lake Shore Dr.

16

Wisconsin

Mohawk

15

13

South Pond

Howe

18 17

Menomonee

14

Ferne Ct.

Sedgwick

Willow

St. Paul

27

Vine

Eugenie

19

20

North Park Ave.

21

Concord Pl.

Wells

La Salle

La Salle Dr.

North Ave.

22

23

28

KEY
Metra Lines

0 ——— 400 yards
0 ——— 440 meters

6 Several doors north is **Bookseller's Row** (2445 N. Lincoln Ave., tel. 312/348–1170), one of several bookstores on the strip, where you'll find used, out of print, and fine books, together with a few new ones as well. **Wax Trax Records** (2449 N. Lincoln Ave., tel. 312/929–0221), the place for everything in popular music, including oldies and imports, is a must stop if you have teenagers with you. **Fiber Works** (2457 N. Lincoln Ave., tel. 312/327–0444) has an attractive selection of clothing and yarns in natural fibers. The **Children's Bookstore** (2465 N. Lincoln Ave., tel. 312/248–2665) is probably the best of its kind in the city. **Finders Keepers** (2469 N. Lincoln Ave., tel. 312/525–1510), a resale shop for the Latin School of Chicago, has the kind of used merchandise also found at the Children's Memorial Resale Shop.

7 Across Lincoln is the **Apollo Theatre Center** (2540 N. Lincoln Ave., tel. 312/935–6100), which offers local productions of Broadway and off-Broadway hit shows.

Time Out If you're hungry for a light snack, pop in at **Periwinkle** (2511 N. Lincoln Ave.), an attractive small café that expands to its adjacent garden in summer. The coffee is outstanding, and the desserts are sinfully rich, although dinner offerings are uneven.

8 **Omiyage** (2482 N. Lincoln Ave., tel. 312/477–1428) is a Japanese shop that has a little of lots of different things: jewelry, plates, cookware, miscellany. The items are attractive and tasteful, the prices reasonable.

Farther south on Lincoln is **Blake** (2448 N. Lincoln Ave., tel. 312/477–3364), a trendy clothing store. If your tastes run to more practical items you might prefer **Uncle Dan's Army Navy Store** (2440 N. Lincoln Ave., tel. 312/477–1918), a trove of camouflage outfits, hats, camp cookware, tents, sleeping bags, duffel bags, foot lockers, and badges.

9 The **Threepenny Theatre** (2424 N. Lincoln Ave., tel. 312/935–5744) used to be a revival house where golden oldies lived again, but that business died when VCRs became ascendant. The Threepenny now shows second-run films.

10 The buildings at **2312–2310 North Lincoln Avenue** were designed by Adler & Sullivan in the 1880s. **Wise Fools Pub** (2270 N. Lincoln Ave., tel. 312/929–1510) is one of the few remaining places on Lincoln Avenue to hear folk and blues. The **John Barleycorn Memorial Pub** (636 W. Belden Ave., tel. 312/348–8899) is one of Chicago's better-known pubs; it's filled with ship models, and classical music accompanies a continuous show of art slides.

11 Some of the best submarine sandwiches in town are available at the **Potbelly Sandwich Works** (2264 N. Lincoln Ave., tel. 312/528–1405), which is worth a visit even if you're not hungry. The walls are decorated with old-fashioned signs, the tables are covered in tile. Vintage malted-milk machines whir behind the counter. A massive old Toledo scale sits against the wall. In the oaken loft is a player piano and a small potbelly stove. The centerpiece of the restaurant is a huge potbelly stove that you'll have to walk around to get to the service counter.

Across the street are **The Body Politic** and the **Victory Gardens Theatre** (2261 N. Lincoln Ave., tel. 312/871–3000), two long-established and respected small theater groups; like many others, they share space and facilities to reduce expenses.

This ends our tour of Lincoln Avenue. At this point you'll want to either retrieve your car or jump on the Lincoln Avenue bus (No. 11) and go south to Lincoln and Armitage avenues (2000 N.). At Armitage Avenue turn left and continue to Clark Street to reach the imposing classical-style building that houses the

⓬ **Chicago Academy of Sciences.** Despite its scholarly name, this is not an institution of higher learning but a museum specializing in the natural history of the Midwest. The permanent exhibits include dioramas showing the ecology of Chicago millions of years ago, before it was settled by man, and back-lit ceiling images of the night sky seen from Chicago. Special exhibits are mounted regularly. *2001 N. Clark St., tel. 312/871–2668. Admission: $1 adults, 50¢ children and senior citizens, free Mon. Open daily 10–5.*

Old Town Triangle Old Town Triangle is filled with courts and lanes that run for only a block or so; to complicate matters, many of the streets have been made one-way in a pattern that can make it difficult to get from one place to another. (Urban planners commonly use this device in redeveloped areas to discourage the inflow of unwanted traffic.) Therefore, if you're driving, you may find it easier to park your car near the start of the tour and explore on foot. If you came by public transportation, you are now rewarded by not having to find a place to park.

To reach Old Town Triangle, take Clark Street or Lincoln Avenue south to Wisconsin Street, turn west, and proceed to Lincoln Park West. Be sure to have a look at the elegant row of gracious old painted-brick buildings at **1850–1858 North Lincoln Avenue.**

A left turn onto Lincoln Park West will lead you to two marvel-
⓭ ous frame houses at **1838 and 1836 North Lincoln Park West.** Frame houses are relatively uncommon in Lincoln Park, in part because of the restrictions on wood construction that went into effect following the Chicago Fire in 1871. (Some poorer areas in the southwest of Lincoln Park do have extensive frame construction; the regulations were not always strictly enforced.)

The smaller of the two buildings, 1836, was built just after the fire; it has narrow clapboards, bay windows, leaded glass, and decorative iron grillwork around the miniature widow's walk above the front entrance. Note also the decorative cutouts in the wood over the front door. The exterior painting has been done in contrasting brown, beige, and white to reveal the details of the woodwork.

The larger house, 1838, is a grand structure built of wider clapboards and painted—in true Victorian style—in vividly contrasting gray, green, and salmon. Ornaments and traceries are outlined. (The painter, James F. Jereb, has signed his work at the south end of the house, a foot or so above the ground.) Notice, too, the overhanging veranda, the twin attic windows, and the ornately carved supports under the veranda and eaves. The style of the wrought-iron fence is of the appropriate period.

Continue south, turn west on Memomonee and go one block to Sedgwick Street. On the southwest corner of the intersection

⑭ is **Marge's Pub** (1750 N. Sedgwick St., tel. 312/944–9775), the oldest commercial property in Lincoln Park and a good place to stop for a beer. The building, with its redbrick construction, decorated in stone around the windows, is a familiar style in older Lincoln Park buildings.

⑮ Turn right onto the **1800 North Sedgwick Street** block and proceed about halfway up the block. On the right you will notice a change from the traditional brick architecture. The materials used to build these houses begin with handsome contemporary red brick and move on to poured concrete, oddly colored brick, and gray wood. This strip may be the most expensive in Chicago. Each of the houses was custom-designed for its owner at an astronomical price by a different world-renowned architect. Such were the egos involved that the architects could agree on nothing—not style, not materials, not lot size, not even the height of the buildings. Although some of the structures might look good on another site, particularly if surrounded by some land, here they look like transplanted misfits, jammed in together, out of character with the neighborhood and with each other. Despite their monetary value, little about them is aesthetically pleasing.

⑯ Continue on Sedgwick Street to the intersection with Wisconsin Street. On the north side of **Wisconsin Street,** extending west to Hudson Avenue, is another example of new construction, a massive condominium complex that fails aesthetically for just the opposite reason that the Sedgwick Street custom-designed buildings fail. Here the architect has augmented basic redbrick construction with virtually every design element one might see in turn-of-the-century buildings of the neighborhood, including bays and huge arched windows. The mammoth scale of the building is an anachronism; worse, the overuse of traditional stylistic elements makes the building look like a parody of, rather than a complement to, the buildings it seeks to imitate. Look at the period brick building on the northeast corner of Sedgwick and Wisconsin streets for a reminder of how satisfying elegant simplicity can be.

⑰ Walk west on Wisconsin Street, turn south on Hudson Avenue, and proceed one block to Menomonee Street. The Oriental-looking building where the street curves is the **Midwest Buddhist Temple** (435 W. Menomonee St., tel. 312/943–7801). In mid-June, Old Town Triangle hosts the Old Town Art Fair, which claims to be the oldest juried art fair in the country, and the Midwest Buddhist Temple is one of the most popular food vendors at the fair.

⑱ Before you turn on Menomonee Street, regard the half-timber house at the corner, **1800 North Hudson Avenue,** a particularly handsome example of a style that's unusual for Lincoln Park.

⑲ Go west one block on Menomonee then south on Cleveland Avenue to Eugenie Street and **St. Michael's Church** (458 W. Eugenie St., tel. 312/664–1511). This massive, ornate Romanesque building was constructed on land donated in the 1850s by Michael Diversey (the early beer baron after whom Diversey Parkway was named) to provide a church where the area's German community could worship. The structure partially withstood the fire of 1871, and the interior of the church was restored after the fire by the German residents of the neighborhood. Their work is a legacy of exquisite craftsmanship.

Outside, notice the classical columns of different heights, the elaborate capitals, the many roofs with stonework at the top, and the elegant spire.

㉚ Walk east on Eugenie Street about five blocks and turn left onto **Crilly Court,** one of the oldest streets in Chicago. For nearly half a century this little enclave was also one of Chicago's stablest neighborhoods, with residents who had lived here for more than 40 years. A few years ago, the buildings were acquired by developers, who converted them into condominiums. The existing tenants were given the option to buy, but most of them—some quite elderly—could not afford to and were forced to move.

㉑ When you come to St. Paul Avenue, turn east, proceed to Wells Street, and turn right. **Green, Inc.** (1716 N. Wells St., tel. 312/266–2806) is a plant-lover's delight, with shrubs and trees set out on the sidewalk in good weather and a marvelous selection of cacti, many of which are displayed in the window. The building that houses the stores on this block has designs stamped in tin between the upper and lower bay windows. The building to the south has several more shops.

Time Out For a pick-me-up, stop at **Savories** (1700 N. Wells St.), a coffee, tea, and spice shop that also sells pots, mugs, and other accessories. The coffee is fresh and delicious (try the daily special), and so are the iced coffees and teas. Sample one of the rich scones or the sour-cherry cobbler; the muffins, buns, and pastries, too, are delectable.

Lincoln Park With Old Town Triangle behind us, we re-enter Lincoln Park, where we ended our tour of North Lincoln Avenue with a visit to the Academy of Sciences (*see above*). For those who've followed the tour to this point, go south on Wells Street, turn left on North Avenue, and walk east to Clark Street. If you're just picking up the tour at this point, you can reach Lincoln Park by taking the No. 151 Sheridan Road bus north from North Michigan Avenue. Get off at North Avenue. If you're driving, take Lake Shore Drive to the La Salle Street/North Avenue exit. Make a right turn onto Stockton Drive and look for metered parking. The area can be extremely congested, especially on weekends, so driving is not recommended.

㉒ The massive Romanesque structure on the west side of Clark Street is **Moody Memorial Church** (1630 N. Clark St., tel. 312/943–0466), one of the largest Protestant churches in the nation. The nondenominational church, named after 19th-century evangelist Dwight L. Moody, is associated with the Moody Bible Institute (*see* Tour 5).

㉓ Across Clark is the southwestern entrance to the park. First pay a visit to the **Chicago Historical Society,** which stands at the northeast corner of North Avenue and Clark Street. The original stately brick Georgian structure was built in 1932, and if you walk around to the eastern side (facing the lake) you can see what it looked like at the time. On the Clark Street side the original facade has been covered by a sparkling all-glass addition, which contains a café at its south end (the curved portion). In the café's north wall is a terra-cotta arch designed by Daniel Burnham more than 100 years ago. The historical society's permanent exhibits include the much-loved diorama room that portrays scenes from Chicago's history and has been a part of the lives of generations of Chicago children. Other highlights include collections of costumes and the famous statue of Abraham Lincoln, whose nose gleams from having been rubbed by countless children. In addition the society mounts temporary exhibitions; its Civil War installation, "A House Divided," will run for the next several years and shouldn't be missed by Civil War buffs. *1601 N. Clark St., tel. 312/642–4600. Admission: $3 adults, $2 senior citizens, $1 children, free Mon. Open Mon.–Sat. 9:30–4:30, Sun. noon–5.*

All of Chicago's parks, and **Lincoln Park** in particular, are dotted with sculptures—historical, literary or just plain fanciful. East of the historical society is one of the most famous, a standing figure of Abraham Lincoln, completed in 1887 by the noted American sculptor Augustus Saint-Gaudens, whose portrayals of military heroes and presidents adorn almost every major city east of the Mississippi River. The sculptor used a life mask of Lincoln's face and casts of his hands that were made before he became president.

Wandering north through the park along Stockton Drive will
㉔ bring you to **Lincoln Park Zoo,** one of the finest small urban zoos in the country. (Look for the red barn, home of "Farm in the Zoo": The main entrance is just north of it.) Begun in 1868 with a pair of swans donated by New York's Central Park, the 35-acre zoo grew through donations of animals from wealthy Chicago residents and the purchase of a collection from the Barnum and Bailey Circus. Many of the big houses, such as the lion house and the elephant house, are built in the classical brick typical of 19th-century zoos. The older buildings are surrounded by newer outdoor habitats that try to re-create the animals' natural, wild surroundings. Outside the lion house there's a window that lets zoo visitors stand almost face to face with the tigers (if the giant cats are in the mood).

Lincoln Park Zoo is noted for its Great Ape House; the 23 gorillas are considered the finest collection in the world. Since most of them have been bred in captivity, there are always several babies about. It's fascinating to spend an hour watching the members of each community interact. In addition to the reptile house, the large mammal house (elephants, giraffes, black rhinos), the monkey house, the bird house, the small-mammal house, and a huge polar-bear pool with two bears, the zoo has several rare and endangered species. The Spectacle Bear (named for the eyeglasslike markings around its eyes) from Peru is one; another, China's Père David's deer, has been extinct in the wild for centuries. The latter is unlike any deer you've seen before, with backward antlers, big feet, and a horselike face. Several koalas live in a "koala condo" in the same building as the main gift shop. Youngsters will enjoy the children's zoo, the Farm in the Zoo (farm animals and a learning center with films and demonstrations), and the Kids' Corner Discovery Place, with hands-on activities. *2200 N. Cannon Dr., tel. 312/294–4660. Admission free. Open daily 9–5.*

The homely bronze figure at Stockton Drive opposite Dickens Street is Hans Christian Andersen, seated there since 1896. Beside him is the beautiful swan from his most famous story, "The Ugly Duckling."

Also near the zoo, at the western edge of the park, opposite
㉕ Belden Avenue, is the **Shakespeare Garden,** featuring flowers
and plants mentioned in the bard's works. The bronze statue
of the author was sculpted by William Ordway Partridge in
1894, after he had exhibited a plaster model of the work at the
Columbian Exposition.

㉖ North of the zoo is the **Lincoln Park Conservatory,** which has a
palm house, a fernery, a cactus house, and a show house in
which displays are mounted: the azalea show in February, the
Eastern show in March or April, the chrysanthemum show in
November, and the Christmas show in December.
Grandmother's Garden, between Stockton Drive and Lincoln
Park West, is a collection dating from 1893 of informal beds of
perennials, including hibiscus and chrysanthemums. A large
outdoor garden has flowering plants. *2400 N. Stockton Dr., tel.
312/294–4770. Admission free. Open Sun.–Thurs. 10–6, Fri. 10–
9. Hours vary during shows.*

In the conservatory garden is an uncommonly joyful fountain
where bronze storks, fish, and small mer-boys cavort in the
spraying water. The 1887 **Bates Fountain** was the collaborative
effort of Saint-Gaudens and his assistant, Frederick MacMon-
nies.

At Fullerton turn right and walk under Lake Shore Drive to
the lakefront. From here you can stroll in either direction for
㉗ several miles. **North Avenue Beach** is likely to be thronged on
summer weekends but sparsely populated at other times. To
get back to the Near North Side, about 2 miles from here, walk
south past North Avenue Beach and follow the lakefront
promenade. Notice the blue-and-white beach house, its port-
holes and "smokestacks" mimicking an old ocean liner. At the
㉘ south end of the beach stop by the **chess pavilion** to watch people of all ages engrossed in intellectual combat. The pavilion is
1950s vintage. Look for the carved reliefs along its base and
the king and queen that flank it on either side.

If you don't feel like a walk on the beach, go west from Fullerton
Avenue to Stockton Drive and catch the No. 151 bus southbound, which will take you back to Michigan Avenue. The No.
22 and No. 36 buses on Clark Street will also take you back to
the Near North or the Loop.

Tour 7: North Clark Street

A car or bus ride up North Clark Street north of Lincoln Park
provides an interesting view of how cities and their ethnic
populations grow and change. Before the late 1960s the Clark
Street area was solidly white middle class. Andersonville, the
Swedish community centered at Foster Avenue (5200 N.) and
Clark Street, extended north half a mile and included residential buildings to the east and west as well as a vital shopping
strip on Clark Street. Then, in the early 1970s, immigration
from the Far East began. Chicago's first Thai restaurant
opened at 5000 North Clark Street. (Chicago's Thai population
has since dispersed itself throughout the city without estab-
lishing a significant concentration here.) The Japanese community, which had shops and restaurants at the northern end
of the North 3000s on Clark Street, became more firmly en-
trenched, joined by substantial Korean immigration. Korean
settlement has since grown to the north and west, along north

Lincoln Avenue. As the 1970s ended, the Asian immigrants were being joined by newcomers from the Middle East. Together these groups have moved into the neighborhood, in classic fashion, as the old established group (the Swedish community) moved out to the suburbs. Today the shops on North Clark Street bear witness to the process of ethnic transition.

You can board the northbound Clark Street (No. 22) bus on Dearborn Street in the Loop or on Clark Street north of Walton Street. Or you can drive to Clark Street and North Avenue, where we'll begin our ride. North Avenue (1600 N.) is the southern boundary of the Lincoln Park neighborhood, which extends north to Diversey Avenue (2800 N.). The drive through Lincoln Park affords views of handsome renovated housing, housing in the process of being restored, upscale shops, and youthful joggers.

As you cross Belmont (3200 N.), you'll notice that the character of the neighborhood has changed. In the 3300 North block of Clark Street the **Happi-Sushi** restaurant and the **Suehiro** restaurant provide for Japanese tastes in food and are long-time denizens of this strip. You can get all the ingredients for authentic Japanese dishes at **Star Market** (3349 N. Clark St.), including exquisitely fresh (and astronomically expensive) fish to be used raw, sliced thinly, for sashimi.

Continuing north to the intersection with Addison Street, you'll find **Wrigley Field,** the home of the Chicago Cubs. The surrounding neighborhood of Wrigleyville is the last solidly white middle-class neighborhood remaining on this strip. Until the summer of 1988, area residents were successful in fighting the installation of lights for night games at Wrigley Field, and the Cubs played all their home games in the afternoon.

At Clark Street and Irving Park Road (4000 N.), you'll find **Graceland Cemetery,** the final resting place of many 19th-century millionaires and other local luminaries. In the 4500 N. block are **K-World Trading** and **Bee Tradin' Co.,** and a bit farther north is **Nice Trading Co.** All are East Asian import and export firms that aren't much to look at—they don't do business with the public—but their names speak volumes.

North of Wilson Avenue, **Charming Woks** (4628 N. Clark, tel. 312/989–8768) prepares Hunan and Szechuan food. **Tokyo Marina** restaurant (5058 N. Clark), comes up on your left (*see* Chapter 6).

Foster Avenue is the old southern boundary of Andersonville. Around the corner on Foster Avenue, west of Clark Street, is the **Middle Eastern Bakery and Grocery** (1512 W. Foster Ave.). Here are falafel, meat pies, spinach pies, *baba ghannouj* (eggplant puree dip), oil-cured olives, grains, pita bread, and a seductive selection of Middle Eastern sweets—flaky, honey-dipped, nut-filled delights. In the 5200 North block just north of Foster Avenue, the **Beirut Restaurant** serves *kifta* kebabs (grilled meatballs), baba ghannouj, *kibbee* (ground lamb with bulghur wheat), falafel, meat and spinach pies, and more. Across the street the original **Ann Sather's** restaurant, with its white wood on red brick storefront, specializes in Swedish cuisine and generally does a good business. South of Ann Sather the **Mediterranean Snack Shop and Grill** advertises steak sandwiches, Italian beef, burritos, and tacos; the specials of the day are potato stew with rice, *kheema* (ground beef) stew with rice, okra stew with rice, and other traditional dishes of the Mideast and Indian subcontinent.

Across the street on the same block the **Byblos I Bakery and Deli** offers Lebanese Middle Eastern bread and groceries. If you arrive at the right time, you'll see the window filled with pita breads still puffed. Opposite the bakery, the **Swedish-American Museum Center** has beautifully decorated papier-mâché roosters and horses, place mats, craft items, tablecloths, and candelabras. North of the Byblos Bakery is the **Scandinavian Furniture Center.** The wares of **Nelson's Scandinavian Bakery** are classic European pastries: elephant ears and petit fours with chocolate, for example. The **Svea Restaurant** has pretty blue and white tablecloths and a counter. **Erickson's Delicatessen** has glögg in bottles, crispbreads, Ramlösa, hollandaise sauce mix, and homemade herring and imported cheese.

Just north of Erickson's the **Andersonville Artists Original Arts and Crafts Display** features the work of local artisans, which includes hand-painted china, small sculptures, and paintings. On the other side of the street, the shelves of **Wikstrom's Gourmet Foods** contain Wasa bread, Swedish pancake mix, coffee roll mix, lingonberries, dilled potatoes, and raspberry dessert. Just north of Wikstrom's is **G. M. Nordling Jeweler.** At **Reza's Restaurant** (5255 N. Clark) you can dine on kebabs, *must* and *khiyar* (yogurt and cucumber), pomegranate juice, charbroiled ground beef with Persian rice, and other Middle Eastern entrées in an attractive setting.

On the 5400 North block are the **Phil Asia Food Market** and the **Kotobuki Japanese Restaurant.**

Phil House (5845 N. Clark) is a Philippine market stocking fresh fish, taro root, fresh shrimp of all sizes, crayfish, langostinos, *longaniza* (Philippine sausage), and a huge selection of spring roll skins. Chicago is home to a very large group of Philippine immigrants, but like the Thais (and unlike the Indians and the Koreans) they have not concentrated in a single area.

Here ends our ride up Clark Street, an urban tour through time and the waves of ethnic migration and replacement. In that respect, Clark—like north Milwaukee Avenue, which has gone from being Polish to Hispanic to Polish again as new immigrants have arrived in the 1980s—is a microcosm of the city of Chicago and the continuing ebb and flow of its populations.

Tour 8: Argyle Street and Uptown

In many cities, *uptown* suggests an elite residential area, as opposed to *downtown*, the central business district. Something like that must have been in the mind of the Californian who bought Chicago's Uptown National Bank sight unseen a few years ago; ever since he got a look at his property and its neighborhood, he's been trying to sell it. In Chicago, Uptown—an area bounded by Irving Park Road (4000 N.) on the south, Foster Avenue (5200 N.) on the north, the lake on the east, and Clark Street and Ravenswood Avenue (1800 W.) on the west—is the home of the down-and-out: Appalachians who came to

Chicago in search of jobs following World War II, blacks, Native Americans, families on welfare, drug addicts, winos, and others of Chicago's most disadvantaged residents live here. The neighborhood is rough and the rents are low.

Given the characteristics of the neighborhood, numerous social service agencies are located here. Because of that, and the low rents, Uptown is where Vietnamese immigrants were placed when they began arriving in Chicago in substantial numbers following the end of the Vietnam War. Hmong refugees from Vietnam likewise joined a polyglot community whose common bond, if any, was a shared destitution.

Yet the arrival of the Vietnamese groups brought interesting developments in Uptown. The first years were difficult: Although some of the families were educated and well-to-do in Vietnam, they came here with no money and no knowledge of English. The Hmong were further disadvantaged by having had no urban experience; these tribal mountain people were transplanted directly from remote, rather primitive villages into the heart of a modern urban slum. Nonetheless, like earlier immigrants who came to America, these people arrived with the determination to make new lives for themselves. They took any job that was offered, no matter how menial or how low the pay, and they worked two jobs when they could find them. From their meager earnings, they saved money. And they did two other important things: They sent their children to school and zealously oversaw their studies, and they formed self-help associations. Through the associations, they used pooled savings as rotating funds to set one, then another, up in business: grocery stores and bakeries to sell the foods that tasted like home, clothing shops and hairdressing salons to fill the needs of the community, and finally restaurants that attracted not only people from the old country who were beginning to have discretionary funds but also Americans from all over the city.

As their businesses prospered, they bought property. And the property they bought was the cheapest they could find, on the most depressed street in this crumbling neighborhood, Argyle Street (5000 N.). Today Argyle Street, a two-block strip between Broadway on the west and Sheridan Road on the east, is thriving. Its commercial buildings have been upgraded, thereby attracting the shops and restaurants of other Asian communities in Chicago, principally the Chinese and Thai. As "New Chinatown" or "Chinatown North," the area became so attractive that the old Chinatown merchant's association, representing the stores along Wentworth Street on the south side, considered relocating there en masse. While that plan fell through, some stores moved on their own. The Argyle Street group has been so successful that there is now a rivalry between the two Chinatowns for the customers of the Asian (and American) communities in Chicago.

If you've never been to Southeast Asia, a walk down Argyle Street is the next best thing. The neighborhood bustles with street traffic, and the stores are crowded with people buying fresh produce, baked goods, kitchen equipment, and 50-pound sacks of rice. Few signs are in English, though merchants know enough English to serve customers who don't speak their native language. Often older children and teenagers who learned English in school are pressed into service to help visitors. If you've been to Southeast Asia and long again for those tastes, smells, and sights, you must visit Argyle Street. Only here will you find, for example, the wonderful, vile-smelling durian fruit—an addiction for many, anathema to some—and other staples of Southeast Asian cuisine. Here, too, you will find many of the best Vietnamese restaurants in the city, including **Mekong** (4953 N. Broadway) and **Hue** (1138 W. Argyle St.; *see* Chapter 6), as well as Chinese restaurants serving noodles and barbecued duck and pork (which you might enjoy munching as you walk).

Today, fueled in part by the success of the Vietnamese and, more generally, the prosperity that that success has brought, Uptown is changing. Renovators are buying once fine old properties and restoring them, and young middle-class folk, driven here by the high prices in such neighborhoods as Lincoln Park to the south, are beginning to move in. The area has become a political battleground between those who claim to represent the poor and downtrodden and those who believe that the undeniable social costs of rehabbing are less than the social costs of allowing the neighborhood to fall further and further into decay.

A walk on Argyle Street is one of the most complex experiences you can have in Chicago. You'll become totally immersed in the tastes and sounds of another culture; you'll see the classic immigrant pattern, the process of successful Americanization; and you'll appreciate the pushes and pulls at work as cities decay, are restored, and grow again.

Tour 9: Devon Avenue

As immigration laws were made more lenient in the 1970s and 1980s, the number of immigrants arriving in Chicago increased substantially. In the 1970s, newcomers from the Indian subcontinent began to arrive, and in the 1980s they were followed by Asians from Thailand, Korea, the Philippines, and Vietnam; as well as large numbers from the Middle East, including Palestinians, Syrians, Lebanese, and Turks. The Soviet relaxation of restrictions on Jewish emigration shortly before the breakup of the Soviet Union turned many Jewish refuseniks into American residents.

Several of these diverse cultures mingle along a mile-long strip of Devon Avenue between Sacramento and Oakley streets, near the northern edge of the city. A stroll down the strip on any sunny Sunday afternoon or hot summer evening will allow you to appreciate the avenue's variety of cultures. At the eastern end is the hub of the Indian community, with stores catering to both Muslims and Hindus. As you walk west, you will see saree stores give way to Korean restaurants and Russian grocery stores. At the western end is an Orthodox Jewish neighborhood, dotted with kosher bakeries and butchers, and religious bookstores.

To get to Devon Avenue (6400 N.), take Lake Shore Drive north to Hollywood Avenue. Stay in one of the left lanes and go west on Hollywood Avenue to Ridge Avenue. Turn right on Ridge Avenue and head north for about a mile to Devon Avenue. Turn left on Devon Avenue, drive about 2 miles west to Oakley Street (2200 W.), and park your car. Your tour will take you down Devon Avenue as far as Sacramento Avenue (3000 W.).

Starting on the south side of Devon Avenue at Oakley Street, you'll see **Farm City Meats** (2255 W. Devon Ave.), purveyors of *Halal* meat, from animals slaughtered according to the provisions of Islamic law. The store sells baby goat meat, as well as a large selection of fish. As you walk west, you'll see many stores, such as **Video Palace** (2315 W. Devon Ave.), that sell or rent Indian and Pakistani movies and videotapes.

There are also at least a dozen stores that sell the colorful sarees worn by Indian women, including the **Taj Saree Palace** (2553 W. Devon Ave.), **Sarees Sapne** (2623 W. Devon Ave.), **Sharada Saree Center** (2629 W. Devon Ave.), and **ISP Indian Saree Palace** (2536 W. Devon Ave.).

Numerous grocery stores along your route sell Indian foods, condiments, and kitchenwares; the exotic smells are enticing. Take a look at the **Middle East Trading Co.** (2505 W. Devon Ave.), **Patel Brothers** (with three locations at 2542, 2600, and 2610 W. Devon Ave.), and **Foods of India** (2331 and 2614 W. Devon Ave.).

For a quick snack, try the Indian food at **Chat and Chat** (6357 N. Claremont Ave., at the corner of Devon Ave.), or **Annapurna Fast Food Vegetarian Snacks and Sweets** (2608 W. Devon Ave.).

Several Indian restaurants along Devon Avenue are good choices for a meal, including **Viceroy of India** (2518 W. Devon Ave.), **Moti Mahal** (2525 W. Devon Ave.), and the vegetarian **Natraj** (2240 W. Devon Ave.). Try the tandoori chicken or fish, which is marinated and grilled, the *sagh paneer* (a creamy mixture of spinach and cheese), or the *dal* (a lentil puree).

Several stores specialize in Russian cuisine and are easily recognized by the signs in Cyrillic writing hanging outside. Among them are **Globus International Foods and Delicatessen** (2909 W. Devon Ave.), **Three Sisters Delicatessen** (2854 W. Devon Ave.), and **Kashtan Deli** (2740 W. Devon Ave.). Three Sisters has a large selection of *matrioshkas* (the popular Russian dolls that are stacked one inside another). At 2845 West Devon Avenue, you'll see the **Croatian Cultural Center.**

When you reach the western end of Devon Avenue, notice the many stores and restaurants catering to the orthodox Jewish community. The restaurants and bakeries are good bets for either a sit-down meal or a snack to eat while you walk. Watch for **Miller's Market** (2727 W. Devon Ave.), **Tel Aviv Kosher Bakery** (2944 W. Devon Ave.), **The Bagel Restaurant** (3000 W. Devon Ave.), **Kosher Karry** (2828 W. Devon Ave.), and **Levinson's Bakery** (2856 W. Devon Ave.). The **Midwest Fish Market** (2942 W. Devon Ave.) has lox and other smoked fish for sale.

Several stores along the way sell Hebrew books and sacramental items, including **Rosenblum's Hebrew Bookstore** (2910 W. Devon Ave.) and the **Chicago Hebrew Bookstore** (2942 W. Devon Ave.). Rosenblum's has a large selection of unusual cookbooks, including several on Yemeni and Sephardic cuisine.

Chicago for Free

Like all great cities, Chicago offers a wealth of things to see and do that cost no more than the price of transportation to them.

Concerts **Chicago Cultural Center** (78 E. Washington St., tel. 312/269–2900 or 312/346–3278) presents the Dame Myra Hess Memorial Concert Series Wednesday at 12:15, a program of recitals by rising professional classical musicians.

Petrillo Bandshell in Grant Park is the site of summertime concerts sponsored by the Chicago Park District. In mid-June the Jazz Fest and the Gospel Fest are three-day events in which numerous performances take place on several stages. The Grant Park Symphony Orchestra and Chorus perform three to four times a week, late June through August. The Blues Festival comes to town in late August and early September. *The Reader* (free at stores and other locations in The Loop, Near North Side, Lincoln Park, and Hyde Park on Thursday and Friday) gives program details and performance times.

Daley Plaza (Washington between Clark and Dearborn Sts.) and **First National Bank of Chicago Plaza** (Dearborn to Clark Sts. between Monroe and Madison Sts.) have performances of light music, including folk and pop, during the noon hour in the summertime.

Chicago Chamber Orchestra (tel. 312/922–5570), under the direction of Dieter Koeber, gives free chamber concerts throughout the year at various locations. The performances are funded by corporate and foundation grants and individual memberships; the organization's goal is to bring live performances of fine music to those who cannot afford to pay for them.

Many Chicago churches offer free concerts, frequently organ recitals, choral programs, and gospel music. *The Reader* lists programs and locations.

Museums Several Chicago museums do not charge admission fees, among them: **Chicago Public Library Cultural Center, Czechoslovakian Society of American Heritage Museum and Archives, DuSable Museum of African American History, Museum of Broadcast Communications, Mexican Fine Arts Center Museum, Oriental Institute, Polish Museum of America.** Of the museums that have admission fees, many of them schedule one day a week when admission is free to all: **Art Institute of Chicago** (Tuesday), **Chicago Academy of Sciences** (Monday), **Chicago Historical Society** (Monday), **Chicago Children's Museum** (Thursday) **Field Museum of Natural History** (Thursday), **Museum of Contemporary Art** (Tuesday), **John G. Shedd Aquarium** (Thursday) and **Museum of Science and Industry** (Thursday). Though there is a fee for the Sky Show, the exhibits are free at the **Adler Planetarium.**

Music School Chicago has several fine music schools and university depart-
Programs ments of music, where faculty and students frequently give recitals (public performances are often a part of degree requirements).

University of Chicago Concert Office (tel. 312/702–8068) schedules concerts by a number of performing ensembles: the Motet Choir, the University of Chicago Chorus, the University of Chicago Orchestra, and the Collegium Musicum (an instrumental and vocal ensemble that performs music of the Renaissance and Baroque periods).

American Conservatory of Music (16 N. Wabash Ave., Suite 1850, tel. 312/263–4161) offers student and faculty recitals, at noon and in the evening, when school is in session. A program is scheduled almost every day except Sunday, and most performances are free.

DePaul University School of Music (804 W. Belden Ave., tel. 312/341–8373) has concerts by a chorus, an orchestra, a jazz band, and other performing ensembles as well as recitals. There are daily events throughout the school year.

Chicago Musical College of Roosevelt University (Rudolf Ganz Memorial Hall, 430 S. Michigan Ave., tel. 312/341–3780) schedules recitals and orchestral, chamber, woodwind, and jazz concerts. Early in the semester there are two to three events a week; later there's something every day.

Sherwood Conservatory of Music (1014 S. Michigan Ave., tel. 312/427–6267) has faculty and student recitals most Sunday afternoons and some Saturdays.

Picnics Between April and October, picnicking can be delightful almost anywhere along the lakefront. Favorite spots include Grant Park and Navy Pier.

Tours Many institutions offer free guided tours of their operations; most require reservations.

Chicago City Hall (121 N. La Salle St., tel. 312/744–2725) has one tour daily at 10 AM that takes in the City Council chambers and an exhibit of gifts presented to the late Mayor Harold Washington. City council meetings are open to the public and are famous for their often heated debates. Call 312/744–3081 for meeting times.

The main **U.S. Post Office** in Chicago (433 W. Van Buren St., tel. 312/765–3802), the largest postal facility in the world, offers tours of its mail processing division weekdays at 10:30 and 12:30. Call one week in advance; no children under nine.

Federal Reserve Bank (230 S. La Salle St., tel. 312/322–5111) explains how checks are processed and how money travels; tours are given daily 9–1. Call two weeks in advance for reservations. No children under 17 admitted. There's a public tour Tuesdays at 1 that requires only one day's advance notice; it's also worth calling to see if you can squeeze into an already booked "private" tour that has fewer than the 20-person limit. A visitors center in the lobby has permanent exhibits of old bills, counterfeit money, and a million dollars in one-dollar bills (though to thwart would-be thieves, most of the stash is in dollar-size scraps of paper). *Open Mon.–Fri. 8:30–5:30.*

What to See and Do with Children

Among the outstanding activities Chicago has in store for family groups are several museums that provide hours of fascination for youngsters, where dozens of exhibits not only don't forbid you to touch them but actually require that you interact with them.

Adler Planetarium (*see* Tour 4: South Lake Shore Drive, *above*). The Sky Shows enthrall young and old alike.

Brookfield Zoo (*see* Chapter 9: Excursions, *below*). Here are elephants, dolphins, a rain forest, and animals enough to keep you busy all day.

Chicago Academy of Sciences (*see* Tour 6: Lincoln Park, *above*) has many exhibits that will fascinate children.

Chicago Children's Museum (*see* Tour 5: Near North, *above*). Designed specifically for very young children, this museum at North Pier has many things to see and touch.

Chicago Public Library Cultural Center (*see* Tour 1: Downtown, *above*). Programs for youngsters take place throughout the year.

Children's Bookstore (2465 N. Lincoln Ave., tel. 312/248–2665). Browsing is encouraged among a superb collection of carefully selected books for children; story hours for children under six are scheduled several times a week.

Field Museum of Natural History (*see* Tour 4: South Lake Shore Drive, *above*). Three rooms are filled with the touchy-feely stuff that small folk love, and many of the regular exhibits have considerable appeal for children.

57th Street Books (*see* Tour 3: Hyde Park and Kenwood, *above*). In addition to the excellent selection of children's books, the store has a play and reading area where youngsters can browse or grownups can read to them.

Harold Washington Library Center (*see* Tour 1: Downtown, *above*) offers a variety of children's activities, including story time for preschoolers, film programs, theater and music performances, and tours.

John G. Shedd Aquarium (*see* Tour 4: South Lake Shore Drive, *above*). The display of sea creatures is guaranteed to captivate every visitor, regardless of age.

Lincoln Park Zoo (*see* Tour 6: Lincoln Park, *above*). The Children's Zoo, the Farm-in-the-Zoo, and the Kids' Corner Discovery Place are the special attractions prepared just for youngsters.

Museum of Science and Industry (*see* Tour 3: Hyde Park and Kenwood, *above*). Children and parents may find themselves competing here to see who gets to use the instruments or take part in the activities first.

Off the Beaten Track

If you're at McCormick Place, take a walk on the promenade that runs between the convention center and the lake. You can watch small planes take off from and land at tiny Meigs Field and, in the summer, observe the sailboats as they bob in Burnham Harbor.

The **Trompe l'Oeil Building** (1207 W. Division Street) is on the northeast corner of La Salle and Division streets, but you should study its appearance from a block east, at Clark and Division Street, or approach it from the south for the full effect of its rose window, ornate arched doorway, stone steps, columns, and sculptures. As you move closer to the building, you'll discover that an ordinary high rise has been elaborately painted to make it look like an entirely different work of architecture.

Olive Park juts out into Lake Michigan a block north of Lake Point Towers (505 N. Lake Shore Dr.); to find it, walk east on

Grand Avenue, pass under Lake Shore Drive, and bear left. It has no roads, just paved walkways and lots of benches, trees, shrubs, and grass. The marvelous and unusual views of the city skyline from here, in addition to the absence of vehicular traffic, make it seem as though you're miles from the city, not just blocks from the busy Near North side.

Slightly northwest of Hyde Park, at the corner of Drexel Boulevard and 50th Street, is the headquarters of **Operation PUSH** (930 E. 50th St., tel. 312/373–3366), Jesse Jackson's black self-help organization. A former synagogue, you'll recognize the building by its splendid columns before you see its colorful cloth banner. Three blocks east and one block north you'll find **4995 South Woodlawn Avenue,** the home of the controversial black leader Louis Farrakhan, who has made it a headquarters of the Nation of Islam. The great house was built by Elijah Mohammed, the Nation's founder; its $3 million funding was rumored to have come from the Libyan despot Muammar Khadafi.

Nearby, at 49th Street and Kenwood Avenue, stand two early works by Frank Lloyd Wright, **Blossom House** (4858 S. Kenwood Ave.) and **MacArthur House** (4852 S. Kenwood Ave.), both built in 1892. Across from Blossom House is **Farmers' Field,** a park where animals grazed as recently as the 1920s. A few blocks away, at 49th Street and Ellis Avenue, (4901 S. Ellis Ave.), is the 22-room Prairie Style **Julius Rosenwald mansion** built by the Sears Roebuck executive in the early 1900s. After a stint as a home for boys, followed by years of disuse, the mansion was purchased by a family and extensively restored.

A treeless hill near Lincoln Park's **Montrose Harbor** draws kiteflying enthusiasts of all ages on sunny weekends. Take Lake Shore Drive north from the Loop about 5 miles, exit at Montrose, turn right into the park, and look for colorful stunt kites on your left. Windsurfers often practice at nearby **Montrose Beach.**

If you're interested in the social history of the late 19th century, there's no place that exemplifies the era better than the planned community of **Pullman** on the far south side. Built in 1880 by railcar tycoon George M. Pullman for the workers at his Palace Car Company, the town had its own hotel, hospital, library, shopping center, and bank. The styles of the homes reflect the status of their original occupants: Workers' homes are simple, those of skilled craftsmen slightly fancier, and executive housing more elaborate still. The town was the site of the famous Pullman strike of 1894 and also its partial cause, because the company cut wages without reducing the rents for workers in company-owned housing. The factory is closed now, but the houses are occupied and the community is thriving. To get to Pullman, take I–94 (Dan Ryan Expy.) south, exit at 111th Street, and turn right. For more information, call the Historic Pullman Foundation (tel. 312/785–8181).

Sightseeing Checklists

Historical Buildings and Sites

This list of Chicago's principal buildings and sites includes both attractions that were covered in the preceding tours and additional attractions that are described here for the first time.

Amoco Building (Tour 1: Downtown)

Art Institute of Chicago (Tour 1: Downtown)

Associates Center (Tour 1: Downtown)

Auditorium Theatre (Tour 1: Downtown)

Biograph Theatre (Tour 6: Lincoln Park)

Blackstone Hotel (Tour 2: Downtown South)

Blackstone Theatre (Tour 1: Downtown)

Buckingham Fountain (Tour 1: Downtown)

Carbide and Carbon Building (Tour 1: Downtown)

Carson Pirie Scott (Tour 1: Downtown)

Chevrolet Building (Tour 3: Hyde Park and Kenwood)

Chicago Academy of Sciences (Tour 6: Lincoln Park)

Chicago Board of Trade (Tour 1: Downtown)

Chicago City Hall–Cook County Building (Tour 1: Downtown)

Chicago Hilton and Towers (Tour 2: Downtown South)

Chicago Historical Society (Tour 6: Lincoln Park)

Chicago Mercantile Exchange (Tour 1: Downtown)

Chicago Public Library Cultural Center (Tour 1: Downtown)

Chicago Temple (Tour 1: Downtown)

Chicago Theatre (Tour 1: Downtown)

Chicago Theological Seminary (Tour 3: Hyde Park and Kenwood)

Civic Opera House (Tour 1: Downtown)

Clarke House (1800 S. Prairie Ave., tel. 312/922–8687). Chicago's oldest building, Clarke House was constructed in 1836 in Greek Revival style. Period furniture enlivens the interior. Part of the Prairie Avenue Historical District. Closed Monday, Tuesday, and Thursday.

Crilly Court (Tour 6: Lincoln Park)

Daley Center (Tour 1: Downtown)

Dearborn Park (Tour 2: Downtown South)

Dearborn Station (Tour 2: Downtown South)

Donohue Building (Tour 2: Downtown South)

Drake Hotel (Tour 5: Near North).

Federal Center and Plaza (Tour 1: Downtown)

Fine Arts Building (Tour 1: Downtown)

First National Bank of Chicago (Tour 1: Downtown)

Fisher Building (Tour 1: Downtown)

Franklin Building (Tour 2: Downtown South)

Glessner House (1801 S. Prairie Ave., tel. 312/922–8687). The only surviving building in Chicago by the architect H. H. Richardson, Glessner House was designed in 1886. Part of the Prairie Avenue Historic District. Closed Monday, Tuesday, and Thursday.

Heller House (Tour 3: Hyde Park and Kenwood)

Hull House (800 S. Halsted St., tel. 312/413–5353). The columned, redbrick, turn-of-the-century Hull House seems out of place on its site, surrounded by the massive and modern buildings of the University of Illinois campus. Here Jane Addams wrought social work miracles in a neighborhood that was then a slum. Here, too, Benny Goodman learned to play the clarinet. Open to the public at no charge weekdays 10 AM–4 PM, Sunday noon–5. Closed Saturday and most holidays.

Illinois Institute of Technology (31st–35th Sts. on S. State St., tel. 312/567–3000). The campus was designed principally by Mies van der Rohe, with participation by Friedman, Alschuler and Sincere; Holabird and Roche; and Pace Associates. Built between 1942 and 1958, the structures have the characteristic box shape that is Mies's trademark. Unlike most of his work, they are low-rise buildings. Crown Hall (3360 S. State St.) is the jewel of the collection; the other buildings have a certain sameness and sterility.

International House (Tour 3: Hyde Park and Kenwood)

John Hancock Center (Tour 5: Near North)

Joseph Regenstein Library (Tour 3: Hyde Park and Kenwood)

Julius Rosenwald Mansion (Off the Beaten Track)

Laird Bell Law Quadrangle (Tour 3: Hyde Park and Kenwood)

Lutheran School of Theology (Tour 3: Hyde Park and Kenwood)

Main Post Office (Tour 1: Downtown)

Marquette Building (Tour 1: Downtown)

McCormick Seminary (Tour 6: Lincoln Park)

Metropolitan Detention Center (Tour 1: Downtown)

Midway Plaisance (Tour 3: Hyde Park and Kenwood)

Monadnock Building (Tour 1: Downtown)

Moody Bible Institute (Tour 5: Near North)

Museum of Science and Industry (Tour 3: Hyde Park and Kenwood)

Northwestern Atrium Center (Tour 1: Downtown)

One Financial Place (Tour 1: Downtown)

Orchestra Hall (Tour 1: Downtown)

Oriental Institute (Tour 3: Hyde Park and Kenwood)

Page Brothers Building (Tour 1: Downtown)

Palmer House (Tour 1: Downtown)

Promontory Apartments (5530 S. South Shore Dr.). The building, designed by Mies van der Rohe in 1949, was named for Promontory Point, which juts out into the lake just east of here.

Quaker Oats Building (Tour 5: Near North)

Railway Exchange Building (Tour 1: Downtown)

Reliance Building (Tour 1: Downtown)

River City (Tour 2: Downtown South)

Robie House (Tour 3: Hyde Park and Kenwood)

Rockefeller Memorial Chapel (Tour 3: Hyde Park and Kenwood)

The Rookery (Tour 1: Downtown)

The Sanctuary (Tour 6: Lincoln Park)

Sears Tower (Tour 1: Downtown)

State of Illinois Center (Tour 1: Downtown)

333 West Wacker Drive (Tour 1: Downtown)

Tribune Tower (Tour 5: Near North)

Union Station (Tour 1: Downtown)

University of Illinois at Chicago (705 S. Halsted St., tel. 312/996–7000). Designed by Walter Netsch, of Skidmore, Owings & Merrill, the university buildings seem to surge and weave toward each other.

Water Tower (Tour 5: Near North)

Windermere House (1642 E. 56th St.). This was designed in 1920 by Rapp and Rapp, known generally for their movie palaces. Notice the grand gatehouse in front of the sweeping semicircular carriage path at the entrance; notice also the heroic scale of the building, with its ornate carvings.

Wrigley Building (Tour 5: Near North)

Xerox Building (Tour 1: Downtown)

Museums and Galleries

Museums **Adler Planetarium.** (Tour 4: South Lake Shore Drive)

American Police Center and Museum. The museum's exhibits are concerned with police work and relationships between the police and the public. Safety, crime and punishment, and drugs and alcohol are among the subjects. One exhibit shows how the police communication system works; another details the history of the Haymarket Riot. A memorial gallery is dedicated to policemen who have lost their lives in the line of duty. *1717 S. State St., tel. 312/431–0005. Admission: $2 adults, $1.50 senior citizens, $1 children 6–11. Open weekdays 8:30–4.*

Art Institute of Chicago (Tour 1: Downtown)

Balzekas Museum of Lithuanian Culture. The little-known Balzekas Museum offers a taste of 1,000 years of Lithuanian history and culture on its three floors. You'll find exhibits on rural Lithuania; concentration camps; rare maps, stamps, and coins; textiles; and amber. The library can be used for research. *6500 S. Pulaski Rd., tel. 312/582–6500. Admission: $4 adults, $3 students and senior citizens, $1 children under 12; free Mon. Open daily 10–4 (Fri. until 8).*

Chicago Academy of Sciences (Tour 6: Lincoln Park)

Chicago Children's Museum. (Tour 5: Near North)

Chicago Historical Society (Tour 6: Lincoln Park)

Chicago Public Library Cultural Center (Tour 1: Downtown)

Czechoslovakian Society of America Heritage Museum and Archives. The collections of the Czechoslovakian Society include crystal, marble, dolls, musical instruments, china, ornamented eggs, vases, paintings, and statues. A library is part of the museum. *2701 S. Harlem Ave., Berwyn, tel. 708/795–5800. Admission free. Open most weekdays 10–noon and 1–4; call ahead to check.*

David and Alfred Smart Museum of Art (Tour 3: Hyde Park and Kenwood)

DuSable Museum of African American History. A 10-foot mural in the auditorium of the museum, hand-carved by Robert Witt Ames, depicts black history from Africa to the 1960s. Another gallery features great history makers: Martin Luther King, Jr., Rosa Parks, Paul Robeson, Sojourner Truth, and others. Special exhibits change frequently; a recent one on the cultural history of Haiti included paintings, papier-mâché crafts, flags, and other cultural artifacts. *740 E. 56th Pl., tel. 312/947–0600. Admission: free. Open daily 10–4.*

Field Museum of Natural History. (Tour 4: South Lake Shore Drive)

International Museum of Surgical Sciences. The surgical sciences museum has medical artifacts from around the world. *1524 N. Lake Shore Dr., tel. 312/642–6502. Admission free. Open Tues.–Sat. 10–4, Sun. 11–5.*

John G. Shedd Aquarium. (Tour 4: South Lake Shore Drive)

May Weber Museum of Cultural Arts (Tour 5: Near North)

Mexican Fine Arts Center Museum. The exhibits of the work of contemporary Mexican artists change every two to three months. *1852 W. 19th St., tel. 312/738–1503. Admission free. Open Tues.–Sun. 10–5.*

Museum of Broadcast Communications. (Tour 1: Downtown)

Museum of Contemporary Art. (Tour 5: Near North)

Museum of Holography. Holograms are three-dimensional images produced by lasers. If you have never seen a hologram, consider this museum a must stop; the images seem to leap out at you from their frames. The exhibits of holographic art from around the world include computer-generated holograms, moving holograms, pulsed portraits of people, and color holograms. Two or three special exhibits are mounted annually. *1134 W. Washington Blvd., tel. 312/226–1007. Admission: $2.50. Open Wed.–Sun. 12:30–5.*

Museum of Science and Industry. (Tour 3: Hyde Park and Kenwood)

Newberry Library. This venerable research institution houses superb book and document collections in many areas and mounts exhibits in a small gallery space. *60 W. Walton Dr., tel. 312/943–9090. Admission free. Closed Sun.*

Oriental Institute (Tour 3: Hyde Park and Kenwood)

Polish Museum of America. Dedicated to collecting materials on the history of the Polish people in America, the Polish Museum has an eclectic collection that includes an art gallery, an exhibit on the Shakespearean actress Modjeska, one on the American Revolutionary War hero Tadeusz Koscziusko, and another on the pianist and composer Ignaczi Paderewski that includes the last piano on which he performed and the chair he carried everywhere and without which he could not perform. The Stations of the Cross from the first Polish church in America (which was located in Texas) are on display. A library is available. *984 N. Milwaukee Ave., tel. 312/384–3352. Admission $2 adults, $1 senior citizens and students. Open daily noon–5.*

Spertus Museum of Judaica (Tour 2: Downtown South)

Swedish-American Museum Association of Chicago. Permanent exhibits here include a history of Swedish immigrant travel to the United States and a survey of the textile arts and industry in Sweden. Special exhibits, often on loan from other museums, come every six weeks. *5211 N. Clark St., tel. 312/728–8111. Admission: $1. Open Tues.–Fri. 11–4, Sat. 11–3.*

Terra Museum of American Art. (Tour 5: Near North)

Ukrainian Institute of Modern Art. Located in the heart of Ukrainian Village on the west side, this museum focuses on contemporary paintings and sculpture by artists of Ukrainian descent. *2320 W. Chicago Ave., tel. 312/227–5522. Admission: free. Open Tues.–Sun. noon–4.*

Galleries Chicago has more art galleries than any American city after New York. Most galleries are open weekdays and Saturday 10–5 or 11–5 and at other times by appointment. The largest concentrations of galleries are in the River North area and on Superior and Ontario streets east of Michigan Avenue. The Near North tour in this chapter points out many of the buildings that house galleries. Because the galleries and their shows change frequently, the prospective visitor should consult the *Chicago Gallery News* for a full current listing.

Churches, Temples, and Mosques

For many decades the immigrants who settled in Chicago came principally from Ireland, Germany, Italy, and the Catholic countries of Eastern Europe. They struggled to build temples to their faith in the new neighborhoods, and churches where the faithful could be uplifted and carried away from the often grinding struggles of their daily lives. As new waves of immigrants arrived, the churches became places where the ethnic community gathered to reinforce its cultural and artistic traditions as well as its faith. In this sense, it has been observed that the history of Chicago's churches is the history of the city.

Today many of the exquisite churches and the historical repositories they represent are threatened; indeed, the churches may have fulfilled their function and outlived it, for the communities they were meant to serve are gone. It is rumored that as many as 25 old neighborhood ethnic churches may be demolished over the next 10 years. Ironically, while churches in the ethnic neighborhoods languish, others—the Fourth Presbyterian Church on Michigan Avenue's Magnificent Mile, for example—whose congregations are well able to support them, are threatened because of the tremendous underlying value of the property on which they stand.

Many of Chicago's most beautiful churches may not be around much longer, and the wise visitor will take the opportunity to see these treasures while it is still possible. Always remember to call ahead before planning to visit a church; economic constraints have forced many churches to restrict the hours during which they are open to the public.

Baha'i House of Worship (Chapter 9, Excursions from Chicago)

Bond Chapel (Tour 3: Hyde Park and Kenwood)

Fourth Presbyterian Church (Tour 5: Near North)

Holy Name Cathedral (Tour 5: Near North)

Holy Trinity Cathedral (1121 N. Leavitt Ave., tel. 312/486–6064). This Russian Orthodox church was designed by Louis Sullivan, who also did the Carson Pirie Scott building. It is said that Czar Nicholas of Russia contributed $4,000 to the construction. The interior, elaborately detailed and filled with icons, contains no pews; worshipers stand during the services.

Midwest Buddhist Temple (Tour 6: Lincoln Park)

Moody Memorial Church (Tour 6: Lincoln Park)

Nativity of the Blessed Virgin Mary Ukrainian Catholic Church (4952 S. Paulina St., tel. 312/737–0733). Note the Byzantine domes. The interior is richly ornamented with murals, icons, chandeliers, and stained glass.

Old St. Patrick Church (718 W. Adams St., tel. 312/782–6171). This is the oldest church in Chicago; built in 1852–1856, it withstood the Chicago Fire. Located just west of the west Loop redevelopment area and the huge Presidential Towers highrise development, Old St. Patrick's is in the happy (and unusual) situation of finding its membership increasing. The towers, one Romanesque and one Byzantine, are symbolic of West and East.

Our Lady of Mt. Carmel Church (690 W. Belmont Ave., tel. 312/525–0453). Mother church for the north side Catholic parishes, Mt. Carmel is a serene oasis in the midst of urban cacophony.

Rockefeller Memorial Chapel (Tour 3: Hyde Park and Kenwood)

St. Alphonsus Redemptorist Church (1429 W. Wellington Ave., tel. 312/525–0709). Having originally served a German neighborhood, the Gothic St. Alphonsus is now in the heart of the redeveloping Lincoln Park. The beautiful interior has a vaulted ceiling and stained glass.

St. Basil Church (1824 W. Garfield Blvd., tel. 312/925–6311). Originally an Irish church, St. Basil's congregation tried unsuccessfully to stave off the white flight that hit this west side neighborhood in the 1960s.

St. Clement's Church (642 W. Deming Pl., tel. 312/281–0371). Combining both Roman and Byzantine elements in its design, St. Clement's has beautiful mosaics and lavish stained glass.

St. Gabriel Church (4522 S. Wallace, tel. 312/268–9595). Situated in the heart of the Irish Bridgeport neighborhood, St. Gabriel was designed more than 100 years ago by Daniel Burnham and John Root. Unlike many of Chicago's neighborhoods, Bridgeport has remained the Irish community it was 100 years ago, despite expansionist pressures from Hispanic Pilsen to the northwest and Chinatown to the northeast.

St. James Cathedral (Tour 5: Near North)

St. Michael's Church (Tour 6: Lincoln Park)

St. Michael's Italian Roman Catholic Church (2325 W. 24th Pl., tel. 312/847–2727). The beautifully ornate St. Michael's is now in a Hispanic parish in the neighborhood of Pilsen.

St. Nicholas Ukrainian Catholic Cathedral (2238 W. Rice St., tel. 312/276–4537). The Byzantine St. Nicholas is situated in the heart of Ukrainian Village, an ethnic enclave.

St. Thomas the Apostle (Tour 3: Hyde Park and Kenwood)

Second Presbyterian Church (1936 S. Michigan Ave., tel. 312/225–4951). Located in a black neighborhood just south of Downtown South, this handsome Victorian church endured years of struggles to stay afloat. The church has lovely stained glass, and oak is used lavishly throughout the interior.

Unity Temple. (Chapter 9, Excursions from Chicago)

Parks and Gardens

Thanks to the Lakefront Protection Ordinance, most of Chicago's more than 20 miles of lakefront is parkland or beach reserved for public use. Visitors to the city tend to concentrate on the lakefront, even though the Chicago Park District maintains hundreds of parks in neighborhoods throughout the city.

Chicago Botanic Garden (Chapter 9, Excursions from Chicago)

Garfield Park Conservatory, perhaps the largest in the world, keeps more than 5 acres of plants and flowers indoors in near-tropical conditions throughout the year. Here are a palm house, a fern house, an aeroid house (which includes such plants as dieffenbachia and antherium), and others. By car, take I–290 (Eisenhower Expressway) to Independence Boulevard. Turn right onto Independence and go north to Lake Street. Turn right on Lake Street and left at the first traffic light. *300 N. Central Park Blvd., tel. 312/533–1281. Admission free. Open daily 9–5, with extended hours during shows.*

Grant Park (Tour 2: Downtown South)

Jackson Park, just south of the Museum of Science and Industry, features an island known as Wooded Island and a Japanese Garden with authentic Japanese statuary.

Lincoln Park (Tour 6: Lincoln Park)

Morton Arboretum (Chapter 9, Excursions from Chicago)

Zoos

Brookfield Zoo (Chapter 9, Excursions from Chicago)

Lincoln Park Zoo (Tour 6: Lincoln Park)

4 Shopping

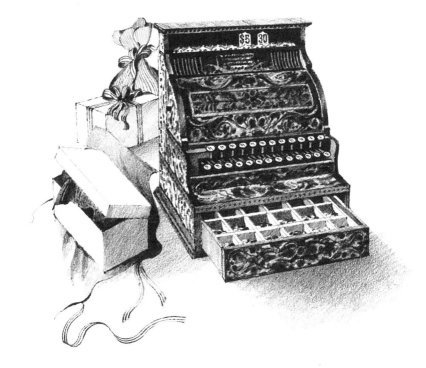

Updated by Mary Wagner

Chicago is a shopper's smorgasbord, serving up something for every taste and pocketbook. You can select from a host of possibilities, ranging from tony purveyors of clothing and jewelry rivaling the wares of Rodeo Drive to bargain-packed discount outlets. Most major credit cards are welcome, as are traveler's checks in most stores. An 8.75% state and county sales tax is added to all purchases except groceries and prescription drugs.

Many stores, particularly on north Michigan Avenue and the north side, are open on Sunday; call ahead for Sunday hours.

The Reader, a free weekly paper available in stores and restaurants in the downtown, Near North Side, Lincoln Park, and Hyde Park areas, carries ads for smaller shops. Sales at the large department stores are advertised in the *Chicago Tribune* and the *Chicago Sun-Times.*

There are far too many stores in Chicago to attempt a complete or fully descriptive listing here. The following pages offer a general overview of the more popular shopping areas and list some of the stores where certain items can be found. If you're looking for something in particular, check the Yellow Pages classified phone directory, but if you have no concrete shopping goals, simply choose any one of the major shopping districts and browse to your heart's content.

Major Shopping Districts

The Loop—the region so named for the elevated train track that encircles it—is the heart of Chicago business and finance. The city's two largest department stores, Marshall Field's & Co. and Carson Pirie Scott, anchor the Loop's State Street–Wabash Avenue area, which has declined since the years when it was known as "State Street, that great street." (Four of State Street's largest retailers—Sears, Montgomery Ward, Wieboldt's, and Goldblatt's—have closed their doors in the last decade.) Several Loop buildings, including the Stevens Building (17 N. State St.) and the Mallers Building (5 S. Wabash Ave.), contain groups of small shops on their upper floors, and there are a number of interesting specialty stores on the west end of the Loop. Most stores in the Loop are closed on Sunday except during the Christmas season.

The Magnificent Mile, Chicago's most glamorous shopping district, stretches along Michigan Avenue from the Chicago River (400 N.) to Oak Street (1000 N.). The street is lined on both sides with some of the most sophisticated names in retailing: Tiffany (715 N.), Gucci (900 N.), Chanel (990 N.), and Ralph Lauren (960 N.), to name just a few. Look on the Mag Mile for stores offering clothing, shoes, jewelry, and accessories, as well as for several art galleries.

Aside from dozens of designer shops, Michigan Avenue also features three "vertical malls." **Water Tower Place** (835 N. Michigan Ave.) contains branches of Lord & Taylor and Marshall Field's, as well as seven floors of specialty stores. Branches of national chains, such as The Gap, Banana Republic, The Limited, Casual Corner, Hoffritz for Cutlery, Benetton, and Rizzoli Books are all represented; the Ritz-Carlton Hotel sits atop the entire complex.

Shopping North

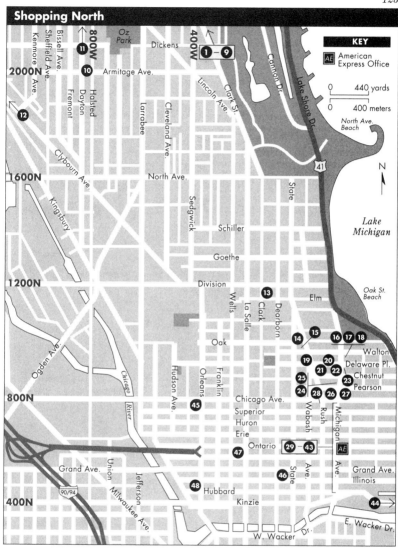

KEY

AE American Express Office

0 — 440 yards
0 — 400 meters

Abraham Lincoln Bookstore, **45**
Accent Chicago, **27**
The Alley, **6**
Ann Taylor, **14, 29**
Bally, **17**
Barney's, **15**
Bloomingdale's, **21**
Brittany Ltd., **16**
The Chalet, **19**
Chernin's, **11**
The City of Chicago Store, **44**
Cole-Haan, **35**
Convito Italiano, **21**

Crate & Barrel, **38**
FAO Schwarz, **25**
Flashy Trash, **7**
Florsheim, **36**
Florsheim Thayer McNeill, **31**
Hammacher Schlemmer, **37**
Hanig, **34**
Hello Chicago, **42**
Henri Bendel, **20**
Herman's, **26**
Jazz Record Mart, **46**
Land's End Outlet, **22**
Le Grand Tour, **3**

Lori's Discount Designer Shoes, **10**
Mark Shale, **18**
MC/Mages Sports, **47**
Neiman Marcus, **30**
Nike Town, **40**
Nuts on Clark, **1**
People Like Us Books, **8**
Rand McNally, **39**
Reckless, **9**
Saks Fifth Avenue, **26**
The Season's Best, **43**
Sony, **41**
Sportmart, **4, 48**

The Stars Our Destination, **5**
Stuart Brent, **33**
Tiffany & Co., **32**
The Tourist Information Center, **24**
Tower Records/Video/ Books, **2**
Treasure Island, **13**
Waterstone's Booksellers, **23**
Williams-Sonoma, **22**
Wolf Camera and Video, **28**

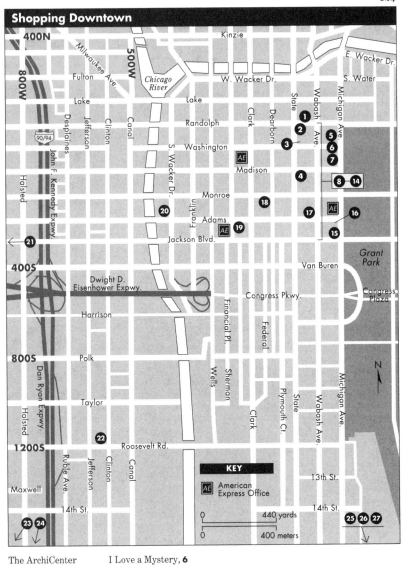

Shopping Downtown

The ArchiCenter
Store, **15**

The Art Institute, **16**

Bennett Brothers, **17**

Brooks
Brothers, **7, 19**

Capper & Capper, **10**

Carl Fischer, **14**

Carson Pirie Scott, **4**

Central Camera, **13**

Chernin's, **22**

Crate & Barrel, **9**

Eddie Bauer, **8**

57th Street Books, **25**

Helix, **21**

I Love a Mystery, **6**

Jos. A. Bank, **3**

Kroch's &
Brentano's, **11**

Marshall Field's, **2**

Powell's, **26**

Rand McNally, **20**

Rose Records, **12**

Savvy Traveller, **5**

Sears, **24**

Seno Formalwear, **1**

The Sharper Image, **18**

Spiegel, **23**

University of Chicago
Bookstore, **27**

The **Avenue Atrium** (900 N. Michigan Ave.) houses the Chicago branches of Bloomingdale's and Henri Bendel, along with dozens of smaller boutiques and specialty stores. Generally, the merchandise found here is more sophisticated, and more expensive, than in Water Tower Place. The Atrium also has a hotel on top—the lavish Four Seasons. The restaurants and movie theaters found in both malls are a good option for entertainment during inclement weather. The third, **Chicago Place** (700 N. Michigan Ave.), has Saks Fifth Avenue, women's clothiers Ann Taylor and Talbots, along with many specialty stores and a food court on the top floor.

There's another cluster of shops at the **Merchandise Mart,** including a branch of Carson Pirie Scott.

Oak Street, between Michigan Avenue and Rush Street, is populated with stores selling designer clothing and European imports. Designers with Oak Street addresses include Giorgio Armani (113 E. Oak St.), Gianni Versace (101 E. Oak St.), Sonia Rykiel (106 E. Oak St.), and Ultimo (114 E. Oak St.).

The upscale residential neighborhoods of **Lincoln Park** and, to the north, **Lakeview** offer several worthwhile shopping strips. **Clark Street** between Armitage (2000 N.) and Diversey (2800 N.) avenues is home to a number of clothing boutiques and specialty stores. The shopping continues north of Diversey Avenue to School Street (3300 N.), with several large antiques stores, more boutiques, and some bookstores. **Broadway** between Diversey Avenue and Addison Street (3600 N.) also offers a variety of shops. The **Century Mall,** in a former movie palace at Clark Street, Broadway, and Diversey Parkway, houses a variety of national outlets and small specialty stores. Take the Clark Street bus (No. 22) at Dearborn Street or the Broadway bus (No. 36) at State Street north to reach this neighborhood.

The **North Pier** development, on the lake, at 435 E. Illinois St. is teeming with fascinating small shops, including a seashell store, a hologram showroom, and a store in which you can record your own music video.

Contained by the Chicago River on the south and west, Clark Street on the east, and Oak Street on the north, **River North** boasts a profusion of art galleries, furnishing stores, and boutiques. The *Chicago Gallery News,* available from the tourist information center at the Water Tower (Michigan Ave. and Pearson St.), provides an up-to-date listing of current art gallery exhibits.

Chicago is famed for its wealth of ethnic neighborhoods, allowing visitors to shop the globe without actually leaving the city. Here are three popular ones: **Chinatown** has a dozen or more shops along a four-block stretch of Wentworth Avenue south of Cermak Road. The range of Far Eastern imports ranges from jade to ginseng root to junk. The **northside Lincoln Square neighborhood,** a stretch of Lincoln Avenue between Leland and Lawrence avenues, offers German delis, imported toys, and European-made health and beauty products. And many non-U.S. visitors make the trek to a cluster of dingy but well-stocked electronics stores in an Indian neighborhood on the city's far north side, on Devon Avenue between Western and Washtenaw avenues, to buy electronic appliances that run on 220-volt currency. Because the United States has no value-added tax—as of yet—it's often cheaper for international visitors to buy here than at home.

Department Stores

Bloomingdale's (900 N. Michigan Ave., tel. 312/440–4460). Unlike both its Michigan Avenue neighbors and its New York City sibling, this branch of Bloomie's, built in a clean, airy style that is part Prairie School and part postmodern, gives you plenty of elbow room to sift through its selection of designer labels. The adjacent six-floor Avenue Atrium offers a profusion of specialty stores and boutiques.

Carson Pirie Scott (1 S. State St., tel. 312/641–7000). Second only to Field's for many years, Carson's was operating at a loss when it was acquired in 1989 by P.A. Bergner, a Milwaukee-based retail chain. Though the main floor of this venerable Chicago emporium is looking a bit tired, it still carries a full line of clothing, housewares, accessories, cosmetics, and more. The building itself, the work of famed Chicago architect Louis Sullivan, is protected by landmark status. It's worth visiting just to see the northwest door at the corner of State and Madison streets; the iron scrollwork here shows Sullivan at his most ornate.

Marshall Field's & Co. (111 N. State St., at the corner of Randolph St., tel. 312/781–1000). Though there are branches at several other locations in Chicago and its suburbs, the State Street Field's is the granddaddy of them all. Founder Marshall Field's catchphrase was "Give the lady what she wants!" and, for many years both ladies and gentlemen have been able to find everything they want, from furs to riding boots to padded hangers, on one of Field's nine floors. After a period of decline, Field's recently completed a $110-million renovation that has glamorously restored the building to its original splendor. The bargain basement has been replaced with "Down Under," a series of small boutiques that sell clothing, luggage, picture frames, Chicago memorabilia, and Field's famous Frango mints, which many consider to be Chicago's greatest edible souvenirs. You'll find restaurants on the seventh floor and in the basement. Architecture buffs will admire the Tiffany glass dome that tops the store's southwest atrium. Usually closed Sundays, Field's State Street store holds a monthly "Super Sunday" affair featuring superdeep discounts. Call for exact dates.

Neiman Marcus (737 N. Michigan Ave., tel. 312/642–5900). Neiman's prices may be steep, but browsing here is fun. Be sure to take a look at the graceful four-story wood sculpture that rises between the escalators of this branch of the famous upscale Dallas department store.

Saks Fifth Avenue (700 N. Michigan Ave., tel. 312/944–6500) is a smaller and less elaborate cousin to the original New York store. It offers the same upscale men's and women's clothing.

Specialty Stores

Books
General Interest
Kroch's & Brentano's (29 S. Wabash St., tel. 312/332–7500). The most comprehensive branch of this local chain, the Wabash Street flagship store will special-order any book. The city's largest selection of technical books shares the lower level with an impressive paperback department. Upstairs, Kroch's col-

lection of hardcover books is extensive and includes several sale tables of remaindered and slightly damaged books. There's a foreign-language department on the mezzanine and a large selection of magazines and newspapers.

57th Street Books (1301 E. 57th St., tel. 312/684–1300). Wood floors, brick walls, and books from the popular to the esoteric distinguish this Hyde Park institution. An excellent place to while away the hours on a rainy Sunday afternoon.

Stuart Brent (670 N. Michigan Ave., tel. 312/337–6357). A Chicago literary landmark, Stuart Brent carries an extensive and tasteful, if sometimes quirky, collection of hardcover and paperback books, as well as a good selection of music and art books. The walls are covered with photographs of well-known authors posing with owner Mr. Brent, who for years has been prominent in the Chicago literary scene.

University of Chicago Bookstore (970 E. 58th St., tel. 312/702–8729). Aside from the expected selection of textbooks, this bookstore also carries many works of general interest, with an emphasis on cooking and computer books. Closed Sunday.

Waterstone's Booksellers (840 N. Michigan Ave., tel. 312/587–8080). This branch of the renowned British chain has more than 100,000 titles and an entire floor of fiction.

Specialty **I Love a Mystery** (55 E. Washington St., tel. 312/236–1338). This shop specializes in—you guessed it—mysteries.

Le Grand Tour (3229 N. Clark St., tel. 312/929–1836). Foreign-language books are the specialty here, but there's a large selection of English volumes and an eclectic assortment of periodicals, as well. There's also a great selection of travel books.

People like Us Books (3321 N. Clark St., tel. 312/248–6363). Here you'll discover a wide selection of gay and lesbian books and periodicals.

Rand McNally (150 S. Wacker Dr., tel. 312/332–2009 and 444 N. Michigan Ave., tel. 312/321–1751). Maps for everywhere from Manhattan to the moon, as well as travel books and globes, are available in abundance here.

Savvy Traveller (upstairs at 50 E. Washington St., tel. 312/263–2100). Aside from a full range of travel books, the Savvy Traveller also carries a number of odds and ends that can come in handy on the road.

The Stars Our Destination (1021 W. Belmont Ave., tel. 312/871–2722). Science fiction fans will find a large selection of their favorites, along with the latest news on local sci-fi happenings.

Used **Abraham Lincoln Bookstore** (357 W. Chicago Ave., tel. 312/944–3085). Civil War buffs will want to visit this shop, which specializes in Lincolniana and Civil War books.

Powell's (1501 E. 57th St., tel. 312/955–7780). Powell's Hyde Park store has one of the largest and most diverse selections of used books in town.

Camera and Electronic Equipment **Central Camera** (230 S. Wabash Ave., tel. 312/427–5580). This store, stocked to the rafters with cameras and darkroom equipment, is a Loop institution.

Helix (310 S. Racine St., tel. 312/421–6000). Off the beaten track in a neighborhood west of the Loop, this warehouse store sells and rents all manner of camera and darkroom paraphernalia at competitive prices. A good selection of used equipment is also available. Helix has two smaller branches in the Loop, at 70 West Madison Street (tel. 312/444–9373) and 440 South La Salle Street (tel. 312/663–3650).

Wolf Camera and Video (750 N. Rush St., tel. 312/943–5531). A block west of Michigan Avenue, there's a great array of film and cameras, and one-hour film processing is available daily.

Catalogue Stores/Factory Outlets **Bennett Brothers** (30 E. Adams St., tel. 312/263–4800). Primarily a catalogue store, Bennett's sells jewelry, silverware, kitchen appliances, cameras, and electronic equipment at discount prices. The store's second-floor showroom displays some of the merchandise available in the catalogue.

Land's End Outlet (men's, 2241 N. Elston Ave., tel. 312/276–2232; women's, 2317 N. Elston Ave., tel. 312/384–4170). This Wisconsin mail-order firm sells casual and business wear, luggage, housewares, and outdoor gear. The quality of the stock may be inconsistent at these outlet stores, but the discount savings can be considerable.

Sony (663 N. Michigan Ave., tel. 312/573–0059) sells electronics in a rarified atmosphere of almost hushed elegance.

Spiegel (1105 W. 35th St., tel. 312/254–0091) and **Sears** (5555 S. Archer Ave., tel. 312/284–3200) both operate warehouse stores on the city's south side. The two famous mail-order establishments have ever-changing inventories of clothing, appliances, and housewares, and can offer fabulous bargains to the sharp-eyed and flexible shopper. Don't expect elegant surroundings or helpful salespeople, and do check your merchandise thoroughly before you take it home.

Clothing The major department stores are good sources of mainstream sportswear, and the smaller boutiques of the Avenue Atrium, Water Tower Place, River North, Oak Street, and Lincoln Park can provide you with more unique designer clothing.

Business Clothing **Brooks Brothers** (209 S. La Salle St., tel. 312/263–0100 and 713 N. Michigan Ave., tel. 312/915–0060), **Capper & Capper** (1 N. Wabash Ave., tel. 312/236–3800), **Brittany Ltd.** (999 N. Michigan Ave., tel. 312/642–6550), and **Mark Shale** (919 N. Michigan Ave., tel. 312/440–0720): All four of these stores are good sources of high-quality business attire.

Jos. A. Bank (25 E. Washington St., tel. 312/782–4432), which is its own manufacturer, offers high-quality business attire for about 10%–15% less than you'll find elsewhere.

Men's **Barney's** (25 E. Oak St., tel. 312/587–1700) is a smaller version of the New York store that's a paean to high style in men's and women's fashions.

Women's **Ann Taylor** (103 E. Oak St., tel. 312/943–5411 and Chicago Place, 700 N. Michigan Ave., tel. 312/335–0117) offers a selection of classic, upscale women's wear.

Henri Bendel (900 N. Michigan Ave., tel. 312/642–0140) is an excellent source for high-priced, high-style women's clothes and accessories.

Vintage **The Alley** (858 W. Belmont St., tel. 312/883–1800). You'll find some secondhand denim here and a great selection of alternative fashion.

Flashy Trash (3524 N. Halstead St., tel. 312/327–6900). Come on in to browse through several generations of styles at bargain prices.

Food **The Chalet** (40 E. Delaware Pl., tel. 312/787–8555). This store is one of a chain that has several branches on the near north and north sides. All stores offer a large selection of wines, beers, cheeses, coffee, and other gourmet items.

Convito Italiano (11 E. Chestnut St., tel. 312/943–2983). Both a restaurant and an Italian food shop, Convito Italiano sells olive oil in porcelain vessels, an array of wines, Saronno biscuits, cookbooks, and enormous selection of pastas, and ready-to-eat carryout items. Elegant party trays can be ordered.

Nuts on Clark (3830 N. Clark St., tel. 312/549–6622). This warehouse, located just a few blocks from Wrigley Field, displays bins full of nuts, as well as an assortment of candies, spices, jams and jellies, coffee, tea, mustards, and more.

Treasure Island (75 W. Elm St., tel. 312/440–1144, and 680 N. Lake Shore Dr., tel. 312/664–0400). This Chicago institution is a combination supermarket/gourmet store. Any of its branches is ideal for buying the makings for a gourmet picnic or an elegant, edible house gift.

Gifts Water Tower Place, the Avenue Atrium, Michigan Avenue, and the larger department stores are likely places to find gifts and toys. For artsy gifts with a twist, try the River North art galleries and boutiques.

The Sharper Image (55 W. Monroe St., tel. 312/263–4535) and **Hammacher Schlemmer** (618 N. Michigan Ave., tel. 312/664–9292). Both stores are great for browsing and can provide upscale gadgets and unusual gifts.

Tiffany & Co. (715 N. Michigan Ave., tel. 312/944–7500) is the spot for impeccably correct crystal, silver, and jewelry.

Kitchenware **Crate & Barrel** (101 N. Wabash Ave., tel. 312/372–0100, 646 N. Michigan Ave., tel. 312/787–5900. Warehouse store: 800 W. North Ave., tel. 312/787–4775). One of the first "lifestyle" cookware, glassware, and furniture stores, the Crate remains one of the best. There are large branches on Michigan Avenue and in the Loop and a warehouse store at North Avenue and Halsted Street where you may pick up a good bargain.

Williams-Sonoma (17 E. Chestnut St., tel. 312/642–1593; 700 N. Michigan Ave., tel. 312/787–8991). The selection of kitchenware and cookbooks is excellent, and if you're there during an equipment demonstration you get to taste the results.

Music **Carl Fischer** (312 S. Wabash Ave., tel. 312/427–6652). This venerable store carries the largest selection of piano, vocal, choral, and band sheet music in Chicago.

Jazz Record Mart (11 W. Grand Ave., tel. 312/222–1467). This specialty store stocks one of Chicago's largest collections of records, in addition to compact discs and tapes. Jazz and blues fanciers will find the rare and the obscure here.

Reckless (3157 N. Broadway, tel. 312/404–5080). This is one of the city's leading alternative and secondhand record stores.

Rose Records (214 S. Wabash Ave., tel. 312/987–9044). This chain's main store on Wabash Avenue has three floors of records, tapes, and compact discs. If you're looking for movie sound tracks or Broadway musicals, Rose has an exceptionally large selection. One entire floor is devoted to "cut-outs," budget labels, and other bargains.

Tower Records/Videos/Books (2301 N. Clark St., tel. 312/477–5994). Abandon hope, all ye (music fans) who enter here. Tower's selection of 150,000 titles is a surefire way to torpedo a vacation budget. Open until midnight.

Shoes There are a great many shoe stores along Michigan Avenue, including several in Water Tower Place. Large selections can be found at **Florsheim** (622 N. Michigan Ave., tel. 312/787–0779), **Florsheim Thayer McNeill** (727 N. Michigan Ave., tel. 312/649–9619), **Hanig** (660 N. Michigan Ave., tel. 312/642–5330), **Bally** (919 N. Michigan Ave., tel. 312/787–8110), **Cole-Haan** (645 N. Michigan Ave., tel. 312/642–8995), and **The Season's Best** (645 N. Michigan Ave., tel. 312/943–6161).

Chernin's (606 W. Roosevelt Rd., tel. 312/922–4545). Chicago's famous bargain shoe outlet is all that remains of a once flourishing Roosevelt Road shopping district. If you're in the market for lots of shoes, it may be worth a trip down here. There's a branch in Lincoln Park at 2665 North Halsted Street (tel. 312/404–0005).

Lori's Discount Designer Shoes (808 W. Armitage Ave., tel. 312/281–5655). Located in Lincoln Park, this store offers women's designer shoes below department store prices.

Souvenirs **The Tourist Information Center** (163 E. Pearson Ave., tel. 312/467–5305). This is an excellent source for postcards and souvenirs, as well as maps and city guides.

Accent Chicago (Water Tower Place, 835 N. Michigan Ave., 7th Floor, tel. 312/944–1354), **Down Under at Marshall Field's** (111 N. State St., basement, tel. 312/781–1000), and **Hello Chicago** (700 N. Michigan Ave., 8th floor, tel. 312/787–0838). All three are good spots to shop for Chicago memorabilia. Accent Chicago has branches at Sears Tower (tel. 312/993–0499) and the Chicago Hilton (tel. 312/360–0115).

The ArchiCenter Store (224 S. Michigan Ave., tel. 312/922–3432). A large selection of books, posters, T-shirts, toys, mugs, and other souvenirs with architectural themes can be found here.

The City of Chicago Store (435 E. Illinois St., tel. 312/467–1111). This shop carries merchandise from 35 of the city's cultural institutions and organizations, including the Art Institute and the Lincoln Park Zoo. There's also an eclectic collection of restored artifacts, such as traffic lights, ballot boxes, parking meters, and manhole covers, culled from 12 city departments.

The Art Institute (S. Michigan Ave. at Adams St., tel. 312/443–3535). There's no charge to enter the enormous gift shop, which has an extensive collection of museum reproductions in the form of posters, books, and more.

Sporting Goods **Eddie Bauer** (123 N. Wabash Ave., tel. 312/263–6005). You'll find clothing for the outdoors and some camping equipment at this chain's Wabash Avenue store. Another branch at Water Tower Place carries mostly sportswear.

Herman's (111 E. Chicago Ave., tel. 312/951–8282). Part of a national chain, Herman's carries a respectable selection of shoes, tennis rackets, golf clubs, skis, and workout wear.

MC/Mages Sports (620 N. La Salle St., tel. 312/337–6151). Be sure to look at the "Wall of Fame" outside the store that shows the handprints of famous Chicago sports figures such as baseball's Ryne Sandberg and hockey's Stan Mikita. Inside you will find six floors of reasonably priced sporting and camping equipment, shoes, and clothing.

Nike Town (669 N. Michigan Ave., tel. 312/642–6363) glorifies athletic shoes and the people who wear them in a store-as-entertainment setting.

Sportmart (3134 N. Clark St., tel. 312/871–8500 and 440 N. Orleans St., tel. 312/222–0900). These large emporia, one in Lakeview and the other in River North, offer low prices and good selections as long as you're not looking for uncommon sizes.

Toys **FAO Schwarz** (840 N. Michigan Ave., tel. 312/587–5000) is a fantasy toy emporium that's only a little smaller than the chain's New York flagship.

5 Sports, Fitness, Beaches

Participant Sports and Fitness

Bicycling The lakefront bicycle path extends about 20 miles along Chicago's lakefront, offering a variety of scenic views. The prospect of the harbor, created with landfill a few years ago when Lake Shore Drive's notorious S-curve between Monroe Street and Wacker Drive was straightened, is lovely. Be careful: A few blocks to the north, Grand Avenue is one of a few places along the route where the path crosses a city street (two others are parallel to Lake Shore Drive in the downtown area). Rent a bike for the day as you enter Lincoln Park at Fullerton Avenue or from **Village Cycle Center** (1337 N. Wells St., tel. 312/751–2488). **Turin Bicycles** (435 E. Illinois St., tel. 312/923–0100) at North Pier also rents bikes by the hour or the day. There are many other scenic routes in the Chicago area. For information, contact the **Chicagoland Bicycle Federation** (Box 64396, Chicago, IL 60664, tel. 312/427–3325).

Boating The lakefront harbors are packed with boats, but if you're not familiar with Great Lakes sailing, it's best to leave the navigating to an experienced skipper. Sailboat lessons and rentals are available from the **Chicago Sailing Club** (Belmont Harbor, tel. 312/871–7245) or **Sailboats Inc.** (400 E. Randolph St., tel. 312/861–1757). Plenty of folks stand ready to charter boats if you're interested in fishing for coho or chinook salmon, trout, or perch. Call the **Chicago Sportfishing Association** (Burnham Harbor, tel. 312/922–1100).

For a more placid water outing, try the paddleboats at Lincoln Park Lagoon. Rentals are located at the lagoon just north of Farm-in-the-Zoo.

Golfing The Chicago Park District (tel. 312/753–8670) maintains six golf courses, five of them with nine holes and one (Jackson Park) with 18, and two driving ranges, one in Jackson Park and one at Lake Shore Drive and Diversey Avenue (where there is a miniature 18-hole course). The Jackson Park facilities are located two and three blocks east of Stony Island Avenue at 63rd Street.

Suburban Chicago abounds with public golf courses—more than 125 of them, with greens fees ranging from $10 to nearly $100. Most accept reservations up to a week in advance; some require a credit card deposit. Following are a few of the more highly rated ones. **Cantigny** (27 W. 270 Mack Rd., Wheaton, tel. 708/668–8463) won *Golf Digest*'s 1989 "Best New Public Course of the Year" award. A wealth of mature trees await you on each of Cantigny's 27 holes. **Cog Hill Golf and Country Club** (12294 Archer Ave., Lemont, tel. 312/242–1717 or 708/257–5872), with four different 18-hole courses, hosts the PGA tour's Western Open in early July. **Kemper Lakes** (Old McHenry Rd., Long Grove, tel. 708/540–3450) is one of the region's most expensive courses ($95 with mandatory cart rental included) and is the only local public course to have hosted a major PGA championship. **Village Links of Glen Ellyn** (220 S. Park Blvd., Glen Ellyn, tel. 708/469–8180) has 27 holes and a driving range.

Ice Skating During the winter months there is ice skating at the **Daley Bicentennial Plaza,** Randolph Street at Lake Shore Drive. A small fee is charged, and skate rentals are available (tel. 312/294–4790).

In-Line Skating In-line skating has become a popular lakefront pastime in recent years. You can rent blades from both branches of **Londo Mondo Motionwear** (247 E. Ontario St., tel. 312/751–1446; 1100 N. Dearborn St., tel. 312/751–2794). Rates are $7 per hour; $20 for 24 hours. There's also a rental stand during peak times (roughly Memorial Day through Labor Day and later if the weather's nice) near the North Avenue beach house, though hours are unpredictable. Keep to the right and watch your back for bicyclists. Stretches of bumpy pavement make wristguards, helmets, and kneepads a good idea.

Jogging The lakefront path accommodates both joggers and bicyclists, so you'll need to be attentive. You can pick up the path at Oak Street Beach (across from the Drake Hotel), at Grand Avenue underneath Lake Shore Drive, or by going through Grant Park on Monroe Street or Jackson Boulevard until you reach the lakefront.

On the lakefront path, joggers should stay north of McCormick Place; muggers sometimes lurk in the comparatively empty stretch between the convention center and Hyde Park. Loop streets are a little spooky after dark and too crowded during the day for useful running. In the Near North, joggers will want to stay east of Orleans Street.

Swimming Lake Michigan provides wonderful swimming opportunities between Memorial Day and Labor Day, particularly toward the end of the summer, when the lake has warmed up (*see* Beaches, *below*).

Tennis The Chicago Park District maintains hundreds of tennis courts, most of which can be used free of charge. The facility at the **Daley Bicentennial Plaza,** Randolph Street at Lake Shore Drive, is the closest to downtown and Near North hotels; it's a lighted facility that can be used at night; there is a modest hourly fee; and reservations are required (tel. 312/294–4790). The **Grant Park** tennis courts, at 9th Street and Columbus Drive (between Michigan Avenue and Lake Shore Drive), are also lighted, and there is a modest fee; reservations are not required.

Spectator Sports

Chicago's loyal sports fans turn out regularly, year after year, to watch what are not the most winning teams in professional sports (with the exception, in recent years, of the Chicago Bulls). At press time, the Cubs and the White Sox were continuing their standard pattern of mediocrity punctuated by the occasional brief winning streak. The White Sox won a lone division championship during the 1980s, and the Cubs won two, though neither was able to capture a league title.

Baseball The **Chicago Cubs** (National League) play at Wrigley Field (1060 W. Addison St., tel. 312/404–2827); the baseball season begins early in April and ends the first weekend in October. Wrigley Field is reached by the Howard Street El line; take the B train to Addison Street. Wrigley Field finally received lights in 1988, the last major-league ballpark in the nation to be lighted for night games. But the Cubs still play most of their home games during the day, and the bleachers are a great place to get a tan while listening to Chicagoans taunt the visiting outfielders. The grandstand offers a more sedate atmosphere. Most games start at 1:20 PM, but call for exact starting times.

The **Chicago White Sox** (American League) play at Comiskey Park (333 W. 35th St., tel. 312/924–1000 or 312/559–1212 for ticket information). Games usually start at 7:30 PM. Take an A or B Dan Ryan El train to 35th Street.

Basketball The **Chicago Bulls** play at the Chicago Stadium (1800 W. Madison St., tel. 312/943–5800 or 312/559–1212 for ticket information); the basketball season extends from November to May, and games usually start at 7:30 PM. Avoid leaving the game early or wandering around this neighborhood at night.

Football The **Chicago Bears** play at Soldier Field (425 E. McFetridge Dr., tel. 312/663–5100) from August (preseason) through January (postseason, if they're lucky). While subscription sales generally account for all tickets, you can sometimes buy the tickets of a subscriber who can't use them at the stadium shortly before game time. To reach Soldier Field, take the Jeffery Express (No. 6) bus to Roosevelt Road and Lake Shore Drive and follow the crowd. The stadium is just south of the Field Museum of Natural History.

Hockey The **Chicago Blackhawks** play at the Chicago Stadium (1800 W. Madison St., tel. 312/733–5300) from October to April. Games usually start at 7:30 PM. Again, avoid leaving the game early or wandering around the neighborhood at night.

Horse Racing Hawthorne Race Course (3501 S. Laramie Ave., tel. 708/780–3700), just beyond the Chicago city limits in Cicero, features **flat racing** October–December.

Arlington Park has **flat racing** May–October (N. Wilke Rd. at West Euclid Ave., Arlington Heights, tel. 708/255–4300). Sportsman's Park (3301 S. Laramie Ave., tel. 312/242–1121) has **flat racing** February–May and **harness racing** May–October. Maywood Park (North and Fifth Aves. in Maywood, tel. 708/343–4800 or 312/626–4816), has **harness racing** February–May and October–December.

Beaches

Chicago has some 20 miles of lakefront, most of it sand or rock beach. Beaches are open to the public daily 9 AM–9:30 PM, Memorial Day–Labor Day, and many beaches have changing facilities. The **Chicago Park District** (tel. 312/294–2333) provides lifeguard protection during daylight hours throughout the swimming season. The water is too cold for swimming at other times of the year.

Along the lakefront you'll see plenty of broken-rock breakwaters that warn "no swimming or diving." Although natives frequently ignore these signs, you should heed them: The boulders below the water are slippery with seaweed and may hide sharp, rusty scraps of metal, and the water beyond is very deep. It can be dangerous even if you know the territory.

Oak Street Beach (600–1600 N.) is probably Chicago's most popular, particularly in the 1000 North area, where the shoreline curves. You can expect it to be mobbed with trendy singles and people-watchers on any warm day in summer. There are bathrooms here, but for changing facilities you'll have to make the walk to the North Avenue Beach bathhouse. The concrete breakwater that makes up the southern part of Oak Street Beach is a popular promenade on hot summer nights. You can walk along the water all the way to Grand Avenue, where you'll find both Navy Pier and Olive Park.

North Avenue Beach (1600–2400 N.) is heavily used; the crowd tends to be more family oriented than the crowd at Oak Street Beach. There are bathrooms, changing facilities, and showers. The southern end of this beach features lively volleyball action during the summer and fall.

South Shore Country Club Beach (7100 S.), Chicago's newest and one of the nicest beaches, is quite pretty and not over-crowded. There are bathrooms, changing facilities, and showers. Enter through the South Shore Country Club grounds at 71st Street and South Shore Drive; you may see the police training their horses in the entry area.

Other Chicago beaches are:
Foster Beach (5200 N.), changing facilities.
Jackson Beach, Central (5700–5900 S.), changing facilities.
Leone/Loyola Beach (6700–7800 N.), changing facilities.
Montrose Beach (4400 N.), changing facilities.
12th Street Beach (1200 S. at 900 E., just south of the planetarium), changing facilities.
31st Street Beach (3100 S.), changing facilities.

6 Dining

*The restaurants
were selected by
Phil Vettel,
restaurant critic of
the* Chicago
Tribune.

However you judge a city's restaurant scene—by ethnic diversity, breadth and depth of high-quality establishments, or nationally prominent chefs—Chicago ranks as one of the nation's finest restaurant towns. Here you'll find innovative hot spots, lovingly maintained traditional establishments, and everything in-between.

Chicago's more than 7,000 restaurants range from those ranked among the best in the nation—and priced accordingly—to simple, storefront ethnic eateries and old-fashioned pubs offering good food in unpretentious settings at modest prices. Our listing includes the restaurants we recommend as the best within each price range.

It's wise to reserve ahead; many restaurants require reservations, and at others, no reservation means a long wait for a table. Ordinarily, reservations can be made a day or two ahead, or even on the afternoon of the same day, but securing a table at the more popular restaurants may take more planning, especially on weekend evenings. Some of the trendiest restaurants don't accept reservations; at such places, a wait of an hour or more on weekends is common.

As a rule, you should expect to tip 15% in restaurants in the Inexpensive and Moderate price categories. The Chicago meal tax is 8 1/2%, and you can double that amount for a 17% tip when you feel generous and don't want to have to do higher math. Expensive and Very Expensive restaurants have more service personnel per table, who must divide the tip, so it's appropriate to leave 20%, depending on the quality of the service. An especially helpful wine steward should be acknowledged with $2 or $3.

This guide divides the restaurants of Chicago into three areas, each with its own dining map that locates the restaurants: (1) Near North, River North, and Lincoln Park; (2) North; and (3) Downtown and South. Several noteworthy suburban restaurants appear at the end, with no map. Within each area, the restaurants are grouped by type of cuisine. Restaurants serve lunch and dinner daily except where noted. And casual attire is fine, except where noted.

Restaurant price categories are based on the average cost of a dinner that includes appetizer, entrée, salad, and dessert. Prices are for one person, food alone, not including alcoholic beverages, tax, and tip.

The following credit card abbreviations are used: AE, American Express; D, Discover; DC, Diners Club; MC, MasterCard; V, Visa.

Highly recommended restaurants are indicated by a star ★.

Category	Cost*
Very Expensive	over $45
Expensive	$30–$45
Moderate	$18–$30
Inexpensive	under $18

*per person, excluding drinks, service, and sales tax (8 1/2%)

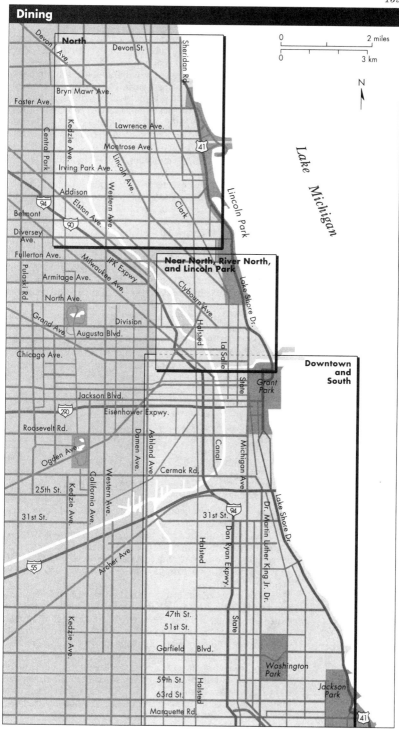

Dining

North

Devon St.

Devon Ave.

Bryn Mawr Ave.

Foster Ave.

Central Park

Kedzie Ave.

Lawrence Ave.

Montrose Ave.

Irving Park Ave.

Lincoln Ave.

Western Ave.

Addison

Elston Ave.

Belmont

Diversey Ave.

Fullerton Ave.

Pulaski Rd.

Armitage Ave.

Milwaukee Ave.

North Ave.

Grand Ave.

Division

Augusta Blvd.

Chicago Ave.

Jackson Blvd.

Eisenhower Expwy.

Roosevelt Rd.

Ogden Ave.

Damen Ave.

Ashland Ave.

Kedzie Ave.

California Ave.

Western Ave.

Cermak Rd.

Canal

25th St.

31st St.

Archer Ave.

47th St.

51st St.

Garfield Blvd.

59th St.

63rd St.

Marquette Rd.

Kedzie Ave.

Halsted

Dan Ryan Expwy.

State

Michigan Ave.

Dr. Martin Luther King Jr. Dr.

Lake Shore Dr.

Washington Park

Jackson Park

Near North, River North, and Lincoln Park

Clybourn Ave.

Halsted

La Salle

Lincoln Park

Sheridan Rd.

Clark

Lake Shore Dr.

Lake Michigan

Downtown and South

State

Grant Park

0 — 2 miles

0 — 3 km

N

Near North, River North, and Lincoln Park

American **Seasons.** This hotel restaurant has become a stop on the gourmet circuit thanks to the creativity of executive chef Mark Baker. New England and Asian influences give the creations here, such as papardelle with grilled Maine lobster and pesto-crusted rack of lamb, a distinct spark. The opulent dining room offers unmatched comfort and plenty of room to relax. Seasons also produces Chicago's best (and most expensive) Sunday brunch. *Four Seasons Hotel, 120 E. Delaware Pl., tel. 312/280–8800. Reservations strongly advised. AE, D, DC, MC, V. Very Expensive.*

★ **Charlie Trotter's.** This tastefully renovated town house accommodates only 20 closely spaced tables, serving many fewer people than would like to eat here. The owner and chef, Charlie Trotter, prepares the newest of new American cuisine with hints of Asian flavors incorporated into classic European dishes. Menus, which change daily, have included such appetizers as red snapper carpaccio with Asian noodle salad and sesame mayonnaise, and foie gras ravioli with mango and lemongrass sauce. Entrées have included mahimahi with leek and sorrel sauce and mushroom ravioli, garlic-laced veal chop with wild mushrooms and eggplant tartlet, and lasagna of sea scallops with squid-ink pasta and saffron sauce. It's a good idea to make reservations well in advance. *816 W. Armitage Ave., tel. 312/248–6228. Jacket required. Reservations required. AE, DC, MC, V. No lunch. Closed Sun., Mon. Expensive–Very Expensive.*

Arnie's. Stained glass, Tiffany lamps, and Art Deco accents are highlights of this venerable restaurant's decor. Various ethnic influences determine the appetizer and soup offerings; entrées are more dependably American, and beef dishes are always a good bet. Live music, from casual piano music to more complex acts, is a daily feature. *1030 N. State St., tel. 312/266–4800. Jacket and tie required. Reservations advised. AE, D, DC, MC, V. Closed Mon., Sat. lunch. Expensive.*

★ **Gordon.** For more than 16 years this has been one of the most innovative restaurants in Chicago. Gordon's kitchen features a light, uncomplicated cooking style, revealed in such dishes as crispy shallot ravioli and sherry-vinegar jus. The four-course prix-fixe dinner is a very good value. Desserts are outstanding, ranging far beyond the usual chocoholics-only selection. Half-size portions are also available. The restaurant's decor is rococo, with Oriental rugs, swag curtains alongside each table, and dark wood surrounding tables set with white cloths and centerpieces of fresh flowers. Service is exceptional here, and on weekends there's dancing. *500 N. Clark St., tel. 312/467–9780. Jacket required. Reservations required. AE, DC, MC, V. Closed holidays. Expensive.*

Michael Jordan's Restaurant. He defies gravity, he wins championships, and now...he slings hash. Michael Jordan's Restaurant, which opened during the '93 playoffs, is a typical sports-theme restaurant in most respects. The all-American menu is dominated by meat offerings, and a massive bar area doubles as a memorabilia-laden shrine to pro sports. What's different, of course, is that it's Michael's—and Michael dominates just about anything he puts his mind to. His Royal Airness even stops in from time to time; MJ holds court in a private dining room, visible to his fans unless some spoilsport draws the curtains. Naturally, there's a large retail store by the entrance. *500 LaSalle St., tel. 312/644–3865. Reservations not accepted. AE, D, DC, MC, V. Expensive.*

The Pump Room. Probably Chicago's most famous restaurant name among out-of-towners, the Pump Room has in recent years augmented its traditional menu with dishes representing a fresh, new style of cooking. The years-loyal clientele keeps coming back for the steaks and baked Alaska, while a newer breed of customer enjoys such dishes as pine-nut-breaded sole with infused oils. Celebrity photos line the walls. *Omni Ambassador East, 1301 N. State Pkwy., tel. 312/266–0360. Reservations strongly recommended. AE, D, MC, V. Expensive.*

The Eccentric. Restaurateur Richard Melman has teamed with talk-show star Oprah Winfrey to open this aptly named adventure in dining. The combination French café/Italian coffeehouse/English pub can seat 400 diners and is decorated with the works of local artists. The food is surprisingly good, given the novelty of the enterprise. Don't miss the excellent steaks and chops, as well as Oprah's mashed potatoes with horseradish. And keep an eye out for Oprah. *159 W. Erie St., tel. 312/787–8390. Reservations accepted for 6 or more. AE, D, DC, MC, V. No lunch weekends. Moderate–Expensive.*

★ **Blackhawk Lodge.** Rustic, vacation-lodge decor sets this American regional restaurant apart. Hickory-smoked cuisine is something of a specialty—the ribs are particularly good— and the aromas coming from the kitchen are just about irresistible. *41 E. Superior St., tel. 312/280–4080. Reservations accepted. AE, D, DC, MC, V. Moderate.*

Gypsy. Mediterranean influences abound in the decor and menu of this eclectic American restaurant. Potatoes and smoked salmon head the list of intriguing pizza toppings, and a roasted artichoke stuffed with Brie makes a great shared appetizer. Chicken cacciatore with whole wheat pasta and grilled tuna with Mediterranean vegetables are representative entrées. Portions are very large, making this one of the most value-conscious restaurants in town. The Sunday brunch is very good, too. *215 E. Ohio St., tel. 312/644–9779. Reservations advised. AE, D, DC, MC, V. Moderate.*

Hard Rock Cafe. Street signs, musical instruments, and posters adorn this branch of the London-based Hard Rock Cafe chain. Music blares over the din of 275 diners (or is it 1,000?). Hamburgers, lime-barbecued chicken, and Texas-style barbecued ribs are among the house specialties, but does anyone come to the Hard Rock Cafe for the food? *63 W. Ontario St., tel. 312/943–2252. Reservations accepted Mon.–Thurs. for lunch only; no reservations other times; the wait can be substantial. AE, MC, V. Closed some holidays. Moderate.*

Jaxx. This American restaurant delights with occasional British influences. Wood-grilled and -roasted meats and fish are the specialties, but don't forget the side dishes, notably the sinfully rich mashed potatoes. Small pizzas, great salade Niçoise, and steak-and-kidney pies help make Jaxx a popular lunch spot. *Hyatt Regency Suites, 676 N. Michigan Ave., tel. 312/266–3020. Reservations recommended. AE, D, MC, V. Moderate.*

Jimo's Cafe. Live music, long hours, and a melting-pot clientele help make this energetic café popular. The menu is eclectic— expect anything from Cajun chicken salad to sautéed soft-shell crab—and so are the customers; expect everything from shorts with cowboy boots to jacket-and-tie. *1576 N. Milwaukee Ave.,*

Dining Near North, River North, and Lincoln Park

KEY

AE American Express Office

0   440 yards
0   400 meters

N

tel. 312/278–2424. Reservations accepted for 6 or more. AE, MC, V. Moderate.

Relish. The important thing to remember here is to save room for dessert. It's wonderful, even if you find it awkward ordering something like the Very Chocolate Orgasm. (If you do, stick to the free-form ice-cream sandwich.) The wide-ranging American menu offers plenty of predessert temptations as well. Sunday brunch is very pleasant in this airy, open dining room. *2044 N. Halsted St., tel. 312/868–9034. Reservations advised. AE, DC, MC, V. No lunch. Moderate.*

Robinson's No. 1 Ribs. Just about everything in this tiny restaurant is barbecued or deep-fried. Ribs (baby backs, tips) head the menu, followed by barbecued chicken, hot links, jumbo shrimp, pork and beef, cracklin' Louisiana catfish, and batter-dipped shrimp. Choose from side orders of natural-cut fries, coleslaw, baked beans, and corn on the cob. A spinach salad and Robinson's No. 1 salad (a chef's salad) are offered for militant cholesterol watchers. *655 W. Armitage Ave., tel. 312/337–1399. AE, MC, V. No lunch weekends. Inexpensive-Moderate.*

Al's Italian Beef. This tiny spot on busy Ontario Street is one of the best in Chicago for those two local delicacies—"Italian beef" (thinly sliced, well-done beef, served on a bun with its juice and as many toppings of hot peppers, onions, ketchup, mustard as you like), and the Chicago-style hot dog (hot dog with toppings in the same manner). You can get Italian sausage and meatball sandwiches here, too, as well as fries, sweet peppers, hot peppers, and chili. Eat at one of the tiny, cramped tables or order carryout. *169 W. Ontario St., tel. 312/943–3222. No credit cards. Inexpensive.*

Billy Goat Tavern. A favorite hangout for reporters, this self-service bar and grill just across the street and down the stairs is the columnist Mike Royko's second office. Don't come here if you're watching your cholesterol level: The famed "chizboogers" are held together with grease. Do come for the atmosphere, a quick bite, and a cold one that won't set you back a day's pay. *430 N. Michigan Ave. (lower level), tel. 312/222–1525. No credit cards. Inexpensive.*

★ **Ed Debevic's.** Half serious, half tongue-in-cheek, this imitation 1950s diner packs them in from morning till midnight. The signs are an important part of the decor: "If you don't like the way I do things—buy me out"; "If you're not served in 5 minutes—you'll get served in 8 or 9. Maybe 12 minutes. Relax." The menu features eight types of hamburger; a sandwich selection that includes tuna salad, chicken salad, chicken BLT, and Sloppy Joe; four chili preparations (plain, with macaroni and cheese, the same plus onion, and with onion and beans); five hot dog offerings; and a selection of "deluxe plates": meat loaf, pot roast, breaded pork loin, and chicken pot pie, all served with bread, butter, and choice of soup, slaw, or salad. The banana cream pie, coconut cream pie, and pecan pie are homemade. Unlike a real 1950s diner, Ed's has a selection of cocktails, wines, and Ed Debevic's Beer, Aged in Its Own Bottle. *640 N. Wells St., tel. 312/664–1707. No reservations; the wait may be substantial. No credit cards. Closed some holidays. Inexpensive.*

Chinese **Tang Dynasty.** Lavishly appointed Tang Dynasty is the best-looking Chinese restaurant in the area. It also offers some of the best cooking. Alongside the usual pot stickers, wonton soup, and hacked chicken are many innovative dishes that change at the chef's whim. All are carefully prepared and professionally served. *100 E. Walton St., tel. 312/664–8688. Reservations advised. AE, DC, MC, V. Closed Sun. lunch. Expensive.*

★ **House of Hunan.** The original Magnificent Mile Chinese restaurant, House of Hunan continues to please. The large, elegantly decorated dining area is appointed with porcelains and carvings. With offerings from the four principal Chinese culinary regions—Mandarin (from Beijing), Hunan, Szechuan, and Canton—the enormous menu offers a satisfying dinner to anyone who enjoys Chinese food. Spicy hot dishes are plentiful, but so are mild ones. Pot stickers, scallop roll, satay beef, buns filled with minced pork and crabmeat, and stuffed crab claws are among the more than a dozen appetizers; cold dishes include drunken chicken, abalone salad, and jellyfish. Noodles, fish, shellfish, pork, duck, chicken, lamb, beef, vegetable, and mu shu (pancake-wrapped) specialties make up the remaining hundred or so preparations. *535 N. Michigan Ave., tel. 312/329–9494. AE, D, DC, MC, V. Moderate–Expensive.*

Eurasian **Le Mikado.** The chef's culinary flights of fancy usually succeed at Le Mikado, another of a growing number of restaurants where the tastes and ingredients of Eastern and Western cuisine merge in unique combinations. Try ravioli filled with Japanese eggplant or pheasant with Chinese cabbage. The two-level dining room offers privacy and refinement befitting the exceptional food. *21 W. Goethe St., tel. 312/280–8611. Reservations advised. AE, D, DC, MC, V. Closed lunch. Expensive.*

French **Ambria.** In the spacious atmosphere of a turn-of-the-century
★ mansion, Ambria serves the most contemporary of French food and light cuisine. Gabino Sotelino, one of Chicago's best chefs, offers menus that change seasonally: A recent spring-summer menu offered terrine of salmon and striped bass with melon, tricolored ravioli of lobster and wild mushroom in lobster broth, sweetbread medallions breaded with pistachio and served with tomato basil sauce, and roast tenderloin of baby lamb with eggplant wrapped in crisp potato and served with couscous. The emphasis here is on using natural juices and vegetable reductions as accompaniments to the entrées, creating delectable food without excessive richness. The assortment of cheeses, sherbets, fruits, and pastries includes a hot soufflé. Ambria is a fine choice for those who want to dine graciously and well but not to excess. *2300 N. Lincoln Park W, tel. 312/472–5959. Reservations required. AE, D, DC, MC, V. Closed lunch, Sun., holidays. Very Expensive.*

★ **La Tour.** One of Chicago's finest and most expensive restaurants, La Tour is a large room done in marble with tones of peach and green; one side looks out on the small Water Tower park and the other is more formal in atmosphere. Tuxedoed waiters serve you from an exquisite French menu that might feature such memorable dishes as swordfish with cabernet sauce and sautéed pineapple with coconut ice cream and burnt-orange sauce. Don't come here when you're slimming. Come here for an elegant, grand splurge. La Tour is also one of the city's premier spots for power breakfasting. *Park Hyatt Hotel, 800 N. Michigan Ave., tel. 312/280–2230. Jacket required at dinner. Dinner reservations required. AE, D, DC, MC, V. Very Expensive.*

Jackie's. This popular French restaurant features the cooking of famed, classically trained chef Jackie Shen. She puts together fascinating combinations of ingredients, such as sea scallops wrapped in phyllo dough with roe, tomatoes, lettuce, and caviar. In many restaurants, such exotic concoctions sound better than they taste, but Jackie's consistently delivers intense and satisfying flavors. If you have room for dessert, the restaurant is famous for its "chocolate bag," a dark chocolate shell filled with white mousse and raspberries. The servers are poised and proper, if occasionally stuffy. *2478 N. Lincoln Ave., tel. 312/880–0003. Reservations required. No denim. AE, D, DC, MC, V. Closed Sun., Mon. Expensive–Very Expensive.*

★ **The Dining Room.** The Dining Room is decorated in a classic French style with walnut paneling, tapestry carpeting, and crystal chandeliers. The food is French with nouvelle accents; a specialty is foie gras salad. Daily specials complement the menu selections. Gracious service and fine food in a beautiful setting make this an outstanding restaurant. *Ritz-Carlton Hotel, 160 E. Pearson St., tel. 312/227–5866. Jacket and tie required. Reservations required. AE, D, DC, MC, V. Closed lunch. Expensive–Very Expensive.*

Bistro 110. Like any good bistro, this place can be noisy and chaotic at times, but third-generation restaurateur Doug Roth presides over the cacophony with élan. Bistro 110 has become a popular gathering place for the city's young executives. Besides the lively bar scene, the real drawing card here is the food from the wood-burning oven. From chicken to seafood, from mushrooms to the whole head of baked garlic placed before diners at the beginning of the meal to be spread on the crusty French bread, the kitchen consistently turns out excellent renditions of French classics, as well as contemporary Franco-American innovations. The Sunday jazz brunch is worth a trip to this restaurant. *110 E. Pearson St., tel. 312/266–3110. Reservations advised for lunch and for 6 or more for dinner. AE, D, DC, MC, V. Expensive.*

Le Perroquet. Years ago, Le Perroquet introduced Chicago to nouvelle cuisine; its historical significance remains, though in recent years other restaurants have eclipsed Le Perroquet's cooking. Today, new ownership and a new, talented kitchen staff deliver an outstanding dining experience, at prices that are neither cheap nor shocking ($38.50 for the four-course dinner). Attentive service is a plus. The wine list is stellar. And the dessert soufflé remains a wonderful, if decadent, way to cap off the evening. *70 E. Walston St., tel. 312/944–7990. Reservations advised. AE, D, DC, MC, V. Closed Sun. Expensive.*

★ **Mirador.** Owned by Amy Morton (daughter of famed Chicago restaurateur Arnie Morton), Mirador is a cheerfully cramped space with high ceilings and textured walls. The menu features provincial French cuisine with Mediterranean accents, such as roasted eggplant salad with grilled radicchio and squab leg confit. A reasonably priced wine list is thoughtfully organized to make it accessible to wine novices. After dinner, head upstairs to the Blue Room, a funky space with live music, imaginative cocktails, and unsurpassed people-watching. In good weather, the outdoor deck is a wonderful place to enjoy a meal. *1400 N. Wells St., tel. 312/951–6441. Reservations advised. AE, MC, V. Closed lunch. Expensive.*

Kiki's Bistro. Country French decor meets urban contemporary cooking in this modern bistro. The kitchen seasons dishes aggressively and likes to experiment, but the food generally stays true to its roots. Grilled rabbit sausage with garlic and rosemary is a fine starter; for an entrée, try grouper served with an herb-scented fish bouillon and vegetable medley. And classics like steak with pommes frites are always reliable. *900 N. Franklin St., tel. 312/335–5454. Reservations accepted. AE, MC, V. Closed Sun., Sat. lunch. Moderate.*

★ **Un Grand Cafe.** This attractive bistro is the casual companion to the elegant Ambria at the same address. Steak frites, cassoulet, and roast chicken are specialties on a menu that reflects the simpler, earthier preparations of the French bistro style while drawing on fresh American produce. Though relaxed in ambience, the restaurant offers the same outstanding quality of food and preparation as does its more formal sibling. *2300 N. Lincoln Park W, tel. 312/348–8886. No reservations; there may be a wait. AE, D, DC, MC, V. Closed lunch. Moderate.*

Yvette. Yvette is the place to go when you want classic French cuisine in a comfortable setting at an affordable price. Appetizers include scallop quenelles with pasta and chives, assorted pâtés and sausages, ballotine of salmon with dill sauce, and sweetbreads with morel mushrooms. There's a warm salad of the day, and soups are prepared daily. For an entrée, you can choose the veal medallions in wild mushroom sauce, the salmon fumé with Oriental-style vegetables, the seafood on fresh pasta (a specialty), or the fish of the day. The informal Yvette's Cafe offers a lighter menu, which emphasizes seafood and salads. *1206 N. State Pkwy., tel. 312/280–1700. Reservations for 6 or more. AE, DC, MC, V. No lunch in the dining room. Moderate.*

German **The Golden Ox.** Dark wood, stained-glass windows, murals on themes from German mythology, a hand-carved bar of golden oak, cheerful waitresses in traditional costume, and strolling accordionists and zither players give this German restaurant—the last remnant of what was once a German neighborhood—an authentically ethnic flavor. White tablecloths laid with platters of pickles and relishes set the tone for leisurely, comfortable dining. The menu offers two dozen German specialties, including four veal preparations, two sausages, smoked pork loin, and several unusual items: roast goose with potato dumplings and red cabbage (Saturday and Sunday only), veal sweetbreads sautéed in butter with mushrooms, and hasenpfeffer (marinated rabbit in cream sauce, served with potato dumpling and red cabbage). This hearty, filling fare leaves you with a contented glow. *1578 N. Clybourn Ave., tel. 312/664–0780. Reservations advised on weekends. AE, D, DC, MC, V. Closed Sun. lunch and Sun. in July and Aug. Moderate.*

Greek **Papagus.** Chicago's best Greek restaurant is a sprawling place,
★ bright and cheerful, rustic and comfortable. The menu focuses on *mezedes*, literally "small plates," or appetizers resembling Spanish tapas. Servers proffer an assortment; you point to what you want and start grazing. There are additional appetizers on the menu, as well as substantial, hearty salads and fairly traditional entrées. Highlights include *tirosalata*, a feta-cheese spread, sensational grilled octopus, and very good lamb chops. Desserts, so often a throwaway on Greek menus, are remarkably good here, especially the unusual dried-cherry-filled baklava. The all-Greek wine list can be daunting, but waiters are knowledgeable enough to provide helpful descriptions and reliable recommendations. *Embassy Suites Hotel, 620 N. State*

St., tel. 312/642–8450. Limited number of reservations accepted. AE, D, DC, MC, V. Moderate.

Indian **Bukhara.** Specializing in the cuisine of northwestern India, Bukhara features an open kitchen, where diners can watch their food prepared in clay ovens. Bread making is particularly theatrical, and the delicious product is likely to be an important part of your meal. Bukhara's food is spicy but not hot, and most dishes are intended to be eaten with the fingers or scooped up on pieces of bread. Plenty of hot towels are provided. Good choices for entrées include *sikandari raan* (leg of lamb marinated in rum and spices and roasted in a clay oven), *khyber tikka* (marinated chicken coated in egg yolk and grilled over charcoal), and the royal Kushan veal chop, seasoned with ginger and garlic. Unless you're extremely hungry, you may want to skip the appetizers, because the main-dish portions are large and often quite rich. As in many Indian restaurants, desserts are very sweet and dense. *2 E. Ontario St., tel. 312/943–0188. Reservations advised. AE, DC, MC, V. Moderate–Expensive.*

★ **Klay Oven.** Quite possibly unlike any Indian restaurant you've ever seen, Klay Oven is a bold experiment in applying fine dining standards to what is all too frequently represented as storefront food. The decor is lovely, the staff is extraordinarily well versed and communicative, and the food, at its best, can dazzle. Such offbeat treats as marinated prawns, mahimahi, rack of lamb, and pork ribs make their way onto the menu here, and all succeed admirably. The prices are relatively high but worth it. *414 N. Orleans St., tel. 312/527–3999. Reservations accepted. AE, DC, MC, V. Moderate.*

Raj Darbar. Raj occupies an important niche in Chicago's Indian dining scene: It is, perhaps, the ideal spot for novices. The menu covers the basics, and the knowledgeable, unintimidating, and mostly American waitstaff serves above-average food. Begin with a traditional sampling of Indian appetizers, move on to the fine curried entrées, and don't fail to sample the soft, delicious Indian breads, such as paratha and naan. Though some dishes are spicy, none is particularly hot. Wine and a wide selection of beer, including three from India, are at bargain prices. *2350 N. Clark St., tel. 312/348–1010. Reservations recommended on weekends. AE, D, MC, V. Moderate.*

International **Foodlife.** Is it a restaurant? Or a food court? Whatever it is, Foodlife threatens to revolutionize mall food. Upon entering, you're issued a credit card, on which you may charge food purchased from any of a dozen food stands (the purchase is magnetically encoded on your card and you pay on the way out). The food is prepared quickly, the tables are bused promptly, and the staff is friendly and helpful. Selections include the standard burgers and pizzas, but there are more enticing options, too: among them a solid Oriental stand with excellent shrimp pot stickers, a grain stand with fresh couscous and grain-crusted salmon, a pasta counter, and a Mexican eatery. Healthful soy and veggie burgers as well as an Enlightened Caesar salad—a low-fat version of the classic—will also tempt you. Most dishes are under $5, and take-out is available. *Water Tower Place, 845 N. Michigan Ave., tel. 312/335–3663. Reservations not accepted. AE, D, DC, MC, V. Inexpensive.*

Italian **Spiaggia.** Luxury-level Italian dining that is unsurpassed in the
★ city. The decor is elegant and modern, with marble-clad columns, stylish table appointments, and pink and teal colors; a

three-story bank of windows overlooks Michigan Avenue and Lake Michigan. The food, as opulent and complex as its surroundings, includes such dishes as a veal chop coddled in a luscious vodka-cream sauce. The menu features several elaborate, filled pasta dishes. The dessert list is compact but delightful. The scholarly wine list is no place for bargain hunters, but there are some remarkable wines available. Note: A downscaled taste of Spiaggia's wonders is available next door at Cafe Spiaggia, a lower-priced, casual sidekick. *980 N. Michigan Ave., tel. 312/280–2750. Reservations advised. Jacket required; no denim. AE, D, DC, MC, V. Closed Sun. lunch. Very Expensive.*

★ **Avanzare.** A handsome pair of marble, carpeted rooms, one raised a few steps above the other, is dominated by traditional brass accents, leather banquettes, and a full-length mirrored bar between the rooms. Tables are topped with white butcher paper over cloth. The main room tends to be quite noisy, the mezzanine somewhat less so. Avanzare offers a wide-ranging menu of pastas, unusual salads, and entrées. Try an appetizer of tuna carpaccio—paper-thin slices of raw tuna in soy sauce with avocado and sweet onions. A dozen carefully prepared pastas appear in the regular menu, but the best pasta offerings come from the list of daily specials. Among the entrées, try one of the unusual game dishes, a tempting seafood special, or the unsurpassed veal chop. Though expensive, Avanzare is consistently one of the best Italian restaurants on Chicago's Near North side. The freshness and quality of the ingredients shine through the preparations. *161 E. Huron St., tel. 312/337–8056. Reservations advised. AE, D, DC, MC, V. No lunch weekends. Expensive.*

Bice. This is the ultimate see-and-be-seen Italian eatery; a strip of mirrored glass at eye level gives even diners with their back to the room an opportunity to watch the goings-on. The food at Bice (pronounced Bee-chay) is quite good, especially the carefully prepared pastas with innovative sauces. Lapses in service seem de rigueur, but there's plenty of action to amuse you during the often interminable waits between courses. *158 E. Ontario St. tel. 312/664–1474. Reservations advised for inside dining room. Jacket and tie required. AE, DC, MC, V. No lunch Sun. Expensive.*

★ **Coco Pazzo.** The Chicago branch of a very successful Manhattan restaurant, Coco Pazzo succeeds on a largely gimmick-free basis. Service is solid, mature, and professional; the kitchen produces mainly lusty Tuscan creations, seasoned aggressively. Grilled game is a particular strength, as are the risotto dishes. On weekends, the menu is arranged "Coco Pazzo" style, with the dishes portioned for two, three, or four diners. The idea is to encourage family-style dining, although if you really want pasta for one, the kitchen will accommodate you. *300 W. Hubbard St., tel. 312/836–0900. AE, DC, MC, V. Closed Sat. and lunch Sun. Expensive.*

Bella Vista. The owners reportedly spent $2 million converting an old bank building into the colorful, architecturally stunning eatery that greets diners today. Seating is on five levels, and the sight lines allow low-key gawking at the faux-stone walls, restored marble floors, bright-copper trim, and colorful clientele. The food is as eye-opening as the decor, in the way the kitchen puts a nouvelle spin on classic Italian favorites. Pizza is a specialty; the owners of Bella Vista also run the popular Bacino's Pizza chain. The wine list is extraordinary. *1001 W.*

Belmont Ave., tel. 312/404–0111. Reservations recommended on weekends. AE, D, DC, MC, V. No lunch Sun. Moderate–Expensive.

Carlucci. A sophisticated urban Italian restaurant that draws a see-and-be-seen crowd. The food is even better than the people-watching though, and the polished service ensures a terrific dining experience. One of the area's most consistent performers. *2215 N. Halsted St., tel. 312/281–1220. Reservations advised. AE, D, DC, MC, V. No lunch. Moderate–Expensive.*

Harry Caray's. Housed in the handsome, old, ornamented brick building that for years was the Kinzie Steak House, Harry Caray's is one of the new breed of "celebrity" restaurant, this one owned by the famed Chicago Cubs baseball announcer. The interior, completely redone, has a long wood bar, tile flooring, and high tables covered with checkered cloths. Baseball memorabilia decorates the walls, and souvenirs can be purchased from the souvenir stand. The food reflects Harry's own preferences: Steaks and chops share the bulk of the menu with traditional Italian preparations. Salads and cold platters are plentiful. This is a good spot for baseball fans who like to eat and don't take the dining experience too seriously. And, unlike the "name" owners of some celebrity restaurants, Harry really does stop by. Holy cow! *33 W. Kinzie St., tel. 312/465–9269. Lunch reservations advised; no reservations other times. AE, D, DC, MC, V. Moderate–Expensive.*

Maggiano's Little Italy. Red sauce Italian food in a cleverly realized Little-Italy milieu. Maggiano's dishes up enormous portions (hint: Order but two entrées for every three diners in your party) in a wide-open dining room full of cheerfully loud patrons. This is the kind of Italian food we grew up with: brick-size lasagna, chicken Vesuvio, veal scaloppine. It's not inspiring cuisine, but maybe it'll bring back a memory or two. *516 N. Clark St., tel. 312/644–7700. Reservations strongly advised. AE, D, DC, MC, V. No lunch Sun. Moderate–Expensive.*

Trattoria Convito. A marble-top bar complements a dining room with fanciful murals and exposed brick, and the windows give an airy feel to the room. Flowers and a bottle of wine are set on each of the white-clothed tables. An assortment of homemade breads presented at the table makes a seductive start to a regional Italian meal. The menu offers unusual soups, a large selection of salads, and equally interesting pastas: A classic spaghetti with tomato-basil sauce is familiar but fresh; rigatoni in tomato-cream sauce with shrimp, bay scallops, and broccoli is less conventional. Entrées emphasize chicken and veal. Pastas, breads, and pastries are all homemade. The shop below has ingredients for your own Italian picnic and unusual kitchen and gift items. *11 E. Chestnut St., tel. 312/943–2984. Reservations accepted. AE, DC, MC, V. Closed Sun. lunch and holidays. Moderate–Expensive.*

Trattoria Gianni. This Lincoln Park establishment successfully re-creates the homey atmosphere and skillful cooking common in Italian trattorias, though at a higher price. Appetizers are a standout: choose among three antipasto plates—hot, cold, or vegetarian—or crunchy deep-fried squid, zucchini strips, or mussels. The vegetarian plate includes marinated eggplant and zucchini salads and a vegetable frittata. Imaginative and usually well prepared pasta dishes include *rigatoni nocerina* (pasta tubes with cream, mushrooms, and sun-dried tomatoes), *farfalle contadina* (bow-tie macaroni with vegetables), and *gnocchi à la panna-pesto* (potato dumplings with cream-and-pesto sauce). Simple but satisfying entrées include grilled red snapper with herbs and olive oil, and the worthwhile charcoal-grilled Cornish game hen. If you can, save room for desserts. *1711 N. Halsted St., tel. 312/266–1976. Reservations advised. MC, V. Closed weekend lunch and Mon. Moderate–Expensive.*

L'Angolo di Roma. Cotton tablecloths are covered with butcher paper and set with fresh flowers in the brightly lit dining rooms. Cold appetizers on display allow diners to select in advance of ordering among carpaccio, sliced tomato and onion, radicchio salad, fennel salad, and endive with pea pods and tomato. Mussels marinara, baked Little Neck clams, and fried calamari are among the hot appetizers. Individual nine-inch pizzas—with prosciutto, artichoke, mushrooms, olive, and egg; four cheeses; or mussels and calamari in marinara sauce—are a specialty. Pastas and entrées change daily, but they might include *gnocchi* (potato dumplings) sautéed in tomato sauce with Parmesan cheese, topped with mozzarella, and baked; rigatoni with tomato sauce, sausage, mushrooms, and broccoli; whole red snapper baked and served with olive oil, garlic, basil, and parsley; or chicken breast sautéed in Marsala wine with mushrooms and scallions. *2260 N. Clark St., tel. 312/935–8100. Reservations advised for 5 or more. MC, V. Closed lunch and holidays. Moderate.*

Scoozi! You'll recognize Scoozi! by the gigantic tomato over the front door. This is a huge, noisy, trendy place popular with the young professional crowd. Booths flank the walls of a multilevel dining room, and wood beams and ceiling decorations complement the country Italian food. A large selection of antipasti, pizza, and pasta is augmented by a small selection of entrées. Steamed clams in garlic and white wine, steamed mussels in tomato sauce, and osso buco (braised veal shanks in roasted vegetables) appear on a generally attractive menu that invites grazing. Many offerings are available in small or large portions. *410 W. Huron St., tel. 312/943–5900. Reservations accepted for lunch, no reservations for dinner; the wait can be substantial. AE, D, DC, MC, V. Closed weekend lunch and some holidays. Moderate.*

Sole Mio. The warm ambience is created by dark wood teamed with white walls, wood-framed mirrors, and photographs of the Italian countryside. The main dining room is flanked by three smaller rooms, one for nonsmokers. The food, prepared by owner-chefs Dennis Terczak and Jennifer Newbury, is inspired by the cuisine of Northern and regional Italy and enhanced by an imaginative contemporary approach. The individual eight-inch pizzas are outstanding, even the familiar pizza *margherita* with mozzarella, fresh tomato sauce, basil, and sausage. Entrées include the adventurous—*misto alla griglia* is a mixed grill of lamb chop, quail, sausage, lentils, and escarole—and the tried-and-true veal scallops, center-cut veal chop, and grilled T-bone steak with peppercorns. A fresh ocean fish, freshwater fish, and shellfish are available daily, and there are homemade desserts and ices. *917 W. Armitage Ave., tel. 312/477–5858. No reservations (the wait is generally less than half an hour). AE, DC, MC, V. Closed lunch and holidays. Moderate.*

Tucci Benucch. This cozy Italian country kitchen in the Avenue Atrium mall is a pleasant escape from the hustle and bustle of shopping outside its doors. Thin-crust pizzas and pasta dishes feature unusual toppings, such as smoked chicken, red peppers, and Asiago cheese. Red sauces for spaghetti include julienne fresh basil. The grilled eggplant, red pepper, and onion sandwich is rich and crusty. Leave room for dessert, because the gelato is worth a try. *900 N. Michigan Ave., 5th floor, tel. 312/266–2500. No reservations. AE, D, DC, MC, V. Moderate.*

Tucci Milan. A cousin to Tucci Benucch, this contemporary restaurant in trendy River North produces some excellent renditions of Northern Italian pastas and grilled dishes. Bustling and noisy, the restaurant attracts a young, professional crowd with its active bar scene and a late-night crowd at the espresso bar in the front. The food is consistently good. *6 W. Hubbard St., tel. 312/222–0044. Reservations advised on weekends. AE, DC, MC, V. Moderate.*

Vinci. Paul LoDuca, who served as chef at many of Chicago's finest restaurants, has now struck out on his own to create this very impressive, stylishly casual restaurant. Decor is all faux finishes and rustic touches; the menu offers robust regional Italian dishes such as grilled pork chops with fennel and garlic. Pizzas are creative; one combines Fontina cheese, roasted garlic, bitter greens, and tomato. The restaurant has quickly achieved popularity, especially among the pretheater crowd. *1732 N. Halsted St., tel. 312/266–1199. Reservations strongly advised. AE, MC, V. No lunch. Closed Mon. Moderate.*

Centro. There's little chance you'll secure a reservation at this megahot restaurant, which draws trendies like moths to a flame. There's even less chance your reservation will be honored: VIPs arrive on a regular basis and force ordinary folk farther down the waiting list. Those who stick it out are rewarded with stupendously portioned pastas and a smattering of other traditional Italian dishes such as grilled pork chops with fennel and garlic. Prices are surprisingly reasonable. *710 N. Wells St., tel. 312/988–7775. Limited reservations accepted. AE, D, DC, MC, V. Closed Sun., Sat. lunch. Inexpensive–Moderate.*

Pizzeria Uno/Pizzeria Due. This is where Chicago deep-dish pizza got its start. Uno has been remodeled to resemble its franchised cousins in other cities, but its pizzas retain their light crust and distinctive taste. Those not accustomed to pizza on a Chicago scale may want to skip the salad to save room. Beer and soft drinks can be ordered by the pitcher. You'll usually have a shorter wait for a table at Pizzeria Due (same ownership and menu, different decor and longer hours), a block away. Some say Uno's pizza is better, but the product at both establishments is among the best in town. *Uno: 29 E. Ohio St., tel. 312/321–1000. Due: 619 N. Wabash Ave., tel. 312/943–2400. No reservations, but phone-ahead orders are accepted weekdays only. AE, D, DC, MC, V. Inexpensive.*

Japanese **Benkay.** In part because of a limited market, and in part because of the cost of buying and preparing the highest-quality ingredients in Japanese style, few Japanese restaurants in the country offer authentic Japanese high cuisine in an elegant setting. Benkay is one that does. Choose between the serenely beautiful 50-seat main dining room served by tuxedoed waiters, the 20-seat sushi room, one of six traditional tatami rooms (foot wells make them as comfortable for Americans as for Japanese) served by kimono-clad waitresses, a teppan-yaki room (in which chefs do their work inconspicuously, so as not to intrude on diners' conversations), and two private Western-style dining rooms. The extensive menu is printed in English and Japanese. A full selection of appetizers, soups, sashimi *(raw fish)*, *ni-mono* (steamed) dishes, *yaki-mono* (grilled) dishes, *age-mono* (fried) dishes, *sunomono* (vinegared) dishes, rices, noodles, and desserts is offered. The restaurant's specialty is its *Kaiseki* menu (three full-course dinners that include at least one item from each of the traditional Japanese styles of cooking). These dinners show the art as well as the refinement and elegance of classical Japanese dining. *Hotel Nikko, 320 N. Dearborn St., tel. 312/836–5490. Jacket and tie required at lunch and dinner. Reservations required. AE, D, DC, MC, V. Closed holidays. Very Expensive.*

★ **Hatsuhana.** Hatsuhana has a long, angled sushi bar and wood tables set on purple carpeting; its white stucco walls are hung with Japanese lanterns. Sushi and sashimi lovers have long esteemed this restaurant as the best in Chicago for these Japanese vinegared rice and raw fish delicacies. The printed menu lists numerous appetizers (broiled spinach in sesame-soy sauce, fried bean curd with sauce, steamed egg custard with shrimp, fish, and vegetables) and only a few entrée selections. An extensive and unusual specials menu supplements the printed menu and has included steamed baby clams in sake, broiled king mackerel with soybean paste, boiled snails in sweet sauce, and chicken wings in special sauce. A small selection of moderately priced complete dinners is available. *160 E. Ontario St., tel. 312/280–8287. Reservations advised. AE, DC, MC, V. Closed Sat. lunch, Sun., and holidays. Moderate–Expensive.*

Honda. Owned and operated by a Tokyo restaurateur, Honda offers one of the most extensive Japanese menus in the city. Its sushi and sashimi are among the city's best, and it also features the country's first *kushi* bar, where morsels of meat, seafood, and vegetables are grilled or deep-fried. Diners have the option of sitting at the kushi bar or in one of Honda's several dining rooms. You can call a day in advance to reserve a traditional tatami room (foot wells under the low tables let you stretch your legs). The many authentic dishes include *chawan mushi* (steamed vegetables and fish in an egg custard). Sukiyaki is prepared at your table. *540 N. Wells, tel. 312/923–1010. Reservations accepted. AE, DC, MC, V. Closed Sat. lunch and Sun. Moderate–Expensive.*

Mediterranean Cuisines. Chicago's first upscale, fine-dining Mediterranean restaurant successfully weds an informal cuisine to formal dining standards. The subdued elegance of the dining room makes this a very comfortable place to eat—a little less light and it would be downright romantic. Italian influences dominate the menu, but there are other choices, including a particularly good paella and one of the kitchen's tastes-of-four-nations appetizers. Desserts are merely perfunctory, but diners are treated to a complimentary plate of fresh fruit. The large, easy-to-interpret wine list is dominated by French and American vintages; you'll find more of a Mediterranean statement on the by-the-glass list. *Stouffer Riviere Hotel, 1 W. Wacker Dr., tel. 312/372–7200. Reservations accepted. AE, D, DC, MC, V. Closed weekend lunch. Expensive.*

★ **Tuttaposto.** Tony Mantuano made his reputation as an Italian chef; his latest restaurant sees him branching out a bit. Besides Italian, there are Greek, French, Portuguese, and North African dishes here. Wood-roast snapper is outstanding. The colorful decor is invigorating, and large windows revealing the rather gritty street scene outside give the restaurant an energetic urban feel. *646 N. Franklin St., tel. 312/943–6262. Reservations advised. AE, D, DC, MC, V. Closed weekend lunch. Moderate.*

Mexican **Topolobampo.** Located next door to Frontera Grill, Topolo-
★ bampo shares more than just the same entrance with its sister restaurant. It has the same owners, the same kitchen, and the same dedication to quality. Everything that can be said for Frontera can be said at least as strongly about Topolobampo, which may be the best Mexican restaurant in the nation. More expensive than Frontera, Topolobampo offers a more stately atmosphere, accepts reservations, and, most important, affords the chef the opportunity to experiment with more expensive ingredients. The ever-changing menu features game, seasonal fruits and vegetables, and exotic preparations that almost always taste even better than they sound: homemade tortillas with pumpkinseed sauce and pheasant roasted in banana leaves are two examples. Good service and an interesting wine list complete the scenario. *445 N. Clark St., tel. 312/661–1434. Reservations recommended. AE, D, DC, MC, V. Closed Sun., Mon. Expensive.*

★ **Frontera Grill.** Chef/owner Rick Bayless and his wife, Deann, literally wrote the book on Mexican cuisine—*Authentic Mexican*—and that's what you'll find at this casual café, along with a tiled floor, bright colors, and Mexican folk art. The Baylesses learned about regional Mexican cuisine by tramping across Mexico, hanging out in markets, eating in restaurants, and talking with the cooks. They serve a sampling of what they learned, and what a sampling it is—from charbroiled catfish, Yucatán style (with pickled red onions and *jicama* salad), to garlicky skewered tenderloin, Aguascalientes style (with poblano peppers, red onion, and bacon)! The menu changes frequently, and weekly specials are often the most tempting dishes. This place proves once and for all that Mexican cuisine is anything but limited and boring. *445 N. Clark St., tel. 312/661–1434. Reservations for 6 or more only; expect a long wait. AE, D, DC, MC, V. Closed Sun., Mon. Moderate.*

Hat Dance. Look for the Indian-style carvings in the imitation adobe exterior of the building to tell you that you've come to the right place. Inside, you'll find umbrellas hanging from the ceiling along with antique chandeliers, pillars sprouting into palm trees, women diving out of trees, animals in bas relief, and a great trompe l'oeil that gives the illusion of a marble wall. Hat Dance, a creation of the Lettuce Entertain You group in partnership with radio personality Steve Dahl, is designed to appeal to trendy, upscale young professionals who enjoy crowds and noise as part of the dining experience. Appetizers include a selection of ceviches, sashimi, and tartares, as well as an assortment of quesos, quesadillas, carnitas, tacos, and guacamole. Entrées lean toward "nouveau" preparations. To the classic carne asada is added, for example, tuna asada (grilled tuna steak served rare, accompanied by chili-papaya relish). A chili relleno is stuffed with chicken, olives, raisins, and onions in a tomato-cinnamon broth. A good selection of desserts includes a vanilla-cinnamon pudding, a rice pudding, chocolate-coconut flan, and assorted pastries. *325 W. Huron St., tel. 312/649–0066. Reservations advised. AE, D, DC, MC, V. Closed weekend lunch. Moderate.*

Polish American **Busy Bee.** Busy Bee is one of the best of the many storefront Polish restaurants to be found throughout Chicago. Two large storefronts have been divided into one room with a large U-shaped counter and booths and a second that is carpeted and furnished with well-spaced, cloth-covered tables. What makes this and other restaurants of its type special are the generous quantities of pleasing, stick-to-the-ribs food at very low prices. *Pierogi* (dumplings stuffed with your choice of meat, potato and cheese, or potato and sauerkraut) are served with sour cream or applesauce. Homemade mushroom soup, barley soup, and *czarnina* (duck gravy soup) are among the daily specials. *Bigos* (hunter's stew), Polish sausages, boiled beef brisket, boiled short ribs, tripe stew, and roast duck are among the entrées. Plenty of standard American dishes are also available, satisfying finicky youngsters while parents enjoy ethnic specialties. Service can be somewhat slow. *1546 N. Damen Ave., tel. 312/772–4433. Reservations not required. No credit cards. Closed some holidays. Inexpensive.*

Seafood **Catch Thirty Five.** A lot of money went into making this one of the most handsome restaurants in Chicago. Situated on one side of the lobby of the new Leo Burnett Building, this restaurant takes its name from its address and the 35 different types of fresh seafood featured daily. The chef (known simply as Eak) mixes such Asian flavorings as curry sauce with such Latin influences as cilantro sauce to create innovative dishes with classic French overtones. The decor is also born of a Western and Eastern mixture, in this case West Coast and East Coast. A huge sculpture projecting a pattern of colored lights hangs over the piano bar, and to the right, the bird's-eye, maple-paneled dining room affords everyone a great view for people-watching. An "ad wall" displays photographs from well-known ad campaigns. The restaurant has yet to ignite with the trendy set to make people-watching a prime sport here, but with such intriguing dishes as wok-steamed striped bass with black bean and ginger sauce, this seafood extravaganza will surely have a bright future. *35 W. Wacker Dr., tel. 312/346–3500. AE, DC, MC, V. Reservations accepted. Closed weekend lunch. Expensive.*

★ **Shaw's Crab House and Blue Crab Lounge.** Here is an East Coast–style oyster bar, in exposed brick and wood, with a wood bar adjoining the main restaurant, again in wood, softly lit, with models of fish on the walls. Preparations tend toward the simple and the classic. Appetizers include french-fried calamari, steamed blue mussels, and Maryland crab cakes. An oyster special of the day offers regional varieties that Midwesterners might not otherwise have a chance to sample. Crab, lobster, and shrimp offerings are standard on the menu; the fresh fish daily specials might include grilled Hawaiian tuna with purslane and tomato relish or a grilled Pacific king salmon with herb marinade. A few obligatory chicken and beef items are offered on the menu as well. *21 E. Hubbard St., tel. 312/527–2722. Reservations advised for lunch. AE, D, DC, MC, V. Closed weekend lunch; lounge closed Sun. Moderate–Expensive.*

Bub City Crabshack and Bar-B-Q. You can't help but have fun at this cavernous place, a re-creation of a Gulf Coast crab shack. Decor is playfully rustic—there's even a sink in the middle of the dining room—and the menu teems with sloppy treats, such as pick 'n' lick shrimp, garlic blue crab, and barbecued ribs. The adjacent Club Bub (no cover charge) offers live country music most evenings. *901 W. Weed St., tel. 312/266–1200. Re-*

servations accepted. AE, D, DC, MC, V. Closed weekend lunch. Moderate.

Old Carolina Crab House. This waterside restaurant, with fishing tackle and pictures of fishermen covering the walls, is about as close as Chicago gets to that Southern-style "little crab house on the shore." When you want a break from shopping in the newly developed North Pier, stop in for a laid-back dinner of steamed crab and beer. *In the North Pier complex at 465 E. Illinois St., tel. 312/321–8400. Reservations accepted. AE, MC, V. Closed Mon. Moderate.*

Spanish   **Cafe Ba-Ba-Reeba!** Chicago's best-known exemplar of *tapas* cuisine (small edibles that once were used as covers for the glasses of sherry, wine, or beer that accompanied them), this large, open restaurant, with its prominent bar, is usually crowded with upscale young folk having a very good time. Choose among a large selection of cold and warm tapas, ranging from cannelloni stuffed with tuna, asparagus, and basil, served with tomato basil sauce and white wine vinaigrette, to veal with mushrooms, eggplant, tomato, and sherry sauce. A few soups and salads are available, as is a limited entrée menu that includes two paellas (meat and seafood or seafood only, baked in rice), a baked salmon with mustard topping and vegetable vinaigrette, sautéed pork tenderloin with caramel orange sauce, and two seafood casseroles. There are several desserts for those who have the room. *2024 N. Halsted St., tel. 312/935–5000. Limited reservations; the wait may be substantial. AE, DC, MC, V. Closed lunch, Sun., and holidays. Moderate.*

Steak Houses   **Eli's The Place for Steak.** Enter this Chicago institution
★   through the lounge, where you'll find a piano bar. This room and the dining room beyond are softly lit, done in club style, with lots of leather and warm wood. Eli's developed its outstanding reputation through an unflagging commitment to top-quality ingredients prepared precisely to customers' orders and generously served. A selection of complimentary appetizers appears at your table. Prime aged steaks are the specialty here, among the best in Chicago. You'll also find a superb, thickly cut veal chop (order it medium rare for maximum tenderness and succulence) and a splendid calf liver. For dessert, order Eli's renowned cheesecake, now sold nationally in countless varieties. *215 E. Chicago Ave., tel. 312/642–1393. Reservations required. Jacket required. AE, D, DC, MC, V. Closed weekend lunch, holidays. Expensive.*

★   **Gene & Georgetti.** Would you give your right arm for a good, old-fashioned piece of prime aged beef or a plate of spaghetti with meat sauce and mushrooms? If so, Gene & Georgetti is for you. Here is one restaurant that hasn't fallen prey to trendiness and does what it has always done as it has always done it, to the immense relief of its customers. Service may be brusque. *500 N. Franklin St., tel. 312/527–3718. Reservations recommended. AE, DC, MC, V. Closed Sun., some holidays. Expensive.*

Gibson's. This fairly new steak house, on the site once occupied by the famous nightclub Mr. Kelly's, has caught on fast with the convention crowd. The reasons? Plenty of room, attractive decor, huge portions, and good service. You don't see chopped liver on many appetizer lists these days, but the version here is good. *1028 N. Rush St., tel. 312/266–8999. Reservations strongly recommended. AE, DC, MC, V. Expensive.*

★ **Morton's of Chicago.** It's Chicago's best steak house—and that's no idle statement. Excellent service, classy ambience, and a very good wine list add to the principal attraction: beautiful, hefty steaks, cooked to perfection. It's no place for the budget conscious, but for steak lovers, it's a 16-ounce taste of heaven. *1050 N. State St., tel. 312/266–4820. Reservations required. AE, D, DC, MC, V. No lunch. Expensive.*

Ruth's Chris Steak House. The country's largest fine-dining steak house chain established this Chicago outpost in 1992, and Ruth's Chris quickly demonstrated that it could compete with the best in this definitive steak town. The steaks are excellent, the lobster good (although expensive, largely because the smallest lobster in their tank is about three pounds), and the service is outstanding. There's a pretty good wine list, though the by-the-glass options are paltry. There are more appetizer and side-dish options here than at most steak houses. *431 N. Dearborn St., tel. 312/321–2725. Reservations recommended. AE, D, DC, MC, V. Closed Sun. Expensive.*

Ukrainian **Galans.** In the heart of Ukrainian Village, Galans has two dining rooms, one dark, classic, and simple, the other light and contemporary. White tablecloths are covered with butcher paper and paper napkins. Entertainment is provided, and guests in the mood can try out the dance floor between courses. Start with the *varenyky* (boiled dumplings filled with your choice of potato, meat, or sauerkraut) or the *kartoplyanyky* (oven-browned potato pancakes). Entrées include the house specialty—*kovbassa* and *kapusta* (homemade smoked sausages with sauerkraut and potatoes). The sautéed walleye in mushroom sauce comes wrapped in a potato pancake; the broiled walleye is covered with spicy cabbage on a bed of rice. Truly hungry guests may want to try the "Kozak Feast": borscht, house salad, cabbage rolls, filled dumplings, Ukrainian sausage and sauerkraut, skewered beef and pork, potato pancake, coffee, and dessert. Desserts include European rolled pancakes filled with fruit preserves or cheese, hot apple strudel, cheesecake, and a torte of the day. *2212 W. Chicago Ave., tel. 312/292–1000. AE, DC, MC, V. Closed Mon., holidays. Moderate.*

North

Afghani **The Helmand.** Green plants, wall hangings, Persian rugs, and ★ candles on linen tablecloths make the Helmand unusually inviting. As you would expect from Afghanistan's location, the cuisine is influenced by that of North India, yet Middle Eastern influences are obvious as well. The food is richly seasoned but not spicy hot, a pleasing cuisine for diners looking for something different and not ready for high adventure. Be sure to try the *aushak* (Afghan ravioli filled with leeks, served on yogurt, and topped with ground beef and mint) and the *mantwo* (pastry shell filled with onions and beef, served on yogurt, and topped with carrots, yellow split peas, and beef sauce). The *koufta challow* (lamb and beef meatballs with raisins, turmeric, green pepper, green peas, and fresh tomato sauce, served with rice) is delicious. Vegetable lovers will enjoy an order of *sabzi* (literally, vegetable—here, spinach sautéed with beef and spices), *bendi* (okra cooked to tenderness in a rich sauce), or *shornakhod* (a salad of potato, chickpeas, and scallions served with cilantro vinaigrette). This is satisfying food, graciously

served. *3201 N. Halsted St., tel. 312/935–2447. Weekend reservations accepted. AE, DC, MC, V. Closed lunch, Sun. Moderate.*

American **Star Top Café.** One of the most daring American eateries in
Chicago—especially among those with moderate prices. Star
Top uses seasonings with what seems like wild abandon, but
the combinations nearly always work. If scallops with mint-
Montrachet sauce seems too odd for you, try the sautéed
sweetbreads and shrimp with Chinese mustard and rosemary
or the grilled amberjack with black peppercorns and a mango
glaze. Desserts are more traditional and very good. The dining
room is as eclectic as the menu, with Mylar-finish reptile-pat-
tern tablecloths, turquoise-wash walls, and faux-stone wain-
scoting. You'll find wit and imagination and very little pretense
here. *2748 N. Lincoln Ave., tel. 312/281–0997. Reservations
strongly advised. AE, MC, V. No lunch. Closed Mon. Moderate–
Expensive.*

Brett's. This cute charmer, in a rapidly gentrified neighborhood, is one of the few restaurants in town that bans smoking
entirely. Decor is uncomplicated but cheerful, with soft lighting
and classical music working together to create a mellow environment. Menu is creative American, soups are a particular
strength, and desserts are heavenly. We come here just to
munch on the homemade bread—and that's free. *2011 W.
Roscoe St., tel. 312/248–0999. Reservations recommended on
weekends. MC, V. No lunch. Closed Mon. Moderate.*

The Elbo Room. This very casual eatery specializes in rotisserie-grilled meats and fish, generally liberally seasoned with
garlic. Pastas are good bets, too. Wide-slat wooden blinds give
the simple dining room a dose of charm. The downstairs nightclub features live music and is a good postmeal destination;
restaurant patrons get their cover charge waived or reduced,
depending on the performer. *2871 N. Lincoln Ave., tel. 312/549–
5549. AE, MC, V. No lunch. Closed Mon. Moderate.*

Brazilian **Rio's Casa Iberia.** Two long rooms are softly lit by oil lamps and
★ furbished with white tablecloths, pink napkins, and rose-
rimmed plates. The food spans three cuisines: Brazilian, Portuguese, and northern Spanish. Fresh seafood—mussels,
clams, shrimp, squid—is plentiful in unusual preparations:
Clams are paired with smoked ham and sautéed with onions,
tomato, green pepper, and parsley for one Brazilian appetizer,
and a Spanish entrée has fillet of sole cooked on a green garlic
sauce and served with clams. The classic dishes associated with
Brazil and Portugal are *feijoada* (a stew of black beans with
pork, sausage, bacon, dry meat, and spices on rice) and *bacal-
hau* (grilled salt cod served with a Portuguese-style tomato
sauce). There are several soups and two desserts—the traditional *flan* (caramel custard, served here with whipped cream)
and *torta de laranja* (orange tart with orange liqueur sauce).
*4611 N. Kedzie Ave., tel. 312/588–7800. AE, DC, MC, V. Closed
Sun.; holidays. Moderate.*

Ethiopian **Mama Desta's Red Sea.** Dramatically different from European
cooking, the stewlike dishes at Mama Desta's are intriguing
combinations of herbs and spices with complex aromas and interesting textures. The food here is flavorful, earthy, and simple. There's no silverware; diners use spongy, slightly sour
flat-bread to scoop up the chef's creations. *3216 N. Clark St.,
312/935–7561. Reservations accepted. AE, DC, MC, V. Closed
Mon. lunch. Inexpensive.*

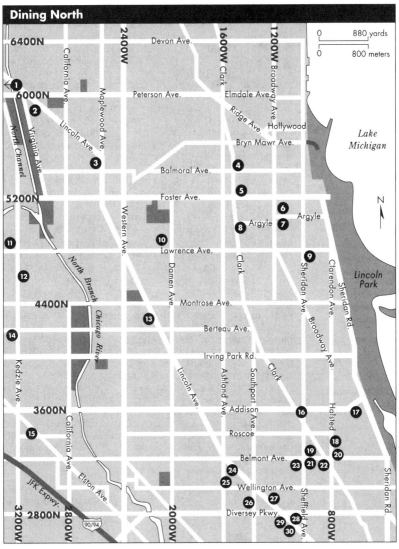

Dining North

Angelina, **17**
Ann Sather, **5, 21**
Arun's, **14**
Bella Vista, **23**
Brett's, **30**
Cozy Thai, **10**
Da Nicolá, **24**
The Elbo Room, **27**
Gin Go Gae, **3**
Heidelberger Fass, **13**

The Helmand, **20**
Jimmy's Place, **15**
Little Bucharest, **25**
Machu Picchu, **4**
Mama Desta's Red
Sea, **19**
Matsuya, **16**
Mekong, **7**
Misto, **28**
Pasteur, **9**

Rio's Casa Iberia, **12**
Shilla, **2**
Star Top Café, **29**
Thai Classic, **22**
Thai Touch, **11**
Tokyo Marina, **8**
Via Veneto, **1**
Yoshi's Cafe, **18**
Zum Deutschen
Eck, **26**

French **Jimmy's Place.** Located in an unprepossessing light-industrial
★ strip, Jimmy's Place serves consistently excellent contemporary French cuisine, with a Japanese accent supplied by the
chef, Kevin Shikami. White tablecloths are adorned with fresh
flowers, and music from grand opera plays softly. Choose from
extensive daily specials, or order from a dinner menu that
changes monthly and might include such appetizers as cold
poached shrimp and avocado with saffron butter, grilled quail
on duck mousse, an assortment of house pâtés and terrines,
and a fresh pasta. A fresh fish entrée is offered daily; other
selections may include braised sweetbreads in applejack cream
sauce with mushrooms and apples, and grilled saddle of lamb
on a bed of roasted peppers with white wine, shallot, and garlic
sauce and sautéed goat cheese. Homemade pastries and desserts with espresso round out a splendid meal. The entire restaurant is smoke free on Saturday nights, but smoking is
allowed in one dining room the rest of the week. *3420 N. Elston
Ave., tel. 312/539–2999. Reservations required. DC, MC, V.
Closed Sat. lunch; Sun. Expensive–Very Expensive.*

★ **Yoshi's Café.** This tiny, simply decorated restaurant, with its
crisp white linen tablecloths, is the establishment of Yoshi Kat-
sumura, one of the best chefs in Chicago. His menu tantalizes
with such appetizers as pheasant pâté with duck liver mousse
and lobster ravioli with champagne-caviar sauce and such entrées as breast of chicken, sweetbreads, and shiitake mushrooms in a phyllo purse with red pepper coulis. Yet the printed
menu tells only half the story, for a daily menu more than doubles the offerings. The soft-shell crab tempura with tomato
cilantro sauce is irresistible, as is a cream soup made with three
types of mushrooms. The entrées emphasize fish and poultry:
steamed woven fillets of fresh Dover sole and salmon on spinach pasta with lobster cream sauce, for example, and grilled
quail and squab salad with radicchio and marinated shiitake
and oyster mushrooms in warm red wine vinaigrette. Soups, a
special salad, and desserts are prepared daily. These are elegant, original creations, skillfully prepared and exquisitely
presented. *3257 N. Halsted St., tel. 312/248–6160. Reservations
required. AE, MC, V. Closed lunch, Mon., and holidays. Expensive–Very Expensive.*

German **Heidelberger Fass.** Although brighter than the typical beer
hall, the Heidelberger Fass, with its stained glass, china, and
menus in medieval German style, evokes the feeling of being
on a street in Germany. The menu includes American favorites
(turkey salad sandwich, poached or pan-fried trout, broiled
filet mignon) and such German delights as liver dumplings,
Kassler ribs (smoked pork loin, cooked to order), two types of
sausage (veal and a veal/pork/beef combination), and sauerbraten. Specialties include the unusual venison schnitzel in mushrooms with red wine sauce, and pheasant braised in its own
gravy. The quality of the food can be uneven. *4300 N. Lincoln
Ave., tel. 312/478–2486. Reservations advised. AE, D, DC, MC,
V. Closed Sun. lunch, Tues. Moderate.*

Zum Deutschen Eck. Here is a cozy German eatery where
stained glass complements dark wood, and costumed
waitresses create a warm, comfortable atmosphere. The fare
includes the typically German homemade *suelze* (head cheese),
herring salad, potato pancakes, *Koenigsberger klops* (German
meatballs), a *schlact platte* combination of bratwurst, knack-
wurst, and smoked pork loin, and *schnitzel à la jaeger* (cutlet

sautéed in red wine with green pepper, onion, fresh mushrooms, and red pepper sauce). Old favorites are also featured: sauerbraten, half roast duckling, Wiener schnitzel. Most entrées are served with whipped potato and sauerkraut; a few come with buttered noodles or spaetzle. *2924 N. Southport Ave., tel. 312/525–8390. Reservations advised. AE, MC, V. Moderate.*

Italian **Da Nicolá.** An Old World kind of restaurant, Da Nicolá rises well above the usual American-style Italian food. Among the excellent pastas are ravioli filled with a puree of *porcini* mushrooms and a *rotolo di pasta* (a large sheet of pasta filled with spinach, ground meat, and cheeses, rolled, poached, then sliced and served). Portions are generous. *3114 N. Lincoln Ave., tel. 312/935–8000. Reservations advised on weekends. AE, MC. No lunch. Closed Tues. Moderate.*

Misto. The word means "mixture," and that's what you get at this stylish restaurant, where the food is Italian with a distinctly Asian accent. The grilled salmon is excellent in all its guises here, and the pastas, including a "crazy spaghetti" laced with chili peppers, are a good bet, too. For a more Oriental touch, try the pork tenderloin, glazed with a Thai barbecue sauce and plated with shredded white ginger-pickled cabbage—the chef's humorous takeoff on coleslaw. Desserts range from tiramisu in a tiny espresso cup (just right if you seek just a taste) to an almost overwhelming chocolate Vesuvio cake with a molten-chocolate interior. *2747 N. Lincoln Ave., tel. 312/281–1400. Reservations advised weekends. D, DC, MC, V. No lunch. Closed Mon. Moderate.*

Via Veneto. This is a tiny, family-run restaurant with simple decor and sophisticated food. Pastas are excellent, and you'll find some daring versions among the daily specials. Desserts have improved enormously of late. The wine list is thoughtful and thorough. Don't bother coming here on Saturday nights, when the crowds are impossible. Friday is a better bet, midweek better. There's a small parking lot in back, but street parking is never a problem in this extremely safe residential neighborhood. *3449 W. Peterson Ave., tel. 312/267–0888. Reservations advised weekends. AE, D, DC, MC, V. No lunch weekends. Moderate.*

Angelina. The high-funk appeal of this restaurant attracts a loyal following among Chicago's hipsters and makes for some fascinating, offbeat people-watching. Pastas, carefully prepared with fresh, high-quality ingredients, are the most reliable choices. The service can be erratic, and the wait may be long. Hang out in Joe's, a friendly neighborhood tavern next door, while waiting for a table. *3561 N. Broadway, tel. 312/935–5933. No reservations. MC, V. Closed lunch, holidays. Inexpensive–Moderate.*

Japanese **Matsuya.** This small, storefront restaurant has a sushi bar, wood paneling, brown tile floor, and a wood floor-to-ceiling screen in front of the kitchen. Sushi and an extensive choice of appetizers dominate the menu: deep-fried spicy chicken wings, steamed spinach with sesame, whitefish with white smelt roe, seafood and vegetables on skewers, and dumplings with sauce are just a few. Tempura, fish, and meat teriyaki dishes, a few noodle dishes, and bowl-of-rice dishes (with toppings of your choice) round out the menu. *3469 N. Clark St., tel. 312/248–2677. Reservations accepted for 4 or more. MC, V. Closed weekday lunch, holidays. Moderate.*

Tokyo Marina. Many Japanese restaurants strive for a gracious, refined atmosphere to complement the careful presentation of a small quantity of rather expensive food. Tokyo Marina is a refreshing contrast to this model, a welcome choice for Americans who want to try Japanese food but are put off by the excessive refinement, delicacy, and price at some establishments. Customers seat themselves at wood tables in this bright, 30-table restaurant and sushi bar. A large menu board covers one wall in the dining area, and Japanese paintings are on other walls. Conversations in Japanese and in English mingle in an amiable din. Like the atmosphere, the food has a certain robustness. Try the *nabe* with crab—the better part of a whole, tender Dungeness crab braised in broth with assorted vegetables, tofu, and noodles; it's succulent, filling, and a bargain at the price. The several dozen entrées include preparations of fresh raw or cooked tuna, yellowtail, mackerel, red snapper, and lobster; "bowl" dishes of beef, chicken, pork, shrimp, or eel served on rice; wheat or buckwheat noodles with assorted ingredients in broth; and the familiar beef or chicken teriyaki, tempuras of all kinds, and sukiyaki. *5058 N. Clark St., tel. 312/878–2900. Reservations not required. MC, V. Inexpensive–Moderate.*

Korean
★
Shilla. Exquisite tropical fish swim in a saltwater tank as you wait to be seated. To your right is the bar; ahead is a large dining room with sushi bar at the front, flanked by individual dining rooms accommodating intimate groups or larger parties. Americans may be steered to one of these rooms on the assumption that they will want mainly grilled foods prepared at their table. Grilled dishes are available in the main dining room, too, and those who prefer dining with other customers and who hope to thus avoid the preparation process should ask for a table in the main room. The menu is enormous; in addition to grilled dishes, there are many noodle preparations, stewlike offerings, and stir-fries. Since the "appetizers" come in entrée-size portions (at entrée-size prices), you will want to exercise caution in the number of dishes you order. The Korean pancake is excellent, and the fried oysters are not to be missed. *Seng sun japtang* is the Korean equivalent of bouillabaisse. Entrées are served with an assortment of Korean relishes, including *kimchee*, the spicy pickled cabbage that accompanies every meal in Korea (ask for it hot if you like it that way). Shilla's food is authentic; the large number of Korean guests attests to that. *5930 N. Lincoln Ave., tel. 312/275–5930. Reservations advised. AE, MC, V. Moderate.*

Gin Go Gae. Two dining rooms—one casual, one more formally done with red carpeting and Oriental art—accommodate a large number of guests, many of them Korean. The food is plentiful and delicious; the servers are warm and attentive. Entrées come with *kimchee* (choose mild or spicy hot) and an assortment of relishes that might make a meal in itself. Try the onion pancakes, here served with a sauce abundant with Oriental vegetables. More adventurous diners can sample the noodles in cold broth. *5433 N. Lincoln Ave., tel. 312/334–3895. AE, MC, V. Inexpensive.*

Peruvian
Machu Picchu. Clean white walls complement beautiful Peruvian rugs; fresh flowers and red napkins adorn each table. The owner, Moses Asturrizaga, refers to the food as "nouveau Peruvian"; its spicy heat has been toned down in deference to American tastes, but all dishes can be ordered extra hot. Ap-

petizers include *ceviche* and *escabeche* (chicken fillet marinated in onion sauce). For an entrée, you might have the duck in Amaretto sauce; in Peru it is served with sliced hot chilies, so that each bite of duck is accompanied by a jab of heat. The less adventurous diner may prefer the fish in tarragon sauce. The bread is heated before serving; the soups and desserts are limited. *5427 N. Clark St., tel. 312/769–0455. Reservations advised. MC, V. BYOB. Closed lunch; Sun., Mon., holidays. Moderate-Expensive.*

Romanian **Little Bucharest.** A cozy, simple room adorned with stained-glass windows, Little Bucharest serves comforting foods Romanian style. The soups are hearty—chicken, oxtail, or veal meatball with dumplings and vegetables; a "European style" salad is the only other appetizer. Veal paprikash, *tocana à la Bucharest*, and beef goulash are prominent on the menu, which includes three veal roll preparations, several baked chicken entrées, four pork chop offerings, two sausage dishes, and the obligatory steak for the diner who will eat nothing else. An attractive entrée selection of stuffed vegetables (choose from eggplant, red peppers, green peppers, and cabbage) is available. Daily specials supplement the menu. *3001 N. Ashland Ave., tel. 312/929–8640. AE, D, MC, V. Inexpensive.*

Southwest **Blue Mesa.** Chicago's first southwestern restaurant (it opened
American 12 years ago) plays to a noisy, casual crowd—reservations are a must on weekends. The menu has plenty of traditional dishes for the timid, but fire-eaters should head for such specialties as jalapeño-grilled shrimp. Fresh fish generally is treated to a chili-rich sauce (plenty of punch, but rarely very hot), such as blackened tuna with sesame-pasilla beurre blanc. The fiery chocolate fritter sundae is topped with a chili-laced chocolate sauce crowned with a thoughtful scoop of vanilla-almond ice cream to cool you down. Sunday brunch is a favorite. *1729 N. Haltsted St., tel. 312/944–5990. Reservations strongly advised on weekends. AE, D, DC, MC, V. No lunch Sat. Moderate–Inexpensive.*

Swedish **Ann Sather.** The large, light, airy Ann Sather restaurants emphasize home-style food and service. Both are popular for weekend breakfasts. Specialties include homemade cinnamon rolls, potato sausage, and chicken croquettes; a full sandwich menu is also offered. A Swedish sampler lets you try duck breast with lingonberry glaze, a Swedish meatball, potato sausage, dumpling, and sauerkraut. Very reasonable entrée prices include an appetizer (Swedish fruit soup and pickled herring are among them), two side dishes (choose from Swedish brown beans, homemade applesauce, mashed or boiled potatoes, pickled beets, and more), and dessert (homemade fruit or cream pies, puddings, cakes, and ice creams). Daily specials augment the standard menu. *5207 N. Clark St., tel. 312/271–6677; 929 W. Belmont Ave., tel. 312/348–2378. MC, V. Closed holidays. Inexpensive.*

Thai **Arun's.** Many think Arun's is the best of Chicago's more than
★ 80 Thai establishments. Influenced by both Chinese and Indian cuisines, Thai food nevertheless has its own characteristics. Lemongrass, *kha* (a type of ginger), lime juice and leaves, and basil figure heavily in the cuisine, as do sauces based on coconut milk. Some dishes are spicy hot; let your server know if you prefer dishes mild or very hot. Appetizers include the familiar pork *satay* (marinated, grilled pork strips served with peanut

sauce and cucumber) and egg rolls and the less familiar *yum wunsen* (glass noodles with cooked shrimp and ground pork, spiced with scallion, cilantro, chili peppers, and lime). Shrimp or fish is a must: Try the garlic prawns, the whole fried red snapper, or the squid in hot pepper sauce with garlic and chili peppers. The extensive basic menu is supplemented by daily specials. The two-level dining room has lots of natural wood, complemented by Thai art and a small art gallery—a far cry from the typical storefront ethnic restaurant. *4156 N. Kedzie Ave., tel. 312/539–1909. AE, D, DC, MC, V. Closed lunch, Mon., and holidays. Expensive.*

Cozy Thai. One of the few storefront Thai restaurants in town to offer live Thai and American music on weekends, Cozy Thai is also one of the city's best. The chef spent several years at Arun's *(see above)*. The atmosphere is sophisticated: fresh flowers decorate each table, and the servers wear black and white. Dishes to try include *kai tod* (crisp fried chicken); spicy pad ped catfish; chicken wings stuffed with ground pork, garlic, bean thread, and black mushrooms; and pork satay. Attractive vegetable garnishes make classic Thai dishes look as good as they taste. *4834 N. Damen Ave., tel. 312/334–7300. Reservations advised. AE, DC, MC, V. Closed weekend lunch. Moderate.*

Thai Classic. This attractive, spotless restaurant just a few blocks south of Wrigley Field features contemporary decor, good service, and meticulously prepared dishes. Bring your own beer or wine; there's a package-liquor store about a block away that's eager for your business (why else would it stock Singha beer?). *3332 N. Clark St., tel. 312/404–2000. Reservations accepted weekends only. AE, MC, V. Closed Mon. lunch. Inexpensive–Moderate.*

Thai Touch. This former luncheonette has been transformed into a lovely, well-appointed dining room. Creatively prepared and beautifully presented Thai food makes this place worth seeking out, even though it's off the beaten restaurant track. All of the traditional Thai dishes are here—the curries are especially good—and presentation goes far beyond the norm. Occasional surprises, such as crab-in-a-basket, are worth trying as well. *3200 W. Lawrence Ave., tel. 312/539–5700. Reservations accepted. MC, V. Inexpensive.*

Vietnamese   **Mekong.** Mekong feels a bit crowded even on the rare occasion
★   when it's empty. Many tables have been squeezed in, the aisles are narrow and winding, and ornate lamps overhang the tables. Masses of people jam the small waiting area on Saturday night, adding to the din of eaters chomping, servers bustling, and dishes clattering in the partly open kitchen. Yet the food is worth the ordeal. Try the lemony Vietnamese-style barbecued beef (not at all like Texas barbecue)—thinly sliced and served just at room temperature with salad—or have the whole crab in sauce, or try one of the many noodle preparations. *4953 N. Broadway, tel. 312/271–0206. AE, DC, MC, V. Closed Mon. Inexpensive–Moderate.*

★   **Pasteur.** Pasteur was opened just a few years ago by a family of Vietnamese refugees who arrived here with few resources, little English, and the need to earn money; their beginning was rocky, but they stuck with it and made it a success. The extensive menu includes appetizers of whole sautéed Dungeness crab, the classic shrimp paste wrapped around sugarcane, and the house specialty—a deep-fried shrimp cake served with fresh salad and special sauce. Noodle lovers will be delighted with the selection: three rice noodle soups, five egg noodle soups, five fried rice noodle dishes, five soft rice noodle dishes, and three fried egg noodle dishes. Shrimp, poultry, beef, pork, and fish selections are available. Many of the translated descriptions of the dishes sound like familiar Chinese preparations, but the difference is in the seasoning and spicing. Vietnamese food relies on lemongrass and fish sauce—two ingredients not used in Chinese cuisine—to give dishes and dipping sauces their distinctive flavor. *4759 N. Sheridan Rd., tel. 312/271–6673. AE, MC, V. Closed Mon., lunch, and some holidays. Inexpensive–Moderate.*

Downtown

American **Buckingham's.** A reliable menu offering well-prepared steaks and seafood, and its proximity to downtown theater and music events, make Buckingham's a destination to consider. The dining room is elegant and classic, the service warm and attentive. *Chicago Hilton and Towers, 720 S. Michigan Ave., tel. 312/922–4400. Reservations recommended. AE, D, DC, MC, V. No lunch. Expensive.*

Prairie. The interior is inspired by the work of Frank Lloyd Wright, and the food by the flavors of the Midwestern states. The result is a thoroughly well conceived American regional restaurant. Meats and game are solid choices, but don't overlook regional fish selections, especially the Lake Superior whitefish. *500 S. Dearborn St., tel. 312/663–1143. Reservations recommended. AE, D, DC, MC, V. Expensive.*

★ **Printer's Row.** The owner and chef, Michael Foley, opened this stylish restaurant when the historic Printer's Row district was just beginning to show signs of a renaissance after decades of decay. Accordingly, his is now the established institution in what has become a very attractive urban neighborhood of renovated loft buildings and gracious older apartment houses. The lounge/entryway and, farther back, the dining room are done in warm woods and brown tones, contrasted by neutral walls and crisp white linens. One of the most interesting and satisfying restaurants in Chicago, Printer's Row continues to unveil fresh and intriguing regional American menus. Game meats receive uncommonly good treatment, as does seafood. And the homemade ice cream is just wonderful. This is one of Chicago's outstanding restaurants, and it is substantially less expensive than many others in its class. *550 S. Dearborn St., tel. 312/461–0780. Jacket advised. Reservations advised, required on weekends. AE, D, DC, MC, V. Closed Sat. lunch, Sun. Expensive.*

Army & Lou's. Soul food at its finest is featured at this venerable south side institution. More than a few hearts were broken when this restaurant closed in 1992, but a trio of investors, who were shrewd enough to coax former owners Charles and Mary Cole out of retirement to serve as consultants, has restored Army & Lou's to its former glory. Fried chicken, barbecued ribs, greens, turkey, and catfish are specialties. *420 E. 75th St., tel. 312/483–3100. Reservations accepted. AE, MC, V. Closed Sun. Moderate–Expensive.*

The Walnut Room. Wood archways and beams and Oriental screens complement this carpeted, Victorian-style dining room at Marshall Field. Long a haven for weary shoppers and business lunchers who seek a relaxing, unhurried spot, the Walnut Room offers beef tenderloin tips Stroganoff, Field's own

Army & Lou's, **31**
The Berghoff, **5**
Buckingham's, **21**
Chon y Chano, **27**
Courtyards of
Plaka, **17**
Emperor's Choice, **25**
Everest, **7**
Greek Islands, **14**
Harold's Chicken
Shack, **29**
Heaven on Seven, **3**
House of Fortune, **26**
Lou Mitchell's, **11**
Maple Tree Inn, **32**
New Rosebud Cafe, **19**
Nick's Fishmarket, **4**
Nuevo Leon, **22**
Pegasus, **13**
Playa Azul, **23**
Prairie, **20**
Primavera, **1**
Printer's Row, **6**
Santorini, **15**
Soul Queen, **34**
Taste of Jamaica, **33**
Taylor Street
Bistro, **16**
Ten-Tsuna, **30**
Three Happiness, **24**
Trattoria No. 10, **9**
Tuscany, **18**
University
Gardens, **28**
Vivere, **8**
Vivo, **12**
The Walnut Room, **2**
Yvette
Wintergarden, **10**

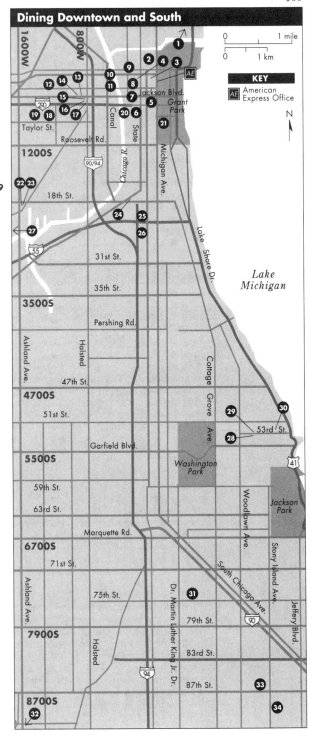

Dining Downtown and South

KEY

AE American Express Office

Lake Michigan

chicken pot pie, roast free-range chicken, scallop and vegetable fettuccine, and a fresh fish of the day, broiled to order. The extensive salad and sandwich selection includes Cobb salad, Szechuan beef and noodle salad served in a crisp potato basket, several hamburger preparations, and a club sandwich. Among the dessert possibilities are puddings, pies, cakes, tortes, and ice cream sundaes. The traditional tea served at 3 PM boasts Field's own Scotch scones with Devonshire clotted cream and jam. Complete bar service is available. *Marshall Field, 111 N. State St., tel. 312/781–1000. AE, MC, V. Closed dinner, Sun, and holidays. Moderate.*

★ **Lou Mitchell's.** Be prepared to stand in line, and be assured that the wait is worth it. Management will give boxes of Milk Duds to the women and girls in your group, and when a spot is available for you, you're likely to be seated at a long communal table (smaller tables may require a longer wait). The waitresses have a rough-and-hearty style that gets everyone served promptly, if brusquely. Fourteen omelets, made from eggs so fresh they remind you how eggs should taste, and cooked in lots of butter, form the centerpiece of a menu that includes pancakes, French toast, and Belgian waffles for breakfast and sandwiches, salads, and a few hot plates for lunch. People flock to Lou Mitchell's because the ingredients are top quality, everything is fresh, and everything is homemade—the Greek bread, the raisin toast, the orange marmalade, the pies, the pound cake, and the pudding with cream. Portions are large, yet the food is so good that people routinely, and with only a little embarrassment, stuff themselves. Breakfast is served all day long. *565 W. Jackson Blvd., tel. 312/939–3111. No reservations. No credit cards. Closed dinner, Sun., and holidays. Inexpensive.*

Cajun **Heaven on Seven.** Officially known as the Garland Building Restaurant, this seventh-floor coffee shop, open daily for breakfast and lunch but never for dinner, would be unremarkable but for the Cajun and Creole specialties that augment the standard menu of egg dishes and sandwiches. Order a shrimp étouffée, and marvel at the full, authentic cuisine served in these simple, incongruous surroundings. At peak lunchtimes, the line snakes out the door and down the corridor to the elevator. (But customers eat quickly, so even a long line often means a wait of merely 15 minutes.) The closest thing to liquor you'll find here is one of several nonalcoholic beers. *111 N. Wabash Ave., tel. 312/263–6443. No reservations. No credit cards. No dinner. Inexpensive.*

French **Everest.** As its name suggests, this restaurant reaches extraor-
★ dinary heights and in more ways than one: First, it is literally 40 stories above the ground and offers a sweeping view of the city's west side. Pricewise, the dinner check here can be formidable (for most people, this is a major-event destination). Cuisinewise, Everest hits highs that most restaurants can't begin to approach. Chef Jean Joho is one of the most creative in town; he takes often-ignored, humble ingredients (particularly favoring foods from his native Alsace) and transforms them into regal and memorable dishes. Past triumphs on this ever-changing menu have included smoked sturgeon with yellow lentil terrine and squid-ink risotto with calamari. The dining room is pleasingly neutral, focusing attention on the kitchen's exquisitely arranged plates; oversize tables provide spaciousness. Service is discreet and very professional. The

wine list has tremendous depth. *440 S. La Salle St., tel. 312/663–8920. Jacket required. Reservations required. AE, D, DC, MC, V. Closed Mon. dinner, Sat. lunch, and Sun. Very Expensive.*

★ **Taylor Street Bistro.** In the heart of Italian-restaurant row sits one of the city's best bistros. The steak au poivre is sensational, the grilled salmon and roast grouper marvelous. Atmosphere is relaxed and friendly. *1400 W. Taylor St., tel. 312/829–2828. Reservations recommended. MC, V. Moderate.*

Yvette Wintergarden. There are few places left where it's possible to dine and dance under one roof. This new restaurant is one of them. There's a large dance floor as well as live music every night in the Top 40/disco mode. The menu, offering a classic bistro selection, is quite good, though the daily fish specials are often your best bet. *311 S. Wacker Dr., tel. 312/408–1244. Reservations recommended. AE, DC, MC, V. Closed Sun., Sat. lunch. Moderate.*

German **The Berghoff.** This Chicago institution has been serving its signature beer since the end of Prohibition (the Berghoff holds city liquor license #1). Long a favorite of the Loop lunchtime crowd, the atmosphere here is bustling and noisy. The oak-paneled interiors are handsome and evoke an authentic, old Chicago feel. You can expect to wait for a table, but then for your meal to proceed rapidly once you're seated. A menu of German classics (Wiener schnitzel, sauerbraten) is augmented by American favorites. The seeded rye bread is outstanding. The food and service (notwithstanding the formal dress of the very correct waiters) are a little too mass-produced for fine dining, and the brisk (some say brusque) efficiency with which orders are taken, food appears, and plates are whisked away does not conduce to lingering over coffee or conversation. Yet the food is competently prepared and occasionally excellent, and the portions are generous. It's no place for a quiet meal, but if you like hearty fare, washed down with excellent beer, you'll love this place. A sister property, Berghoff Brewery and Restaurant (436 W. Ontario St.), features several made-on-premises beers and serves a somewhat similar dinner menu. *17 W. Adams St., tel. 312/427–3170. Reservations accepted for 6 or more. AE, DC, MC, V. Closed Sun. Moderate.*

Greek **Courtyards of Plaka.** With its salmon-colored walls, red-tile floors, aquamarine bar, white-clothed tables, and live music, Courtyards of Plaka is one of the most sophisticated Greek restaurants in Chicago. Friendly servers work hard to make sure everyone has a good time. Appetizers include the ubiquitous *saganaki* (fried cheese), *melizzanoszlata* (a purée of lightly spiced eggplant to be spread on Greek bread), and *taramosalata* (fish roe salad). Also available, though it doesn't appear on the menu, is *skordalia* (garlic-flavored mashed potatoes). *340 S. Halsted St., tel. 312/263–0767. Reservations not required. AE, D, DC, MC, V. Moderate.*

Greek Islands. This large, colorful, and noisily cheerful restaurant is located in the heart of Greektown. Food is good and service fast. This restaurant draws lots of large parties, probably because the waiters know how to make things comfortable and fun for groups. *200 S. Halsted St., 312/782–9855. Reservations not accepted on weekends. AE, D, DC, MC, V. Moderate.*

Santorini. Don't come to this spacious and friendly spot expecting the tourist's typical Greek restaurant; instead, come for the impeccably fresh and well-prepared seafood. Be sure to try the charcoal-grilled octopus appetizer. *138 S. Halsted St., tel. 312/829–8820. Reservations accepted weekdays. AE, MC, V. Closed Mon. Moderate.*

Pegasus. Greektown's newest restaurant features a lovely interior: French doors overlook the street, architectural details enliven the pure white walls and ceilings, and a striking mural covers two walls. Greek standbys such as stuffed grape leaves, lamb dishes, and spinach pie are reliable here, but the daily specials generally offer the most intriguing choices. *130 S. Halsted St., tel. 312/226–3377. Reservations recommended. AE, D, DC, MC, V. Inexpensive.*

Italian **Primavera.** Once known exclusively for its singing waiters, this hotel restaurant now has a kitchen that can match the service in theatrics. The something-for-everyone menu has plenty of pastas, and the veal chop is excellent; the restaurant also boasts the best (and largest) cappuccino in town. *Fairmont Hotel, 200 N. Columbus Dr., tel. 312/565–6655. Reservations recommended. AE, D, DC, MC, V. Expensive.*

Trattoria No. 10. Quarry-tile floors, theatrical lighting, and a burnt-orange, red, and ocher color scheme combine to give this former basement boiler room the charm and warmth of an outdoor café. One of the signature dishes at this eclectic Italian restaurant is ravioli with exotic fillings of lobster or mushrooms. The pastas are fresh, and the interesting antipasti include sea scallops with orange-fennel relish, and *rotolo di mozzarella* (homemade mozzarella cheese rolled around layers of pesto and prosciutto). The steaks, chops, and fish dishes are good but are not standouts on the menu. For dessert, try the *tiramisu* (liqueured ladyfingers topped with mascarpone cheese) or the triple-chocolate cannoli. *10 N. Dearborn St., tel. 312/984–1718. Reservations advised. AE, MC, V. Closed weekend lunch and Sun. Expensive.*

★ **Vivere.** The old Florentine Room, on the middle floor of the venerable three-restaurant Italian Village, has been transformed into a palace of modern Italian dining. The decor alone is worth the visit: the designers have made sure there isn't an uninteresting view in the house. The menu takes traditional recipes and gives them a slight nouvelle spin, and nearly everything works beautifully. *71 W. Monroe St., tel. 312/332–7005. Reservations recommended. AE, DC, MC, V. Closed Sun.; Sat. lunch. Expensive.*

New Rosebud Cafe. This extremely popular restaurant specializes in good old-fashioned, Southern Italian cuisine. One of the best red sauces in town can be found here, and the roasted peppers, homemade sausage, and exquisitely prepared pastas are not to be missed. The wait for a table can stretch to an hour or more, despite confirmed reservations, but those with patience will find that the meal is well worth the wait. *1500 W. Taylor St., tel. 312/942–1117. Reservations advised. AE, DC, MC, V. Closed Sat. lunch and Sun. Moderate.*

Tuscany. As the name suggests, this restaurant focuses on hearty flavors and simple preparations. The rotisserie-grilled chicken is especially good. The Taylor Street neighborhood, just west of the Loop, is a popular destination at lunchtime. *1014 W. Taylor St., tel. 312/829–1990. Reservations recommended. AE, MC, V. Moderate.*

Vivo. Well off the beaten path, but one of the city's leading see-and-be-seen restaurants, Vivo is the darling of the high-fashion set. The people-watching (okay, gawking) is fascinating. Striking visuals and attentive service (the waiters themselves are rather stylishly turned out) are more memorable than the rather unadventurous menu, which, though certainly contemporary Italian, offers nothing that can't be found elsewhere. *838 W. Randolph St., tel. 312/733–3379. Reservations strongly advised. AE, D, DC, MC, V. Closed weekend lunch. Moderate.*

Seafood **Nick's Fishmarket.** A dark, sumptuous room filled with leather and wood, Nick's caters to the high-powered business set as well as to romantic couples. Anyone, in fact, who appreciates overwhelmingly attentive service (and is willing to pay accordingly) will enjoy Nick's, where tuxedoed waiters greet you like a valued regular even if it's your first visit. Nick's is best known for its wide assortment of fresh seafood, particularly for its Pacific catches; the menu recently has been readjusted to include more Italian specialties and lighter seafood-pasta pairings. Massive steaks are always available, too. Nick's Fishmarket in Rosemont (10275 W. Higgins Rd.), near O'Hare airport, is a virtual carbon copy of the downtown location. *1 First National Plaza, tel. 312/621–0200. Jacket and tie advised. Reservations advised. AE, D, DC, MC, V. Closed Sun.; Sat. lunch. Very Expensive.*

South

American **Harold's Chicken Shack.** The name says it all: This cramped hole-in-the-wall carryout serves up perhaps the best fried chicken in the city, crisply coated on the outside and moist and tender within. Although the restaurant is part of a chain, Harold maintained control of all the branches and insisted that his techniques and recipes be followed everywhere. For an unusual snack treat, try the deep-fried gizzards in hot sauce (they can become an addiction). If you can wait that long, take your bag to the University of Chicago quadrangle or Promontory Point and have a picnic on the grass. *1364 E. 53rd St., tel. 312/667–9835. No credit cards. Inexpensive.*

Cajun/Creole **Maple Tree Inn.** A renovated three-floor building is the home ★ of this south side jewel; owner Charlie Orr was cooking Cajun long before it was trendy and kept doing it long after the fashionable set moved on. A third-floor bar makes the long waits (guaranteed on weekends) tolerable. And, yes, the food is worth waiting for. The New Orleans barbecue shrimp is a messy, finger-licking delight; the homemade andouille sausage is properly incendiary; and the pecan pie brings the meal to a sweet, smooth finish. *10730 S. Western Ave., tel. 312/239–3688. Reservations accepted for 4 or more with credit card deposit. AE, MC, V. Closed Mon. and Tues. Moderate.*

Caribbean **Taste of Jamaica.** If you've traveled in the Caribbean and eaten indigenous food there, one look at this menu will activate your salivary glands. There are no appetizers; instead, try one of the soups: pumpkin, pepper pot, manish water, conch, red peas, pigeon gungu peas, or tripe. Then move on to the curried goat, the oxtail and broad beans, the jerk chicken, or the brown-stewed fish. Nowhere else in Chicago can you find codfish and ackee or codfish and *callaloo* (that wonderful spinachlike vegetable). Entrées are served with rice, salad, and fried plantain. Side orders include rice and peas, yam, green banana dumpling, fried plantain, patties (meat pies), codfish fritters, johnny cake (chewy deep-fried-dough bread), and an astonishing variety of buns, flavored breads, and cakes (carrot, banana, dark wine rum fruitcake, coconut drops). Soursop and other juices, fruit nectars, frosties, lemonade and limeade, and tamarind-passion fruit drink are available. *1448 E. 87th St., tel. 312/978–6300. Reservations advised on Sun. No credit cards. BYOB. Closed holidays. Inexpensive.*

Chinese **Emperor's Choice.** This sophisticated but comfortable restaurant sets out to demonstrate that Chinese seafood specialties can go well beyond shrimp with Chinese vegetables. It succeeds admirably; the seafood dishes are fresh and expertly prepared. *2238 S. Wentworth Ave., tel. 312/225–8800. Reservations not required. AE, D, MC, V. Moderate.*

House of Fortune. Elegant and spotless, this restaurant has a particularly large menu, offering more than 250 entrées, including such relatively uncommon items as tripe and sea cucumber. Not to worry; there are plenty of more familiar dishes. *2407 S. Wentworth Ave., tel. 312/225–0880. Reservations accepted. AE, MC, V. Inexpensive–Moderate.*

Three Happiness. It's possible for folks to eat lunch and dinner at Three Happiness, but those in the know go for the Sunday dim sum brunch, served from 10 AM to 2 PM. The restaurant opens at 10 AM, the crowd having begun to form at 9:30, and both floors of the spacious restaurant are full within minutes of opening. Try for a table near the door; that's closest to where the serving carts emerge from the kitchen. Servers wheel the carts around the dining room, stopping when you flag them down. Each cart is laden with six or so individual orders of dim sum—bite-size morsels of noodle dough wrapped around various fillings of pork or shrimp, then steamed or fried; deep-fried taro root stuffed with pork; rice cake filled with barbecued pork and steamed in banana leaf; and countless other varieties. Each cart carries different items, so be sure to investigate all of them. A few items are prepared to order at a grill in the dining room; walk around and see what they're making. Each order typically contains three individual dim sum; when you go with a group, you can mix and match. Servers tally your purchases on a "scorecard" at your table; you probably won't be able to keep track of what you've ordered or what it should cost, but don't worry, it's difficult to eat more than $10 worth before becoming stuffed. *2130 S. Wentworth Ave., tel. 312/791–1229. AE, D, DC, MC, V. Inexpensive.*

Japanese **Ten-Tsuna.** Cloth napkins, wood tabletops, soft lighting, and a quietly attentive staff attired in traditional Japanese kimonos make this the restaurant to come to when you're ready to leave the clamor of your day behind. Take a table if you want a full-course meal, or choose the sushi bar for a lunch or dinner of the delicacies made of vinegared rice and raw fish. The sashimi is fresh and delicious, The *gyoza* (fried dumplings) are crispy outside and juicy within. The *nabeyaki udon* (noodles, vegetables, and egg in broth) delights the eye as well as the palate. Order the *shabu-shabu* if you prefer to have your waitress prepare your meal at tableside, quickly simmering vegetables, tofu, and noodles in broth. A good selection of Japanese beer and wine is available. *Harper Court, 5225 S. Harper Ave., tel. 312/493–4410. AE, D, MC, V. Closed weekend lunch. Moderate.*

Mexican **Playa Azul.** You will find wonderful fresh oysters at both the original 18th Street location and the sister house on North Broadway. You will also find a full selection of fish and seafood soups, salads, and entrées, including abalone, octopus, shrimp, crab, clams, and lobster. Red snapper Veracruzaná (deep-fried) or *al mojo de ajo* (in garlic sauce) are house specialties, both delectable. Grilled meat dishes and chilies rellenos are available for those who don't want fish, and there are Mexican beers. *1514 W. 18th St., tel. 312/421–2552. No reservations. No credit cards. Closed Sun. Inexpensive–Moderate.*

Chon y Chano. This clean, well-lighted place is the only U.S. outpost of a popular Mexico City chain, and it attracts diners from all over Chicago. Most of the menu is devoted to make-your-own tacos, with delicious and occasionally exotic fillings: grilled cactus, beef marrow, steak, barbecued pork, beans, and sausage, to name a few. You can watch the chef make the fresh corn tortillas that wrap the tacos. A house specialty—Aztec soup—consists of chunks of chicken breast in broth, with strips of tortilla and crumbled white cheese. A large toasted chili pepper is served on the side, and you can crumble as much of it into your soup as you wish. *3901 W. 26th St., tel. 312/522–0041. No reservations. MC, V. Inexpensive.*

Nuevo Leon. The simple storefront Nuevo Leon restaurant offers a pleasant atmosphere in which to enjoy familiar or less familiar dishes and come away satisfied. Appetizers include nachos, guacamole, quesos, and quesadillas with chili sauce. In addition to a large selection of enchiladas, tacos, tostadas, and tamales, you'll find such less familiar items as rich and flavorful *menudo* (tripe soup), several beef soups, pork stew, chicken in mole sauce, tongue in sauce, and chopped steak simmered with tomatoes, jalapeño peppers, and onion (a house specialty). Not all servers are fluent in English, but cheerful goodwill prevails. *1515 W. 18th St., tel. 312/421–1517. No credit cards. Inexpensive.*

Middle Eastern **University Gardens.** Once inside this dimly lit restaurant, you're transported immediately to the Middle East. Arabic music plays in the background, prayer rugs adorn the walls along with Arabic movie posters, and the Formica-top tables are placed close together. The service is genial but not always speedy. Use the pita-pocket bread, baked here daily, to dip in hummus or to surround falafel, lettuce, and tomato for a Middle Eastern sandwich. For dinner, choose a kebab plate, the lamb shank braised with Middle Eastern spices, or the spinach stew with meat. Ask for an order of pickled vegetables. The tea is seasoned with sage, for a most unusual flavor. Finally, be sure to sample one of the pastries arrayed at the back. *1373 E. 53rd St., tel. 312/684–6660. No credit cards. BYOB. Inexpensive.*

Soul Food **Soul Queen.** Come to Soul Queen for the food, not the ambience. Plentiful quantities of Southern-style entrées and down-home specials are available on a large buffet: channel catfish steaks served with Mississippi hush puppies, ham hock with fresh greens or peas and candied yams, and stewed chicken with homemade dumplings, greens, and deep-dish apple pie. *9031 S. Stony Island Ave., tel. 312/731–3366. No credit cards. Closed some holidays. Inexpensive.*

The Suburbs

French **Carlos.** Under the watchful eyes of owner Carlos Nieto (himself ★ a Le Francais graduate) and his wife, Deborah, Carlos continues to challenge Le Francais (*see below*) for the title of best French restaurant in the area. Service is particularly good—Carlos himself gets involved in the front-room operations—but even the lowest-ranking assistant has a firm grasp of the menu, can explain preparation methods, and can even offer informed wine recommendations. Recent remodeling has updated the decor a bit. The contemporary French menu changes frequently and invariably offers an array of delights, such as rabbit tournedos with creamed leeks and truffles, and squab ravioli with garlic sauce. Desserts are heavenly. The substantial wine list includes some magnificent vintages, although at eye-popping prices. *429 Temple, Highland Park, tel. 708/432–0770. Reservations required. Jacket and tie required. AE, D, DC, MC, V. Closed lunch and Tues. Very Expensive.*

★ **Le Francais.** The husband-wife team of Roland and Mary Beth Liccioni has Le Francais, in many eyes Chicago's finest restaurant, running beautifully. Roland rules the kitchen, turning out Oriental-influenced contemporary French creations. His plates are visual masterpieces, and portions are substantial for cuisine this fine. Mary Beth is arguably the city's finest pastry chef; her desserts are unparalleled and her chocolates—now available on a retail basis—are equally superb. A veteran wait staff inspires confidence and imparts conviviality; intimidation isn't part of the experience. Lunch at Le Francais is one of Chicago's great gastronomic events and substantially less expensive than dinner. *269 S. Milwaukee Ave., Wheeling, tel. 708/541–7470. Reservations required. AE, D, DC, MC, V. Closed Sun., lunch Sat., and Mon. Very Expensive.*

7 Lodging

American Express offers Travelers Cheques built for two.

American Express® Cheques *for Two*. The first Travelers Cheques that allow either of you to use them because both of you have signed them. And only one of you needs to be present to purchase them.

Cheques *for Two* are accepted anywhere regular American Express Travelers Cheques are, which is just about everywhere. So stop by your bank, AAA* or any American Express Travel Service Office and ask for Cheques *for Two*.

By Elizabeth Gardner and Mary Wagner

Chicago is the nation's most popular convention destination, particularly for large shows that demand the vast caverns of McCormick Place (due to become even more vast through yet another expansion slated for 1997). This popularity is both good and bad news for pleasure travelers.

On one hand, when there's no major show in town, hotel occupancy droops to 40%, creating a buyer's market. Virtually every hotel offers weekend packages and corporate rates, and many give discounts for auto club members, senior citizens, the clergy, educators, and military personnel. Sometimes you can get a better price just by asking for it. Don't be afraid to shop around. On the other hand, when a big show's in town, the city's 25,000-odd hotel rooms fill to the rafters, and you're lucky to get a closet next to the ice machine at an airport motel. Some hotels charge a premium over their normal rate.

When Not to Go

If you're coming to Chicago just to enjoy the city, it's best to avoid the larger trade shows. A few dates to eschew in 1994: January 16–19 (National Housewares Manufacturers Association), February 28–March 3 (Analytical Chemists Annual Meeting), May 1–4 (Food Marketing Institute), June 4–7 (Consumer Electronics Show), June 20–24 (Plastics Expo), and November 27–December 2 (Radiological Society of North America). The 1994 World Cup soccer matches are to be held on June 17–July 2, but it's hard to say what effect they'll have on hotel occupancy. Meeting dates are subject to change, and new ones are added periodically, so it's a good idea to check with the Chicago Convention and Tourism Bureau (tel. 312/567–8500).

Choosing a Neighborhood

Hotels are clustered primarily in three locations: the Loop, the Near North Side, and the airport. They're listed below by location and then by price category within each location.

For business travelers, Loop hotels offer ready access to the financial district and government offices. Major cultural institutions are found here as well: The Art Institute, the Symphony, and the Lyric Opera. The Field Museum, Shedd Aquarium, and Adler Planetarium are just a short bus or cab ride away. DePaul University's downtown campus is on South Wabash Avenue. And then there are the skyscrapers that have put Chicago on the architectural map of the world. Loop hotels tend to be older and somewhat less expensive than those in the Near North. The main drawback to staying here is that it gets deserted and a little spooky late at night. Women traveling alone may prefer the brighter lights of North Michigan Avenue or the neighborhood quality of the Gold Coast.

In addition to safety, dining and shopping are the big draws in the Near North, where hotels line both sides of Michigan Avenue as well as the side streets. Association headquarters, art galleries, advertising agencies, and media companies are located here. Hotels range from high tech to homey. A bit north of Michigan Avenue is the Gold Coast, a stately residential neighborhood where the hotels are quiet and dignified.

If you're coming to Chicago to see the city, don't stay out by the airport, even though prices are lower than in downtown hotels. It's drab and depressing and far from the center of the action. And the trip into town can take an hour or more during rush hour, bad weather, or periods of heavy construction on the Kennedy Expressway.

Bed-and-Breakfasts Lodging in someone's home is a good way to stay in residential neighborhoods that you might not otherwise see and lends a personal touch to your visit. You may save some money over many of the downtown hotels as well. Bed & Breakfast/Chicago (Box 14088, Chicago 60614, tel. 312/951–0085) is a clearinghouse for more than 50 options ranging from a guest room in someone's home to a furnished apartment to a full-fledged inn. Most cost less than $100 a night and are concentrated in the Near North or Lincoln Park, though some are as far away as Indiana. Most require a two-night minimum, and weekly or monthly rates are available for some. Reservations can be made by phone (weekdays 9–5) or by mail. The office will send out sample listings and a reservation form on request.

Hostels and Student Accommodations If you're truly budget conscious and don't mind sharing a bathroom, try these three places—one near the northern border of the city, one in Lincoln Park, and the third in Hyde Park.

Arlington House. Choose either dormitory or double rooms in this hostel on a quiet street in Lincoln Park. It's handy to north side dining and nightlife and near El and bus lines to downtown. Linens are available for rental. IYH and AYH cardholders get a discount. *616 W. Arlington Pl., Chicago 60614, tel. 312/929–5380 or 800/538–0074. 75 dormitory beds, 20 double rooms. Facilities: kitchen, laundry, bicycle rental, 24-hour check-in. DC, MC, V. Inexpensive.*

Chicago International Hostel. These dormitory-style accommodations are near Loyola University in Rogers Park, with several beds in a room. Linens are provided. IYH cardholders get a discount. Nearest mass transit is the Loyola stop on the Howard Street elevated line. *6318 N. Winthrop Ave., Chicago 60660, tel. 312/262–1011. 100 beds. Facilities: kitchen, laundry. No credit cards. Inexpensive.*

International House. On the campus of the University of Chicago, rooms are single; baths are shared. Towels and sheets are provided. There's a weight room. Availability varies with the season; fall is the busiest time. *1414 E. 59th St., Chicago 60637, tel. 312/753–2280, fax 312/753–1227. 500 rooms. MC, V. Inexpensive.*

Booking Your Room Hotel price categories in this chapter are based on the standard weekday rate for one room, double occupancy. These are the rack rates—the highest price at which the rooms are rented. As noted above, lower rates are often available. Weekend packages can offer real bargains. But note that, unlike standard rates that are quoted *per room,* package rates are often quoted *per person, double occupancy.*

When you make your reservation, be sure to get a reservation number and keep it with you for reference. Notify the hotel if you anticipate arriving later than 5 PM; many hotels will guarantee your reservation to your credit card and have a room waiting for you even if you arrive at 2 AM. Should you need to cancel your reservation, notify the hotel as soon as possible—and be sure to get a cancellation number. Otherwise, you may be responsible for at least one night's charge.

Most hotels offer room service, as well as laundry and dry cleaning. We list this only if the service is particularly good: round-the-clock room service and same-day laundry. When health club access is available, there's usually a daily fee ranging from $5 to $10. A few hotels charge for using their own health club.

Category	Cost*
Very Expensive	over $200
Expensive	$150–$200
Moderate	$100–$150
Inexpensive	under $100

All prices are for a standard double room, excluding 12.4% tax and service charges.

The following credit card abbreviations are used: AE, American Express; D, Discover; DC, Diners Club; MC, MasterCard; V, Visa.

Highly recommended hotels are indicated by a star ★.

O'Hare Airport

Very Expensive **Hyatt Regency O'Hare.** You can't miss the four shiny towers of this airport-area landmark, which is adjacent to the O'Hare Expocenter, a popular meeting spot. Inside, the grimness of the concrete atrium is only partly relieved by hanging plants; the mood is impersonal, unmanageable, and confusing. Contemporary, mauve-and-beige-tone rooms are large and recently renovated, with sitting areas. For the price, you'd expect more amenities and fewer extra costs; every other airport hotel has free parking. Unless business calls you here, you'll get more for less elsewhere. *9300 W. Bryn Mawr Ave., Rosemont 60018, tel. 708/696–1234 or 800/233–1234, fax 708/698–0139. 1,100 rooms, 57 suites. 666 nonsmoking rooms, 7 disabled-accessible rooms. Facilities: 4 restaurants, 24-hour room service, same-day laundry/dry cleaning, concierge, garage, business center, free airport shuttle, pool, exercise room. AE, D, DC, MC, V.*

Expensive **Embassy Suites.** If you've ever stayed at one of these cookie-cutter all-suite hotels, you know what to expect: generic two-room suites, adequate space, a refrigerator, a coffeemaker, and phones in every room—including the bathroom. Living room sofas fold out to queen-size beds. Rooms open onto a central, skylighted atrium. A big plus is the free full breakfast: omelets, French toast, and yogurt and fruit for the health conscious. The pool is suitable for lap swimming and there are a few exercise machines. Nick's Fishmarket, a stellar seafood restaurant, is across the street. *6501 N. Mannheim Rd., Rosemont 60018, tel. 708/699–6300 or 800/548–4193, fax 708/699–0617. 299 suites, 164 nonsmoking suites, 7 disabled-accessible suites. Facilities: pay movies, hair dryers, complimentary breakfast, restaurant, bar, pool, exercise room, free airport shuttle, same-day laundry/dry cleaning. AE, D, DC, MC, V.*

★ **Hotel Sofitel O'Hare.** Several Parisian touches—a map of the Métro in the lobby, a boulangerie/patisserie, nightly turndown with a rose, and a complimentary baguette at checkout—give the Sofitel unexpected charm, at least for an airport hotel. The staff is well-informed and enthusiastic. Room decor is a reasonably successful copy of country French, with blond-wood furniture and floral print fabrics. Overall, rooms are spacious and comfortable. Other thoughtful details include irons and boards, extra pillows and blankets, hair dryers, and telephones equipped for modems. The health club is small but well equipped and includes a lap pool and a sundeck. The French theme also carries through to the restaurant and the café. *5550 N. River Rd., Rosemont 60018, tel. 708/678–4488 or 800/233– 5959, fax 708/678–4244. 304 rooms, 9 suites. 150 nonsmoking rooms, 8 disabled-accessible rooms. Facilities: 2 restaurants, bar, bakery, minibars, 24-hour room service, pay movies, laundry/dry cleaning, indoor pool, health club, concierge, garage, business center, free airport shuttle. AE, D, DC, MC, V.*

★ **O'Hare Marriott.** On the outside, this 1960s concrete building is aging more gracefully than most; inside, it's pure 1990s. Two low-rise buildings and one 12-story high rise were revamped in 1992. Smallish rooms are elegantly appointed with floral-print fabrics and dark-wood furnishings. There are a few off-beat amenities, including a Video on Demand movie service that lets guests choose from among 60 offerings in English, Spanish, and Japanese. Other highlights are the five different restaurants, including one Japanese and one Polynesian, and a superb health club, with a whirlpool, a tanning booth, separate men's and women's saunas, a masseur, and a large, circular indoor/outdoor pool. *8535 W. Higgins Road, Chicago 60631, tel. 312/693–4444 or 800/228–9290, fax 312/714–4297. 681 rooms, 25 suites. 340 nonsmoking rooms, 27 disabled-accessible rooms. Facilities: 5 restaurants, health club, 2 pools, concierge, valet parking, laundry/dry cleaning, hair dryers, ironing boards/irons, free airport shuttle. AE, D, DC, MC, V.*

Radisson Plaza O'Hare. This low-rise hotel's two-room suites are furnished in a homey style with blond-wood furniture. Living rooms have sofa beds as well as kitchen areas, each with a wet bar, a refrigerator, a microwave, and a dining table. Each suite also has two TVs and two telephones. Full breakfast in the morning and two hours of free cocktails in the evening are complimentary. Rooms open onto an interior courtyard. The health club includes a pool, a whirlpool, weight machines, and a sauna. *5500 N. River Rd., Rosemont 60018, tel. 708/678–4000 or 800/333–3333, fax 708/671–3059. 296 suites. 40 nonsmoking suites, 4 disabled-accessible suites. Facilities: restaurant, bar, minibars, pay movies, same-day laundry/dry cleaning, health club, pool, concierge, garage, free airport shuttle. AE, D, DC, MC, V.*

Westin O'Hare. The interior is a hodgepodge, blending the 1820s and 1950s, with some Oriental influences. Surprisingly, it works well to give this concrete high rise much more character than the average airport hotel. The green-and-peach lobby has a bakery counter that will set you up with a tasty box lunch to go. Rooms are roomy, done in green and beige with dark-wood furniture and botanical prints. Each has a small desk and a sitting area. Extra blankets and a generous selection of movies are standard. A small TV in the bathroom keeps you tuned in at all times. The well-equipped health club charges guests a nominal admission fee. *6100 N. River Rd., Rosemont 60018, tel. 708/698–6000 or 800/228–3000, fax 708/692–5490. 525 rooms, 28 suites. 192 nonsmoking rooms, 10 disabled-accessible rooms. Facilities: 2 restaurants, café, 24-hour room service, minibars, pay movies, same-day laundry/dry cleaning, indoor lap pool, health club, racquetball, basketball, sauna, concierge, valet parking, business center, free airport shuttle. AE, D, DC, MC, V.*

Moderate **Holiday Inn O'Hare.** A little tired on the outside, this familiar 1960s hostelry was refurbished in 1993. The atrium lobby is built around the indoor pool, over which appear exposed white girders. You can take in this weird lesson in postindustrial architecture while sipping cocktails, snug in your bamboo lounge chair. Rooms are in the unexciting tradition of Holiday Inns, with pink-and-blue color schemes and plenty of space. Several restaurants and a 1950s-style bar provide entertainment. *5440 N. River Rd., Rosemont 60018, tel. 708/671–6350 or 800/465–4329, fax 708/671–5406. 507 rooms, 16 suites. 119 nonsmoking rooms, 4 disabled-accessible rooms. Facilities: 2 restaurants, food court, lounge, pay movies, minibars, 2 pools, exercise room, concierge, garage, free airport shuttle. AE, D, DC, MC, V.*

O'Hare Hilton. A multimillion-dollar renovation in 1992 turned this former airport dumping ground into a pleasant haven for business travelers. A dramatic high-ceilinged lobby eschews the usual institution-pastel hues in favor of a snappy red-and-black color scheme. The small rooms have that slightly dreary airport-hotel feel to them, but they're suitably equipped and innocuous. The hotel management has been considering a health club expansion to include a pool and locker rooms. Day rates, presumably for travelers with short stopovers, are available. As the only hotel physically in the airport, the Hilton is extremely convenient; for some flights, you can actually check your bags at the hotel and walk to your gate unencumbered by Samsonite. *Box 66414, O'Hare International Airport, Rosemont 60666, tel. 312/686–8000 or 800/445–8667, fax 312/686–0073. 858 rooms, 18 suites. 575 nonsmoking rooms, 16 disabled-accessible rooms. Facilities: restaurant, bar, minibars, pay movies, 24-hour room service, exercise room, business center. AE, D, DC, MC, V.*

Ramada Hotel O'Hare. The interior of this sprawling low-rise harkens back to the late 1970s, with greens, beiges, and exposed faux brick. A current remodeling project should spruce up some of the worn public areas. The Lilliputian rooms aren't conducive to lounging, but there are indoor and outdoor pools, an exercise room, tennis courts, and a 9-hole pitch-and-putt golf course to keep you busy. *6600 N. Mannheim Rd., Rosemont 60018, tel. 708/827–5131 or 800/272–6232, fax 708/827–5220. 723 rooms, 45 suites. 72 nonsmoking rooms, 4 disabled-accessible rooms. Facilities: 2 restaurants, entertainment lounge, pay movies, same-day laundry/dry cleaning, concierge, business center, 2 pools, exercise room, golf, tennis, free airport shuttle. AE, D, DC, MC, V.*

Inexpensive **Comfort Inn O'Hare.** For an economical price, this 1988 low-rise packs a punch, offering 24-hour airport shuttle; free coffee, juice, and doughnuts in the morning; and a spa with several exercise machines and a whirlpool. Teal-and-pink rooms are spotless and surprisingly quiet, considering the hotel's location at a busy intersection. An adjacent coffee shop provides room service. *2175 E. Touhy Ave., Des Plaines 60018, tel. 708/635–1300 or 800/222–7666, fax 708/635–7572. 148 rooms, 8 suites. 85 nonsmoking rooms, 15 disabled-accessible rooms. Facilities: coffee shop, exercise machines, dry cleaning, free airport shuttle. AE, D, DC, MC, V.*

Downtown

Very Expensive **The Fairmont.** This neoclassic pink-granite tower was built in
★ 1987 as part of the sterile Illinois Center complex, but it's much
more inviting than the glass boxes surrounding it. Whoever
designed the 45-story Fairmont must have been tall, because
rooms are on a grand scale with extra-long beds and plenty of
space. Windows can be opened to catch the lake breezes, a rare
feature in high-rise hotels. The building's relative isolation
gives it spectacular views in almost any direction. Warm, neutral color schemes are accented by live plants and marble-top
dark-wood furniture. Bathrooms have separate showers and
oversize tubs, TVs, phones, scales, hair dryers, and robes. Antiques and art grace the common areas. The main restaurant,
Primavera, is known for both excellent food and an operatic
wait staff. There's no health club, but guests get a discount at
the superb facility in nearby Illinois Center ($12 per day).
There are also plans to build a nine-hole golf course on the
scruffy vacant lot between the Fairmont and Lake Shore Drive.
*200 N. Columbus Dr., Chicago 60601, tel. 312/565–8000 or
800/527–4727, fax 312/856–1032. 692 rooms, 72 suites. 200 nonsmoking rooms, 7 disabled-accessible rooms. Facilities: 2 restaurants, cabaret lounge, lobby lounge, minibars, 24-hour room
service, health club nearby, pay movies, same-day laundry/dry
cleaning, concierge, garage. AE, D, DC, MC, V.*

Hyatt Regency. The two-story greenhouse lobby is decked with
trees, palms, gushing fountains, and a bar overlooking the
whole scene. A cozy hideaway it's not: between the sound of
crashing water and the traffic from the hotel's many meeting
rooms, a dull roar permeates. It's alarmingly easy to get lost
in the labyrinth of halls and escalators that snake through the
Hyatt's two towers. Rooms, furnished in classic contemporary
decor, feature phone voice mail and built-in hair dryers. The
Illinois Center location, steps from Michigan Avenue and equi-
distant from State Street and North Michigan Avenue shopping, is very convenient. But unless you're attending a meeting
in the Hyatt, a quieter atmosphere for the same price, or less,
can be had at the nearby Fairmont or Swissôtel. *151 E. Wacker
Drive, Chicago 60601, tel. 312/565–1234 or 800/233–1234, fax
312/565–2966. 2,019 rooms, 175 suites. 500 nonsmoking rooms,
25 disabled-accessible rooms. Facilities: 4 restaurants, 5
lounges, 24-hour room service, minibars, pay movies, access to
nearby health club, same-day laundry/dry cleaning, concierge,
business center, garage. AE, D, DC, MC, V.*

Stouffer Riviere. Opened during the 1991 recession, this white
stone-and-glass north Loop property has a fanciful 1990s exterior. But the interior tries, with varying degrees of success,
to evoke the rococo splendor of a turn-of-the-century hotel.
Lavish floral carpets, tapestry upholstery, crystal-beaded
chandeliers, and vaguely French Provincial furniture create
opulent public areas. Bellhops dress in traditional waistcoats
and pillbox hats. The floral theme, in neutral tones, is carried
through in the rooms, which aren't large but contain sitting
areas. Many have spectacular river views. Amenities include
robes and complimentary shoeshines. The riverfront location
is particularly handy to the north Loop and the Merchandise
Mart. *1 W. Wacker Dr., Chicago 60601, tel. 312/372–7200 or
800/468–3571, fax 312/372–0093. 565 rooms, 40 suites. 300 nonsmoking rooms, 29 disabled-accessible rooms. Facilities: 2 res-*

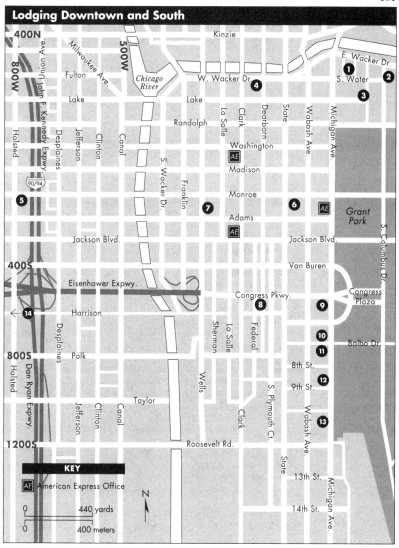

Lodging Downtown and South

Blackstone Hotel, **10**

Chicago Hilton and Towers, **11**

The Congress Hotel, **9**

Essex Inn, **12**

The Fairmont, **3**

Grant Park Hotel, **13**

Hyatt on Printer's Row, **8**

Hyatt Regency, **1**

Inn at University Village, **14**

The Midland, **7**

The Palmer House Hilton, **6**

Quality Inn Downtown, **5**

Stouffer Riviere, **4**

Swissôtel, **2**

taurants, lobby bar with live entertainment, health club, pool, sauna, concierge, minibars, pay movies, 24-hour room service, same-day laundry/dry cleaning, valet parking. AE, D, DC, MC, V.

Expensive   **Chicago Hilton and Towers.** The Hilton, built in 1927, is a vast
★   convention hotel, with the largest exhibit space, the largest health club (28,000 square feet), and the largest and grandest ballroom of any hotel in the city. Its $180 million renovation, completed in 1986, is still holding up well. The lobby is a sea of green-and-mauve marble with gilt and crystal galore. The first-floor concourse is abuzz with activity, and you may need a map at first to find your way around. To get away from it all, try ducking into the English-style tavern, Buckingham's, or the second-story lounge area, featuring chairs designed for the French ocean liner *Normandie.* The pampering continues in the guest rooms, which are done in muted pastels and cherrywood and have marble bathrooms with built-in hair dryers. Kitty O'Shea's, the hotel's Irish bar and restaurant, offers live entertainment and a rollicking good time. *720 N. Michigan Ave., 60605, tel. 312/922–4400 or 800/445–8667, fax 312/922–5240. 1,543 rooms, 149 suites. 416 nonsmoking rooms, 11 disabled-accessible rooms. Facilities: 3 restaurants, 2 lounges, minibars, 24-hour room service, pool, health club, concierge, same-day laundry/dry cleaning, hairdresser, garage, business center, bus shuttle to shopping areas. AE, D, DC, MC, V.*

Hyatt on Printer's Row. A series of three older buildings form this small European-style hotel, previously called the Hotel Morton. Rooms are done in soft gray-greens with black-lacquer furniture and tapestry-style bedspreads. Bathroom amenities include scales, hair dryers, phones, and TVs. Room sizes and shapes vary depending on which building you're in, but they're generally spacious and many have 12-foot ceilings and large windows. Service is prompt and genial. The hotel restaurant, Prairie, serves top-notch New American cuisine. This Hyatt is an excellent alternative to the noisy Hilton and just a few blocks away from the financial center. *500 S. Dearborn St., Chicago 60605, tel. 312/986–1234 or 800/233–1234, fax 312/939–2468. 161 rooms, 4 suites. 72 nonsmoking rooms, 1 disabled-accessible room. Facilities: restaurant, bar, minibars, pay movies, VCR rental, concierge, health club nearby, garage. AE, D, DC, MC, V.*

The Midland. This small hotel in the heart of the financial district was built as a men's club in the 1920s. The exuberant beaux-arts-style lobby has vaulted arches and a gold-leaf ceiling. Rooms are nondescript, with beige and mauve accents and acoustical tile ceilings; the canyonlike neighborhood of tall buildings stifles potential views. Rooms are each configured a little differently; if you prefer a tub, be sure to ask. Service is sanguine and unobtrusive, but amenities are a bit lacking given the rates. The Midland's London taxi whisks guests to and from various downtown locations; it also transports joggers to the lakefront path at 6:30 AM. A tiny exercise room is available, too. A coffee shop serves good omelets, and there's a more upscale restaurant and a bar. A breakfast buffet is included. *172 W. Adams St., tel. 312/332–1200 or, outside Illinois, 800/621–2360, fax 312/332–5909. 257 rooms, 4 suites. 125 nonsmoking rooms, 4 disabled-accessible rooms. Facilities: 2 restaurants, bar, concierge, barber, exercise room, free shuttle to downtown locations. AE, D, DC, MC, V.*

★ **Swissôtel.** The triangular Harry Weese design makes for some oddly shaped rooms in this concrete-and-glass high rise, but the penthouse health club, with a sizable pool and extensive equipment, offers panoramic lake views. Despite its size and 1988 vintage, the Swissôtel wears a quiet European ambience. Each of the spacious guest rooms has its own doorbell, a superb city or lake view, a sitting area, a marble bathroom with separate tub and shower, and two-line phones. The restaurant, Land of Plenty, specializes in regional American cooking. There are also a snug bar off the lobby and a bakery where you can buy fresh bread and pastries. *323 E. Wacker Dr., 60601, tel. 312/565–0565 or 800/654–7262, fax 312/565–0540. 636 rooms, 32 suites. 282 nonsmoking rooms, 9 disabled-accessible rooms. Facilities: 2 restaurants, bar, bakery, minibars, 24-hour room service, pay movies, same-day laundry/dry cleaning, concierge, garage, health club, pool, business center. AE, D, DC, MC, V.*

Moderate **Blackstone Hotel.** Built in 1910, the Blackstone's Second Empire decor makes it look 60 years older. The appointments of a bygone era include chandeliers and marble statues in the lobby and original brass hardware glowing against warm mahogany doors. Since it was built, every American president except Bill Clinton has stayed here, and the place fairly reeks of history. The passage of time has left a mark here or there, and the usual newfangled amenities are missing—even shampoo. But the doorman will bring ice on request; the rooms have high ceilings and big closets; and the Jazz Showcase, one of the city's premier clubs, is just off the lobby. Developers occasionally threaten to refurbish the Blackstone, but most prefer to keep it—along with its reasonable prices—just as is. *636 S. Michigan Ave., Chicago 60605, tel. 312/427–4300 or 800/622–6330, fax 312/427–4300. 305 rooms, 25 suites. 80 nonsmoking rooms, 5 disabled-accessible rooms. Facilities: restaurant, lounge, jazz club, theater, access to business center and health club at the nearby Hilton, same-day laundry/dry cleaning, valet parking. AE, D, DC, MC, V.*

The Congress Hotel. The original building opened in 1893, and its public areas still retain touches of that ornate period. More recent additions have added little personality. An overflow hotel for the nearby Chicago Hilton and Towers, the Congress is favored by convention-goers, tour groups, and airline crews. Rooms are clean, secure, and relatively inexpensive. Some are quite roomy, and those facing east, though more expensive, have views of the lake and Grant Park. Except for these features and the hotel's location near McCormick Place and the museums, there's little reason to stay here. *520 S. Michigan Ave., 60615, tel. 312/427–3800 or 800/635–1666, fax 312/427–4840. 818 rooms, 30 suites. 80 nonsmoking rooms, 25 disabled-accessible rooms. Facilities: 2 restaurants, VCR rental, valet parking. AE, D, DC, MC, V.*

Grant Park Hotel. This Best Western hotel is a good value for travelers attending functions at nearby McCormick Place. The mauve-and-gray rooms are plain and smallish but clean and functional. The south Loop location is near Printer's Row as well as the cluster of museums at the south end of Grant Park. *1100 S. Michigan Ave., Chicago 60605, tel. 312/922–2900 or 800/528–1234, fax 312/922–8812. 172 rooms. 24 nonsmoking rooms, 1 disabled-accessible room. Facilities: restaurant, small exercise room, outdoor pool, valet parking for $6.60 per day. AE, D, DC, MC, V.*

★ **Inn at University Village.** Two miles west of the Loop, this 1988 redbrick property attracts people visiting the University of Illinois or Rush Presbyterian St. Lukes Medical Center, which owns the hotel. As befits its hospital ownership, public areas are completely disabled accessible. The lobby's dark-wood antiques, reproductions, and velvet sofas and chairs give it an unexpectedly clubby feel. Guest rooms, however, have a more modern decor: blond-wood furnishings with black accents, ceramic pieces resembling fragments of Egyptian friezes overhanging the beds, and tabletops and bathroom sinks made from granite and marble. The restaurant, Benjamin's, specializes in "heart-healthy" cuisine and will provide you a nutritional analysis of anything you order. Little Italy is a few blocks south on Taylor Street. The neighborhood has some unsavory spots, though, and walkers should stay off side streets after dark. A free shuttle bus takes guests to the Loop. *625 S. Ashland Ave. (corner of Harrison St.), Chicago 60607, tel. 312/243–7200 or 800/622–5233, fax 312/243–1289. 114 rooms, 5 suites. 65 nonsmoking rooms, 4 disabled-accessible rooms. Facilities: restaurant, small exercise room, health club privileges at University of Illinois, valet parking, pay movies. AE, D, DC, MC, V.*

★ **The Palmer House Hilton.** Built more than 100 years ago by Chicago merchant Potter Palmer, this landmark hotel in the heart of the Loop has some of the most ornate and elegant public areas in the city. The main lobby, up a floor from the marble street-level shopping arcade, has 21 ceiling murals by Louis Rigal, lots of gilding, Victorian velvet, brocade furniture, crystal chandeliers, and a late-19th-century patina. Upstairs, rooms are much less spectacular but still pleasant, with beige or peach color schemes and reproduction antique furniture. Rooms have several different configurations, but most have plenty of elbow room. Like most big-meeting hotels, the Palmer House gets hectic at times, and service can be brusque. *17 E. Monroe St., Chicago 60603, tel. 312/726–7500 or 800/445–8667, fax 312/263–2556. 1,669 rooms, 88 suites. 800 nonsmoking rooms, 20 disabled-accessible rooms. Facilities: 6 restaurants, bar, minibars, concierge, barber, garage, health club, pool, business center. AE, D, DC, MC, V.*

Inexpensive **Essex Inn.** Two-thirds of the Essex's guests are in town for trade shows at Chicago's McCormick Place convention center, which is not a surprise given the hotel's South Michigan Avenue location. The plain but pleasant motel-modern lobby was last renovated in 1992, and rooms in the same style are refurbished regularly. Come here for basic facilities and amenities and few frills at a low price. *800 S. Michigan Ave., Chicago 60605, tel. 312/939–2800 or 800/821–6909, fax 312/939–1605. 255 rooms, 16 suites. 2 disabled-accessible rooms. Facilities: restaurant, lounge, minibars, concierge, outdoor pool, valet parking, free shuttle to North Michigan Avenue shopping. AE, D, DC, MC, V.*

Quality Inn Downtown. Don't be fooled by the name: This oddly situated property is almost a mile west of anywhere that could be considered downtown. The exterior resembles a Moscow housing project and you have to enter through the parking garage, but once inside, you'll find a pleasant lobby, a cozy restaurant and cordial service. The rooms are heavy on Formica but roomy and clean, and many have terrific views of I–290. The neighborhood looks seedy but is well populated and safe enough during the day and early evening; don't walk around late at night though. Greektown restaurants are convenient; everything else is a trek away. *1 S. Halsted St., tel. 312/829–5000 or 800/221–2222, fax 312/829–8151. 406 rooms, 5 suites. 90 non-smoking rooms, 8 disabled-accessible rooms. Facilities: restaurant, laundry room, pool, health club privileges at University of Illinois, garage, pay movies. AE, D, DC, MC, V.*

Near North

Very Expensive **The Drake.** The grande dame of North Michigan Avenue, the ★ Drake opened in 1920 and has been the choice of visiting heads of state ever since. Built in the style of an Italian Renaissance palace, it went onto the National Register of Historic Places in 1981. The oak-paneled lobby has a lavish red carpet, crystal chandeliers, a marble fountain, and a palm court where high tea is served in the afternoon. The rooms resemble those in an English country house: reproduction antique furniture, marble bathrooms, striped wallpaper, and floral bedspreads. Each is a little different, but all have sitting areas and ample space. For a slight premium, you can get a room with a lake view. Service is courteous and enthusiastic. The Drake's restaurants include the quaint street-level Cape Cod Room and the gracious Oak Room, which has a view of the lake. Oak Street Beach, with a lakefront bicycle/jogging path, is across the street and through a pedestrian underpass. *140 E. Walton St., Chicago 60611, tel. 312/787–2200 or 800/553–7256, fax 312/951–5803. 535 rooms, 65 suites. 200 nonsmoking rooms, 2 disabled-accessible rooms. Facilities: 3 restaurants, 2 lounges, minibars, 24-hour room service, pay movies, business center, shopping arcade, same-day laundry/dry cleaning, concierge, barber, valet parking, exercise room, access to nearby health club. AE, D, DC, MC, V.*

Embassy Suites. Built in 1991, these Embassy Suites were instantly successful. Already, some of the furniture in the handsome salmon-tint and blond-wood-furnished rooms shows effects of heavy traffic. Microwave ovens, minirefrigerators, phones, and coffeemakers are standard. Rooms are arranged around an 11-story atrium overlooking a plant-filled, multilevel courtyard, complete with decorative pool and fountain. That's where guests are served a complimentary full breakfast each morning and cocktails each evening during the manager's reception. There are a small fitness center and a lap pool. The top floor has a laundry room. Papagus, a popular Greek-style restaurant that also serves Continental cuisine, is just off the lobby. *600 N. State St., Chicago 60610, tel. 312/943–3800 or 800/362–2779, fax 312/943–7629. 358 suites. 275 nonsmoking suites, 18 disabled-accessible suites. Facilities: restaurant with bar, minibars, pay movies, health club, pool, same-day laundry/dry cleaning, concierge, laundry facilities, valet parking. AE, D, DC, MC, V.*

★ **The Four Seasons.** Visiting celebrities stay here for one reason: They need pampering. And it's no exaggeration to claim the Four Seasons aims to treat every guest like a celebrity—service is of paramount importance here. The Four Seasons sits atop the stores of the Avenue Atrium, but inside it feels more like a grand English country house than an urban skyscraper. The lobby, which has the only wood-burning fireplace in a Chicago hotel, has cabinets stocked with antique Minton china and contains a marble fountain that was imported from Italy. This

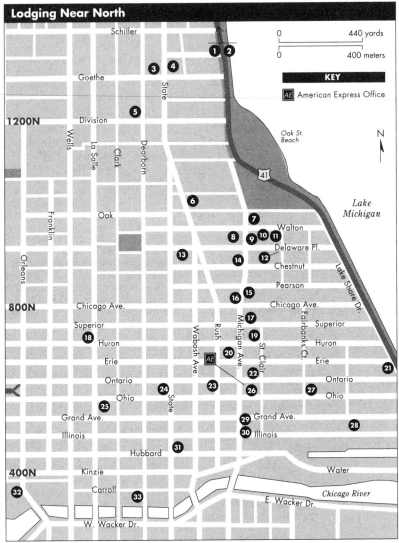

Lodging Near North

1200N

Oak St. Beach

Lake Michigan

800N

400N

Chicago River

The Barclay
Chicago, **17**

Claridge Hotel, **5**

Comfort Inn of
Lincoln Park, **1**

Courtyard by
Marriott, **31**

Days Inn Chicago, **21**

The Drake, **7**

Embassy Suites, **24**

Forum Hotel
Chicago, **29**

The Four Seasons, **8**

Guest Quarters Suites
Hotel, **11**

Holiday Inn Chicago
City Centre, **27**

Holiday Inn Mart
Plaza, **32**

Hotel Inter-
Continental
Chicago, **30**

Hotel Nikko, **33**

Hyatt Regency
Suites, **20**

Inn of Chicago, **26**

The Knickerbocker, **10**

La Salle Hojo Inn, **18**

Le Meridien, **6**

Lenox House, **23**

The Margarita—
A European Inn, **2**

Omni Ambassador
East, **4**

Park Hyatt, **16**

Radisson Plaza
Ambassador West, **3**

The Raphael, **12**

Richmont, **22**

The Ritz-Carlton, **15**

River North Hotel, **25**

Sheraton Chicago
Hotel and Towers, **28**

Sheraton Plaza, **19**

The Talbott, **13**

The Tremont, **14**

The Westin Hotel, **9**

is a suitable setting for afternoon tea, which is served daily. The Old World feeling continues in the elegant furnishings of the pastel-toned guest rooms, decorated with Italian marble, handcrafted woodwork, custom-woven rugs, and botanical prints. Bathrobes, multiple phones, hair dryers, unusually lavish bath supplies, and well-stocked minibars and snack stations are standard in the rooms. *120 E. Delaware Pl., Chicago 60611, tel. 312/280–8800 or 800/332–3442, fax 312/280–9184. 343 rooms, 121 suites. 65 nonsmoking rooms, 8 disabled-accessible rooms. Facilities: 2 restaurants, bar, 24-hour room service, minibars, pool, health club, same-day laundry/dry cleaning, concierge, business center, valet parking. AE, D, DC, MC, V.*

Guest Quarters Suite Hotel. The striking lobby here is neither brass-and-glass contemporary nor traditional; it has a post-modern look, with a bow in the direction of arts and crafts. Like the other hotels flanking Michigan Avenue, it's a big weekend travel destination for shoppers. The two-room standard suite is snug, probably with no more floor space than one room at most hotels in the same price category, but families may prefer that setup because parents can have a bedroom to themselves while children sleep (free to kids 18 and under) on a living room sofa bed. Rooms have wet bars, coffeemakers, TVs in both rooms, two phones, and good-size bathrooms. *198 E. Delaware Pl., Chicago 60611, tel. 312/664–1100 or 800/424–2900, fax 312/664–9881. 345 suites. 17 disabled-accessible rooms. Facilities: 2 restaurants, bar, 24-hour room service, health club with pool, business center, concierge, valet parking. AE, D, DC, MC, V.*

★ **Hotel Inter-Continental Chicago.** Built in 1929 as the Medinah Athletic Club, which underwent several incarnations as a lodging before Inter-Continental overtook and overhauled it in 1990. The Michigan Avenue location is within walking distance of the Loop and Near North business districts. Unlike most grand hotels, this one has a low-ceilinged lobby in dark green and dark wood, with an intimate bar to the left and a long lounge area to the right. Rooms are done in beige and green in 1920s neoclassical style; the furniture was designed specifically for the hotel. Bathrooms are roomy and nicely appointed. Amenities include robes, scales, and padded-silk hangers. The "executive" level has a spectacular skylighted lounge, with terrific views of several neighboring Gothic-style skyscrapers. The showpiece of the Inter-Continental is its Italianate junior Olympic-size swimming pool, fit for an Esther Williams water ballet. *505 N. Michigan Ave., Chicago 60611, tel. 312/944–4100 or 800/327–0200, fax 312/944–3050. 338 rooms, 30 suites. 100 nonsmoking rooms, 3 disabled-accessible rooms. Facilities: restaurant, bar, 24-hour room service, minibars, pay movies, lap pool, health club, same-day laundry/dry cleaning, concierge, garage, valet parking, business center. AE, D, DC, MC, V.*

★ **Hotel Nikko.** The Nikko provides a glimpse of Japanese culture in the middle of Chicago, and indeed, the large, low-ceilinged lobby is a model of understated Asian elegance. The polished granite, black-lacquer, and mahogany interior looks out through floor-to-ceiling windows over a rock garden. Rooms, furnished in either contemporary or traditional Japanese, have marble baths, bathrobes, dressing areas, and three phones. Complimentary coffee and newspaper are available and there is nightly turndown service. There are a fully equipped business center—open during business hours—and a full-service health club. Two restaurants, one Japanese and one Continental, serve breakfast, lunch, and dinner; the Continental Celebrity Café has a renowned Sunday Jazz brunch. Most rooms have river views. *320 N. Dearborn St., Chicago 60610, tel. 312/744–1900 or 800/645–5687, fax 312/527–2650. 425 rooms, 25 suites. 108 nonsmoking rooms, 20 disabled-accessible rooms. Facilities: 2 restaurants, lounge, 24-hour room service, minibars, pay movies, fitness center, same-day laundry/dry cleaning, concierge, business center, valet parking. AE, D, DC, MC, V.*

Hyatt Regency Suites. The predictable contemporary style of the hotel's fourth-floor lobby gives no hint of the comfortable, clubby-looking, forest-green guest suites above. The amenities are first-rate: suites have two TVs, ironing boards, coffeemakers, and exceptionally well stocked minibars. Bathrooms feature kimonos and built-in hair dryers. Jaxx, the hotel's restaurant, has fantastic views of Michigan Avenue; be sure to sit near the windows. Suites geared toward business travelers have upgraded amenities, such as in-room faxes. Three spectacular suites are decorated in the styles of (and named after) architects Ludwig Mies van der Rohe, Charles Rennie MacIntosh, and Frank Lloyd Wright. *676 N. Michigan Ave., Chicago 60611, tel. 312/337–1234 or 800/233–1234, fax 312/266–3017. 347 suites. 140 nonsmoking suites, 8 disabled-accessible suites. Facilities: restaurant, bar, 24-hour room service, minibars, pay movies, health club, pool, same-day laundry/dry cleaning, concierge, valet parking. AE, D, DC, MC, V.*

★ **Le Meridien.** Air France has an equity interest in this hotel, which may explain its almost intimidating chic. Visiting entertainers favor the hotel, whose sleek, European style has Art Deco overtones. Rooms are done up in hues of gray, black, and white; many feature original Robert Mapplethorpe photos. Entertainment centers—including VCRs, CD players with several compact discs, radios, and TVs—are standard in every room, and the hotel maintains a video library. The bathrooms are equipped with terry cloth robes, hair dryers, and a separate tub and shower. And if you're a chocoholic, don't leave without visiting the Saturday afternoon chocolate buffet in the hotel's restaurant, the French-style Brasserie Bellevue. *21 E. Bellevue Pl., Chicago 60611, tel. 312/266–2100 or 800/543–4300, fax 312/266–2141. 247 rooms, 41 suites. 90 nonsmoking rooms, 15 disabled-accessible rooms. Facilities: restaurant, bar, 24-hour room service, minibars, step aerobics setups available in rooms on request, access to nearby health club, same-day laundry/dry cleaning, concierge, business services, valet parking. AE, D, DC, MC, V.*

★ **Park Hyatt.** You'll pay a stiff tariff here, but it's worth it to most corporate travelers. The contemporary classic decorating scheme has striking Oriental touches, and the whole establishment is impeccably maintained. Eighty percent of hotel guests are corporate travelers. Coffee and tea in the lobby are standard, as are fax machines and multiple phones in each room; complimentary cookies, fruit, and bottled water daily; and bathrooms with robes, scales, phones, and TVs. The lobby lounge features live music nightly, and the hotel's restaurant, La Tour, is one of the city's finest. A caveat: The building's mostly glass outer wall doesn't adequately drown out traffic sounds from nearby Chicago Avenue. *800 N. Michigan Ave., Chicago 60611, tel. 312/280–2222 or 800/233–1234, fax 312/280–*

1963. 255 rooms, 40 suites. 160 nonsmoking rooms, 12 disabled-accessible rooms. Facilities: restaurant, 2 lounges, 24-hour room service, minibars, pay movies, access to nearby health club, exercise equipment set up in room on request, 24-hour concierge, valet parking. AE, D, DC, MC, V.

★ **The Ritz-Carlton.** The Ritz-Carlton, which is run by the Four Seasons and not the Ritz-Carlton hotel chain, spent $340,000 on floral arrangements last year, and that was just to adorn the common areas. The Ritz's 12th-floor lobby sits above Water Tower Place, one of the Mag Mile's vertical shopping malls. The two-story greenhouse lobby, which serves tea in the afternoon and one of the area's few late-night dinners in the evening, is dressed in wicker and palms; a fountain makes a crashing backdrop. Upstairs there's luxury: Hair dryers, bathrobes, multiple telephones, and lighted makeup mirrors are standard. A $17 million renovation, completed in 1991, outfitted the spacious rooms in a blend of European styles with fine mahogany furniture, cherry Chippendale-style armoires, floral pattern wallpaper with border prints, and such comfy touches as wing chairs. The full-service health club has a lap pool. *160 E. Pearson St., Chicago 60611, tel. 312/266–1000 or 800/691–6906, fax 312/266–9498. 431 rooms, 72 suites. 372 nonsmoking rooms, 30 disabled-accessible rooms. Facilities: 3 restaurants, bar, 24-hour room service, minibars, health club, pool, same-day laundry/dry cleaning, concierge, valet parking. AE, D, DC, MC, V.*

★ **Sheraton Chicago Hotel and Towers.** In 1991, during the construction of this imposing postmodern edifice, about the last thing Chicago needed was another dizzyingly large convention hotel. Fortunately, its vastness is manageable, and the Sheraton is far more appealing than its competitor across the river, the Hyatt Regency. Bountiful use of warm woods and art deco–style patterns give the 34-floor Sheraton a 1930s feel that's rare in this city. Rooms are on the diminutive side, mirroring the lobby's peachy tones. With no neighboring skyscrapers, most rooms and all public areas have spectacular river, city, or lake views. There are two lobby bars—one with a piano—and several restaurants. Service is efficient and cheerful; most employees braved long lines, stiff competition, and frigid weather to obtain employment here during the winter of 1992. The Sheraton is near Michigan Avenue, the North Pier complex on Illinois Street, and the Illinois Center office complex. *Cityfront Plaza, 301 E. North Water St., Chicago 60611, tel. 312/464–1000 or 800/325–3535, fax 312/464–9140. 1,200 rooms, 76 suites. 480 nonsmoking rooms, 50 disabled-accessible rooms. Facilities: 3 restaurants, 2 bars, 24-hour room service, pay movies, minibars, health club, pool, concierge, same-day laundry/dry cleaning, valet parking, garage, business center. AE, D, DC, MC, V.*

Expensive **The Barclay Chicago.** A small, intimate lobby paneled in blond oak sets the tone for this hotel's pure, traditional look. It's an all-suite establishment, but some suites seem to be no more than slightly extended rooms. Many do, however, have kitchens, and the management will stock the refrigerator on request. Some rooms and upstairs public areas are looking worn. Phones in bathrooms are standard, as are built-in hair dryers. One block off the Magnificent Mile, the Barclay caters to business travelers during the week and packs in shoppers on the weekend. *166 E. Superior St., Chicago 60611, tel. 312/787–6000 or 800/621–8004, fax 312/787–4331. 120 suites. 30 nonsmoking suites, 1 disabled-accessible suite. Facilities: restaurant, 2* *lounges, VCR rental, pool, exercise bikes in room on request, access to nearby health club, concierge, valet parking. AE, D, DC, MC, V.*

Forum Hotel Chicago. Adjoining the more opulent Hotel Inter-Continental, this mid-priced high-rise business hotel is run by the same company. The 1960s building was completely renovated in 1990. Both the guest rooms and public areas are done in grays and other cool neutrals. Furniture is modern and nondescript, but the spacious bathrooms include full-length mirrors, the rooms have large desks, and the more expensive rooms have views of Lake Michigan. For a fee, Forum guests may use the Inter-Continental's health club, including the spectacular pool, and may sign for meals at the Inter-Continental's restaurants. *525 N. Michigan Ave., Chicago 60611, tel. 312/944–0055 or 800/327–0200, fax 312/944–3050. 517 rooms, 6 suites. 115 nonsmoking rooms, 5 disabled-accessible rooms. Facilities: restaurant, bar, 24-hour room service, minibars, pay movies, access to Inter-Continental health club and pool, same-day laundry/dry cleaning, concierge, garage, valet parking, business center. AE, D, DC, MC, V.*

The Knickerbocker. This 1927 hotel offers some of the nearby Drake's charm and tradition, but without the high rates. The Knickerbocker signed a new management contract in 1993 with Maryland-based Grand Heritage Hotels, an operator of historic hotels, and was embarking on a renovation that the management swears will be completed by January 1994. Though well maintained, the rooms' traditional decor could use brightening up. The marble bathrooms are small, a legacy of the days before bathrooms emerged into the sybaritic palaces they are today. But the location is great for North Michigan Avenue shopping, and the Limehouse Pub, the oak-paneled bar off the lobby, is one of the coziest hotel bars in the city. *163 E. Walton Pl., Chicago 60611, tel. 312/751–8100 or 800/621–8140, fax 312/751–0370. 254 rooms, 25 suites. 46 nonsmoking rooms, 1 disabled-accessible room. Facilities: 2 restaurants, access to nearby health club, concierge, same-day laundry/dry cleaning, valet parking. AE, D, DC, MC, V.*

Omni Ambassador East. The renowned Pump Room restaurant, a favorite of the glitterati, put the Ambassador East on the map; elegance, charm, and gracious service keep it there. In the quiet residential Gold Coast, this 1920s small hotel is a 10- to 15-minute cab ride from the Loop; it's popular with movie stars and business travelers who want to get away from the bustle of Michigan Avenue. The lobby has an Old World elegance, with crystal chandeliers, marble floors, and curving banisters. Rooms vary in size, shape, and decor; some have reproductions of 19th-century American antiques; others have more of a 1950s feel. *1301 N. State Pkwy., Chicago 60610, tel. 312/787–7200 or 800/842–6664, fax 312/787–4760. 275 rooms, 52 suites. 120 nonsmoking rooms, 3 disabled-accessible rooms. Facilities: restaurant, 24-hour room service, minibars, pay movies, same-day laundry/dry cleaning, concierge, barber, valet parking, access to nearby health club. AE, D, DC, MC, V.*

Sheraton Plaza. The Sheraton Plaza courts the individual business traveler and the shopper. While the newly opened Sheraton Hotel and Towers is outshining its older cousin, the Plaza does offer location—one block east of Michigan Avenue—and pleasant if undistinguished rooms, last refurbished in 1988. There's a pleasant second-story lounge above the rather small first-floor lobby for meeting, relaxing, and reading the newspaper. *160 E. Huron St., Chicago 60611, tel. 312/787–2900 or 800/325–3535, fax 312/787–5158. 334 rooms, 88 suites. 167 non-smoking rooms, 1 disabled-accessible room. Facilities: Restaurant, bar, minibars, coffeemakers, pay movies, outdoor pool, access to nearby health club, concierge, business center, parking. AE, D, DC, MC, V.*

The Talbott. Female travelers especially gravitate toward this small, homelike, and secure European-style hotel. Most of the rooms feature full kitchens, a legacy from the 1927-vintage structure's earlier life as an apartment building. Some rooms are in need of redecorating, a process that was ongoing in 1993. The traditional decor of the guest rooms is carried over into the twin parlors at the front of the hotel, facing onto Delaware Street; they're filled with a mixture of antique and reproduction furnishings. Though there's no restaurant, the room-service menu is extensive. *20 E. Delaware Pl., Chicago 60611, tel. 312/944–4970 or 800/621–8506, fax 312/944–7241. 147 rooms, 28 suites. 10 nonsmoking rooms, 2 disabled-accessible rooms. Facilities: bar, complimentary Continental breakfast, minibars, full kitchen, access to nearby health club, garage. AE, DC, MC, V.*

The Tremont. This small, European-style hotel is one of several of its type tucked away near North Michigan Avenue. It pulls in mostly independent business types and is not at all family oriented: Most guests are repeaters. In 1993, the hotel was in the midst of redoing its guest rooms by brightening up the colors but keeping the traditional Williamsburg-style decor and Baker furniture. Some of the rooms are small, so be sure to ask about size. The staff is multilingual. Cricket's, the hotel's restaurant, has lately begun targeting a broader audience, in the past having been a major watering hole for Chicago's beautiful people. *100 E. Chestnut St., Chicago 60611, tel. 312/751–1900 or 800 621–8133, fax 312/280–3078. 127 rooms, 10 suites. 20 non-smoking rooms, 1 disabled-accessible room. Facilities: restaurant with bar, 24-hour room service, pay movies, access to nearby health club, concierge, same-day laundry/dry cleaning, valet parking. AE, D, DC, MC, V.*

Moderate **Claridge Hotel.** If you're looking for something simple but com-
★ fortable that won't eat up your entire travel budget, this small, recently renovated 1930s hotel is a superb value. Its Gold Coast location is quiet but convenient to the singles scene on nearby Division Street and other Near North nightlife. Public areas are tastefully decorated in dark wood and green marble; guest rooms tend toward mauves, grays, and other neutral colors. Rooms that don't get direct sunlight are done in deep jewel tones to liven things up. In-room amenities aren't lavish, but almost any toilet article is available from the front desk. Standard rooms are smallish; deluxe rooms are large enough to have a sitting area. Continental breakfast is included. The Claridge offers limousine service to business districts and shopping areas. *1244 N. Dearborn Pkwy., Chicago 60610, tel. 312/787–4980 or 800/245–1258, fax 312/266–0978. 173 rooms, 3 suites. 60 non-smoking rooms, 4 disabled-accessible rooms. Facilities: restaurant, bar, minibars, 24-hour room service, pay movies, VCR rental, access to nearby health club, limousine service, hairdresser, garage. AE, D, DC, MC, V.*

Courtyard by Marriott. Parent corporation Marriott Hotels and Resorts launched the Courtyard concept after surveying business travelers about what they wanted in a hotel. The re-

sult: soothing, large rooms that feature desks, well-lighted
work areas, and voice mail on every phone. A spacious marble-
floor lobby opens onto a lounge with a bar, and the restaurant
is a few steps away. If you feel like venturing out, you can bill
dinner to your room at nearby Shaw's Crab House and Tucci
Milan, two popular downtown eateries. And if you're staying
in, there are an exercise facility, a lap pool, and an extensive
pay-movie selection. Seventy percent of the rooms are designated for nonsmokers. Opened in 1992, the Courtyard is one of
Chicago's newest hotels and still looks brand-new. *30 E. Hubbard St., Chicago 60611, tel. 312/329–2500 or 800/321–2211, fax
312/329–0293. 336 rooms. 235 nonsmoking rooms, 18 disabled-
accessible rooms. Facilities: restaurant, lounge with bar, pay
movies, same-day laundry/dry cleaning, garage, valet parking.
AE, D, DC, MC, V.*

Days Inn Chicago. Lakefront access is the best thing about this
concrete high rise, though rooms were redone in 1992 in greens
and jewel tones and are pleasant and sunny. Rooms have either
two double beds or one king-size bed. Half have lake views; the
others look out on the city, and most aren't too badly blocked
by surrounding skyscrapers. The North Pier complex is right
around the corner, and there's a small beach just two blocks
south. Amenities aren't lavish, but nor is the price high. *644 N.
Lake Shore Dr., Chicago 60611, tel. 312/943–9200 or 800/325–
2525, fax 312/943–9200, ext. 3108. 578 rooms, 6 suites. 60 nonsmoking rooms, 8 disabled-accessible rooms. Facilities:
restaurant, lounge, pay movies, outdoor pool, exercise room, garage. AE, D, DC, MC, V.*

Holiday Inn Chicago City Centre. Offering value and comfort
over glitz, this busy hotel is serious about exercise. It's connected to McClurg Court, one of the city's biggest health clubs,
and club visits are free to guests. It's also close to the jogging
path along nearby Lake Michigan. That's probably why the
hotel was selected by *Fitness* magazine last year as one of the
nation's top ten hotels for fitness-minded business travelers.
There are great city views from almost every room, each of
which has functional decor. *300 E. Ohio St., Chicago 60611, tel.
312/787–6100 or 800/465–4329, fax 312/787–6259. 500 rooms, 9
suites. 110 nonsmoking rooms, 1 disabled-accessible room. Facilities: restaurant, 2 bars, free health club access, pool, same-
day laundry/dry cleaning, coin-op laundry, concierge, garage.
AE, D, DC, MC, V.*

Holiday Inn Mart Plaza. Perched atop the Apparel Center and
next to Merchandise Mart, this 16-year-old hotel is off the
beaten track for purposes other than business in the neighborhood. The rooms, ringed around a multistory atrium, are pleasant, if small and completely unremarkable. Free hors d'oeuvres
are served in the lobby at night. There's no fitness center, but
there is a big indoor pool. An assortment of interesting stores
is in the Shops at the Mart complex on the floors below the
hotel. The Michigan Avenue and State Street shopping areas
are a brief hike away, though the River North gallery district
is closer. *350 N. Orleans St., Chicago 60654, tel. 312/836–5000 or
800/465–4329, fax 312/222–9508. 524 rooms, 18 suites. 163 nonsmoking rooms, 2 disabled-accessible rooms. Facilities: 2 restaurants, 2 lounges, pay movies, pool, small exercise room,
same-day laundry/dry cleaning, garage. AE, D, DC, MC, V.*

Inn of Chicago. The hotel dates back to 1927, but it became a
Best Western property only recently. One block east of Michigan Avenue, it's a bargain for visitors who want to be near the

Magnificent Mile without paying the usual high price. Rooms are spotless, if spartan, and if you don't feel pampered, you'll be comfortable. The busy lobby—often crowded with tour groups—has live piano music playing during cocktail hour. An extra $10 gets you a first-class upgrade, including drinks in the hotel lounge, breakfast in the restaurant, a morning newspaper, and a suite based on availability. *162 E. Ohio St., Chicago 60611, tel. 312/787–3100 or 800/528–1234, fax 312/787–8236. 357 rooms, 26 suites. 76 nonsmoking rooms, 18 disabled-accessible rooms. Facilities: restaurant with bar, pay movies, same-day laundry/dry cleaning, access to nearby health club, valet parking. AE, D, DC, MC, V.*

Lenox House. Most suites in this all-suite hotel are actually just one large room with a Murphy bed, a queen sleeper-sofa and a wet-bar kitchenette. All the same, you can sleep four people in these rooms without difficulty, and the Water Tower area location is convenient to shopping and nightlife. Public areas verge on quaint, but guest rooms are generic 1980s. *616 N. Rush St., Chicago 60611, tel. 312/337–1000 or 800/445–3669, fax 312/337–7217. 325 suites. 75 nonsmoking suites, 4 disabled-accessible suites. Facilities: restaurant, bar, concierge. AE, D, DC, MC, V.*

Radisson Plaza Ambassador West. This 1920s European-style hotel's marble-and-oak lobby is loaded with antiques and reproductions, and the smallish rooms retain some vintage flavor with maroon-and-beige color schemes and hunting prints on the walls. The residential Gold Coast location is quiet but handy to Near North nightlife. The hotel sometimes acts as home away from home for movie people shooting films in Chicago. *1300 N. State Pkwy., Chicago 60610, tel. 312/787–7900 or 800/333–3333, fax 312/787–6235. 220 rooms, 50 suites. 55 nonsmoking rooms, 1 disabled-accessible room. Facilities: restaurant, bar, minibar, pay movies, concierge, valet parking, access to McClurg Court health club. AE, D, DC, MC, V.*

★ **Raphael.** This small European-style hotel on a side street near the John Hancock Building attracts devoted regulars who appreciate its spacious, comfortable rooms, obliging service, and extremely reasonable prices. Most rooms are actually 1 ½- or 2-room suites with sitting areas; some have chaise lounges for extra relaxation. The lobby and wide, floral-carpeted hallways have a turn-of-the-century feel. A cozy restaurant off the lobby beckons you for a nightcap or a bite to eat. *201 E. Delaware Pl., Chicago 60611, tel. 312/943–5000 or 800/821–5343, fax 312/943–9483. 98 rooms, 75 suites. 36 nonsmoking rooms, 1 disabled-accessible room. Facilities: restaurant with bar, minibars, 24-hour room service, access to nearby health club, same-day laundry/dry cleaning, valet parking. AE, D, DC, MC, V.*

Richmont. Cabaret music echoes softly through the corridors of this charming small hotel a block from Michigan Avenue. There are other Parisian touches as well: a bistro-style restaurant, turn-of-the-century French advertisement posters, and excruciatingly slow elevators. Standard rooms can't fit much more than the usual complement of a bed, a dresser, and a nightstand, so if you lean to claustrophobia or plan to spend a lot of time in your room, spring for the "deluxe" accommodations—they're still a relative bargain. Continental breakfast and afternoon wine-tasting and hors d'oeuvres are complimentary. *162 E. Ontario, Chicago 60611, tel. 312/787–3580 or 800/621–8055, fax 312/787–1299. 193 rooms, 26 suites. 60 nonsmoking rooms, 15 disabled-accessible rooms. Facilities: restaurant,* *piano bar, minibars, pay movies, same-day laundry/dry clean-ing, access to nearby health club, garage. AE, D, DC, MC, V.*

River North Hotel. This Best Western property, with its undistinguished exterior and lobby, has surprisingly stylish rooms decorated in tones of black, white, mauve, and gray. The rooms are large and well maintained, perhaps because the general manager was for ten years the head housekeeper at the Chicago Hilton and Towers. There are a large indoor pool, small game and exercise rooms, and a sundeck on the roof, as well as a VCR in each room. Across the street is Chicago's famous Rock 'n' Roll McDonald's, one of the busiest in the world. *125 W. Ohio St., Chicago 60610, tel. 312/467–0800 or 800/727–0800, fax 312/467–1665. 148 rooms, 58 suites. 115 nonsmoking rooms, no rooms with disabled access. Facilities: restaurant with bar, VCRs and video rental, pool, exercise room, same-day laundry/dry cleaning, free parking. AE, D, DC, MC, V.*

The Westin Hotel. Visiting pro-sports teams often stay here, but signs in the lobby ask you not to snap photos of the players. With more than 700 rooms, it's a tourist warehouse, but the brass-and-glass contemporary decor is pleasant enough. A new feature on room phones is AT&T's Language Line, a translation service for foreign travelers. The Westin's big draw is its great location on the Magnificent Mile. *909 N. Michigan Ave., Chicago 60611, tel. 312/943–7200 or 800/228–3000, fax 312/943–9347. 743 rooms, 45 suites. 165 nonsmoking rooms, 4 disabled-accessible rooms. Facilities: 2 restaurants, bar, 24-hour room service, minibars, pay movies, health club, same-day laundry/dry cleaning, concierge, valet parking, business center. AE, D, DC, MC, V.*

Inexpensive **Comfort Inn of Lincoln Park.** It's a motel. You park your own car in a lot visible from your room, and the price is about what you'd expect for clean, no-frills lodging. The lobby is unexpectedly quaint, with wood-and-brass decor and a small sitting area. The residential Lincoln Park neighborhood is a bit far north of all the downtown hoopla, but it's packed with small shops and restaurants that are interesting in their own right, and it's close to Wrigley Field. *601 W. Diversey, Chicago 60614, tel. 312/348–2810 or 800/727–0800, fax 312/348–1912. 71 rooms, 3 suites. Facilities: Continental breakfast included, parking lot. AE, D, DC, MC, V.*

The Margarita—A European Inn. Actually in Evanston, one town north of Chicago, the Margarita is a perfect choice if you need a break from the city. It's within walking distance of Northwestern University and close to Evanston's many shops, restaurants, and art galleries. The Margarita is smaller than most hotels but larger than a typical bed-and-breakfast. The parlor of this former women's boarding house, built in 1915, shows off the hotel's European-style elegance and intimacy: Sunlight gushes through several arched floor-to-ceiling windows, showing off a smattering of antiques and houseplants. Rooms are not large but are decorated tastefully. Continental breakfast is included. The French-influenced Northern Italian restaurant, Va Pensiero, is one of the area's finest eateries. *1566 Oak Ave. (2 blocks from train/bus), Evanston 60201, tel. 312/869–2273. 10 rooms with bath, 39 rooms share bath. Facilities: restaurant, library, rooftop sundeck, off-street parking. AE, MC, V.*

8 The Arts and Nightlife

The Arts

*Updated by
Elizabeth Gardner
and Mark Kollar*

Chicago is a splendid city for the arts. In addition to dozens of classical music organizations, including a world-class symphony orchestra and opera company, there are hundreds of clubs featuring jazz, rock, folk, and country music; some 50 theaters; an outstanding dance company; and movie theaters that show everything from first-run features to avant-garde films. For complete music and theater listings, check the two free weeklies *The Reader* and *New City*, the Friday and Sunday editions of the *Tribune* and *Sun-Times*, and the monthly *Chicago* magazine.

Ticket prices vary wildly depending on whether you're seeing a high-profile group or venturing into more obscure territory. Chicago Symphony tickets go from $16 to $65, Lyric Opera from $20 to more than $100 (if you can get them). Smaller choruses and orchestras charge from $10 to $25; watch the listings for free performances. Commercial theater ranges from $15 to $60; smaller experimental ensembles might charge $5, $10, or pay-what-you-can. One group lets you roll dice to determine your ticket price. Movies vary from $6.50 to $7.50 for first-run houses and as low as $2 at some suburban second-run houses. Some commercial chains take credit cards.

Music

The Chicago Symphony is internationally renowned, and Chicago's Lyric Opera may be the best opera company in America today. Season subscribers take virtually all the tickets to these performances, but subscribers who can't use their tickets sometimes return them to the box office. If you go to the opera house or Symphony Hall a half hour before performance time, you may find someone with an extra ticket to sell.

Orchestras **Chicago Symphony** (220 S. Michigan Ave., tel. 312/435–6666). The season at Symphony Hall extends from September through May, with music director Daniel Barenboim conducting. In the summer you can see and hear the Chicago Symphony at Ravinia Park in suburban Highland Park, under the direction of James Levine. It's a trip of about 25 miles from Chicago, accessible by train. The park is lovely, and lawn seats are always available even when (rarely) those in the Shed and the smaller Murray Theatre are sold out. Performances usually feature one or more notable soloists. For program, ticket, and travel information, tel. 312/728–4642.

Grant Park Symphony Orchestra (tel. 312/294–2420). Sponsored by the Chicago Park District, the Grant Park Symphony gives free concerts during the summer at the James C. Petrillo Bandshell in Grant Park, between Michigan Avenue and Columbus Drive at about Adams Street (enter from Monroe Street and follow the crowd). Performances usually are on Wednesday, Friday, Saturday, and Sunday evenings. The weekly *Reader* or a daily newspaper will have details of programs and performance times.

Concert Halls **Orchestra Hall** (220 S. Michigan Ave., tel. 312/435–8122). A variety of concerts and recitals are programmed during the year.

Mandel Hall (57th St. at University Ave., tel. 312/702–8068). Guest orchestras and performers are scheduled on a regular basis at this hall on the University of Chicago campus.

Smaller halls in the Loop/Near North area include **Curtiss Hall** in the Fine Arts Building (410 S. Michigan Ave., tel. 312/483–6730), **Fullerton Hall** in the Art Institute (Michigan Ave. at Adams St., tel. 312/443–3600), the **Newberry Library** (60 W. Walton Ave., tel. 312/943–9090), and the **Three Arts Club** (1300 N. Dearborn Pkwy., tel. 312/944–6250).

Choral and Chamber Groups The **Chicago Children's Choir** (tel. 312/324–8300) is one of the country's premier children's choral groups, with members drawn from a broad spectrum of racial, ethnic, and economic groups. Performances are given each year during the Christmas season and in early June; other concerts are scheduled periodically.

Concertante di Chicago (tel. 312/454–3030) is an excellent small orchestra specializing in 20th-century chamber music. It performs at the DePaul University Concert Hall (800 W. Belden).

Music of the Baroque (tel. 312/986–3236), the granddaddy of independent ensembles in Chicago, is a nationally known, highly polished professional chorus and orchestra concentrating on the works—particularly the choral works—of the Baroque period. It schedules eight concerts a year, with performances at various locations.

The **William Ferris Chorale** (tel. 312/527–9898), a distinguished choral ensemble that focuses on 20th-century music, gives concerts throughout the year.

Oriana Singers (tel. 312/262–4558) is an outstanding a cappella sextet with an eclectic classical repertoire.

Opera **Chamber Opera Chicago** (tel. 312/822–0770). A relatively new troupe, the Chamber Opera performs major works in English.

Chicago Opera Theatre (2936 N. Southport Ave., tel. 312/663–0048). The Chicago Opera specializes in English-language productions of smaller works suited to the intimate setting of the comfortable church auditorium in which it performs. Its 1993 season included *Don Giovanni.*

Lyric Opera of Chicago (20 N. Wacker Dr., tel. 312/332–2244). The season at the Civic Opera House runs from September through January; the tickets are difficult to come by.

Light Opera **The Light Opera Works** (tel. 708/869–6300). Gilbert and Sullivan operettas and other light operas are performed during a June–December season.

Theater

While road-show productions of Broadway hits do come to Chicago, the true vigor of its theater scene springs from the multitude of small ensembles that have made a home here. They range from the critically acclaimed Steppenwolf and the Goodman Theatre to fringe groups that specialize in experimental work.

Many smaller companies perform in tiny or make-shift theaters, where admission prices are moderate to quite inexpensive. You can save money on seats at **Hot Tix** (108 N. State St.), where unsold tickets are available at half price (plus a small service charge) on the day of performance; you can't learn what's available until that day, and you have to pay cash. The Hot Tix booth is open Monday noon–6, Tuesday–Friday 10–6, and Saturday 10–5; tickets for Sunday performances are sold on Saturday. When the temperature is below freezing, Hot Tix gives theatergoers a break and allows them to call 312/977–1755 to reserve tickets. At other times, calling that number activates a recorded message about shows available that day.

Theater groups from throughout the world perform at the annual International Theatre Festival (tel. 312/664–3370), held every other year in the spring. In 1992 the big draws were *Macbeth* and *Twelfth Night* by the English Shakespeare Company, and *Waiting for Godot* from Dublin's Gate Theater. For 1994, the probable festival dates are May 24–June 19. At press time (spring 1993), the Fest had booked a Canadian production of Robert LePage's *Needles and Opium* and a British production of Alan Ayckbourn's *A Word from Our Sponsor.*

Commercial Theater Most of the houses listed here are hired by independent producers for commercial (and sometimes nonprofit) productions; they have no resident producer or company.

Apollo Theater Center (2540 N. Lincoln, tel. 312/935–6100). This modern space is located in one of Lincoln Park's few strip malls.

Auditorium Theater (50 E. Congress Pkwy., tel. 312/559–2900). Acoustics and sight lines are excellent in this Louis Sullivan architectural masterpiece. You're likely to see touring productions of Broadway hits like *City of Angels* and *Miss Saigon.*

Briar St. Theater (3133 N. Halsted St., tel. 312/348–4000). Local productions of hit Broadway plays often find their way to this modest space in Lakeview.

Candlelight Dinner Playhouse (5620 S. Harlem Ave., Summit, tel. 708/496–3000). Just over the city line in Summit, the Candlelight usually offers superb productions of classic Broadway musicals. The food is edible, and the dinner/theater package is a good deal, or you can just go for the show. **The Forum,** a smaller theater, is next door.

Chicago Theater (175 N. State St., tel. 312/443–1130). This former movie palace and vaudeville house was gaudily but lovingly restored in 1986, and ran into financial trouble shortly thereafter. It's now open sporadically for national tours of musicals and various types of performances.

Halsted Theater Center (2700 N. Halsted St., tel. 312/348–0110). This new complex has two small theater spaces, with an adjacent parking lot.

Mayfair Theater (Blackstone Hotel, 636 S. Michigan Ave., tel. 312/786–9120). The audience-participation mystery *Shear Madness* has been playing here since 1982 and shows no signs of closing.

Merle Reskin–Blackstone Theater (60 E. Balbo, tel. 312/362–8455). This grand and ornate space is owned by DePaul University and used for productions by its theater school.

Organic Theater (3319 N. Clark St., tel. 312/327–5588). Once a theater company in its own right, the Organic is now largely just another performance space.

Royal George Theater Center (1641 N. Halsted St., tel. 312/988–9000). A new building, the Royal George has one large, gracious theater, one smaller studio theater, a cabaret space, and a restaurant.

Shubert Theater (22 W. Monroe St., tel. 312/977–1700). A grand 19th-century-style theater, the Shubert is one of the few remaining remnants of the Loop's once-thriving theater district.

Wellington Theater (750 W. Wellington St., tel. 312/975–7171). The former Ivanhoe Theater (explaining the exterior's medieval half-timbered look) was refurbished and reopened in 1989.

Performing Groups Chicago's reputation as a theatrical powerhouse was born from its dozens of small not-for-profit theater companies that produce everything from Shakespeare to Stephen Sondheim. The groups listed below do consistently interesting work, and some have gained national attention. Some, such as Steppenwolf and the Remains Theater Company, are ensemble troupes; others, notably the Goodman, the Court, and the Body Politic, are production companies that use different casts for each show. Keep an open mind when you're choosing a show to see; even a group you've never heard of may be harboring one or two underpaid geniuses. *The Reader* carries complete theater listings and reviews of the more avant-garde shows.

Body Politic/Victory Gardens (2257–61 N. Lincoln Ave., tel. 312/871–3000). These two venerable institutions have traditionally offered polished productions of both modern American plays and works of Shakespeare and Shaw. The Body Politic, however, recently underwent a change of artistic directors and has lately—along with Victory Garden—been presenting more original scripts by local authors.

Court Theater (5535 S. Ellis Ave., tel. 312/753–4472). On the University of Chicago campus, the Court revives classic plays with varying success.

Goodman Theater (200 S. Columbus Dr., tel. 312/443–3800). One of the oldest and best theaters in Chicago, the Goodman is known for its polished performances of contemporary works starring well-known actors. Now situated behind the Art Institute, it's scheduled to move into two former movie palaces in the north Loop in 1996.

Interplay (Pilsen East Center for the Arts, 1935 S. Halsted St., tel. 312/243–6240). This small theater stands in a developing artists' neighborhood, which is still far from gentrification, southwest of the Loop.

Neo-Futurists (5153 N. Ashland Ave., tel. 312/275–5255). Performing in a space above a funeral home, this group's long-running cult hit is *Too Much Light Makes the Baby Go Blind*, a series of 30 two-minute plays whose order is chosen by the audience.

Next Theater Company (Noyes Cultural Arts Center, 927 Noyes, Evanston, tel. 708/475–1875). Founded by an Evanston woman who thought it would be fun to produce plays (and evidently was right), the Next specializes in rarely performed scripts.

Pegasus Players (1145 W. Wilson Ave., tel. 312/271–2638). Pegasus tackles interesting and difficult works, usually producing at least one Stephen Sondheim musical each season. The spacious theater is at the city's Truman College.

Remains Theater (1800 N. Clybourn, tel. 312/335–9800). Remains specializes in original scripts by American writers, featuring gritty acting in the Steppenwolf tradition. Cofounder William Petersen turns up in the movies now and then.

Shakespeare Repertory (2939 N. Broadway, tel. 312/281–1878). This extremely talented group is almost single-handedly keeping the Bard's flame alive in the Chicago area.

Steppenwolf (1650 N. Halsted St., tel. 312/335–1650). The nationally known Steppenwolf company brings a dark, brooding, Method-acting style to its consistently successful productions. Illustrious alumni include John Malkovich, Joan Allen, and Laurie Metcalf. Its Broadway production of John Steinbeck's *The Grapes of Wrath* won a Tony award in 1990 for best play.

The Theatre Building (1225 W. Belmont Ave., tel. 312/327–5252). This rehabbed warehouse provides a permanent home for half a dozen small companies of local renown, including Bailiwick Repertory, Lookingglass Theatre, and New Tuners Theatre.

Touchstone Theater (2851 N. Halsted St., tel. 312/404–4700). This company took over the Steppenwolf company's former space in Lakeview and specializes in 20th-century works.

Wisdom Bridge Theater (1559 W. Howard St., tel. 312/743–6000). Wisdom Bridge's innovative productions are too varied to pigeonhole, but usually worth seeing.

Dance

Though there are fewer organized dance troupes in Chicago than one might expect to find in a city so renowned for music and theater, there are several companies that perform regularly. The most popular dance performance space is the Civic Opera House (20 N. Wacker Dr.).

Ballet Chicago (222 S. Riverside Plaza, tel. 312/993–7575) is the city's only resident classical ballet troupe and has received critical acclaim for its work. The group currently conducts spring seasons only.

Chicago's most notable success story in dance is the **Hubbard St. Dance Company** (tel. 312/663–0853), whose contemporary, jazzy vitality has made it extremely popular. Another company worth seeing is the **Joseph Holmes Dance Theater** (1935 S. Halsted Ave., tel. 312/942–0065).

Film

Many cinemas on the near north side offer first-run Hollywood movies on multiple screens, including **Chestnut Station** (830 N. Clark St., tel. 312/337–7301), **Water Tower Theater** (845 N. Michigan Ave., tel. 312/649–5790), **900 N. Michigan Theater** (tel.

312/787–1988), and **McClurg Court** (330 E. Ohio St., tel. 312/642–0723).

The **Esquire** (58 E. Oak St., tel. 312/280–0101), an Art Deco landmark, recently underwent a renovation that preserved its facade but divided it into four theaters.

A north-side first-run movie house of some historical interest is the **Biograph Theatre** (2433 N. Lincoln Ave., tel. 312/348–4123); gangster John Dillinger was shot in front of the Biograph by FBI agents in 1934. If you ask around, you may be able to find a local who can show you the bullet marks in the side of the building.

The most convenient first-run movie theater for those staying in the south Loop is the recently built **Burnham Plaza** (826 S. Wabash Ave., tel. 312/922–1090).

For something a bit different, try **The Fine Arts Theatre** (418 S. Michigan Ave., tel. 312/939–3700), whose four screens show independent, foreign, and avant-garde films.

The Film Center of the Art Institute (Columbus Dr. at Jackson Blvd., tel. 312/443–3737) specializes in unusual current films and revivals of rare classics. The program here changes almost daily, and filmmakers sometimes give lectures at the Film Center.

Facets Multimedia (1517 W. Fullerton Ave., tel. 312/281–4114) presents a variety of rare and exotic films; call and see whether a particular day's fare appeals to you. The basement has a videotape-rental library.

The Music Box Theatre (3733 N. Southport Ave., tel. 312/871–6604) is a small and lovingly restored 1920s movie palace. Programs at this richly decorated theater change nightly, except for special runs; the theater shows a mix of classics and outstanding recent films, emphasizing independent filmmakers. The theater organ is played during intermission at special events and as an accompaniment to silent films. If you love old theaters and old movies, don't miss a trip here.

Nightlife

Chicago comes alive at night, with something for everyone, from loud and loose to sophisticated and sedate. *The Reader* and *New City* (available Thursday and Friday in Lincoln Park and Hyde Park) are your best guides to the entertainment scene. The *Chicago Tribune* and the *Chicago Sun-Times* on Friday are good sources of information on current shows and starting times. Shows usually begin at 9 PM; cover charges generally range from $3 to $7, depending on the day of the week; Friday and Saturday nights are the most expensive. There's a free concert hot line (tel. 312/666–6667).

If you want to find "Rush Street," the famous Chicago bar scene, don't bother looking on Rush Street itself. Most of the nightlife is now located on Division Street between Clark and State streets, having been pushed north by office and apartment development. Among the better-known singles bars are **Mother's** (26 W. Division St.), featured in the motion picture *...About Last Night;* and **Butch McGuire's** (20 W. Division St.). If you are in the mood for dancing, try **Eddie Rocket's** (9

W. Division St.). This area is particularly festive on warm weekend nights, when the street adopts a carnival-like atmosphere.

You can find a similar atmosphere in the establishments at the North Pier development (455 E. Illinois St.), notably the **Baja Beach Club** and **Dick's Last Resort.** North Pier is the center of a growing nightlife scene just north of the Loop and east of Michigan Avenue.

The list of blues and jazz clubs includes several South Side locations, and visitors to Chicago should be cautious about transportation here late at night, since some of these neighborhoods are dangerous. Drive your own car or a previously reserved cab or limo, and avoid public transportation. Some clubs provide guarded parking lots or can arrange cab service for visitors. Parking in North Side neighborhoods, particularly Lincoln Park and Lakeview, can be scarce on weekends. If you're visiting nightspots in these areas, consider leaving your car behind and taking cabs or public transportation.

Music

Blues In the years following World War II, Chicago-style blues grew into its own musical form. Blues flourished here in the 1950s, then faded in the 1960s with the advent of rock and roll. Today Chicago blues is coming back, although more strongly on the trendy North Side than on the South Side where it all began.
Blue Chicago (937 N. State St., tel. 312/642–6261). This large room has a good sound system and attracts a cosmopolitan, heterogeneous crowd. The same management runs **Blue Chicago on Clark** (536 N. Clark St., tel. 312/661–0100). Minimum.
B.L.U.E.S. (2519 N. Halsted St., tel. 312/528–1012). The best of Chicago's own musicians play here and attract a large, friendly crowd.
B.L.U.E.S. Etcetera (1124 W. Belmont Ave., tel. 312/525–8989). A spacious and comfortable change from overcrowded spots.
Buddy Guy's Legends (754 S. Wabash Ave., tel. 312/427–0333). One of Chicago's own blues legends is part-owner of this converted double storefront in the south Loop and often sits in. It's spacious, with good sound, good sight lines, and weekday sets that start at 8:30 PM. Cover charge varies.
Kingston Mines (2548 N. Halsted St., tel. 312/477–4646). One of the North Side's oldest spots, the Mines attracts large numbers of blues lovers and cruising singles, the first because of its continuous live weekend entertainment on two stages, the second because of its late closing (4 AM Friday, 5 AM Saturday).
Lilly's (2513 N. Lincoln Ave., tel. 312/525–2422). Lilly's is tiny, warm, and friendly.
New Checkerboard Lounge (423 E. 43rd St., tel. 312/624–3240). Although the neighborhood is rough, this remains one of the great old South Side clubs. The music by name performers is usually worth the trip.
Rosa's Lounge (3420 W. Armitage St., tel. 312/342–0452). Expect good music at this homey spot in a Hispanic and Polish neighborhood. No cover Monday.
Wise Fools Pub (2270 N. Lincoln Ave., tel. 312/929–1510). The intimate room is an old-time Lincoln Park spot that books name performers. Minimum Saturday.

Jazz **Andy's** (11 E. Hubbard St., tel. 312/642–6805). Once just a big old friendly neighborhood bar in the shadow of the IBM Building, Andy's has become one of Chicago's best spots for serious jazz. The jazz at noon is a boon for music lovers who aren't night owls. No cover at noon.

The Bop Shop. (1807 W. Division St., tel. 312/235–3232). Small groups play in an intimate setting at this Wicker Park club.

The Bulls (1916 N. Lincoln Park West, tel. 312/337–3000). This small club showcases the best of local groups.

The Cotton Club (1710 S. Michigan Ave., tel. 312/341–9787). This spot is a favorite of upscale young black professionals.

Dick's Last Resort (435 E. Illinois St., tel. 312/836–7080). This crowded, raucous North Pier fixture has hot Dixieland jazz most nights.

Gold Star Sardine Bar (680 N. Lake Shore Dr., tel. 312/664–4215). Housed in a splendid renovated building that once was the Chicago Furniture Mart, this tiny spot books top names that attract a trendy clientele. Minimum. Jacket required.

The Green Mill (4802 N. Broadway, tel. 312/878–5552). This Chicago institution, off the beaten track in untrendy Uptown, has been around for most of this century and has been skillfully renovated to look as if it hasn't been redecorated since it opened. The entertainment ranges from good to outstanding, and the club can get crowded on weekends. On Sunday evenings, the Uptown Poetry Slam, a competitive poetry reading, takes center stage.

Jazz Showcase (636 S. Michigan Ave., tel. 312/427–4300). Nationally known acts perform in the once elegant but decaying setting of the Blackstone Hotel. A no-smoking policy is strictly enforced.

Milt Trenier's Lounge (610 Fairbanks Ct., tel. 312/266–6226). Cabaret acts are augmented by Milt himself, who plays with his jazz quintet on weekends.

Oz (2917 N. Sheffield Ave., tel. 312/975–8100). An intimate, crowded neighborhood bar, Oz features quality local performers Thursday–Saturday, plus one of the city's biggest assortments of cognacs and Armagnacs.

Pops for Champagne (2934 N. Sheffield Ave., tel. 312/472–1000). Despite the incongruous name, this is a good spot for serious jazz fans. Pops sports a popular champagne bar.

Rock **Avalon Niteclub** (959 W. Belmont Ave., tel. 312/472–3020). The building's been around for a long time; the acts are up and coming.

Cabaret Metro (3730 N. Clark St., tel. 312/549–0203). The Metro presents a wide range of artists, from the nationally known to the cream of the local crop, and a wide range of rock styles. People come for a specific show, so the crowd will vary according to the attraction. There's dancing in the Smart Bar, downstairs.

China Club (616 W. Fulton St., tel. 312/466–0812). If you can't do without New York–or L.A.–style glitz and are willing to risk rejection by the doorman, this huge complex in River West may be just the thing. Open Wednesday–Saturday until 4 AM.

Club Dreamerz (1516 N. Milwaukee Ave., tel. 312/252–1155). Rising young local talent is presented here.

Cubby Bear (1059 W. Addison St., tel. 312/327–1662). A variety of acts play this scruffy but roomy venue across the street from Wrigley Field. The music usually starts around 10 PM. During baseball season, the Cubby Bear opens in the afternoon to give Cub fans another place to drown their sorrows.

Lounge Ax (2438 N. Lincoln Ave., tel. 312/525–6620). A mix of local rock, folk, country, and reggae acts is presented here nightly.

The Wild Hare (3530 N. Clark St., tel. 312/327–4273). Local groups perform reggae; a Caribbean decor adds to the atmosphere.

Folk and Ethnic **Abbey Pub** (3420 W. Grace, tel. 312/478–4408). Irish music by Irish performers is the fare at this neighborhood establishment.

Cafe Continental (5515 N. Lincoln Ave., tel. 312/878–7077). Up in the German Lincoln Square neighborhood, this club's regular acts include the Maxwell St. Klezmer Band. Closed Monday and Tuesday. Minimum.

Deni's Den (2941 N. Clark St., tel. 312/348–8888). This large, attractive spot features Greek performers. Until 4 AM Friday, 5 AM Saturday.

Kitty O'Shea's (720 S. Michigan Ave., tel. 312/922–4400). This handsome room in the Chicago Hilton and Towers recreates an Irish pub, complete with Irish music and food by Irish chefs.

No Exit (6970 N. Glenwood Ave., tel. 312/743–3355). Folk, jazz, and poetry readings are offered in a comfortable coffeehouse setting reminiscent of the late 1960s. Backgammon and chess sets are available.

Old Town School of Folk Music (909 W. Armitage Ave., tel. 312/525–7793). Chicago's only folk music school, Old Town offers outstanding folk performances.

Tania's (2659 N. Milwaukee Ave., tel. 312/235–7120). This Cuban restaurant becomes a nightclub with salsa bands on weekends. No cover or minimum; no jeans.

Country There isn't much country music in Chicago, but you might try one of these places:

Carol's Pub (4659 N. Clark St., tel. 312/334–2402).

Clearwater Saloon (3937 N. Lincoln Ave., tel. 312/549–5599).

Emerald Point Lounge (3432 W. Irving Park Rd., tel. 312/539–5229).

Lakeview Lounge (5110 N. Broadway, tel. 312/769–0994).

Whiskey River (1997 N. Clybourn Ave., tel. 312/528–3400).

For country music with food, try **Bub City Crabshack and Barbecue** (901 W. Weed St., tel. 312/266–1200).

Eclectic Clubs in this category don't limit themselves to a single type of music. If you have a strong preference for the kind of music you're going to hear, you will want to call ahead to learn what's playing.

Abbey Pub (3420 W. Grace St., tel. 312/478–4408). This neighborhood establishment features Irish music Wednesdays and Sundays, with a mix of folk, rock, and blues the rest of the week.

At the Tracks (325 N. Jefferson St., tel. 312/332–1124). An upstairs location affords a fantastic view of the maze of railroad tracks coming into the city from the west. The music is usually excellent, the food pretty good.

The Beat Kitchen (2100 W. Belmont Ave., tel. 312/281–4444). A good sound system and varied local acts make this small club in Bucktown popular. Cover and minimum.

Biddy Mulligan's (7644 N. Sheridan Rd., tel. 312/761–6532). The neighborhood ambience attracts a nice mix of customers. Biddy's started out as a blues bar but has branched out into rock and reggae, so there's no telling what you'll find here.

Fitzgerald's (6615 W. Roosevelt Rd., Berwyn, tel. 708/788–2118). Though a bit out of the way, Fitzgerald's draws crowds from all over the city and suburbs with a mix of folk, jazz, and blues and a homey summer-cabin ambience.

The Hothouse (1565 N. Milwaukee Ave., tel. 312/235–2335). An arty crowd flocks to this cavernous room in Wicker Park to hear everything from heavy metal to Brazilian samba, with the occasional evening of performance-art thrown in.

Park West (322 W. Armitage Ave., tel. 312/929–5959). Shows here tend to be name acts glossily performed; expect high cover and drink prices. The hall itself is large, with good sight lines and acoustics. Jacket required; no jeans.

The Vic (3145 N. Sheffield Ave., tel. 312/472–0366). This former movie palace advertises "all ages" shows, heavy on rock and R&B. Sunday through Wednesday is "brew and view"—current movies with beer.

Dance Clubs

Asi Es Colombia (3910 N. Lincoln Ave., tel. 312/348–7444). Good salsa bands attract good dancers. Jacket required.

Eddie Rockets (9 W. Division St., tel. 312/787–4881). Dance till dawn with a young singles crowd. Open until 4 AM Friday, 5 AM Saturday.

Excalibur (632 N. Dearborn St., tel. 312/266–1944). This River North brownstone hides a super-disco with multiple dance floors and bars, a games room, and a restaurant. Popular with young adults, it attracts a large suburban crowd on weekends. Open Fri. till 2 AM, Sat. till 3 AM. No cover.

Gordon (500 N. Clark St., tel. 312/467–9780). Principally a fine restaurant, Gordon has a very good jazz combo that plays after 9 PM Saturday for dancing.

Neo (2350 N. Clark St., tel. 312/528–2622). Neo is loud but not way out. Open until 4 AM Friday, 5 AM Saturday.

Riviera Night Club (4750 N. Broadway, tel. 312/275–6800). Laser beams and name bands are the attractions at this cavernous former movie palace. Open until 4 AM Friday, 5 AM Saturday.

Piano Bars

Coq d'Or at the Drake Hotel (140 E. Walton St., tel. 312/787–2200). Chicago legend Buddy Charles holds court here Wednesday–Saturday nights.

Four Seasons (120 E. Delaware, tel. 312/280–8800). Enjoy drinks or dessert to the sounds of jazz piano.

Pump Room (Omni Ambassador East Hotel, 1301 N. State Pkwy., tel. 312/266–0360). You can still dance cheek-to-cheek at this long-time celebrity hangout. Jacket required.

The Salon at the Park Hyatt (800 N. Michigan Ave., tel. 312/280–2222). The Salon is an intimate, elegant spot.

Sports Bars

Sluggers (3540 N. Clark St., tel. 312/248–0055). Across from Wrigley Field, this roomy, comfortable bar is packed after Cub games, and the players themselves make occasional personal appearances. Check out the fast- and slow-pitch batting cages on the second floor.

Coffeehouses

During the past few years, cafés have sprung up throughout the lakefront to accommodate those who wish to hang out and talk without necessarily drinking alcohol. Most offer the full gamut of coffees and teas, as well as gooey desserts. Some have small menus of real food too. Yuppie to arty, there's a coffeehouse for every taste. Here are just a few:

Café Voltaire (3231 N. Clark St., tel. 312/528–3136). With exposed brick and a vegetarian menu in addition to the usual coffee and desserts, this place caters to artists and entertains everyone else. A space downstairs doubles as a theater.

Coffee Chicago (801 N. Wabash Ave., tel. 312/664–6415; 2922 N. Clark St., tel. 312/327–3228; 3323 N. Clark St., tel. 312/477–3323; 6744 N. Sheridan Rd., tel. 312/274–1880; 1561 N. Wells St., tel. 312/787–1211). A chain, but it doesn't look like one. All five locations are quiet and congenial, decorated in tasteful Laura Ashley prints. Scones and tortes are especially good.

Java Jive (909 W. School St., tel. 312/649–3500). This place is popular with the all-in-black crowd. There are a piano, board games, and a fortune teller who drops in occasionally. The artwork on the walls is usually for sale.

Kopi, a Traveler's Cafe (5317 N. Clark St., tel. 312/989–5674). The first café in Andersonville, it has a selection of travel books and artifacts from foreign lands, artfully painted tables, and outrageous cakes.

Third Coast Café (888 N. Wabash Ave. at Delaware, tel. 312/664–7225; 1260 N. Dearborn St., tel. 312/649–0730). The Dearborn location is cavernous and open 24 hours Tuesdays through Saturdays; it sometimes has live entertainment. The Delaware location has indoor and outdoor tables. You can spend the day in either, sipping and talking.

Comedy Clubs

Improvisation has long had a home and a successful following in Chicago; stand-up comedy has fared less well. Up-and-coming local talent has brightened the scene in recent years.

All Jokes Aside (1000 S. Wabash Ave., tel. 312/922–0577). This is the only stand-up outpost in the south Loop.

ComedySportz (Congress Hotel, 520 S. Michigan Ave., tel. 312/549–8080). Specializing in "competitive improv" (two teams vie for the favor of the audience), this troupe has had many homes over the past several years, but now seems more or less firmly situated. Cover and minimum.

Funny Firm (318 W. Grand St., tel. 312/321–9500). This popular club books both local and national stand-up talent.

Improvisation Institute (2319 W. Belmont Ave., tel. 312/929–2323). The resident improv group is very good.

Improvisations (504 N. Wells St., tel. 312/782–6387). When you tire of the comedy here, you can munch dim sum in the attached restaurant. Cover charge and minimum.

Second City (1616 N. Wells St., tel. 312/337–3992). An institution for more than 30 years, Second City has spawned some of the hottest comedians around. Yet in recent years the once bitingly funny, loony improvisation has given way to a less imaginative and more raunchy style.

Zanies (1548 N. Wells St., tel. 312/337–4027). Perhaps Chicago's best stand-up comedy spot, Zanies books outstanding national talent. Reservations recommended.

Gay/Lesbian

Chicago's gay nightlife scene is diverse; its bars appeal to mixed crowds and tastes. Most are on North Halsted Street (3200 N. and above), an area appropriately named "Boys Town." Bars generally stay open until 2 AM weekends, but a few keep the lights on until 5 AM Sundays. The *Windy City Times* and *Gay Chicago Magazine* list nightspots, events, and gay and lesbian resources.

AA Meat Market—A Butcher Bar (2933 N. Lincoln Ave., tel. 312/528–2933). A "rough-and-rowdy" leather bar, known for its "full-moon" and "lights-out" parties. What to wear? Don't worry: Plans to open a leather boutique are in the works.

Baton Show Lounge (436 N. Clark St., tel. 312/644–5269). This popular drag show caters mostly to curious out-of-towners. Even so, it's a fun spot and some of the regular performers, such as Chili Pepper, have become Chicago cult figures.

Berlin (954 W. Belmont Ave., tel. 312/348–4975). A video bar that's hot with the fast-lane set from the futures exchanges. Wednesdays are a big night: The last one of every month is "Disco Wednesday," and the first and third ones are predominately lesbian.

Big Chicks (5024 N. Sheridan Rd., tel. 312/728–5511). The bar sponsors several men's and women's sports teams, so it's a favorite spot with alternative jocks. The crowd is mixed but caters mostly to gays. Great jukebox and fun-loving staff, even though the location's a bit of a hike.

Charlie's (405 W. Ontario St., tel. 312/642–0050). The biggest gay bar, ergo the biggest country-and-western gay bar, in Chicago. You can dance nightly to achy-breaky tunes. It's mostly a suburban boots-and-denim crowd on weekends, but even hard-core urbanites rate it high on their cruising lists.

The Closet (3325 N. Broadway, tel. 312/477–8533). A small neighborhood bar, which locals call a "friendly joint." Don't miss the infamous "Bloody Sundays," for what are hailed as the best Bloody Marys in town. Mixed crowd.

Gentry (712 N. Rush St., tel. 312/644–1033). This piano bar draws the "coat-and-tie" set. Regulars sing along to show tunes. Two separate bars—one video, one intimate—provide meeting spots to dish. One of the few gay bars either Near North or downtown.

Little Jim's (3501 N. Halsted St., tel. 312/871–6116). Another neighborhood bar with a good mix of regulars. Video screens show films of varying repute. Wednesday is bingo night.

Paris Dance (1122 W. Montrose Ave., tel. 312/769–0602). This spirited, lesbian dance club plays Top-40 music but also features disco and salsa nights. The place rocks on weekends.

Roscoe's Tavern and Cafe (3354–56 N. Halsted St., tel. 312/281–3355). This crowded yuppy bar has great dance music, outdoor patios, and a late-night café, famed for its desserts.

Sidetrack (3349 N. Halsted St., tel. 312/477–9189). A major stand-and-pose scene where the boys usually serve more fashion than fun. Popular in summer because of its patio. Clientele tends toward young and beautiful, so it seems to think.

Vortex (3631 N. Halsted St., tel. 312/975–6622). A pulsating disco of bulked-up men. Live entertainment has included Marky Mark, Ru Paul, and gaggles of go-go boys.

9 Excursions from Chicago

The Western Suburbs

Chicago's western suburbs, particularly those near the city, are quite different from the sumptuous enclaves of the North Shore. Gracious villages that date from the 1800s mingle with more modest developments from the postwar housing boom. Our tour of the western suburbs includes a visit to Oak Park, one of the most interesting neighborhoods of residential architecture in the United States. A little farther west is the planned community of Riverside, designed by Frederick Law Olmsted and Calvert Vaux, who laid out New York's Central Park. Riverside's neighbor, Brookfield, has one of the country's foremost zoos. We'll also stop at two nature preserves, one a restored prairie, the other a spectacular arboretum. Finally, we'll visit Wheaton and the estate of one of Chicago's most influential citizens earlier in the century, *Tribune* publisher Robert McCormick.

Tourist Information

The **visitors center** at the Pumping Station (Michigan Ave. at Pearson St., tel. 312/280–5740) and the Cultural Center (78 E. Washington St.) have some information on major attractions in the western suburbs, as does the **Illinois Tourist Information Center** (310 S. Michigan Ave., tel. 800/233–0121). Also check with the **Chicago Architecture Foundation** (tel. 312/922–8687) and the **Oak Park Visitors Center** (tel. 708/848–1500).

Getting There

By Car This excursion is best done by car. The main arteries serving the western suburbs are the Eisenhower Expressway (I–290), which goes west from the Loop; the Tri-State Tollway (I–94/294), which circles the region from north to south; and newly built I–355, which connects I–290 with I–55, the road from Chicago to St. Louis.

By Train You can take **Metra** commuter trains (tel. 312/322–6777) to in-
Commuter dividual attractions. The Metra Chicago and Northwestern Line departs from **Northwestern Station** (500 W. Madison St.) and stops in Oak Park and Wheaton. The Burlington Northern line departs from **Union Station** (210 S. Canal St.) and stops at Riverside, Brookfield, and Lisle.

El Train The Lake Street line of the **Chicago Transit Authority's** El train goes to Oak Park, but it's not recommended because of the high number of crimes reported on it. The Congress line also stops in Oak Park, but several miles south of the historic district.

Guided Tours

The Chicago Architecture Foundation (*see* Tourist Information, *above*) has occasional tours of the western suburbs, and the Oak Park Visitors Center (*see* Tourist Information, *above*) has self-guided tours of Oak Park and adjacent River Forest, as well as information on guided tours.

Exploring the Western Suburbs

Numbers in the margin correspond to points of interest on the Northeastern Illinois map.

Oak Park Ernest Hemingway once called **Oak Park**—his birthplace and
❶ childhood home from 1899 to 1917—a town of "broad lawns and narrow minds." The ethnic and political leanings of this village have diversified since Hemingway played on its streets, however, due in part to the past decade's influx of young professionals fleeing the city with their children in search of safer streets, better public schools, and easy access to the Loop.

Founded in the 1850s, just west of the Chicago border, Oak Park is not only one of Chicago's oldest suburbs, but also a living museum of American architectural thought. It has the world's largest collection of Prairie School buildings, an architectural style created by Frank Lloyd Wright, to reflect the expanses of the Great Plains. Constructed from materials indigenous to the region, Prairie School houses hug the earth with their emphatic horizontal lines; inside, open spaces flow into each other, rather than being divided into individual rooms.

To get to the heart of Oak Park, take the Eisenhower Expressway (I–290) west to Harlem Avenue and exit to the left. Turn right at the top of the ramp, head north on Harlem Avenue to Chicago Avenue, turn right, and proceed to Forest Avenue.

On the southeast corner of Forest and Chicago avenues you'll see the **Frank Lloyd Wright Home and Studio.** In 1889, the 22-year-old Wright began building his own Shingle Style home, financed by a $5,000 loan from his then-employer and mentor, Louis Sullivan. Over the next 20 years, Wright expanded his business as well as his original modest cottage, establishing his own firm in 1894 and adding a studio in 1898.

In 1909 Wright left his wife and six children for the wife of a client; the focus of his career changed, too, as he spread his innovative designs across the United States and abroad. Sold by Wright in 1925, his home and studio were turned into apartments that eventually fell into disrepair. In 1974, a group of local citizens calling itself the Frank Lloyd Wright Home and Studio Foundation, together with the National Trust for Historic Preservation, embarked on a 13-year, $2.2 million restoration that returned the building to its 1909 appearance.

Wright's home, made of brick and dark shingles, is filled with natural wood furnishings and earth-tone spaces; Wright's determination to create an integrated environment prompted him to design the furniture as well. The leaded windows have colored art glass designs, and several rooms feature skylights or other indirect lighting. A spacious playroom on the second floor is built to a child's scale. The studio is made up of four spaces—an office, a large reception room, an octagonal library, and an octagonal drafting room that uses a chain harness system rather than traditional beams to support its balcony, roof, and walls. *951 Chicago Ave., tel. 708/848–1500. Admission: $6 adults, $4 senior citizens and children 10–18. Tours weekdays at 11 AM, 1 PM, and 3 PM, and continuously on weekends 11–4. Reservations required for groups of 10 or more.*

Several other examples of Wright's work are within easy walking or driving distance from his home and studio. Except for the Unity Temple, though, these are all private homes, so you'll have to be content with what you can view from the outside. One block left on Chicago Avenue takes you past **1019, 1027,** and **1031 Chicago Avenue.** Turn left on Marion Street and then left again on Superior Street to reach **1030 Superior Street.** Continue down Superior Street, turn right onto Forest Avenue, and take a look at **333, 318, 238,** and **210 Forest Avenue.** Head left for a detour to **6 Elizabeth Court.** Follow Forest Avenue a few blocks south to Lake Street and turn left.

On the corner of Lake Street and Kenilworth Avenue is **Unity Temple** (875 Lake St., tel. 708/383–8873), built for a Unitarian congregation in 1905. The stark, concrete building consists of two spaces, a sanctuary and a parish house, connected by the low-ceilinged main entrance. The cubical sanctuary is lit by high windows of stained glass. Wright would no doubt be delighted to find his original furniture still in use here.

Hemingway fans may want to head back up Forest Avenue to Chicago Avenue. One block east and two blocks north brings you to **Ernest Hemingway's boyhood home** (600 N. Kenilworth). This gray stucco house is privately owned and not open to the public.

Maps, tour information, and multilingual recorded tours of other historic buildings in the River Forest/Oak Park area (including those by Prairie School architects E. E. Roberts and George Maher) are available through the **Oak Park Visitors Center** (158 N. Forest Ave., tel. 708/848–1500).

Riverside/
Brookfield Area
❷

The planned community of **Riverside** is the next stop. The village was founded in the 1860s, when the beautiful Des Plaines River setting inspired a group of Eastern businesspeople to finance the development of a resort-style suburb. They hired Frederick Law Olmsted and Calvert Vaux, designers of New York City's Central Park and a large percentage of memorable land on the East Coast, to create their "village in a park." The name is apt, since Olmsted and Vaux gave Riverside five large parks and 41 smaller ones. Housing construction continued through the 19th century and the first quarter of the 20th.

Today, Riverside is an affluent suburb whose 9,000 residents are passionate about their town, designated a National Historic Landmark in 1970. The village declined federal aid intended to help repave a road because intersections would have had to be converted to safer (but less aesthetically pleasing) 90-degree angles. The Frederick Law Olmsted Society offers occasional walking and biking tours (tel. 708/447–1158) and crusades against unwelcome modernization.

To get to Riverside, return to Harlem Avenue and drive south to the Eisenhower Expressway, taking it west to 1st Avenue. Go south on 1st (also called Golfview and Forbes at various points) past 31st Street. (To get to Brookfield Zoo, *see below,* turn right on 31st.) Turn left onto Forest Avenue and right onto Longcommon Road. (Notice the Swiss Gothic water tower.) Turn right just beyond the train station onto Barrypoint Road and right onto Bloomingbank Road. As you curve around, the river is on your right and stunning Victorian houses are on your left. At the stop sign, turn left onto Scottswood Road.

At 300 Scottswood is one of Frank Lloyd Wright's finest works, the **Avery Coonley House.** Built in 1908 as the centerpiece of a large estate, the house has a raised ground floor, with most of the principal rooms on the second floor. The house is privately owned, so you can view it only from the outside. The original complex included a garage and formal gardens, but the lot was subdivided for other buildings.

As you drive through Riverside (or park your car for a walk), notice the curving streets and generous parklands, in contrast to the strict rectangles of Oak Park.

Return to 31st Street and go directly west until you see signs for **Brookfield Zoo.** (Alternately, to reach the zoo from Chicago by train, take the Burlington Northern train from Union Station to Hollywood Avenue, also known as the zoo stop; it's a walk of about 1/2 mile from the station to the zoo.) You can easily spend an entire day here. Established in 1934, the zoo has more than 2,000 animals, inhabiting naturalistic settings that give visitors the sense of being in the wild rather than in a zoo environment. One exhibit, simulating a tropical rain forest, comprises the world's largest indoor zoo of mixed species. Monkeys, otters, birds, and other rain-forest fauna cavort in a carefully constructed setting of rocks, trees, shrubs, pools, and waterfalls. Thunderstorms occur at random intervals, although visitors on the walkways are sheltered from the rain. In the **Aquatic Bird House** visitors can test their "flying strength" by "flapping their wings" on a machine that simultaneously measures wing action and speed and decides what kind of bird you are, based on how you flap. A new 5-acre Habitat Africa has a water hole and rock formations characteristic of the African savanna. Here, visitors can see tiny animals such as klipspringer antelope, which are only 22 inches tall, and rock hyraxes, which resemble prairie dogs. The daily dolphin shows, a highlight of the zoo, are a favorite even among jaded adults, and the new show-area accommodates 2,000 spectators. Seals and sea lions inhabit a rocky seascape-exhibit that simulates a Pacific Northwest environment, and there's a splendid under-water viewing-gallery. From late spring through early fall the "motorized safari" tram will carry you around the grounds; in wintertime the heated *Snowball Express* does the job. *8400 W. 31st St., Brookfield, tel. 708/485–0263 or 312/242–2630. Admission: $4 adults, $1.50 senior citizens and children 3–11, under 3 free; free Tues. Parking: $4 ($3.50 Tues.).* Children's zoo: *$1 adults, 50¢ senior citizens and children 3–11, under 3 free; free Nov.–Feb. Dolphin shows: $2 adults, $1.50 senior citizens and children 3–11, under 3 free.* Motorized safari: *$2 adults, 75¢ senior citizens and children 3–11, under 3 free. Open Memorial Day–Labor Day, daily 9:30–5:30; Labor Day–Memorial Day, daily 10–4:30. Rental strollers and wheelchairs available.* Snowball Express *free.*

Before the Midwest was plowed and planted to feed the nation, tall-grass prairie stretched from Illinois to the Rocky Mountains. To see what the state of Illinois looked like until the 1800s, stop off at **Wolf Road Prairie.** This 80-acre black-soil prairie has been painstakingly restored by volunteers to its original array of tall grasses, wildflowers, and other characteristic plants. Birds and other wildlife are especially active at dawn and twilight. From Brookfield Zoo drive west about 10 miles on 31st Street to Wolf Road. Park on the north side of 31st Street just west of Wolf Road.

Lisle To reach the next stop go north on Wolf Road to I–290, and almost immediately get on I–88 (the East–West Tollway), going west (toll: 40¢). Take it to Route 53 north and go about ❺ ½ mile to the **Morton Arboretum.** Established by salt magnate Joy Morton in 1922, it consists of 1,500 acres of woody plants, woodlands, and outdoor gardens. The complex also includes a library and a gift shop, a restaurant that serves lunch, and a coffee shop. It's possible to drive through, but you really should get out and walk some of the 25 miles of trails. Most are short and take 15–30 minutes to complete; some are designed around themes, such as conifers or plants from around the world. Trees ran in the Morton family: Joy's father, J. Sterling Morton, originated Arbor Day. In the spring, the flowering trees are spectacular. Tours and special programs are scheduled most Sunday afternoons. *Rte. 53, Lisle, tel. 708/968–0074. Admission: $5 per car, walk-ins free. Open daily 9–7.*

Wheaton For the last stop, take Route 53 south to Warrenville Road, turn right, and follow it for about 10 miles. Turn right onto Winfield ❻ and go about 4 miles to the entrance of **Cantigny,** the former estate of Col. Robert McCormick, editor and publisher of the *Chicago Tribune* from 1925 to 1955. (Don't turn in at the "Cantigny Golf" sign unless you wish to play golf; *see* Sports, *above.*) Splendid formal gardens, a restored 1870s mansion, and a tank park are a few of the attractions here. McCormick's will left his 500-acre estate to be maintained as a public park. The estate is named after the village of Cantigny, France, which McCormick helped capture in World War I as a member of the U.S. army's first division. There's a museum devoted to the history of the first division from 1917 to Desert Storm. The tank park contains tanks from World War II, the Korean War, and the Vietnam War. Children are encouraged to play on the tanks, which are surrounded by soft wood chips. The first and second floors of the Georgian-style mansion are open to the public and are furnished with antiques and artwork collected by Colonel McCormick's two wives. There's also a beautiful wooded picnic area. *15151 Winfield Rd., tel. 708/668–5161. Admission free. Parking $3 per car. Park open daily 7 AM–dusk. Mansion and museum open Memorial Day–Labor Day, Tues.–Sun. 10–5; Labor Day–Dec. and Mar.–Memorial Day, Tues.–Sun. 10–4; Feb., weekends 10–4.*

To get back to Chicago, take Winfield Road south to Butterfield Road and turn left. At Naperville Road, turn right to return to I–88, which merges with I–290 and takes you back to the Loop.

Dining

Note: Berwyn is directly south of Oak Park. Hillside and Oak Brook are west of Brookfield. For price categories, *see* Chapter 6.

Berwyn **Capri.** This old-fashioned Italian dining room has a loyal local following that comes for the steamed mussels in white or red sauce, pastas, and desserts. *3126 Oak Park Ave., tel. 708/484–6313. Reservations advised. AE, MC, V. Closed Mon. Moderate.* **Salerno's.** People from nearby towns make pilgrimages here expressly for the purpose of eating the thick-crust pizza, which ranges in size from "baby" to extra large. The pastas are good, too, as is the veal marsala. *6633 W. 16th St., tel. 708/484–3400. Reservations advised. AE, DC, MC, V. Inexpensive.*

Hillside **La Perla.** An eclectic menu offers Mediterranean dishes from France, Spain, Italy, Greece, and Morocco. Fresh fish and seafood entrées change daily, and there are plenty of pastas and pizzas, as well. The white-painted, colorfully tiled interior is in keeping with the cuisine. The lounge has music (piano jazz, flamenco, and blues) Thursday through Saturday. *2135 S. Wolf Rd. at 22nd St., tel. 708/449–1070. Reservations advised. AE, D, DC, MC, V. Closed Sun. Moderate.*

Oak Brook **Zarrosta Grill.** An eclectic menu, a wood-burning pizza oven, and a rotisserie set this pleasant spot apart from most restaurants you find in shopping-mall and office-park territory. Try the roasted chicken and California-style pizzas on foccacia bread. *118 Oak Brook Center Professional Bldg., Cermak Rd. and Rte. 83, tel. 708/990–0177. Reservations advised. AE, MC, V. Moderate.*

Oak Park **Philander's.** This hotel dining room has the feel of a classy tavern, and its reliable fish and seafood have recently been supplemented with nonfish items. One of Oak Park's few fine-dining spots, Philander's usually has a crowd. A more casual café, Poor Phil's, is adjacent. *Carlton Hotel, 1120 Pleasant St., tel. 708/848–4250. Reservations advised. AE, D, DC, MC, V. Closed lunch and Sun. Moderate.*

Robinson's No. 1 Ribs. Meaty ribs, barbecued chicken wings, baked beans, and coleslaw are the stars at this eat-in/takeout storefront. Robinson's tangy sauce has won top honors at the *Chicago Tribune's* Labor Day Ribfest. *940 W. Madison St., tel. 708/383–8452. AE, MC, V. Inexpensive.*

Sheridan Road and the North Shore

The shore of Lake Michigan north of Chicago has well-to-do old towns with gracious houses, on lots ever larger and more heavily wooded the farther you travel north. The first stop here is polyglot Evanston, which sits on the northern border of Chicago and is the home of Northwestern University. First settled in 1826, Evanston is also the headquarters of the Women's Christian Temperance Union. Even today it's tough to find a drink here.

Hollywood films have helped make the North Shore synonymous with the upper middle class through such hit films as *Home Alone* (filmed in Winnetka), *Ordinary People* (Lake Forest), and *Risky Business* (Glencoe). The farthest suburbs on our tour, Lake Forest and Lake Bluff, were first settled in the 1830s and grew to prominence as summer settlements for wealthy Chicagoans.

Beyond the borders of suburbia is Illinois Beach State Park, where you can see a somewhat wilder version of Lake Michigan's shore. A detour west brings you to Gurnee, home of a huge theme park and an equally huge shopping mall.

The drive up Sheridan Road, in most spots a stone's throw from the lakefront, is pleasant in itself, even if you don't stop. It's particularly scenic in spring, when the trees flower profusely, and in the fall, when their foliage is downright gaudy.

Tourist Information

Call the **Illinois Tourist Information Center** (310 S. Michigan Ave., tel. 800/233–0121) or the **Lake County Convention and Tourism Bureau** (tel. 708/662–2700).

Getting There

By Car This excursion is designed as a driving tour, although you can take a commuter train to individual attractions (*see below*). The route follows Sheridan Road along the lakeshore. The other major artery serving the North Shore is the Edens Expressway (I–94).

By Train The **Metra Chicago/Northwestern line** (tel. 312/322–6777) de-
Commuter parts from the Northwestern station at 500 West Madison Street and stops in Evanston (Davis St.), Wilmette, Glencoe, Ravinia Park (special trains on concert nights), Highland Park, Highwood, Fort Sheridan, Lake Forest, Waukegan, and Zion.

El Train The **CTA's** Howard line will take you as far as Wilmette, with multiple stops in Evanston. Board it northbound along State Street in the Loop or at Chicago Avenue and State Street in the Near North. Change at Howard for the Evanston shuttle. To reach the Northwestern campus, get off at Foster and walk east to Sheridan Road. The Howard line is not recommended after dark.

Guided Tours

The **Chicago Architectural Foundation** (tel. 312/922–8687) has occasional walking, bicycle, and bus tours of parts of the North Shore. The **office of undergraduate admissions** at Northwestern University (tel. 708/491–7271) offers tours of the campus, weekdays, at 1:30 PM.

Exploring Sheridan Road and the North Shore

Take Lake Shore Drive north to its end, at Hollywood Avenue, and turn right onto Sheridan Road. Follow it through a zone of 1960s high rises, past Mundelein College, and into Rogers Park, home of Loyola University. A few blocks north of Loyola, the road runs along the lake, and there's a cemetery on the left. Beyond the cemetery is the Evanston town limit.

Although Sheridan Road goes all the way to the Wisconsin border, it twists and turns and occasionally disappears. Don't lose hope; just look for small signs indicating where it went. When in doubt, keep heading north, and stay near the lake.

As you wind through the Victorian, Prairie Style, and Queen **7** Anne–style houses of **Evanston,** look for Greenwood Street, one block north of Dempster. Turn right and proceed to 225 Greenwood, where you'll enter the grounds of the **Evanston Historical Society,** housed in the châteaulike former home of Nobel prize winner Charles Gates Dawes, vice president under Calvin Coolidge. The 28-room mansion has been restored to its 1920s appearance and has vaulted ceilings, stained-glass windows, and period furniture. The historical society also maintains a costume collection and research facilities on the premises. *225 Greenwood Ave., tel. 708/475–3410. Admission: $3 adults, $1 students and senior citizens. Open Mon.–Tues. and Thurs.–Sat., 1–5.*

At the junction of Sheridan Road and Clark Street is the southern edge of **Northwestern University.** Founded in 1855, Northwestern has 7,400 undergraduates and 4,300 graduate students at its Evanston campus, which stretches along the lakefront for 1 mile. Its schools of business, journalism, law, and medicine are nationally known, and its school of speech has graduated many leading actors. Its football team is a perennial underdog in the Big Ten midwestern conference, in which Northwestern is the only private school.

The visitor's center is in the Tudor Revival mansion at the corner of Sheridan and Clark; here you can pick up a map of the campus. The undergraduate-admissions office is directly west at Sheridan and Hinman. Stop here for a complete tour of the campus (*see* Guided Tours, *above*).

To reach the Mary and Leigh Block Gallery, a university-owned fine-arts museum that hosts traveling exhibits, go north on Sheridan until it jogs left at the southern edge of the Northwestern campus. Instead of following it, turn right and look for the arts complex on your left. The gallery shows a variety of exhibits: European Impressionist and American Realist paintings, photography, decorative arts, and modern sculpture. The adjacent sculpture garden has large-scale sculptures by Henry Moore, Joan Miró, and Arnoldo Pomodoro. *1967 Sheridan Rd., tel. 708/491–4000. Admission free. Open late Sept.–May, Tues.–Wed. noon–5, Thurs.–Sun. noon–8; June 9–late Sept., Tues.–Sat. noon–4. The gallery closes periodically to install new exhibits.*

The irregularly shaped white building across the way is the **Pick-Staiger Concert Hall,** with a 1,003-seat auditorium that regularly presents performances by internationally known artists, as well as Northwestern faculty and students, and is acclaimed for its acoustics.

Leaving the arts complex, continue on Sheridan as it travels west and then north. On the right side of Sheridan, between Garrett Place and Haven Street, is the **Shakespeare Garden.** Set back from the street and enclosed by 6-foot hedges, this tranquil refuge is planted with 70 flowers, herbs, and trees mentioned in Shakespeare's plays. Park on the side streets west of Sheridan.

Although it looks placid enough most of the time, Lake Michigan has enough fog, violent storms, and sandbars to make navigation treacherous. **Grosse Point Lighthouse** was built in 1873 to help guide ships into the port of Chicago. The lighthouse was decommissioned in 1935, but the Evanston Historical Society has restored it and offers guided tours of the interior on weekend afternoons from June through September. The surrounding park is open year-round and has a nature center and a community arts center. *2535 Sheridan Rd., tel. 708/328–6961. Admission to lighthouse: $2 adults, $1 children.*

❽ Continue up Sheridan into **Wilmette.** The **Baha'i House of Worship,** at Sheridan Road and Linden Avenue, is a sublime nine-side building that incorporates a wealth of architectural styles and symbols from the world's religions. The temple is the U.S.

center of the Baha'i faith, which celebrates the unity of all religions. The symmetry and harmony of the building are paralleled in the formal gardens that surround it. Begun in 1920, the temple wasn't finished until 1953. Ask at the visitors' center for a guide to show you around. To reach the temple by public transportation, take the Evanston shuttle from Howard Street to the end of the line at Linden Avenue and walk two blocks east. *100 Linden Ave., Wilmette, tel. 708/273–3838.*

Next you will pass through the tiny (population 2,708), wealthy community of **Kenilworth,** marked by gray pillars at its entrance, and the equally lovely but less haughty village of **Winnetka.** The road curves sharply back and forth through the ravine that separates Winnetka from **Glencoe,** so drive carefully and watch for daredevils in sports cars.

At Lake-Cook Road, turn left and drive west past Green Bay Road to the **Chicago Botanic Garden.** It covers 300 acres and has 15 gardens, among them a traditional rose garden, a three-island Japanese garden, a waterfall garden, a sensory garden for the visually impaired, an aquatic garden, a learning garden for the disabled, and a 3.8-acre fruit-and-vegetable garden whose yields are donated to area soup kitchens. Ten greenhouses provide flowers all winter long. Special events and shows are scheduled most weekends, many sponsored by local plant societies. Major shows are the winter orchid show, August bonsai show, daffodil show, cactus-and-succulent show, and Japan Fest in May. To reach the gardens by public transportation take the Evanston shuttle to Davis Street; transfer there for the Nortran (No. 214) bus, which stops at the garden. *Lake Cook Rd., Glencoe, tel. 708/835–5440. Admission: $4 per car. Open summer, daily 7 AM–sunset; winter, daily AM–sunset.*

Backtrack on Lake-Cook Road to Sheridan and turn left. You'll pass the main entrance to **Ravinia Park,** important to remember if you'll be returning here later.

Summer visitors might want to combine a North Shore excursion with an evening trip to the Ravinia Music Festival for an outdoor concert (*see* Chapter 8). You can pack a picnic and blanket and sit on the lawn for about the cost of a movie. (Seats are also available in the pavilion for a significantly higher price.) Picnic fixings can be bought at several spots along the way, including **Plaza del Lago,** a shopping center on Sheridan Road on the border between Wilmette and Kenilworth, and the grocery stores in **Highwood.** There are also restaurants and snack bars on the park grounds. Concerts usually start at 8; plan to arrive at the park no later than 6:30 to allow time for parking, hiking from the parking lot to the lawn, and getting settled.

🔟 At 1145 Sheridan Road in **Highland Park** is the **Willits House,** a 1902 building designed by Frank Lloyd Wright, which has a cruciform plan built around a large fireplace in the center. Wright and other Prairie School architects used this technique frequently. The house is now privately owned.

⓫ The next village north, **Highwood,** is an anomaly on the North Shore, a working-class ethnic community. Highwood was incorporated in 1887, and its fortunes have been entwined with those of the adjacent army post, Ft. Sheridan, which was opened in the same year to maintain an army presence near Chicago in the wake of the labor unrest surrounding the Haymarket Riot.

In the early days Highwood was the only place nearby where soldiers could get a drink, because most of the North Shore suburbs were dry.

A large Italian population has helped make Highwood the restaurant row of the North Shore, although for some reason several of its most famous spots are French (*see* Dining, *below*).

Time Out   Many of Highwood's restaurants are open only for dinner, but you can grab a bite throughout the day at **Mexico Lindo** (830 Sheridan Rd.), **Virginia's Restaurant** (415 Sheridan Rd.), or **Rainbows Bar and Grill** (432 Sheridan Rd.). There are more dining spots on Green Bay Road, a block west of Sheridan Road and across the train tracks. For Italian-style picnic fare try **Bacio Foods** (424 Sheridan Rd.; open Mon.–Sat. 9–6, Sun. 9–2).

As you continue north, you'll see on your right the distinctive **❷** yellow buildings of **Ft. Sheridan.** Designed by the noted Chicago firm of Holabird and Roche, the 54 buildings were constructed of brick that was manufactured on the building site from indigenous clay. At this writing the fort was due to be closed as an army post, and the fate of its prime lakefront site was unclear. But as a National Trust Historic District, its buildings are likely to remain, perhaps as housing for officers stationed at nearby Great Lakes Naval Air Station a little farther north. It's worth turning in at the main gate and asking the military police officer on duty if you can drive around.

The next town north is tony **Lake Forest,** where you'll pass the beautifully landscaped campuses of Lake Forest and Barat colleges, as well as many sumptuous mansions set far back on heavily wooded lots. Beyond Lake Forest is **Lake Bluff,** Chicago's northernmost suburb, which began life in the 19th century as a summer resort and Methodist camp-meeting ground.

About 10 miles north of Lake Bluff, beyond the town of Waukegan and the industrial waterfront of North Chicago, is the **❸** entrance to **Illinois Beach State Park,** in Zion, where you can swim if you're willing to brave the cold water. This beach is wilder than those in Chicago, although you can see signs of industry along the lake in both directions. You'll also see the dune plants that covered the lakefront until the 19th century. The nature preserve at the south end of the park has areas of marsh and forest. The northern section of the park was used as a prisoner-of-war camp during the Civil War and provided a site for army basic training in both world wars. *Sheridan and Wadsworth Rds., tel. 708/662–4811. Open daily.*

At this point you can backtrack on Sheridan Road to return to Chicago or head west on Wadsworth Road from the park's main entrance to I–94 for a quicker ride back to the city. To get to I–94, take Wadsworth to Route 131 (Green Bay Rd.). Turn left and go south to Route 132 (Grand Ave.), and turn right. At the **❹** intersection of Route 132 and I–94 is **Gurnee,** and two places you probably won't have the energy to visit after a day exploring Sheridan Road, but you may want to return another day.

Six Flags Great America has 132 rides, but it specializes in roller coasters. Turn upside-down on the Shock Wave and the Iron Wolf, or go for major ups and downs on the classic wood American Eagle. Warner Brothers characters—Bugs Bunny, Daffy Duck, Sylvester the Cat—prowl the grounds. It's best to arrive early in the morning or late in the day. If the midday crowds wear you out, you can have your hand stamped for free re-admission later and go somewhere else for a while. Hours and prices vary, and sometimes the park is closed for private events, so call ahead. Look for discount coupons in flyers at hotels and tourist offices. *I–94 at Rte. 132 (Grand Ave.), tel. 708/249–1776. Open Late May–mid-June, daily 10–9; mid-June–Aug., daily 10–10; hours and days vary in early June and Sept.*

Shoppers may prefer **Gurnee Mills,** across I–94 from Six Flags. This massive mall combines factory outlets, discount stores, and regular-price stores. Several food courts and a museum-quality collection of prototype automobiles postpone boredom for the nonshopper. *Tel. 708/263–7500. Open Mon.–Sat. 11–9, Sun. 11–6.*

To get back to Chicago, enter I–94 south/east and follow the signs. For the Near North Side, exit at Ohio Street; for the Loop, take any of the eastbound exits between Washington Street and Congress Parkway.

Dining

For price categories, *see* Chapter 6.

Evanston **Oceanique.** As its name suggests, this storefront place special-izes in fish. Grilled dishes such as Scottish salmon and striped bass stand out, but there are also excellent pasta dishes, soups, and sinful chocolate desserts. *505 Main St., tel. 708/864–3435. Reservations advised. AE, D, DC, MC, V. Closed lunch and Sun. Expensive.*

Dave's Italian Kitchen. A traditional hangout for Northwest-ern students, Dave's has a collegiate atmosphere that may bring on nostalgia even among nonalumni. Dishes are large, inexpensive, and successfully lure the clientele away from dorm food. Stick with the reliable pizzas (deep-dish and thin-crust) and pastas. *906 Church St., tel. 708/864–6000. No reserva-tions; expect to wait on weekends. MC, V. Closed weekend lunch. Inexpensive.*

Highwood **Alouette.** The menu changes monthly at this French bistro. There's usually at least one poultry and one fish dish, and the rack of lamb is consistently good. The snails in pastry are an excellent appetizer. The prix-fixe dinner, offered every night but Saturday, is a good deal. *440 N. Green Bay Rd., tel. 708/433–5600. Reservations advised. AE, D, DC, MC, V. No lunch. Moderate.*

Froggy's French Cafe. This comfortable bistro is known for sumptuous six-course, prix-fixe dinners and lunches, excellent cassoulet and other hearty dishes, and a huge wine list. Expect to wait at peak hours. *306 N. Green Bay Rd., tel. 708/433–7080. Reservations accepted for 6 or more. D, DC, MC, V. Closed Sat. lunch and Sun. Moderate.*

Wilmette **Betise.** This bistro in Wilmette's Plaza del Lago shopping cen-ter offers a pastiche of dishes from southern France and Italy, most of them emphasizing tomatoes, potatoes, fish, and roasted chicken. Friday is bouillabaisse night. Cobblestone floors and off-white walls add to the Riviera atmosphere. *1515 Sheridan Rd., tel. 708/853–1711. Reservations advised. D, DC, MC, V. Moderate.*

Walker Bros. Original Pancake House. This traditional breakfast-all-day spot has fluffy omelets, several varieties of pancakes, and fresh-ground coffee served with whipping cream. *153 Green Bay Rd., tel. 708/251–6000. MC, V. Inexpensive.*

Milwaukee

By Don Davenport   Visitors to Chicago are blessed with the exciting option to take in two sharply different cities on one trip. Contrasting with Chicago's enormity and urbanity, Milwaukee is an enclave of distinctly accessible, even local, pleasures. You can easily make a day trip here, but an overnight jaunt will allow you to sample Milwaukee's beer-ocentric nightlife to the fullest.

Set on the shores of Lake Michigan, just a couple of hours north of Chicago, Wisconsin's largest city is an international seaport and the state's primary commercial and manufacturing center. A small-town atmosphere prevails in Milwaukee, which is not so much a city as a large collection of neighborhoods. Modern steel-and-glass high rises occupy much of the downtown area, but the early heritage persists in the restored and well-kept 19th-century buildings that share the city skyline. First settled by Potawatomi Indians and later by French fur traders in the late 18th century, the city boomed in the 1840s with the arrival of German brewers, and their legacy remains.

Milwaukee has also become known as a city of festivals. The **Summerfest** kicks off each summer's activities on the lakefront. Another annual highlight is the **Great Circus Parade,** a July spectacle that features scores of antique circus wagons from the famed Circus World Museum in Baraboo. August brings the **State Fair.**

Tourist Information

Greater Milwaukee: Convention & Visitors Bureau (510 W. Kilbourn Ave., 53203, tel. 414/273–3950 or 800/231–0903).

Getting There

By Car   I–94 runs directly from Chicago into downtown Milwaukee.

By Train   **Amtrak** (tel. 800/872–7245) has service from Chicago to Milwaukee. The round-trip fare is $24; the ride takes 1½ hours.

By Bus   **Greyhound** (tel. 800/231–2222) service connects the two cities. The round-trip fare is $21.50; the ride takes 2 hours.

Getting Around Milwaukee

Lake Michigan is the city's eastern boundary; Wisconsin Avenue is the main east–west thoroughfare. The Milwaukee River divides the downtown area into east and west sections. The East–West Expressway (I–94/I–794) is the dividing line between north and south. Streets are numbered in ascending order from the Milwaukee River west well into the suburbs. Many downtown attractions are near the Milwaukee River and can be reached on foot. **Milwaukee County Transit System** (tel. 414/344–6711) provides bus service. **Taxis** can be ordered by phone or at taxi stands; the fare is $2.50 for the first mile and

$1.25 for each additional mile. The largest firm is **Yellow Cab** (tel. 414/271–1800).

Exploring Milwaukee

Numbers in the margin correspond to points of interest on the Downtown Milwaukee map

Downtown Milwaukee's central business district is a mile long and only a few blocks wide. It is divided by the Milwaukee River. On the east side, the **Iron Block Building** (N. Water St. and E. Wisconsin Ave.) is one of the few remaining ironclad buildings in the United States. Its metal facade was brought in by ship from an eastern foundry and installed during the Civil War. In the 1860s, Milwaukee exported more wheat than any other port in the world, which gave impetus to building the **Grain Exchange Room** in the **Mackie Building** (225 E. Michigan St.). The 10,000-square-foot trading room has three-story-high columns and painted ceiling panels that feature Wisconsin wildflowers.

The **Milwaukee Art Museum,** in the lakefront War Memorial Center designed by Eero Saarinen, houses notable collections of paintings, drawings, sculpture, photography, and decorative arts. Its permanent collection is strong in European and American art of the 19th and 20th centuries. *750 N. Lincoln Memorial Dr., tel. 414/271–9508. Admission charged. Closed Mon.*

Returning to the river, stop a moment at **Cathedral Square.** This quiet park (E. Kilbourn Ave. and Jefferson St.) was built on the site of Milwaukee's first courthouse. Across the street, **St. John's Cathedral,** dedicated in 1853, was the first church built in Wisconsin specifically as a Roman Catholic cathedral.

The banks of the Milwaukee River are busy in summer, especially at noon, when downtown workers lunch in the nearby parks and public areas, such as **Père Marquette Park,** on the river at Old World 3rd Street and West Kilbourn Avenue.

Adjacent to the park, the **Milwaukee County Historical Center** (910 N. Old World 3rd St., tel. 414/273–8288), a museum housed in a graceful former bank building, features early fire-fighting equipment, military artifacts, toys, and women's fashions. It also contains a research library with naturalization records and genealogical resources.

The river is also the departure point for cruises of Milwaukee's harbor and lakefront. **Iroquois Harbor Cruises** (Clybourn St. bridge on the west bank, tel. 414/332–4194) offers harbor cruises aboard a 149-passenger vessel. **Celebration of Milwaukee** (502 N. Harbor Dr., tel. 414/278–1113) and **Edelweiss Excursions** (1110 N. Old World 3rd St., tel. 414/272–3625) offer lunch and dinner cruises.

As you cross the river to the west side, notice that the east-side streets are not directly opposite the west-side streets and that the bridges across the river are built at an angle. This layout dates from the 1840s, when the area east of the river was called Juneautown and the region to the west was known as Kilbourntown. The rival communities had a fierce argument over which would pay for the bridges that connected them; so intense was the antagonism that citizens venturing into rival territory carried white flags. The Great Bridge War was finally settled by

224

Milwaukee

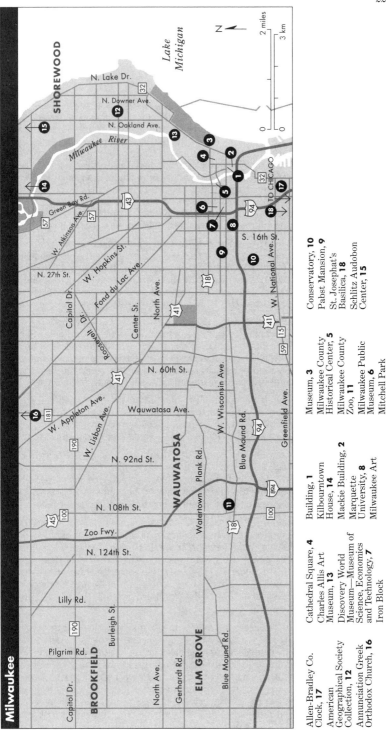

Allen-Bradley Co.
Clock, 17
American
Geographical Society
Collection, 12
Annunciation Greek
Orthodox Church, 16

Cathedral Square, 4
Charles Allis Art
Museum, 13
Discovery World
Museum—Museum of
Science, Economics
and Technology, 7
Iron Block

Building, 1
Kilbourntown
House, 14
Mackie Building, 2
Marquette
University, 8
Milwaukee Art

Museum, 3
Milwaukee County
Historical Center, 5
Milwaukee County
Zoo, 11
Milwaukee Public
Museum, 6
Mitchell Park

Conservatory, 10
Pabst Mansion, 9
St. Josephat's
Basilica, 18
Schlitz Audobon
Center, 15

the state legislature in 1845, but the streets on either side of the river never were aligned.

6 A few blocks west of the river, the **Milwaukee Public Museum** has the fourth-largest collection of natural history exhibits in the country, as well as outstanding fine arts and Native American, African, and pre-Columbian collections. Walk-through exhibits include the "Streets of Old Milwaukee," depicting the city in the 1890s; a two-story rain forest; and the "Third Planet" (complete with full-size dinosaurs), where visitors walk into the interior of the Earth to learn about its history. *800 W. Wells St., tel. 414/278–2702. Admission charged.*

7 Nearby, **Discovery World—Museum of Science, Economics and Technology,** in the Milwaukee Public Central Library, has a wide range of hands-on exhibits on magnets, motors, electricity, health, and computers that introduce youngsters to science, technology, and economics. It also features the "Great Electric Show" and the "Light Wave–Laser Beam Show" on weekends. *818 W. Wisconsin Ave., tel. 414/765–9966. Admission charged. Closed holidays.*

8 Farther west, just off Wisconsin Avenue on the central mall of the **Marquette University** campus, is **St. Joan of Arc Chapel** (601 N. 14th St., tel. 414/288–7039), a small, stone 15th-century chapel moved from its original site near Lyon, France, and reconstructed here in 1964. One of the stones was reputedly kissed by Joan before she went to her death and is said to be discernibly colder than the others. The **Haggerty Museum of Art** (12th St. and Wisconsin Ave., on the mall between Wisconsin Ave. and Clybourn St., tel. 414/288–7290) houses the university's collection of more than 6,000 works of art, including Renaissance, Baroque, and modern paintings, sculpture, prints, photography, and decorative arts; it also offers changing exhibitions.

Other Attractions
9 Away from downtown, the **Pabst Mansion,** built in 1893 for the beer baron Captain Frederick Pabst, is one of Milwaukee's treasured landmarks. The castlelike, 37-room Flemish Renaissance-style mansion has a tan pressed-brick exterior and is decorated with carved stone and terra-cotta ornamentation outside and carved cabinets and woodwork, ornamental ironwork, marble, tile, stained glass, and carved panels inside, all imported from a 17th-century Bavarian castle. *2000 W. Wisconsin Ave., tel. 414/931–0808. Admission charged. Closed weekdays Jan.–mid-Mar.*

10 Milwaukee's unique **Mitchell Park Conservatory** consists of three modern 85-foot-high glass domes housing tropical, arid, and seasonal plant and flower exhibits; its displays of lilies and poinsettias are spectacular at Easter and Christmas. There are picnic facilities on the grounds. *524 S. Layton Blvd., tel. 414/649–9800. Admission charged.*

11 The **Milwaukee County Zoo** houses more than 3,000 wild animals and birds, including many endangered species, displayed in natural environments. It also offers educational programs, a seasonal children's zoo, narrated tram tours, miniature-train rides, picnic areas, and cross-country ski trails. *10001 W. Bluemound Rd., tel. 414/771–3040. Admission charged.*

12 North of downtown Milwaukee, the **American Geographical Society Collection,** housed in the Golda Meir Library on the

University of Wisconsin–Milwaukee campus (2311 E. Hartford Ave., tel. 414/229–6282), has an exceptional assemblage of maps, old globes, atlases, and charts, plus 180,000 books and 400,000 journals. The **University of Wisconsin–Milwaukee Art Museum** (3253 N. Downer Ave., tel. 414/229–5070) displays a permanent collection of Greek and Russian icons and 20th-century European paintings and prints. The **UWM Fine Arts Gallery** (2400 E. Kenwood Blvd.) displays the works of students and faculty members; other changing exhibits are held at the **UWM Art History Gallery** (3203 N. Downer Ave.).

⑬ The **Charles Allis Art Museum** (1801 N. Prospect Ave., tel. 414/278–8295) occupies an elegant Tudor-style house built in 1911 for the first president of the Allis-Chalmers Manufacturing Co. The home has stained-glass windows by Louis Comfort Tiffany and a stunning worldwide collection of paintings and objets d'art, including works by major 19th- and 20th-century French and American painters.

⑭ The Greek Revival cream-colored brick **Kilbourntown House** (4400 W. Estabrook Dr., tel. 414/273–8288), built in 1844, is listed on the National Register of Historic Places and contains an outstanding collection of mid-19th-century furniture and decorative arts.

⑮ The **Schlitz Audubon Center,** 10 mi north of downtown, is a 186-acre wildlife area of forests, ponds, marshland, and nature trails along Lake Michigan. Popular with cross-country skiers and bird-watchers, it has an environmental research and education center. *1111 E. Brown Deer Rd., tel. 414/352–2880. Admission charged. Closed Mon., holidays.*

⑯ The **Annunciation Greek Orthodox Church** (9400 W. Congress St., tel. 414/461–9400) was Frank Lloyd Wright's last major work; the famed Wisconsin architect called it his "little jewel." Since it opened in 1961, the blue-domed, Byzantine-style church has drawn visitors from all over the world.

⑰ Just south of downtown, the **Allen-Bradley Co. Clock** (1201 S. 2nd St.) is a Milwaukee landmark and, according to the *Guinness Book of World Records,* "the largest four-faced clock in the world." Great Lakes ships often use the clock as a navigational reference point.

⑱ Built by immigrant parishioners and local craftsmen at the turn of the century, **St. Josephat's Basilica** (2336 S. 6th St., tel. 414/645–5623) is the first Polish basilica in North America and has a dome modeled after St. Peter's in Rome. The church is adorned with a remarkable collection of relics, portraits of Polish saints and leaders, stained glass, and wood carvings.

Shopping

Stores range from tiny ethnic and specialty shops to enclosed shopping malls featuring large department stores. Using the downtown skywalk system, it's possible to browse in hundreds of stores over several blocks without once setting foot outside. Downtown Milwaukee's major shopping street is **Wisconsin Avenue** west of the Milwaukee River. The **Grand Avenue Mall** is the major downtown retail center, spanning four city blocks. **Historic Third Ward,** a turn-of-the-century wholesale and manufacturing district on the National Register of Historic Places, is bordered by the harbor, the river, and downtown and offers many unusual shops and restaurants. **Jefferson Street,** stretching four blocks from Wisconsin to Kilbourn, offers upscale shops and stores. The **Lincoln Avenue District,** minutes from downtown off I–94, has specialty shops and ethnic restaurants in a quaint, historic Polish and German neighborhood. On Milwaukee's south side, historic **Mitchell Street** is a multicultural blend of retail shops and diverse ethnic restaurants.

Shopping centers in the metropolitan area include **Bayshore** (5900 N. Port Washington Rd.), **Brookfield Square** (95 N. Moorland Rd.), **Capital Court** (5500 W. Capitol Dr.), **Mayfair** (2500 N. Mayfair Rd.), **Northridge** (7700 W. Brown Deer Rd.), **Point Loomis** (3555 S. 27th St.), **Southgate** (3333 S. 27th St.), and **South Ridge** (5300 S. 76th St.).

Dining

Milwaukee's culinary style was shaped to a great extent by the Germans who first settled here. Many restaurants—whether or not they are German—offer Wiener schnitzel or the meringue-based desserts called *schaumtortes.* Rye bread, sometimes crusted with coarse salt, is as common on Milwaukee tables as robins on a spring lawn. Many other ethnic groups have also donated their specialties to Milwaukee's tradition of gemütlichkeit (fellowship and good cheer).

Milwaukeeans like to relax and socialize when they eat out. Fashion isn't as important here as in faster-paced cities. Jackets and ties are customary at the most expensive restaurants, but only a few actually require them. For price ranges, *see* chart in Chapter 6.

Highly recommended restaurants are indicated by a star ★.

Very Expensive **English Room.** Milwaukee's premier hotel restaurant, in the ★ Pfister Hotel, has a dark, Victorian elegance. Chef Édouard Becker's German/American cuisine emphasizes meat dishes, though seafood is also served. Service is formal, with plenty of tableside cooking. *424 E. Wisconsin Ave., tel. 414/273–8222. Reservations advised. Jacket required. AE, D, DC, MC, V. No lunch weekends.*

★ **Grenadier's.** Knut Apitz, chef-owner, serves some of the most elegant food in Milwaukee. Imaginative dishes combine classical European style with Oriental or Indian flavors; offerings include tenderloin of veal with raspberry sauce and angelhair pasta. The three small rooms have an air of matter-of-fact refinement; the handsome, darkly furnished piano bar also has tables. *747 N. Broadway St., tel. 414/276–0747. Reservations advised. Jacket required. AE, DC, MC, V. No lunch Sat.; closed Sun.* **Sanford.** Award-winning chef Sanford D'Amato and his wife, Angie, are at the helm of one of Milwaukee's best and busiest restaurants. The innovative French–New American menu changes daily but may include such specials as seared tournedos of sea scallops. The 50-seat dining room is decorated in understated gray and black. *1547 N. Jackson St., tel. 414/276–9608. Reservations essential. Jacket required. AE, D, DC, MC, V. No lunch; closed Sun.*

Expensive **Boder's on the River.** Tie-back curtains, fireplaces, and lots of knickknacks give the dining rooms in this suburban restaurant a cheerful country look. The menu offers Wisconsin favorites prepared in a straightforward manner, including roast duckling and baked whitefish. *11919 N. River Rd., Mequon, tel. 414/242–0335. Reservations advised. AE, D, DC, MC, V. Closed Mon.*

Giovanni's. At this Old World–style Sicilian place one finds flocked wallpaper, crystal chandeliers, and large portions of rich Italian food. Veal steak Giovanni is excellent, but the pasta is disappointing. *1683 N. Van Buren St., tel. 414/291–5600. Reservations advised. MC, V. No lunch weekends.*

Harold's. Velvet-backed booths, low lighting, etched glass, and rich greenery set a romantic, if slightly generic, mood at this restaurant in the Grand Hotel. Breast of capon with pistachio nuts is representative of the ambitious but sometimes heavy-handed choices on the menu. There is also a selection of "traditional favorites," including steaks and fresh fillet of whitefish. *4747 S. Howell Ave., tel. 414/481–8000. AE, DC, MC, V. No lunch weekends.*

★ **Karl Ratzsch's Old World Restaurant.** In the authentic German atmosphere of this family-owned restaurant, such specialties as schnitzel, roast duckling, and sauerbraten are served by dirndl-skirted waitresses while a string trio schmaltzes it up. The main dining room is decorated with murals, chandeliers made from antlers, and antique beer steins. *320 E. Mason St., tel. 414/276–2720. Reservations advised. AE, D, DC, MC, V. No lunch Mon.*

Mike and Anna's. At this small, trendy restaurant in a working-class neighborhood on the South Side, the changing menu features excellent nouvelle-inspired selections, such as fresh salmon with basil-and-tarragon beurre blanc. Be sure to ask for directions when making reservations. *1978 S. 8th St., tel. 414/643–0072. Reservations advised. MC, V. No lunch.*

★ **Steven Wade's Cafe.** Noted for creative, freshly prepared food, chef and co-owner Steven Wade Klindt operates this establishment in a former suburban paint-and-wallpaper store. The changing menu might include Norwegian salmon fillet poached with vanilla sauce or coconut curried lamb. *17001 W. Greenfield Ave., New Berlin, tel. 414/784–0774. Reservations required. AE, D, DC, MC, V. No lunch Sat.; closed Sun.*

Moderate **Chip and Py's.** In the northern suburbs, this stylish restaurant has light gray dual-level dining rooms, a huge fireplace, and contemporary art. The eclectic menu features chicken, beef, seafood, blackened redfish, and vegetarian entrées. Jazz is offered weekends. *1340 W. Town Square Rd., Mequon, tel. 414/241–9589. AE, D, DC, MC, V. No lunch Sun., no dinner Mon.*

Izumi's. Traditional Japanese dishes, including sushi (and tempura or noodles for those who prefer their food cooked), are the fare at this friendly, well-run restaurant. *2178 N. Prospect Ave., tel. 414/271–5278. Reservations advised. AE, MC, V. No lunch weekends.*

Jake's. There are two locations for this longtime Milwaukee favorite that earned its reputation with perfectly prepared steaks and heaps of french-fried onion rings. The best menu choices include escargot, roast duckling, and Bailey's chocolate-chip cheesecake. *6030 W. North Ave., Wauwatosa, tel. 414/771–0550; 21445 W. Capitol Dr., Brookfield, tel. 414/781–7995. Reservations advised. AE, MC, V.*

Three Brothers Bar & Restaurant. Set in an 1887 tavern is one of Milwaukee's revered ethnic restaurants, serving chicken paprikash, roast lamb, Serbian salad, and homemade desserts at old metal kitchen tables. It's about 10 minutes from downtown on the near South Side. *2414 S. St. Clair St., tel. 414/481–7530. Reservations advised. No credit cards. No lunch; closed Mon.*

Inexpensive **Benjamin's Delicatessen and Restaurant.** You'll find a wide selection of such tasty specialties as matzo ball soup, corned beef sandwiches, and brisket of beef at this neighborhood deli. There are booths, tables, and a counter where the TV is usually tuned to the latest sporting event. *4156 N. Oakland Ave., Shorewood, tel. 414/332–7777. MC, V.*

Crocus Restaurant and Cocktail Lounge. Tucked away on the South Side is this friendly neighborhood restaurant decorated with ethnic paintings and artifacts. Good choices among the homemade Polish dishes are braised-beef roll-ups, stuffed potato dumplings, and pierogi. *1801 S. Muskego Ave., tel. 414/643–6383. No credit cards. No lunch weekends.*

Elsa's on the Park. Across from Cathedral Square Park, this chic but casual place attracts talkative young professionals for big, juicy hamburgers and pork chop sandwiches. The decor is a crisply stylish gray, white, and black. *833 N. Jefferson St., tel. 414/765–0615. No credit cards. No lunch weekends.*

Rudy's Mexican Restaurant. Located in Walker's Point, an area south of downtown inching toward gentrification, Rudy's serves fresh standard Mexican fare, including chile rellenos, enchiladas, and guacamole. *625 S. 5th St., tel. 414/291–0296. AE, D, DC, MC, V.*

Watts Tea Shop. This genteel spot for breakfast or lunch is located above George Watts & Sons, Milwaukee's premier store for china, crystal, and silver. Offerings include simple breakfasts, sandwiches, a juice bar, and the special custard-filled sunshine cake. *761 N. Jefferson St., tel. 414/276–6352. No shorts. AE, MC, V. Closed Sun.*

Lodging

Milwaukee offers a number of options for accommodations, ranging from cozy small motels to executive suites overlooking Lake Michigan and the city. Most downtown hotels are within walking distance of the theater district, the Convention Center and Arena, and plenty of shopping and restaurants. In summer, accommodations should be booked well ahead, especially for weekends. For price ranges, *see* chart in Chapter 7.

Highly recommended hotels are indicated by a ★.

Very Expensive **Pfister Hotel.** Many of the rooms in Milwaukee's grand old
★ hotel, built in 1893, have been combined to make suites with enlarged bathrooms. Rooms in the Tower, built in 1975, are bright and contemporary with a Victorian accent, in keeping with the original hotel. A collection of 19th-century art hangs in the elegant Victorian lobby. *424 E. Wisconsin Ave., 53202, tel. 414/273–8222; fax 414/273–0747. 307 rooms. Facilities: 3 restaurants, nightclub, lounge, indoor pool, health club. AE, D, DC, MC, V.*

Expensive **Embassy Suites Hotel.** The sweeping atrium lobby with foun-
★ tains, potted plants, and glass elevators is the focal point of this hotel in the western suburbs. The one- or two-bedroom suites are decorated in pastels and earth tones with contemporary furnishings. *1200 S. Moorland Rd., Brookfield 53005, tel. 414/782–2900; fax 414/796–9159. 203 suites. Facilities: restau-*

rant, lounge, indoor pool, whirlpool, sauna, exercise room. AE, D, DC, MC, V.

Hyatt Regency. This centrally located high-rise hotel has an 18-story open atrium and a revolving restaurant on top. The rooms are airy and bright, with plush contemporary furnishings. *333 W. Kilbourn Ave., 53203, tel. 414/276–1234 or 800/233–1234; fax 414/276–6338. 484 rooms. Facilities: 3 restaurants, 3 lounges. AE, D, DC, MC, V.*

Marc Plaza. Crystal chandeliers, marble-base columns, and dark woodwork in the lobby give this gracious hotel, built in 1929, a handsome appearance. Traditionally decorated rooms vary quite a bit in size. *509 W. Wisconsin Ave., 53203, tel. 414/271–7250 or 800/558–7708 outside WI; fax 414/271–1039. 500 rooms, 34 suites, Facilities: 2 restaurants, lounge, indoor pool, sauna, exercise room. AE, D, DC, MC, V.*

★ **Wyndham Milwaukee Center.** Part of the city's growing theater district, this hotel is located atop the Milwaukee Center, by the river. The opulent lobby is tiled with Italian marble; guest rooms are contemporary, large and pleasant, with mahogany furnishings. *139 E. Kilbourn Ave., 53202, tel. 414/276–8686; fax 414/276–8007. 221 rooms. Facilities: restaurant, lounge, exercise room, sauna, whirlpool, 2 steam baths, health club, jogging track. AE, DC, MC, V.*

Moderate **Grand Milwaukee Hotel.** Located across from the airport, the Grand is the largest hotel in the state. Renovated in 1992, the bright rooms are decorated in earth tones. The marble-walled lobby is illuminated with chandeliers; a swimming pool cools the central courtyard. *4747 S. Howell Ave., 53207, tel. 414/481–8000 or 800/558–3862; fax 414/481–8065. 510 rooms. Facilities: restaurant, lounge, nightclub, 2 pools, health club, 7 indoor tennis courts, 6 racquetball courts, movie theater. AE, DC, MC, V.*

Ramada Inn Downtown. Rough knotty-pine paneling gives the lobby of this motor hotel a casual feeling. The maroon-toned rooms are furnished in standard Ramada style. *633 W. Michigan St., 53202, tel. 414/272–8410; fax 414/272–4651. 154 rooms. Facilities: restaurant, lounge, outdoor pool, airport transportation. AE, D, DC, MC, V.*

Sheraton Mayfair. This bustling high-rise motor hotel on the west side is convenient to the County Medical Complex and the Milwaukee County Zoo. Guest rooms are bright and airy, with traditional furnishings; those near the top have fine views. *2303 N. Mayfair Rd., Wauwatosa 53226, tel. 414/257–3400 or 800/325–3535; fax 414/257–0900. 150 rooms. Facilities: restaurant, lounge, indoor pool, sauna. AE, D, DC, MC, V.*

Inexpensive **Astor Hotel.** Close to Lake Michigan, the Astor has the not-unpleasant air of a hotel past its heyday, which is documented with photographs of illustrious guests in the large lobby. Many of the rooms have been remodeled and furnished with antiques and period reproductions but retain old bathroom fixtures. *924 E. Juneau Ave., 53202, tel. 414/271–4220, 800/558–0200, or 800/242–0355 in WI; fax 414/271–6370. 96 rooms. Facilities: restaurant, lounge, garage, airport transportation. AE, D, DC, MC, V.*

Motels **Best Western Midway Hotel–Brookfield** (1005 S. Moorland Rd., Brookfield 53005, tel. 414/786–9540 or 800/528–1234; fax 414/786–4561), 125 rooms, restaurant, lounge, indoor pool, saunas, whirlpool, recreation area; moderate. **Holiday Inn–South** (6331 S. 13th St., 53221, tel. 414/764–1500; fax 414/764–6531),

159 rooms, restaurant, lounge, indoor recreation area, heated pool, whirlpool, playground, sports court, jogging track; moderate. **Holiday Inn Express** (11111 W. North Ave., Wauwatosa 53226, tel. 414/778–0333; fax 414/778–0331), 122 rooms; inexpensive.

The Arts and Nightlife

Milwaukee Magazine (on newsstands) lists arts and entertainment events. Also check the Arts section of the Sunday *Milwaukee Journal.*

The Arts Milwaukee's theater district is in a two-block downtown area bounded by the Milwaukee River, East Wells Street, North Water Street, and East State Street. Most tickets are sold at box offices.

The **Riverside Theater** (116 W. Wisconsin Ave., tel. 414/224–3000) and **Pabst Theater** (144 E. Wells St., tel. 414/278–3663) host touring theater companies, Broadway shows, and other entertainment. The **Milwaukee Center** (108 E. Wells St., tel. 414/224–9490) is home to the **Milwaukee Repertory Theater** and the **Milwaukee Chamber Theater.** The **Milwaukee Symphony Orchestra, Milwaukee Ballet Company, Florentine Opera Company,** and **First Stage Milwaukee** are based at the **Performing Arts Center** (929 N. Water St., tel. 414/273–7206). **Lincoln Center for the Arts** (820 E. Knapp St., tel. 414/272–2787) is home to three dance groups: the **Bauer Dance Company, Dancecircus,** and **J.U.M.P. Dance Theater.** The 1927 **Oriental Landmark Theater** (2230 N. Farwell Ave., tel. 414/276–8711) shows foreign and hard-to-find films in an exotic setting.

Nightlife The city offers a variety of nightlife, with friendly saloons (about 1,600 at last count) and a varied music scene. The **Safe House** (779 N. Front St., tel. 414/271–2007), with a James Bond spy hideout decor, is a favorite with young people and out-of-towners. **La Playa** (Pfister Hotel, 424 E. Wisconsin Ave., tel. 414/276–1200) combines a South American atmosphere with the glamour of a supper club. **Major Goolsby's** (340 W. Kilbourn Ave., tel. 414/271–3414) is regarded as one of the country's top 10 sports bars by the jocks and occasional major-league sports stars who hang out here. Jazz fans go to the **Bombay Bicycle Club** (Marc Plaza Hotel, 509 W. Wisconsin Ave., tel. 414/271–7250) or **The Estate** (2423 N. Murray Ave., tel. 414/964–9923), a cozy club offering progressive jazz four nights a week.

Index

Fodor's Travel Guides

Available at bookstores everywhere, or call 1–800–533–6478, 24 hours a day.

U.S. Guides

Alaska

Arizona

Boston

California

Cape Cod, Martha's Vineyard, Nantucket

The Carolinas & the Georgia Coast

Chicago

Colorado

Florida

Hawaii

Las Vegas, Reno, Tahoe

Los Angeles

Maine, Vermont, New Hampshire

Maui

Miami & the Keys

New England

New Orleans

New York City

Pacific North Coast

Philadelphia & the Pennsylvania Dutch Country

The Rockies

San Diego

San Francisco

Santa Fe, Taos, Albuquerque

Seattle & Vancouver

The South

The U.S. & British Virgin Islands

The Upper Great Lakes Region

USA

Vacations in New York State

Vacations on the Jersey Shore

Virginia & Maryland

Waikiki

Walt Disney World and the Orlando Area

Washington, D.C.

Foreign Guides

Acapulco, Ixtapa, Zihuatanejo

Australia & New Zealand

Austria

The Bahamas

Baja & Mexico's Pacific Coast Resorts

Barbados

Berlin

Bermuda

Brazil

Brittany & Normandy

Budapest

Canada

Cancun, Cozumel, Yucatan Peninsula

Caribbean

China

Costa Rica, Belize, Guatemala

The Czech Republic & Slovakia

Eastern Europe

Egypt

Euro Disney

Europe

Europe's Great Cities

Florence & Tuscany

France

Germany

Great Britain

Greece

The Himalayan Countries

Hong Kong

India

Ireland

Israel

Italy

Japan

Kenya & Tanzania

Korea

London

Madrid & Barcelona

Mexico

Montreal & Quebec City

Morocco

Moscow & St. Petersburg

The Netherlands, Belgium & Luxembourg

New Zealand

Norway

Nova Scotia, Prince Edward Island & New Brunswick

Paris

Portugal

Provence & the Riviera

Rome

Russia & the Baltic Countries

Scandinavia

Scotland

Singapore

South America

Southeast Asia

Spain

Sweden

Switzerland

Thailand

Tokyo

Toronto

Turkey

Vienna & the Danube Valley

Yugoslavia

WHEREVER YOU TRAVEL, *H*ELP IS NEVER FAR AWAY.

From planning your trip to providing travel assistance along the way, American Express® Travel Service Offices* are always there to help.

Chicago Area

625 North Michigan Ave.
Chicago
(312) 435-2570

230 S. Clark St.
Chicago
(312) 629-0685

34 N. Clark St.
Chicago
(312) 263-6617

122 South Michigan Ave.
Chicago
(312) 435-2595

Howlett Travel
1629 Orrington Ave., Evanston
(708) 869-6800

Mount Prospect Vacations, Inc.
11 West Prospect Ave.
Mount Prospect
(708) 259-6030

Crossroads Travel Service, Inc.
1010 Lake St., Oak Park
(708) 524-1600

Around The World Travel, Inc.
48 East Palatine Rd.
Palatine
(708) 359-9590

Golfwood Square Mall
604 E. Golf Rd.
Schaumburg
(708) 884-6472

Wilmette Commons
110 Skokie Blvd., Wilmette
(708) 251-7530

For the office nearest you, call 1-800-YES-AMEX.

INTRODUCING

AT LAST, YOUR OWN PERSONALIZED LIST OF WHAT'S GOING ON IN THE CITIES YOU'RE VISITING.

KEYED TO THE DAYS WHEN YOU'RE THERE, CUSTOMIZED FOR YOUR INTERESTS, AND SENT TO YOU BEFORE YOU LEAVE HOME.

EXCLUSIVE FOR PURCHASERS OF FODOR'S GUIDES...

Fodor's WORLDVIEW
TRAVEL UPDATE

Introducing a revolutionary way to get customized, time-sensitive travel information just before your trip.

Now you can obtain detailed information about what's going on in each city you'll be visiting <u>before</u> you leave home—up-to-the-minute, objective information about the events and activities that interest you most.

Your Itinerary:
Customized reports available for 160 destinations

This is a special offer for purchasers of Fodor's guides – a customized Travel Update to fit your specific interests and your itinerary.

Travel Updates contain the kind of time-sensitive insider information you can get only from local contacts – or from city magazines and newspapers once you arrive. But now you can have the same information before you leave for your trip.

The choice is yours: current art exhibits, theater, music festivals and special concerts, sporting events, antiques and flower shows, shopping, fitness, and more.

The information comes from hundreds of correspondents and thousands of sources worldwide. Updated continuously, it's like having your own personal concierge or friend in the city.

You specify the cities and when you'll be there. We'll do the rest — personalizing the information for you the way no guidebook can.

It's the perfect extension to your Fodor's guide and the best way to make the most of your valuable travel time.

Reg
The
in th
domain
tion as
worthwhi
the perform
Tickets are u
venue. Alter
mances are canc
given. For more in
Open-Air Theatre,
NW1 4NP Open Air
Tel: 935-5756. Ends: 9-
International Air Tattoo
Held biennially, the world
military air display in
demostra-
tions, milita
bands

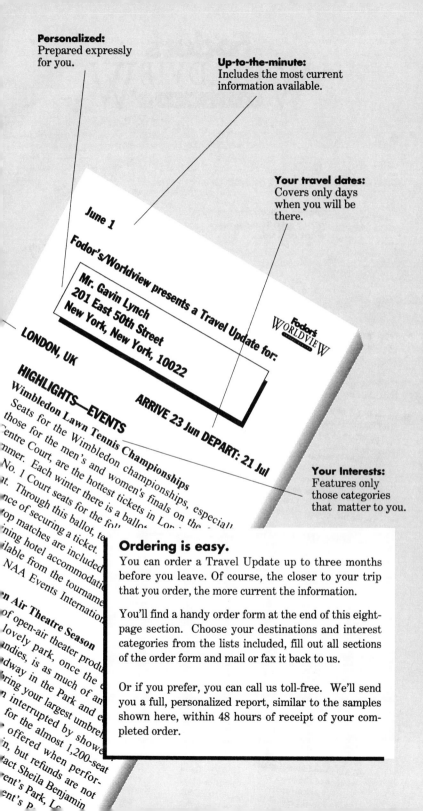

Personalized:
Prepared expressly for you.

Up-to-the-minute:
Includes the most current information available.

Your travel dates:
Covers only days when you will be there.

June 1

Fodor's/Worldview presents a Travel Update for:

Mr. Gavin Lynch
201 East 50th Street
New York, New York, 10022

Fodor's
WORLDVIEW

LONDON, UK

ARRIVE 23 Jun DEPART: 21 Jul

HIGHLIGHTS—EVENTS

Wimbledon Lawn Tennis Championships
Seats for the Wimbledon championships, especially those for the men's and women's finals on the Centre Court, are the hottest tickets in London this summer. Each winter there is a ballot No. 1 Court seats for the following at. Through this ballot, te nce of securing a ticket. top matches are included ning hotel accommodati ilable from the tourname NAA Events Internation

n Air Theatre Season
of open-air theater produ lovely park, once the e ndies, is as much of an dway in the Park and e ring your largest umbrel n interrupted by shower for the almost 1,200-seat offered when perfor in, but refunds are not act Sheila Benjamin ent's Park, L ont's P

Your Interests:
Features only those categories that matter to you.

Ordering is easy.

You can order a Travel Update up to three months before you leave. Of course, the closer to your trip that you order, the more current the information.

You'll find a handy order form at the end of this eight-page section. Choose your destinations and interest categories from the lists included, fill out all sections of the order form and mail or fax it back to us.

Or if you prefer, you can call us toll-free. We'll send you a full, personalized report, similar to the samples shown here, within 48 hours of receipt of your completed order.

**Special interest,
in-depth listings**

**Special concerts—
who's performing
what and where**

**One-of-a-kind,
one-time-only events**

Children — Events

Angel Canal Festival

The festivities include a children's funfai
entertainers, a boat rally and displays on th
water. Regent's Canal. Islington. N1. Tube
Angel. Tel: 267 9100. 11:30am-5:30pm. 7/04

Blackheath Summer Kite Festival

Stunt kite displays with parachuting tedd
bears and trade stands. Free admission. SE3
BR: Blackheath. 10am. 6/27.

Megabugs

Children will delight in this infestation o
giant robotic insects, including a praying
mantic 60 times life size. Mon-Sat 10am-
6pm; Sun 11am-6pm. Admission 4.50
pounds. Natural History Museum, Cromwell
Road. SW7. Tube: South Kensington. Tel:
938 9123. Ends 10/01.

Childminders

This establishment employs only women,
providing nurses and qualified nannies to

Music — Jazz & Blues

Tito Puente's Golden Men of Latin Jazz

The father of mambo and Cuban rumba king
comes to town. Royal Festival Hall. South Bank.
SE1. Tube: Waterloo. Tel: 928 8800. 8pm. 7/15.

Georgie Fame and The New York Band

Riding a popular tide with his latest album, the
smoky-voiced Fame and his keyboard are on a
tour yet again. The Grand. Clapham Junction.
SW11. BR: Clapham Junction. Tel: 738 9000
7:30pm. 7/07.

Jacques Loussier Play Bach Trio

The French jazz classicist and colleagues.
Kenwood Lakeside. Hampstead Lane.
Kenwood. NW3. Tube: Golders Green, then bus
210. Tel: 413 1443. 7pm. 7/10.

Tony Bennett and Ronnie Scott

Royal Festival Hall. South Bank. SE1. Tube:
Waterloo. Tel: 928 8800. 8pm. 7/11.

Santana

Royal Festival Hall. South Bank. SE1. Tube
Waterloo. Tel: 928 8800. 8pm. 7/12.

Count Basie Orchestra and Nancy Wilson Trio

Royal Festival Hall. South Bank. SE1. Tube
Waterloo. Tel: 928 8800. 8pm. 7/14.

King Pleasure and the Biscuit Boys

Royal Festival Hall. South Bank. SE1. Tube
Waterloo. Tel: 928 8800. 6:30 and 9pm. 7/16.

Al Green and the London Community Gospel Choir

Royal Festival Hall. South Bank. SE1. Tube
Waterloo. Tel: 928 8800. 8pm. 7/13.

BB King and Linda Hopkins

Mother of the blues and successor to Bessi
Smith, Hopkins meets up with "Blues Boy
King. Royal Festival Hall. South Bank. SE
King. Royal Festival Hall. 2000. 6:30 and 9pr

Music — Classical

Marylebone Sinfonia

Kenneth Gowen conducts music by P
and Rossini. Queen Elizabeth Hall. 3
Bank. SE1. Tube: Waterloo. Tel: 928
7:45pm. 7/16.

London Philharmonic

Franz Welser-Moest and George Ber
conduct selections by Alexander C
Messiaen, and some of Benjamin's own
positions. Queen Elizabeth Hall. South
SE1. Tube: Waterloo. Tel: 928 8800. 8

London Pro Arte Orchestra and Forest

Murray Stewart conducts selectio
Rossini, Haydn and Jonathan Willcock
Queen Elizabeth Hall. South Bank
Tube: Waterloo. Tel: 928 8800. 7:45pr

Kensington Symphony Orchestra

Russell Keable conducts Dvorak's

Here's what you get . . .

Detailed information about what's going on — precisely when you'll be there.

Show openings during your visit

Reviews by local critics

Exhibitions & Shows—Antique & Flower

Westminster Antiques Fair
Over 50 stands with pre-1830 furniture and other Victorian and earlier items. Thu-Fri 11am-8pm; Sat-Sun 11am-6pm. Admission 4 pounds, children free. Old Royal Horticultural Hall. Vincent Square. SW1. Tel: 0444/48 25 14. 6-24 thru 6/27.

Royal Horticultural Society Flower Show
The show includes displays of carnations, summer fruit and vegetables. Tue 11am-7pm; Wed 10am-5pm. Admission Tue 4 pounds, Wed 2 pounds. Royal Horticultural Halls. Greycoat Street and Vincent Square. SW1. Tube: Victoria. 7/20 thru 7/21.

Hampton Court Palace International Flower Show
Major international garden and flower show taking place in conjunction with the British

Theater — Musical

Sunset Boulevard
In June, the four Andrew Lloyd Webber musicals which dominated London's stages in the 1980s (Cats, Starlight Express, Phantom of the Opera and Aspects of Love) are joined by the composer's latest work, a show rumored to have his best music to date. The 1950 Billy Wilder film about a helpless young writer who is drawn into the world of a possessive, aging silent screen star offers rich opportunities for Webber's evolving style. Soaring, aching melodies, lush technical effects and psychological thrills are all expected. Patti Lupone stars. Mon-Sat at 8pm; matinee Thu-Sat at 3pm. In-person sales only at the box office; credit card bookings, Tel: 344 0055. Admission 15-32.50 pounds. Adelphi Theatre. The Strand. WC2. Tube: Charing Cross. Tel: 836 7611. Starts: 6/21

Leonardo A Portrait of Love
A new musical about the great Renaissance arti and inventor comes in for a London premier tested by a brief run at Oxford's Old Fire Stati autumn. The work explores the relations Vinci and the woman

Spectator Sports — Other Sports

Greyhound Racing: Wembley Stadium
This dog track offers good views of greyhound racing held on Mon, Wed and Fri. No credit cards. Stadium Way. Wembley. HA9. Tube: Wembley Park. Tel: 902 8833.

Benson & Hedges Cricket Cup Final
Lord's Cricket Ground. St. John's Wood Road. NW8. Tube: St. John's Wood. Tel: 289 1611. 11am. 7/10.

Business-Fax & Overnight Mail

Post Office, Trafalgar Square Branch
Offers a network of fax services, the Intelpost system, throughout the country and abroad. Mon-Sat 8am-8pm, Sun 9am-5pm. William IV Street. WC2. Tube: Charing Cross. Tel: 930 9580

Alberquerque • Atlanta • Atlantic City • N
Baltimore • Boston • Chicago • Cincinnati
Cleveland • Dallas/Ft.Worth • Denver • De
• Houston • Kansas City • Las Vegas • Los
Angeles • Memphis • Miami • Milwaukee •
New Orleans • New York City • Milwaukee
Springs • Philadelphia • Phoenix • Orlando •
Portland • Salt Lake • San Antonio • Pittsburg
San Franc • • St. Louis • Tamp
Oslo • Was • • lu • Island •
Hawaii • • Manzanu • Abacos • Bimini •
Ber • • Hamilton • ar
Antigua & B • •

Fodor's
WORLDVIEW
TRAVEL UPDATE

Gorda • Barbados • • Forte
cia • St. Vincent • Dominica • Gren
ymans • Puerto Plata • Trinidad &Tobago
Aruba • Bonaire • Santo Doming
ec City • Montreal • Curacao • St. Ma
Vancouver • Guadeloupe • Ottawa • Toron
elemy • St. Martin • Kingston • Martiniqu
o Bay • Negril • Ocho Rios • Ixta
n • Grand Turk • Providenciales • Ponce
St. John • St. Thomas • Acapulco • S
& Isla Mujeres • Cozumel • Guadal
• Los Cabos • Manzinillo • Mazatl
City • Monterrey • Oaxaca • Puerto
do • Puerto Vallarta • Veracruz • Ix
dam • Athens • Barcelona • F

Interest Categories

For <u>your</u> personalized Travel Update, choose the categories you're most interested in from this list. Every Travel Update automatically provides you with *Event Highlights* – the best of what's happening during the dates of your trip.

1.	**Business Services**	Fax & Overnight Mail, Computer Rentals, Photocopying, Secretarial , Messenger, Translation Services

Dining

2.	**All Day Dining**	Breakfast & Brunch, Cafes & Tea Rooms, Late-Night Dining
3.	**Local Cuisine**	In Every Price Range—from Budget Restaurants to the Special Splurge
4.	**European Cuisine**	Continental, French, Italian
5.	**Asian Cuisine**	Chinese, Far Eastern, Japanese, Indian
6.	**Americas Cuisine**	American, Mexican & Latin
7.	**Nightlife**	Bars, Dance Clubs, Comedy Clubs, Pubs & Beer Halls
8.	**Entertainment**	Theater—Drama, Musicals, Dance, Ticket Agencies
9.	**Music**	Classical, Traditional & Ethnic, Jazz & Blues, Pop, Rock
10.	**Children's Activities**	Events, Attractions
11.	**Tours**	Local Tours, Day Trips, Overnight Excursions, Cruises
12.	**Exhibitions, Festivals & Shows**	Antiques & Flower, History & Cultural, Art Exhibitions, Fairs & Craft Shows, Music & Art Festivals
13.	**Shopping**	Districts & Malls, Markets, Regional Specialities
14.	**Fitness**	Bicycling, Health Clubs, Hiking, Jogging
15.	**Recreational Sports**	Boating/Sailing, Fishing, Ice Skating, Skiing, Snorkeling/Scuba, Swimming
16.	**Spectator Sports**	Auto Racing, Baseball, Basketball, Football, Horse Racing, Ice Hockey, Soccer

Please note that interest category content will vary by season, destination, and length of stay.

Destinations

The Fodor's/Worldview Travel Update covers more than 160 destinations worldwide. Choose the destinations that match your itinerary from this list. (Choose bulleted destinations only.)

United States (Mainland)
- Albuquerque
- Atlanta
- Atlantic City
- Baltimore
- Boston
- Chicago
- Cincinnati
- Cleveland
- Dallas/Ft. Worth
- Denver
- Detroit
- Houston
- Kansas City
- Las Vegas
- Los Angeles
- Memphis
- Miami
- Milwaukee
- Minneapolis/St. Paul
- New Orleans
- New York City
- Orlando
- Palm Springs
- Philadelphia
- Phoenix
- Pittsburgh
- Portland
- St. Louis
- Salt Lake City
- San Antonio
- San Diego
- San Francisco
- Seattle
- Tampa
- Washington, DC

Alaska
- Anchorage/Fairbanks/Juneau

Hawaii
- Honolulu
- Island of Hawaii
- Kauai
- Maui

Canada
- Quebec City
- Montreal
- Ottawa
- Toronto
- Vancouver

Bahamas
- Abacos
- Eleuthera/Harbour Island
- Exumas
- Freeport
- Nassau & Paradise Island

Bermuda
- Bermuda Countryside
- Hamilton

British Leeward Islands
- Anguilla
- Antigua & Barbuda
- Montserrat
- St. Kitts & Nevis

British Virgin Islands
- Tortola & Virgin Gorda

British Windward Islands
- Barbados
- Dominica
- Grenada
- St. Lucia
- St. Vincent
- Trinidad & Tobago

Cayman Islands
- The Caymans

Dominican Republic
- Puerto Plata
- Santo Domingo

Dutch Leeward Islands
- Aruba
- Bonaire
- Curacao

Dutch Windward Islands
- St. Maarten

French West Indies
- Guadeloupe
- Martinique
- St. Barthelemy
- St. Martin

Jamaica
- Kingston
- Montego Bay
- Negril
- Ocho Rios

Puerto Rico
- Ponce
- San Juan

Turks & Caicos
- Grand Turk
- Providenciales

U.S. Virgin Islands
- St. Croix
- St. John
- St. Thomas

Mexico
- Acapulco
- Cancun & Isla Mujeres
- Cozumel
- Guadalajara
- Ixtapa & Zihuatanejo
- Los Cabos
- Manzanillo
- Mazatlan
- Mexico City
- Monterrey
- Oaxaca
- Puerto Escondido
- Puerto Vallarta
- Veracruz

Europe
- Amsterdam
- Athens
- Barcelona
- Berlin
- Brussels
- Budapest
- Copenhagen
- Dublin
- Edinburgh
- Florence
- Frankfurt
- French Riviera
- Geneva
- Glasgow
- Interlaken
- Istanbul
- Lausanne
- Lisbon
- London
- Madrid
- Milan
- Moscow
- Munich
- Oslo
- Paris
- Prague
- Provence
- Rome
- Salzburg
- St. Petersburg
- Stockholm
- Venice
- Vienna
- Zurich

Pacific Rim Australia & New Zealand
- Auckland
- Melbourne
- Sydney

China
- Beijing
- Guangzhou
- Shanghai

Japan
- Kyoto
- Nagoya
- Osaka
- Tokyo
- Yokohama

Other
- Bangkok
- Hong Kong & Macau
- Manila
- Seoul
- Singapore
- Taipei

Fodor's WORLDVIEW Order Form

THIS TRAVEL UPDATE IS FOR (Please print):

Name

Address

City	**State**	**ZIP**

Country	**Tel #** ( ) -

Title of this Fodor's guide:

Store and location where guide was purchased:

INDICATE YOUR DESTINATIONS/DATES: Write in below the destinations you want to order. Then fill in your arrival and departure dates for each destination.

		Month	Day		Month	Day
(Sample) **LONDON**	From:	**6** /	**21**	To:	**6** /	**30**
1	From:	/		To:	/	
2	From:	/		To:	/	
3	From:	/		To:	/	

You can order up to three destinations per Travel Update. Only destinations listed on the previous page are applicable. Maximum amount of time covered by a Travel Update cannot exceed 30 days.

CHOOSE YOUR INTERESTS: Select up to eight categories from the list of interest categories shown on the previous page and circle the numbers below:

1   2   3   4   5   6   7   8   9   10   11   12   13   14   15   16

CHOOSE HOW YOU WANT YOUR TRAVEL UPDATE DELIVERED (Check one):

❏ Please mail my Travel Update to the address above **OR**

❏ Fax it to me at **Fax #** ( ) -

DELIVERY CHARGE (Check one)

	Within U.S. & Canada	Outside U.S. & Canada
First Class Mail	❏ $2.50	❏ $5.00
Fax	❏ $5.00	❏ $10.00
Priority Delivery	❏ $15.00	❏ $27.00

All orders will be sent within 48 hours of receipt of a completed order form.

ADD UP YOUR ORDER HERE. *SPECIAL OFFER FOR FODOR'S PURCHASERS ONLY!*

	Suggested Retail Price	Your Price	This Order
First destination ordered	$13.95	$ 7.95	$ 7.95
Second destination (if applicable)	$ 9.95	$ 4.95	+
Third destination (if applicable)	$ 9.95	$ 4.95	+
Plus delivery charge from above			+
		TOTAL:	$

METHOD OF PAYMENT (Check one): ❏ AmEx   ❏ MC   ❏ Visa   ❏ Discover
❏ Personal Check   ❏ Money Order

Make check or money order payable to: Fodor's Worldview Travel Update

Credit Card #   **Expiration Date:**

Authorized Signature

SEND THIS COMPLETED FORM TO:
Fodor's Worldview Travel Update, 114 Sansome Street, Suite 700, San Francisco, CA 94104

OR CALL OR FAX US 24-HOURS A DAY
Telephone **1-800-799-9609** • Fax **1-800-799-9619** (From within the U.S. & Canada)
(Outside the U.S. & Canada: Telephone 415-616-9988 • Fax 415-616-9989)

(Please have this guide in front of you when you call so we can verify purchase.)

Offer valid until 12/31/94.